With my pistol leveled, I took one wide, leaping side step, moving out to my left where I could see around the corner. *Surprise!* Instead of the dark green uniforms of the Marines of 2d Platoon, there were ten or twelve tan-uniformed, very tough looking enemy troops. They were not alert, a fact that probably saved my life. . . .

I found myself looking almost straight down on two 7.62mm RPD light machine guns. The muzzle of the nearest weapon, which was mounted on its bipod, was less than three feet from my right leg. All of the men squatting there were uniformed, booted, and had helmets, either tipped back on their heads or lying nearby; they were either regular fighters of the interprovincial force Viet Cong or regulars from the North Vietnamese Army.

Without any real pause, I shot the nearest enemy soldier, the closest one who had a light machine gun. The shock of the first round hitting his chest bowled him backward, and for a moment, the other Vietnamese froze as they looked at me. I kept trying to kill as many as possible and shouted to the Marine at the dike to shoot through the bushes at the trail corner. . . .

By Alex Lee
*Published by The Ballantine Publishing Group:*

FORCE RECON COMMAND: *3rd Force Recon Company in Vietnam, 1969–70*
UTTER'S BATTALION: *2/7 Marines in Vietnam, 1965–66*

# UTTER'S BATTALION

*2/7 Marines in Vietnam, 1965–66*

## Lt. Col. Alex Lee, USMC (Ret.)

BALLANTINE BOOKS • NEW YORK

A Ballantine Book
Published by The Ballantine Publishing Group
Copyright © 2000 by Alex Lee

www.randomhouse.com/BB/

Library of Congress Catalog Card Number: 99-91633

ISBN 0-8041-1638-5

Manufactured in the United States of America

First Edition: January 2000

10  9  8  7  6  5  4  3  2  1

This book is respectfully and lovingly dedicated to

Lieutenant Colonel Leon N. Utter
United States Marine Corps

A peerless leader of men in the terrible, shattering inferno of close-range ground combat in the jungles of Vietnam, Lt. Col. Leon N. Utter proved to all who followed him that he was one of the finest infantry battalion commanders ever sent to make war by the United States of America and by the Corps of Marines that serves our nation.

Lieutenant Colonel Utter led us with bravery, with honor, with dignity, and with a deep sense of concern for every man who went forward to the sound of the guns. He never, ever, at any time, ceased teaching us the basic truths of soldiering under fire. By his personal example, he taught us many valuable lessons about how brave men meet the horror and the challenge of combat. His faith in his Marines was evident, and we always did our utmost to live up to his expectations.

Illustrative of our respect and the underlying deeply abiding love for this colonel-of-Marines is the fact that, in the Republic of Vietnam in 1965 and 1966, the Marine officers and enlisted men of his battalion did not say that they were serving in Second Battalion, Seventh Marines, they said, instead:

"I am in Utter's battalion."

and to my mother

Isabel Chamberlain McCoy Lee
September 1910–March 1998

READY FOR ANYTHING,
COUNTING ON NOTHING

Motto: Second Battalion, Seventh Marines
Republic of Vietnam, 1965–1966

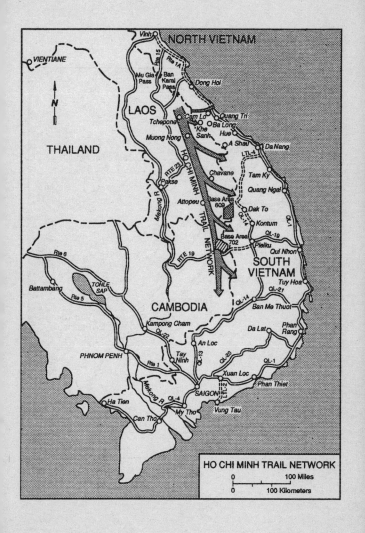

VIENTIANE

NORTH VIETNAM

Vinh

Mu Gia
Pass
Ban
Karai
Pass

Dong Hoi

LAOS

Cam Lo    Quang Tri
Ba Long
Tchepone    Khe
Sanh    Hue
Muong Nong    A Shau    Da Nang

THAILAND    LTL-4

Chavane    Tam Ky

Pakse    Quang Ngai

HO CHI MINH TRAIL NETWORK

Attopeu    Base Area
609    Dak To

Kontum    QL-1

Base Area
702    QL-19
Pleiku
Qui Nhon

SOUTH
VIETNAM

Tuy Hoa

Rte 6    QL-21
TONLE
SAP    Ban Me Thuot
Battambang    RTE 19

Rte 5

CAMBODIA    QL-14

Kampong Cham    Da Lat    Phan
Rang
QL-22
An Loc
PHNOM PENH    Tay    QL-13
Rte 1    Ninh    QL-20    QL-1

Xuan Loc
SAIGON    Phan Thiet

Ha Tien    QL-4    Vung Tau
Can Tho    My Tho

HO CHI MINH TRAIL NETWORK

0         100 Miles

0         100 Kilometers

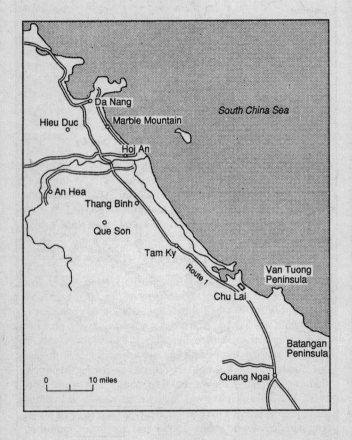

# INTRODUCTION

We Marines have always done our very best to set ourselves apart from the rest of mankind—with good reason. We feel justified in considering ourselves separate because we have always had to live a hard life of service for our civilian masters. Those masters have been, from time to time, great men of sterling character; on other occasions our leaders have been an uninformed, unappreciative, and occasionally, hostile gathering of self-centered political hacks who could not locate a single bone of statesmanship in their bodies. Regardless, all of the nation's leaders have possessed the authority, given them by the Constitution of the United States that Marines swear to "preserve and protect," to happily misuse our capabilities—should they choose to do so. Frequently throughout our history, Marines have been asked to perform the most hazardous service, in far lands against great odds, in furtherance of civilian goals that did not coincide with anyone's understanding of military objectives. Recent historical studies of the Vietnam War era have shown that in the early 1960s the United States was led by men who both lied and made grievous errors in reaching their decisions. Their errors compounded to cost many decent and honorable men their lives, and in the end, their actions cost the nation its good name. Yet, in that era, as in all other times, the Marines sent to war by their masters in Washington did their best to perform the missions that were assigned.

The Marine view of life, which our detractors call "an attitude," is often controversial, but Marines still firmly hold the opinion that our way of doing things has served us well in times of peace and times of war. Being different is not necessarily bad as some believe, but those of us who served in the 2d Battalion, 7th Marines (2/7), between August 1964 and the last day of June 1966 earned the right to believe that we were truly different. Different in a manner worth describing to those who are interested in the history of the American involvement in the war in Southeast Asia.

Every one of the twenty-seven infantry battalions in the United States Marines Corps constantly reminds the men assigned to it that their battalion is unique. This drumbeat "guidance" is intrinsic to the Marine Corps's development within *every* Marine of a deep and abiding loyalty to the Corps. This stern, single-minded, direct, and specifically *personal* loyalty to the Marine Corps as the finest military representative of our nation, has worked for us for more than 220 years. From boot camp to retirement, Marines are told repeatedly that *they* are unique. They become believers and carry on the spirit of the Corps with adherence to that core belief. At the rifle battalion level, Marines use unique historical facts or other aspects of their battalion's accomplishments to make the point that its Marines are the ones who are *really* unique.

As many illustrations have been used to foster the Corps-wide sense of being unique as there are old Marines. One well-used line that comes to mind is, "With 275 million people in the United States of America, less than 200 thousand of them can be Marines." Another is the recruiting slogan of the 1946/1947 period, "Only 100,000 may serve!" Of course, at the time, fewer than 75,000 men could be induced to sign enlistment papers; in the late 1940s, just prior to the Korean War, the Marine Corps languished well below the desired 100,000-man level then authorized by Congress.

The attitude of being unique as Marines is fostered at the "big picture"—Corps-wide—level, and it is carried down the chain to the infantry battalions with great clarity and consistency. It is also frequently carried down to the squad- and fire-team level. For eighty years, men of the battalions of the 5th and 6th Marine Regiments have proudly worn, draped around their shoulders, the braided fourragère presented by the French government for gallantry on the bitter battlefields of France during some of the heaviest fighting of World War I. Men of the infantry battalions of the 5th and 6th Regiments will tell you endlessly that they are very, very different. Of course, the word "different" is just a simple code masking the claim that they are "better" than all the other infantry battalions in other regiments. We Marines always use terms like different and unique to set us apart from non-Marines, to mean exactly the same thing—better.

At all levels, such boasting is often just another means of raising the spirit and enthusiasm of the troops for their particular unit. However, being unique in other ways is possible. It can come with shared sorrow, pain, and anguish. For more than twenty years, the leaders of the three infantry battalions of the 4th Marine Regiment taught the young officers and enlisted men who filled the regimental muster rolls that their units were unique because the regiment was forever disgraced in the eyes of America; beginning after World War II, Marines of the three infantry battalions of the 4th Marine Regiment were told that the regiment could never return to the continental United States because, the story went, we were members of the only Marine unit *ever* to strike its colors to an enemy.

The banning of the regiment from our home nation was alleged to be the result of a formal order of the president of the United States. Although none of us ever saw a copy of the order, we were made to feel that service with the infantry battalions of the 4th Marines was similar to service with the French Foreign Legion. To ease the pain slightly, unit staff noncommissioned officers (SNCOs) and noncommissioned officers (NCOs) often slyly pointed out that our regiment, which had been ordered from duty in China to the Philippines in the last days of 1941, surrendered, after the battles for Bataan and Corregidor, while under the operational control of the U.S. Army. They were implying, with little guile intended, that our dishonor wasn't at all the fault of the Marines involved. Regardless, it was an article of faith among those who served in it that the 4th Marine Regiment could not return, even for training exercises in California, or to any other location in the nation it had failed. *That* kind of heritage made its Marines sorrowful and slightly ashamed. But the challenge of making the nation proud of the regiment drove them to do their best wherever the units were sent. Plainly, the story of the banning of the 4th Marine Regiment was a hoax, but one that, in the telling, was used to show the troops that their regiment was unique. This odd and hurtful motivational technique was still in use when the 4th Marines arrived in the Republic of Vietnam. The story has now been long discarded as a motivational tool, in part because of the regiment's gallant service in the Republic of Vietnam, and because of its very frequent participation, since the war, in training exercises in the continental United States.

Those of us who served in the 2d Battalion, 7th Marine Regiment (2/7), from 1964 to 1966 also had our myths and our realities about the unique nature of our unit. The troops were frequently reminded of the battalion's history in World War II in the Pacific Theater and in the snows of 1950 in Korea. Emphasis was always placed on the battle of the Tok Tong Pass during the Chosin Reservoir battles in Korea during November and December of 1950. At the Tok Tong Pass, Company F of the battalion was commanded by Capt. Bill Barber, who, with two others, won the Medal of Honor during the heavy fighting. Company F held the Tok Tong Pass against vastly superior Chinese forces who attacked and reattacked the beleaguered Marines relentlessly. At the same time that the hordes of Chinese troops were massing for more attacks, Captain Barber and his small band of infantrymen—almost every one of whom was wounded at least once—suffered terrible frostbite injuries from the subzero Korean cold. For fifty years, that bloody fight has been used throughout the Marine Corps as a benchmark against which Marines in the infantry rifle companies are asked to measure themselves.

In the early 1960s, there were still many Marines around who had fought at the Chosin Reservoir in Korea, and they always pointed out that anyone serving in 2/7 was fortunate to be part of that battalion because it had such a great heritage. That heritage was thirteen and one-half years behind us when this story of the 2d Battalion, 7th Marines begins.

My goal is to begin the story of 2/7 during the late summer of 1964 and to carry it to the end of the month of June 1966. The particular coming together of those who were in the battalion during that period of time is an initial aspect of what made the battalion unique—at least unique for the period of the war in the Republic of Vietnam.

Those of us who were assembled to make up 2/7 in August and September of 1964 found that we were taking part in many new and challenging aspects of our military service. The year 1964 was part of a time when unexpected and remarkable changes were taking place within the nation and within its Marine Corps, and many Marine professionals were confused and stunned at the rapidity of those changes. In the civilian community of the United States, society was changing in ways that most Marines ignored. Quite inaccurately, we active duty Marines felt that the sweeping changes were unrelated to our lives as military professionals. While those changes swirled through the civilian world, we often found it easier to hew to the "way things had been." Prior to the war in the Republic of Vietnam, the Marine Corps remained very, very traditional, conducting activities and rituals that dated to times that were more than one hundred years past. Formal calls were made and returned, with engraved calling cards exchanged in the age-old way. The wives of senior officers still felt some responsibility for the actions and thoughts of the wives of the young lieutenants and captains who worked for their husbands. Those older ladies even attempted, on occasion, to exercise control over the younger wives, as their predecessors had exercised social control over them when their husbands were lieutenants.

As an aside, it is important to note that in 1964, a belief in the traditional concepts of the Marine Corps was not always a bad thing. Many fine, dedicated, and capable Marines serving in 1964 loved the old ways and reveled in the military rituals from times past. Tradition and ritual were cited as significant bastions of strength in a time of fluid mores and frustrating changes.

In the 1960s, those of us holding the ranks of sergeant, staff sergeant, captain, and major had been trained under the guidance and leadership of Marines known as the "Old Breed." In 1964, that term covered anyone who had World War II or Korean War combat experience. At almost every level, we were led by, counseled by, and instructed by those hard men who had survived the terrors of Guadalcanal, Tarawa, Iwo Jima, Okinawa, and the three-year debacle of the war in Korea. Those men taught us the ways of the past and worked to make us fully understand our relationship within the hierarchy of the Corps and with its time-tested methods.

For those older Marines, and for most of us as well, the simple sight of fifty women in the battalion parking lot on payday was just one of many shocks pursuant to being present during unexpected and unwanted change. The presence of those women, the wives of junior enlisted Marines, was such an unusual event to us that it jarred our sense of propriety. The young ladies came to collect the payday cash from their husbands—and they wanted it immediately. The presence of these women concerned us because we officers had all grown up with, and had been trained to hold, the deeply ingrained view that wives were not appropriate to junior enlisted men. For those few young Marines who did happen to be married as lance corporals and corporals it was logical, in our view, that their wives stay home. It was almost doctrine to believe that the wives of enlisted men, like those of the few married officers and senior noncommissioned officers, should wait sensibly for their Marine to bring home the cash he was paid by some annoyed, and very worried, second lieutenant on the fifteenth and thirtieth of each month. Yet, by 1964, the new relationship between the Marine Corps and the wives of the junior enlisted Marines was just one of a horde of changes that were engulfing the Corps. It was clear that an ever-increasing portion of the enlisted strength of the rifle battalion was going to consist of married men, not bachelors. No one was really ready for such changes, but we had no choice in the matter. Many other such old views were destroyed in the new ways of life that were coming to be the standard in the civilian world and, by extension, the standard in the United States Marine Corps as well.

Another aspect of those days of professional military service that is difficult to clearly set forth for the reader is the insular nature of Marine Corps life as we lived it in the late 1950s and early 1960s. While today we frequently hear the whining voices of pundits railing against the separation of the military from the nation as a whole, the idea that this is a new situation is utterly false. The separation between our world and that of the civilians outside the gate was, before the war in the Republic of Vietnam, a wide, very deep, and infrequently crossed gulf. Today's Marines are vastly closer to their civilian contemporaries than any of us ever thought possible in 1964. Despite the inane comments of some who describe Marines as being wild-eyed extremists who are far outside the norm, i.e., extreme in the worst sense of the word (as was openly stated in 1998 by some mindless boob in the civilian hierarchy of the U.S. Army), the truth is, that today's Marine Corps is, in no way, as insular as it was thirty-five or more years ago.

To comprehend the story that follows, the reader must understand that, at that time, we and our civilian contemporaries lived very far apart for a number of reasons. Both groups were almost forced by their manner of living to exist in two very, very separate worlds. There was not much meaningful interaction. Most of what happened outside the camp gate had little or no impact on our lives. Those who lived off post came to work each morning through the gates of Camp Pendleton from civilian communities with which they were only minimally involved.

Marine work habits alone tended to set us apart. Most officers and SNCOs were out of their homes, or billeting areas, well before first light, and on most days, they returned well after dark. Saturday was a normal workday for almost everyone on the base, and nobody bothered to question that requirement or to be even mildly surprised at the expectation of our leadership that we be there to get the job done. Our dress, our haircuts, our low incomes, and our personal attitudes also set us at an even greater distance from civilians of the same age group.

By 1964, when this story begins, the "beat generation" had passed by after having had a chance to have its say. In the civilian world, the first of the hippies and their follow-on culture, the flower children, were beginning to appear. Far across a cultural gulf from our Marine Corps, a group of extremely hostile anti-American radicals had banded together in 1962 to create an organization known as Students for a Democratic Society (SDS). Men like Paul Booth worked to coauthor a document called, "The Port Huron Statement" in which the hostility of the SDS to America and to the values held most dear by those of us who served the Corps of Marines was clearly laid out; we remained oblivious to such pronouncements.

In the Fleet Marine Forces where we served, we had no idea about forces working within the nation to foment hatred against us or against our government. For Marines, the SDS and all similar movements were unknown territory. If we had even been aware that they existed, we would have dismissed them as having nothing to do with us or our Marine Corps ways. In 1964, had we thought of them at all, no radical movement would have been considered to have any importance because we could not conceive of such movements having any effect on America. Within the radical groups, the seeming insistence on poor personal hygiene, the bizarre forms of dress, and the weirdly inconsistent and inane use of platitudes all combined to cause Marines of the time to look askance and step back in order to stand clear. Oddly, we failed to notice that those mannerisms were appearing everywhere across the country, coupled with wide drug use and immorality as a way of life. Obviously, those aspects of the new culture clashed bitterly with our more conservative viewpoint. The Marine

Corps of the early 1960s was out of touch with the changing world. We were so conservative that many senior officers still found the idea of short-sleeve uniform shirts for use in hot climates to be a bad thing, an unnecessary departure from traditional Marine standards of dress.

On the other hand, another disturbing thing to Marines of the time was the presence, at very senior levels, of a few men who greatly desired to blur the line between the Marine Corps and the civilian world, a line that most of us felt should be left firmly and properly in place. As an illustration, one very senior general officer issued an order that Marine lieutenants should, henceforth, eschew their traditional "high-and-tight" military haircuts. He wanted their hair to be long enough to comb or to brush into a visible part. His purpose in ordering the change was to illustrate that those young fighting men were, in some unexplained and unrealistic fashion, much the same as civilian men who worked as managers or performed similar administrative functions in the business world. Of all the orders that came from on high in the late 1950s and the early 1960s, that was one of the most ignored. Marine lieutenants had always been taught that their role in life was to lead their platoons from the front, and to die, if necessary, at the place of "gravest danger." Dying on an assault beachhead did not sound to them to be anything even slightly akin to a management job in some corporation. Being looked upon as managers rather than warriors annoyed most of the lieutenants, and some left the service feeling gravely affronted. Almost across the board, young Marine officers sneered at the idea that they should sport a neat and tidy management-style haircut. Some lieutenants even began to shave their heads each week as a response to being told that what they did for a living could be easily compared with civilian management.

Poverty was another factor. In the Marine Corps of that time, everyone, at every rank, earned so little income that he lacked the funds to take a very active part in life outside the gate. For the troops and the junior NCOs there were the temptations of the flesh and the too easy availability of alcohol in Oceanside, California, the town that lay just outside the

Camp Pendleton gate. Their meager monthly incomes would disappear almost immediately into the pockets and purses of the innkeepers and "ladies of the evening." After just a few short hours of liberty on "the beach," most returned to the barracks, flat broke. Many Marines had only two evenings of liberty in each month because after a high-stepping payday night in Oceanside they would be penniless. For the following two weeks they had no choice but to hang around in the barracks each evening as they waited for the next payday.

For the married officers, SNCOs and NCOs, it was a fact that barely "getting by" was the norm. There were many occasions when tuna-and-cheese combinations stood in for the steak that we all wanted to set out on our tables. Twenty years later, when I commanded the 3d Battalion, 1st Marines (3/1) at Camp Pendleton (from 1974 to 1976) many of us marveled at the higher pay rates that had been established for junior Marines. My contemporaries and I worried aloud that, "Perhaps the young Marines these days get paid too well. They clearly get paid all the dollars they will ever need to get themselves into serious trouble. But, they don't get nearly enough money to get themselves back out of their own mess-ups." That remark was a very serious commentary cloaked in mild humor. But the humor vanished quickly; financial difficulty in the ranks was a proven condition to anyone who looked into the parking lot of 3/1 where expensive new four-wheel-drive pickup trucks, fully loaded civilian Jeeps, and powerful late model sports sedans were common, and most were owned by privates, privates first class, lance corporals, corporals, second lieutenants, and first lieutenants, every one of whom was mired in debt to his ears.

Marines in 1964 were as poor as church mice, but they lived by an inflexible honor code relating to debt and payment of obligations. As an example, of one of the deleterious effects that the passage of years has had on the way financial matters were routinely handled in the Marine Corps of the past, I offer the following story. In 1976, one of my second lieutenants in 3/1 averaged no fewer than two credit-problem letters, addressed to me as his commanding officer, every week for five months. In the old Marine Corps, he might well have been cashiered after the very first letter; his dishonorable debt would have been enough to find him to be unfit to hold his commission. In 1976 I could counsel him and mark him down as having poor judgment, but I could not rid the Marine Corps of him and his bad example to his juniors. In fact, I could only beg the adjutant of the 1st Marine Division to haul him out of my unit as quickly as possible. Begging did not work at all, so I arranged a swap with a unit that had a quota to fill for a Marine Corps base assignment. By simple horse trading we were able to rid 3/1 of a chronic credit abuser who lived without any sense of honor or integrity. However, other than completion of a harsh fitness report remark about the officer's unsatisfactory judgment, I could not do very much about his effect on the reputation of the other officers serving in the Marine Corps. It was an ugly, frustrating, and depressing experience to learn that those who met their obligations honorably could not defend themselves or their reputations. Nothing could be accomplished at my level without the action's being crushed by some higher headquarters where my strong and harsh response to the officer's dishonorable conduct was criticized as "unfair."

Overall, the most significant aspect about the Marine Corps of the early 1960s is the woeful truth about the abject poverty, an utter, all-pervasive poverty that intruded into every facet of our lives. The constant concern with money, and the lack thereof, was a corrosive influence on our lives. What we had available to us did not compare in any measurable way with what was needed and desired. Not only were we individual Marines of the 2d Battalion, 7th Marines, personally poor, but the battalion, as a living, breathing entity, was also flat, dead, stony, bare-assed broke. The 7th Marine Regiment, too, had very empty pockets, and—by extension—the 1st Marine Division was also poor, poor, poor! We were serving in a division that was destined to go to war, at a time when the whole Marine Corps was desperately poverty-stricken. Poverty nearly defeated us before we ever left to fight.

Marines have always laughed a bitter laugh about the fact that the Corps is famous for "doing more with less" than anyone on earth. But such remarks have always had the solid ring of truth. Before going to Vietnam, we literally did things on the most worn of shoestrings in our personal lives and in the daily operations of our units. So it should be understood by the reader that critical training and readiness tasks were sometimes left uncompleted because of the horrifying financial state of the Marine Corps—and of those who served in it. No amount of the "Love of Corps and Country" ingrained in us by our drill instructors could help us make "nothing" stretch further.

In 1964, the 2d Battalion, 7th Marines was equipped with the most abysmal equipment imaginable. Only a minuscule quantity of funds was programmed in the battalion budgets for future years to replace the worn-out items or to make needed repairs. It was sad that many officers and SNCOs felt forced to bring in their own tools, their own flashlight batteries, and their own weapons-cleaning gear to help keep the battalion running. That they cared enough to do those things also illustrates the way we lived at the time. Some characterized the life of Marine officers in the late 1950s and the early 1960s as being similar to the lives lived by the Jesuit Fathers. As we saw it, like Marines, the members of the Society of Jesus lived in poverty, worked their asses off for people who just didn't care very much about them, and soldiered with honor for their leaders whenever and wherever the Society ordered them to serve. In our minds, the comparison was not overdrawn; it was the simple truth as we saw it in 1964.

Nothing in the weapons and equipment inventory of the battalion was even in basically acceptable condition. Many items were so worn from years of use as to be fully and completely WOIS, worn out in service. In addition to lousy gear, we had no fuel. The battalion had almost no budget money ("paper" accounting money used to obtain goods and services) for the fuel, known as "mogas," which was needed to run our vehicles during training operations. In 2/7's budget for the year starting 1 October 1964 and ending 30 September

1965, fuel was so limited that half the vehicles often sat dead-lined in the motor pool so that the rest of the vehicles could operate at the minimal rates needed to support training.

With so little fuel available for transportation needs, we inherited another related problem. Just to feed the troops in the field or on training ranges, we often were forced to serve them field rations that had been made in 1952 and 1953. We did that instead of setting up field mess units for troops operating at extended distances from our regimental base at Camp Las Pulgas because we did not have enough gasoline to boil water for the troops to clean their mess kits before and after eating.

Lastly, the poverty of the Marine Corps led to such a short-fall in training ammunition—both live-fire and blank ammunition for training exercises—that the predeployment lock-on phase of training was almost farcical. Troops would dash through the Camp Pendleton scrub growth, shouting with loud and shamefaced bravado, *"Bang! Bang! Bang!"* and "I got you, you bastard!"

Marines have a long tradition of being resourceful, and the training ammunition situation proved that beyond doubt. Every rifle company commander, and his trusted training NCO, had his own personal, illegal stash of training ammunition. They hid the materiel in caves, in tunnels, or under the company commander's desk. Official division, regimental, and battalion orders stated that such storage of blank ammunition, flares, training mines, and the like was against all ammunition-handling and safety regulations. However, the private stashes were ignored by everyone from the regimental commander on down as absolutely necessary evils—if the troops were to be trained at all.

The fall of 1964 was a very interesting time in the 1st Marine Division with regard to the realities of overall combat readiness. Of course, combat readiness was stressed at every level, and that stress was underscored in all official documentation. However, many shortcuts were in place by 1964. These shortcuts were almost always because of the Corps's poverty. Myriad tales were told and retold throughout the division about the horrible state of readiness in the division when it

had deployed a few years earlier for a possible assault landing in Cuba. The departure for Cuba was, it was said, successfully completed with just the bare minimum of the necessary
weapons and equipment. Additionally, the departure was
completed at great personal cost to the Marines who deployed. The division units sailed as ordered, but hundreds of
cars and other items of personal property were scattered
wherever they'd been abandoned across the base. Readiness
to go to war is always the main mission of Marines, but the
problems that surfaced during that short-notice movement
had everyone concerned about what would happen if we were,
again, ordered to war. Vast and complex plans were drawn up
to ensure that the earlier chaotic situations would never be repeated. None of us wanted to be ordered to deploy and discover that the normal cheery, "Aye, aye, sir," response was not
possible because we had, somehow, lost track of some detail
that would screw up the move beyond all belief.

Despite the honest effort devoted by the 1st Marine Division to being continuously deployment ready, it was a very
simple matter to discover a number of areas where readiness
to depart and go fight someone—should the country call—
was lax to utterly nonexistent. For example, the 7th Marine
Regiment had all three of its battalions and its headquarters
company up and operating full blast. All four of these units
had fully manned mess sections with trained cooks, M-1937
field ranges, and all the other paraphernalia needed to feed the
troops fresh rations. Each battalion rated enough equipment
to keep more than sixteen hundred troops well fed in the field.
That large number included the expected reinforcements of
artillery, engineer, communications, motor transport, and reconnaissance Marines who are normally added to each deploying infantry battalion. Such reinforced battalions were
known in those days as battalion landing teams (BLT). With
proper use of the mess section assets, the Marines of 2/7
could be fed fresh food, even while conducting combat operations in the field. That, at least, was the theory behind the
staffing levels for cooks and the equipment lists for field-

mess gear that were published in the official Tables of Organization (T/O) and Tables of Equipment (T/E).

All the mess section's field equipment, the M-1937 field ranges, the refrigerators, the vacuum cans used to move food, and all the other hundreds of bulky items required wooden crating for movement to war aboard amphibious shipping. These crates are called "mount-out boxes." The term *mount-out* was the shorthand of the time for a Marine unit's being ordered to sea for a deployment to fight on some foreign shore. The term was used constantly. It was placed in front of all manner of words. There were mount-out conferences, mount-out stockpiles, mount-out schedules, mount-out ammunition storage, etc. All mount-out boxes were carefully identified by the tactical mark of the unit to which they belonged. Also displayed were the weight of that particular crate, a code for its contents, and the "cube" of the crate (i.e., the volume that the crate would occupy when taken on board ship). All of those markings were, like fingerprints, individualized for each unit. They were carefully coded, as required by the division order covering the tactical marking of all vehicles and equipment for movement aboard ship.

Despite all the emphasis on mounting-out, the three battalions of the 7th Marine Regiment owned just *one* set of crates for *one* infantry battalion's mess-section equipment. Just one! The dour old mess sergeants of the three battalions gleefully swapped the set back and forth when it was needed for an inspection. When the mount-out inspecting officer was due from the 1st Marine Division's embarkation section, the boxes were dragged out, repainted with the tactical markings of the unit to be inspected, and lined up for the officer's approval. For some, the nonsense was just a lark. Fooling the inspector was, in their eyes, another way to have fun. For the rest of us, it was a simple, but clear, portent of very difficult times to come.

As anyone who has experience dealing with life's adversities expects, the moment something very, very bad can happen, it usually does. Despite our best efforts, including a reasonably early solution to the mess section's mount-out box problems, that shortfall was typical of many that plagued us. Shortfalls in readiness, like the mount-out box fiasco, cropped up almost daily to compromise 2/7's "real" readiness posture. Although we had no money for lumber, it was evident that some punitive actions were needed and some lumber for mount-out box construction had to be procured—one way or another. Improving readiness was always the goal, but the almost comical example of the mount-out boxes illustrates why a host of similar poverty-based evils could surface to bedevil us when the entire regiment was ordered to war.

For 2/7, being ordered in May of 1965 to go to the war in Southeast Asia, created the primary condition that really does set our battalion apart as absolutely unique. By unique, I mean that between 1964 and 1966 our battalion *really was* different in a special way from other infantry battalions of the Marine Corps. The 2d Battalion, 7th Marines departed for the war in the Republic of Vietnam with an amazing level of unit integrity and personnel stability. Simply by chance, during the first year of Marine deployment to the Republic of Vietnam, 2/7 possessed more long-term personnel and greater unit integrity than any other infantry unit of the Marine Corps. Nothing changed that fact as the war years passed and the steady flow of individual replacements filled the ranks of the Marine units fighting in Vietnam.

By June of 1966, which is when this book will come to its close, there were many, many Marines serving in 2/7—among both the officers and enlisted men—who had served closely together for almost four full years. No other unit could approach that level of personnel stability. None did at the time, and none ever had any possible opportunity to do so as the war in the Republic of Vietnam wound on, and on, and on to its tortured and shameful conclusion. When the last Marine infantry battalion, the 3d Battalion, 1st Marine Regiment, left Vietnam forever, no other infantry unit deployed to the war had served together as long as had the men of 2/7. Because we had *unique* personnel stability, the story of 2/7 was, and will always be, different from the story of any other battalion that went west to that war.

Our stability gave the unit a tremendous advantage, one made clear when 2/7 was ordered to ready for deployment to war. All the Marines of 2/7 were comfortable with their solid ability to rely, no matter what was happening, on the other men of 2/7. Effective teamwork was facilitated in all aspects of daily life because of the well-understood familiarity that every Marine had with the strengths and weaknesses of the other members of the battalion. Personnel stability is central to effective operations, and every Marine understands that. Because they knew each other so well, the Marines of 2/7 got ready, they got set, and from far away, the powers-that-be in high places said, "Go to war!" Of course, the National Command Authority did not tell us why we were going, they did not give us a meaningful mission, nor did they take the time to mention any understandable national interest. But being professionals, the 2d Battalion, 7th Marines went—as ordered— to war.

It is my most sincere desire to emphasize to the reader that, in every line in this book, I seek to reflect credit on the fighting men of the 2d Battalion, 7th Marines and the lieutenant colonel who commanded them. The men of 2/7 met, more than thirty years ago, the challenge of infantry combat in the Republic of Vietnam. That challenge inflicted on those Marines, and the navy corpsmen who lived and died with them, a life of constant danger, mindless confusion, miserable living conditions, and the vile hatred that awaited them when they returned to the United States. Many men in the battalion died horrible deaths, and many more were gravely wounded and disfigured. All that agony was suffered with nothing, nothing at all, to show for the sacrifices made or the blood shed. That tragic fact is inescapable. Those of us who served in the battalion during 1965 and 1966 in combat in the Republic of Vietnam need only to look into the mirror each morning to feel the pain of our losses. That terrible, lifelong ache is the flip side of the personnel stability of a unit that serves together for a very long time. Every man wounded or killed in 2/7 was a real member of our extended family, a long-known individual, a friend, a comrade, a brother—lost.

Lastly, I would like to explain directly to the reader that there are many, many opinions expressed freely throughout every chapter of this book. These opinions are mine. My opinions did not always coincide with Marine Corps views or policies of the time, and I would very likely be out of step with many of today's policies as well, driven by political correctness as so many of them are. However, the reader should understand the depth of emotion, pent up for more than thirty years, behind many of my comments. The 2d Battalion, 7th Marines, did its very best in the maelstrom of that war. We who served in the battalion saw all of the effort, the pain, the sweat, and the blood wasted. We came home angry. Many of us are still angry!

I apologize beforehand for factual errors that may have found their way into this book. For some reason, the 2/7 historical files are not complete. There are no copies of any of the many reports submitted by the battalion between August 1964 and May 1965. The command chronology for December 31, 1965, begins with 2/7's deployment to the Republic of Vietnam in *May* of that year. Searches by the archivists in Washington did not turn up any of the older records. They could find no reports covering the hard months of training and preparation that 2/7 underwent between August 1964 and May 1965. Even the personal intervention of Mr. Fred Graeboske of the historical branch, who was kind enough to institute several special searches, could not uncover the long-buried documents.

I also greatly appreciate all Mr. Graeboske's help in obtaining copies of all of the after-action reports and command journals for the 2d Battalion, 7th Marines, for the period 30 November 1965 through all but the last few days of June 1966 when this book comes to its close. From those interconnected sources, it was possible to examine the operations of 2/7 in detail and to review for inclusion the various events that combined to affect those of us who served within the battalion. It was a long, hard year in which much was learned and much was suffered.

Important to all of this, and utterly independent of the research done, is that it is entirely possible that other factual errors may exist in this book. This is possible because I may have completely misread some of the source documents that were at hand when a specific chapter was being written. Regardless, this is my story of the 2d Battalion, 7th Marines, covering the period between August 1964 and the end of June 1966. This book is written from the perspective of those of us who were, when we were serving in infantry combat in the Republic of Vietnam, truly, the Marines of Lieutenant Colonel Leon N. Utter, United States Marine Corps.

> Lt. Col. Alex Lee, USMC (Ret.)
> Alpine, California
> October 1998

# 1

# CREATING SOMETHING
# FROM NOTHING

In the early 1960s, the Marine Corps was seeking to develop a number of new, innovative, combat-readiness-based personnel management techniques. Throughout the Corps, it was clear that there was a definite need to improve unit cohesion and efficiency within the infantry formations of the three Marine divisions. Of particular concern were the six infantry battalions that provided the fighting teeth of the 3d Marine Division. As part of the American resolve to remain fully prepared for a possible return to the Korean Peninsula, that division was permanently based in Okinawa, Japan. Replacement of Marines for the division was accomplished through use of the old standard, one-at-a-time individual rotation. This brought troops on individual orders from the various Marine bases in the United States to their overseas assignment. Under this system, each Marine moved when he received his orders and deployed overseas, joining the 3d Division for an unaccompanied (no dependents) tour of thirteen months.

All of the coming and going was typified by constant problems resulting from the personnel turmoil, the staff instability, and the inefficiencies that stem from a total lack of unit cohesiveness. Every single week of their overseas tours, the unit commanders in the 3d Marine Division saw a few new people rotate in and a few old hands rotate out. The result was a destructive interruption of normal daily small-unit routine which, in turn, resulted in an overall disruption of the infantry battalions. Obviously, that way of doing business was not in the best interest of the individuals concerned nor did it serve to enhance, in any way, the combat readiness of the infantry elements of the 3d Division.

At the command level and at the senior staff level, individual rotation was disastrous. Often, orders home took effect while key Marines were taking part in major amphibious exercises or during other large, joint maneuvers. The transfers often happened precisely when those Marines were most needed to supervise their units. This one-at-a-time departure system also denied the affected unit commanders the opportunity to gain experience in their profession by taking part in these larger scale operations. Naval planners could hardly be faulted for failing to schedule the availability of major fleet units and components of the amphibious navy just to coordinate with the assigned rotation dates of Marine infantry commanders or their staff officers.

Everyone wanted a better system, but creating one that would work was difficult in the days when junior officers—reserve lieutenants who made up the majority of movement-ready young officers—served for only two years of active service. Many of the enlisted Marines were also serving on two-year enlistment contracts. So, by the time an officer or enlisted Marine was trained and ready for deployment, he had to be made available to the overseas pipeline very quickly. An overseas slot had to be found, and the individual had to be shipped to his new assignment without undue delay if the Marine Corps was to get a full thirteen month period of service in the Far East from that Marine.

The transplacement system was implemented as a way of providing personnel stability to deployed battalions. To make this new system work, the 1st Marine Division was tasked to train battalions for deployment to Okinawa. These infantry battalions would not deploy by individual rotation, but, instead, would rotate to the Far East as a completely staffed unit. All nine infantry battalions of the 1st Marine Division would take part, and would sequentially replace the six battalions of infantry assigned to the 3d Marine Division in Okinawa.*

Making the grand ideas behind the transplacement system into a realistic way of life at Camp Pendleton was a very, very difficult job. The understrength 1st Marine Division was already hard-pressed to keep up with all of the commitments levied against it. There were units on standby that had to be ready to go to war overnight to Cuba and units standing ready to go to war, almost anywhere, on five days' notice. Always, behind all of the possible subordinate unit readiness requirements, lay the ever-present need for the division to be fully prepared to take everyone and everything, at the drop of a hat, to whatever war might be selected by the National Command Authority. Effectively adding any sort of unit training and rotation work-up system into that already complex readiness situation was not done with the wave of a hand. The pressure to control and manage the transplacement system, that is to make it work, was constantly competing head-to-head with the many other preparedness tasks required of the division.

For all of us assigned to the 1st Division, the transplacement system was just another no-win situation that greatly frustrated even the most ardent and willing Marines. When we were joking around, the whole mountain of division readiness responsibilities was characterized as, "Never mind the horse. Just load the wagon!" Actually, when viewed from the perspective of the 1990s, the number and complexity of commitments assigned to the Marine units then differed only in

*In the 1960s, one-third of the 3d Division, the three battalions of the 4th Marine Regiment, had been detached. The 4th, normally an assigned component of the 3d Marine Division, had spent the preceding several years in Hawaii, at Marine Corps Air Station, Kaneohe, as the ground element of the 1st Air-Ground Task Force, which later became the 1st Marine Brigade. Marines assigned to the 1st Marine Brigade in those days did not transplace. Instead, they rotated in and out of Hawaii on individual orders. Thus, in that era, the 1st Marine Brigade had personnel turbulence and a lack of unit cohesion similar to that which had been taking place on a larger scale in Okinawa. However, on the positive side of the ledger, the Hawaii-based Marines, who were not deployed often beyond the limits of the Hawaiian Island chain, were spared the pains and agonies inherent in supporting the transplacement system.

detail from the deployment pressures and multiple commitments levied on Marine infantrymen today. The 1st Marine Division was, in 1964, expected to be prepared for anything from reaction to civil disorder to a full-scale war. Huge World War II assault landings were still considered possible, as was a return to the snowy mountains of Korea. Overall, it had to be responsive to a hodgepodge of required readiness conditions, a complex reality that confounded us.

Being all things to all men in all situations is not just hard, it is utterly impossible. No one was ever very surprised when some of the high-level decisions setting out the various "top-priority" efforts tended to get mangled and overcome by events in the field. Regardless of what people in Washington thought at the time, it was simply impossible to make every single thing done in the 1st Marine Division a high-priority activity. Honest effort and good intent by the commanding general of the division and his staff officers often ran bitterly aground on reality. For all the fancy readiness policies to be implemented at 100 percent effectiveness would have required the efforts of many, many more men and the availability of much more military materiel than our poor, understrength, overcommitted division could ever have expected to have at hand in the bleak days of 1964.

Marine infantry battalions were, and still are, being deployed to Okinawa as part of the national resolve to maintain forces in the Far East. Then, as now, these forces are prepared to return to Korea should the North Koreans chose to invade South Korea again. At the same time, there remained for those of us in California in 1964 a very basic level of expectation that we would make an amphibious assault into Cuba. We felt this pressure because the 1st Marine Division was still specifically designated as responsible for a high level of readiness for possible deployment to Cuba. If an armed response was ordered to any move by Fidel Castro, we knew that we would be one of the first units sent to deal with him. More than likely, we would have been used to respond to an attack launched against the U.S. Navy's training base at Guantanamo Bay. That base was always under harassment by the Cubans outside the wire, and the possibility of an attack was considered very probable. Only a few years before, the entire division had mounted out, transited the Panama Canal, and prepared to land in Cuba. Assault landings were never ordered, but the division had embarked and sailed to the Caribbean for an extended period of time, leaving chaos at Camp Pendleton. Rumors of another move to Cuba were always abundant, and many expected that we would be ordered soon to go there to "kick Castro's ass." Scuttlebutt (rumor) around the division was that things were building up, and we would probably be off to Cuba no later than the spring of 1965.

All of the readiness plans had as their baseline the task organization of various reinforced infantry units—depending on their overall readiness posture at a given time. Units slated for deployment in the various go-to-war plans were designated to leave the base in accordance with specific departure-time phases. One battalion of the division was always kept on the eight-hour-go. This meant they had to be clear of the base, climbing aboard the transport aircraft at El Toro Marine Corps Air Station within eight hours after receipt of the signal to execute the mission. Of course, this also meant that the men of that battalion had to eat, sleep, and work right next to their already packed and readied equipment. Nobody assigned to be on the eight-hour-go could go home, go to town, or even go to the post exchange.

Keeping up with the commitments required that a second infantry battalion be designated to leave for Cuba by air in twenty-four hours. At the same time, one of the regiments, the "ready regiment," was always on standby to mount out by ship for Cuba within seventy-two hours of the execution order. The entire 1st Marine Division was also expected to be ready to leave for war within five days. Looking at only the first three of these required readiness postures illustrates that the eight-hour-go (one battalion), the twenty-four-hour-go (one battalion), and the ready regiment (3 battalions), consumed five of the nine available infantry battalions of the division. There were also various plans in place for short-notice unit deployments to deal with civil unrest, to fight forest fires, to reinforce the 3d Marine Division overseas, and to take part in all manner of warlike and nonwarlike activities.

While all of the readiness assignments moved each month from unit to unit, the overall feeling in the division was that every last Marine must constantly be ready to go somewhere to fight with little or no prior notice. Adding the requirements of transplacement system to the mix immediately reduced combat readiness within the 1st Marine Division because it took a portion of the division assets out of a readily deployable status. Obviously, a battalion that has just been disassembled on its return from Okinawa, dropping 50 percent of its personnel and joining several hundred new Marines, could not be quickly deployed to any kind of conflict, anywhere.

Joining the 1st Marine Division in the summer of 1964, I was feeling very fortunate and reacted with boundless enthusiasm when I was ordered to report to the 7th Marines for duty with the regiment's 2d Battalion. It was what I wanted to do, and it was what I needed to be doing for professional development. For an infantry captain, being sent to an infantry battalion for duty was far superior to any possible assignment to a billet anywhere on the division staff. A long assignment in special operations, outside the Marine Corps, had sharpened my desire to return to the infantry, and I was very excited about getting back where I could work with my own kind of people. Armed with the adjutant's endorsement on my orders, I headed out that hot dusty summer day to make myself ready to serve in the 7th Marine Regiment.

Arrival at the regimental base area, Camp Las Pulgas, where the regimental headquarters and all three of its infantry battalions were quartered, tempered my excitement to a great degree. While I knew that the battalion I was to join did not exist at the moment, the initial impression I got on arrival at Las Pulgas cooled a great deal of my enthusiasm. Second Battalion, 7th Marines did not exist because the 3d Battalion, 9th Marines (3/9), which had been overseas, had not arrived home to be redesignated as 2/7. Until that happened, the battalion would only be a cadre unit with a skeleton structure of early arriving officers and NCOs. That cadre unit was quartered near the regimental headquarters, and the conditions under which they were living gave me a tremendous shock. The new members of 2/7 were living in what I felt were terrible, substandard conditions. My very first look at the troop billeting in Camp Pulgas, made before turning in my orders, was not conducive to an optimistic outlook!

Before they had become 3/9 in Okinawa for thirteen months, the men of the returning battalion had been at Camp Pendleton in 1962–1963 for a year of "lock-on" training together as 2d Battalion, 1st Marines (2/1). Designation and redesignation of units was standard practice during the time that transplacement system was in operation. It was another confusing aspect of being part of the cycles, and it served to reduce the personal loyalty that Marines developed toward their units. Being redesignated meant that you were no longer a long-term, dedicated member of any one particular infantry battalion. In this system you were expected to be part and parcel—instantly—of some other unit that would immediately expect your fervent loyalty and concern. For many it was hard to shift from being one thing to being another with such frequency.

To report for duty with the battalion, I had to pass through the regimental headquarters to receive the "blessing" of the regimental adjutant as to my assignment. After a short chat, the adjutant endorsed my orders with a stamp and sent me on down to report in at the 2d Battalion headquarters. I was directed to present myself to the "acting" commanding officer of 2/7. I was not told who was acting as the commander, but I did learn that he had few troops to command. So far, not more than about ninety men of all ranks had reported into 2/7. Since not even the advance party from 3/9 had yet returned to Camp Pendleton from the Far East, the battalion area was nearly deserted. Almost all of the barracks doors were still tightly locked, and many windows were boarded over. The view through the windows without boards was discouraging beyond description. The insides of the buildings looked as if bad tempered children had been at work. Piles of lockers, locker-boxes, and various other things were just scattered around within the barracks. Trash was everywhere. There was some vandalism evident, and a great deal of minor repair work was clearly needed to make the barracks habitable. I was willing to accept that the barracks area had been unused for several months, but the idea of it being left in such a disgusting, nonprofessional state by the Marines who had last been billeted there was disconcerting and anger provoking.

Checking in to become a member of 2/7 handed me a very jolting surprise. The acting commanding officer was Capt. Fredrick L. Tolleson, Jr., a Naval Academy graduate from the class of 1955. He was exactly one year senior to me, a point of great importance to his type of officer. I found the captain in a dusty, dark, plywood-paneled office in the middle of the most miserable steel Butler building imaginable. It was dreary, dirty, dark, depressing, and stifling hot in that sheet-iron oven. Even to think about having to work there was depressing. As a command facility, the building was barely more inviting than a spot selected in the rain under a leaky tree. There was nothing about the place that would cause anyone to look forward to attempting to make an infantry battalion come to life with that sad, sad dump as its nerve center. The building was absolutely inadequate. There weren't even fans to move the superheated air from place to place. Worse, it was structurally unfit for use as a command post because it was really nothing but a hollow shell without inner subdivisions for office space. That horrible Butler building remained absolutely unfit for use as a battalion headquarters for the next ten months. Of course, it was used throughout that time as the command post for the 2d Battalion, 7th Marines.

Captain Tolleson and I had served together in the 4th Marine Regiment, he in one battalion, and I in another. During that period of service, we had never been closer than casual acquaintances at the bar in the officers' club. After having been a platoon commander in 3d Battalion, 4th Marines, Tolleson had moved up the staff chain to work in the fiscal office for the commanding general of the 1st Marine Brigade. Our contacts had become even less frequent after he went to the fiscal office. Nevertheless, Captain Tolleson greeted me like a long lost *compañero* and took great and loudly gleeful pleasure in the tremendous surprise that he had handed me. He was probably the last man alive that I had expected to find sitting in the battalion commander's chair. The two of us settled in to make small talk, most of which revolved around how I had looked when I walked in and found him acting as the battalion commander. While he and I were always capable of serious disagreement—we had engaged in some very spirited clashes as lieutenants—we did get on fairly well on a personal basis. Captain Tolleson was not stupid, and he fully understood what had to be done to make things right. It was very reassuring to find that Captain Tolleson was also amazed and sadly disconcerted by the chaos in the battalion area.

As the acting commander of 2/7, Captain Tolleson was free to decide my assignment, firmly underscoring in the process the fact, which we both already knew, that he was senior to me. He directed that I set up camp immediately in the office space, a dreary hole boxed in by some plywood sheets, that he had chosen for the logistics staff section. At the battalion level, this section is known as the S-4. Being an S-4 is not a particularly rewarding assignment at any time, ever. In those days before officer specialization in logistics was created, most captains did their best to avoid the job. My feelings on the matter made little difference, and no appeal was worth the time and energy that it would have taken. Tolleson's decision was made more appealing, but not very much so, by his view that if I filled a staff job in the training phase at Camp Pendleton, I would be a more likely candidate for command of an infantry company in Okinawa during the overseas phase of the transplacement. There was some logic to his view, but none that did anything to soften the blow. I, like any other infantry captain I knew at the time, wanted to command an infantry rifle company during both the Stateside training cycle and the overseas deployment.

Since I was not completely out of touch with reality, I realized immediately that Captain Tolleson was looking for someone to do the scut work that the S-4 would be expected to do—getting the ratty looking place ready to billet a twelve-hundred-man infantry battalion. By throwing me into the S-4 shop, he would have someone available—me—to hand the boring, difficult jobs to when things needed to be done quickly. For him, it was a good deal, failures he could ascribe to me, and successes could be credited himself. This would, of course, be an inversion of many old Marine Corps adages on the application of leadership, however, the decision had been made long before my arrival. There was no recourse. Once forced by Tolleson to leap into the saddle as the S-4, I remained trapped there in the thankless logistic morass until the battalion entered combat in the Republic of Vietnam.

Of course, Captain Tolleson harbored no such logical intentions concerning service on the battalion staff during the Stateside phase for himself. As a senior captain, junior only to Capt. A. J. Doublet who was to be the operations officer (S-3), he was later successful in getting what he wanted. When 2/7 was actually up and running, he obtained command of Company E. Captain Tolleson fluctuated wildly between being a decent, funny sort of guy to being an ambitious "ticket-puncher" who had his thumb on his own number. His variances of attitude befuddled many and annoyed others. Some of the young officers admired his loud, aggressive manner, and others found him to be just another senior captain who was hard to deal with. To everyone who worked with him or for him, it sometimes appeared that he wanted to make sure he got himself taken care of first. His naturally abrasive and somewhat overbearing nature often made doing business with him far more difficult than it should have been. To his credit, Captain Tolleson always felt that whatever he was doing at any time, he was doing it for his Marines, even when it might appear otherwise and might annoy everyone else. He cared deeply about his Marines, and that concern counts for a great deal in the profession of arms.

I had no interest, none whatsoever, in being the S-4 of anything, but that was not pertinent at the moment. What was important was to make something of the mess and to be prepared to receive, billet, and process out to postdeployment home leave some eleven hundred Marines. About half of that number would come back to 2/7 from leave, and the others would carry out orders that would take them home or to other assignments.

Astonishment followed astonishment on my first day with 2/7. By the simple accident of overhearing a conversation in the personnel section (S-1) between S.Sgt. Ah Soon and a corporal, I learned in midafternoon that, within a week, 2/7 would be getting about six hundred newly trained recruits. The new Marines were to arrive about three or four days after 3/9 came home and went on leave. That little tidbit of information added greatly to the immediate pressure of my new job. With so much to do, the logistics section—so far that meant me—had to get busy if it was ever going to be possible to make something out of the absolute "nothing" we new arrivals had inherited.

Good fortune came to me the very next day. On my first full day as the S-4, S.Sgt. Reginald D. Tackett arrived for duty. He was a big man, a smart man, a man who happened to be a bit overweight, and a man who was opinionated as hell. I use this as the polite way of pointing out that Tackett was not afraid to "firmly" state his position when some officer, or senior SNCO, was expressing a countering view. This big, solid, and roughcast man would never have been anyone's idea of a recruiting poster Marine. He was not a pretty boy! Regardless of his personal appearance and his combative demeanor, Staff Sergeant Tackett turned out to be one of the most amazing professionals I have ever encountered. Tackett could do almost anything, and do it with verve! He knew logistics backwards and forwards and was fully trained in the field of embarkation as well—an absolute necessity for 2/7, it later turned out.

Staff Sergeant Tackett would not have been an acceptable Marine if we had been judging him by a 1990s set of criteria. My logistics chief was the kind of Marine who worked at his job, not one who played to the audience of higher rank. Like many of us assigned to 2/7, he made multiple mistakes, almost daily. He made those mistakes while doing his best to accomplish a great deal in a very short time. The loud, aggressive, and constant drumfire of actions by Staff Sergeant Tackett, all for the purpose of getting things accomplished, would never have been possible in a zero-defects world or a political-correctness world. Staff Sergeant Tackett shouted, he cursed, he cajoled, and he even threatened—loudly—but he got what he wanted and what we needed. His tasks were many, and they were done right far more often than not. He could work twenty hours without a meal and stay at his task for sixty to seventy continuous hours without sleep. Staff Sergeant Tackett could keep track of more data in his head than any other Marine I ever met. He was a wonderful man to work with, and his impact on 2/7 lasted until we all departed the battalion, forever, in June 1966.

With Staff Sergeant Tackett and one sergeant clerk-typist, whom I borrowed, we began to attack the mess we faced. All available men were gathered on the parade deck. We created ad hoc fire teams, appointed their leaders, and assigned those teams, as units, to get busy on the major problems—the barracks and the mess hall. Two of the barracks were opened, the trash removed, paint "found" somewhere, and rejuvenation begun. Our immediate need was living space for the new arrivals and for those few Marines from 3/9 who might prefer not to go on leave.

Using every sneaky artifice we could dream up, we went to work. Tackett collected some hard charging Marines who were not part of the ad hoc fire teams, and he shepherded them from task to task, much like a very busy border collie handling his sheep. He was everywhere. He worked on various schemes to make the battalion area more presentable and obtained many needed items far, far outside of normal channels. His hope was to make the billeting areas meet, at the very least, the minimum standards for use by Marines. Those standards would horrify a 1998 Marine who is housed today in what amounts to apartment-style living. But in comparison to the way things were at the inception of the task, the working parties created a decent place for Marines to establish their personal living space.

Billeting was not fancy in 1964. Enlisted Marines lived, by necessity, in old style, low-roofed, concrete barracks. Each barracks building was established with the long rows of double-decked bunks that were typical of open squad-bay style billeting. This kind of billeting was virtually unchanged from that of one hundred years before. It was fairly standard in those days for fifty Marines to live in each open squad bay. The heads (showers and toilets) were in the middle of each barracks building. There were few amenities. All of the Marines in 2/7 would begin their work day on bare concrete decks, and they would bathe in communal showers. Tackett's job was to make sure that those decks were clean and the showers would work. When he was done, the barracks were ready for occupancy.

The battalion had a mess hall to run, too, a structure absolutely no different from any other mess hall designed for the feeding of fifteen hundred to two thousand Marines. The only real difference was that the building was padlocked and it was far, far beyond filthy. Setting in motion a twenty-four-hour-per-day effort, Staff Sergeant Tackett and the gunnery sergeant who was the designated 2/7 mess chief, directed a cleanup effort that began in the upper reaches of the building and finished with the careful waxing of the deck. All of the mechanical elements of the facility were checked, and vast amounts of food were ordered; it would take an enormous amount of food to feed three meals a day to all the Marines of 2/7 and to the regimental headquarters unit that would be eating with us. Again, the efforts of Staff Sergeant Tackett and his superior ability to foresee needed actions resulted in a ready and functioning mess hall when the men of 3/9 arrived at Camp Las Pulgas.

Sadly, the close work with the gunnery sergeant who ran the mess hall made it known to Tackett and me that we had a serious problem. Like all cooks, he was able to get up at 0300 and work for seventeen or eighteen hours without stopping, but he could not do so without the help of very generous doses of cheap bourbon whiskey. By mid to late afternoon each day, he smelled like a distillery and was prone to discipline Marines assigned to help the cooks (called messmen) by hitting them on the head with a large wooden mixing spoon or the side of a meat cleaver. Additionally, when he left the mess hall, he often found it necessary to fill the backseat and trunk of his automobile with steaks and roasts from the meat locker. He probably sold the meat in Oceanside to some restaurant or to a circle of his friends. We had to stop him, so we did. His actions stopped very abruptly about an hour after we learned the truth. The gunnery sergeant was taken directly to jail from the parking area near the back loading dock of the mess hall.

Destroying a staff noncommissioned officer was a very rare action in the Marine Corps of 1964. Both Staff Sergeant Tackett and I were assailed with a torrent of abuse because the gunnery sergeant had seventeen or more years of service behind him. Many thought that he should be given a break. Some of the older enlisted Marines in the 7th Regiment seemed to feel that continued service for an extended period of time was equal to honorable service. At the gunnery sergeant's court-martial, the presiding officer and the members of the court quickly discarded that concept, and the offending Marine was reduced in rank and served a period of time in confinement. After that, he was discharged from the Marine Corps. For months after that incident, many of the other SNCOs in the regiment avoided me and were rude to Staff Sergeant Tackett and to the sergeant who rose from being just another cook to being the new mess sergeant for the battalion.

The newly elevated mess sergeant was a wonder. He had fourteen years of service with more than eight years of flawless performance, without ever having had a single chance for promotion from the rank of sergeant. This was possible because in those days being a cook placed you in one of the slowest promotional fields within the entire Marine Corps. As, in his words, a "kid" in 1950, he had cooked, when he was not acting as a rifleman, at the Chosin Reservoir in Korea. Regardless of his past experiences and his sterling personal quality, the one that made him most valuable to 2/7 was that he did not drink or steal. He just did his job!

Immediately after the completion of the necessary reorganization and the cleanup of the mess hall, the battalion received its first influx of troops. Without so much as a heads up from division, we looked up one afternoon and found more than four hundred young Marines checking into the personnel office. Almost all of the newcomers were fresh out of boot camp or just returning from leave after their initial Marine Corps training. Of those who were not new Marines, there were some communicators, a few more cooks, three or four drivers, and a total of two—just two—experienced infantry corporals.

Those two corporals probably never worked harder in their lives. It fell to them to manage all of the movements of all the new men, to see that they got bedding, to assign them specific bunks in the company areas, and to see that they were properly fed and watered. With great aplomb, the two young Marines took complete charge and quickly got everything sorted out. When complimented, they joked that they merely applied the same leadership skills that they had acquired as fire-team leaders and rifle-squad leaders in their previous units. By the end of the second day, each of the four rifle company barracks was inhabited by a cadre of hardworking young men who would get the tired old buildings shipshape in nothing flat.

While everyone in 2/7 was busy, the Headquarters and Service Company (H & S) had the most difficult company-level task. Because most of the men of that company work for the staff and support sections of the headquarters, their time is not always available to the company commander. In an H & S company there are many NCOs and few privates and privates first class to assign to cleanup and working parties. Thus, experienced Marines, the battalion drivers, communicators, cooks, clerks, supply clerks, mortarmen, antitank assault men, and the like had to work at the cleanup side by side with the new arrivals to the Corps. In the 2/7 H & S Company, a set of corporal chevrons was not enough to keep anyone from swabbing decks, painting, or cleaning. Under the leadership of Capt. James M. Nolan the H & S area soon sparkled.

Captain Nolan was a very careful and positive officer who went to great lengths to see that the Marines worked cooperatively and that the barracks and grounds cleanup went on full blast. Any headquarters company is hard to command because not only are most of the Marines in the company NCOs, but a lot of them work directly for officers who are senior to the company commander. Sorting out all his difficulties, Captain Nolan was exceptionally successful in creating a very superior, squared-away, capable company. With all cadres of the rifle companies working equally hard, the battalion area began to look like the home of a working organization. Everyone was fully occupied in making something viable out of the mess that we had found on arrival.

When 3/9 did arrive home from Okinawa, we met them only briefly as they wanted to process and get on their way as quickly as possible. The S-1 was buried for hours under the deluge of orders and other paperwork. But, in an amazingly short time, all those who were going to other units had been processed, and those who were going on leave had departed for the bus depot or for the airport. Working in the dark and dust-filled gloom of the 2/7 command post, 1st Lt. Nate Jolley and his cadre of S-1 clerks did a magnificent piece of work. The men of 3/9 vanished quickly because they were processed by motivated Marines, all of whom did more than their share to make it happen smoothly and with minimal hassle.

Two weeks passed, and we began to expect that some of the experienced members of 3/9 would begin returning from their leave. Despite all the turmoil, we concluded that things were looking pretty decent for 2/7. At the rate things were going, we were going to have a fully functional battalion area for the Marines to return to after their leave period. Our small moment of self-congratulation was shattered when we learned that the requirement for 2/7 to support the operations of other units had not been considered. When we came to the conclusion that things were going well, we did not have all the facts. The 1st Division headquarters had additional work for us to do. The 2d Battalion, 7th Marines (at the time still a mythical unit) was designated as the enemy aggressor force to be deployed to oppose an assault landing by the historically famous 5th Marine Regiment. The division wanted about five hundred men for the aggressor force, and they wanted them in the field, ready to fight, in two days. With all the new young Marines now entrusted to our care, a force of that size could be assembled easily. But, that force would be almost all brand-new Marines. Nobody in any higher headquarters seemed to care that we would be struggling to accomplish this unexpected task without any officers or any NCOs. The job was just dumped on the battalion, and it became 2/7's job to respond, without comment, to the directive from above.

Our aggressor capability was augmented the following morning by the arrival of six very nervous second lieutenants who were newly graduated from the most recent class at the Basic School in Quantico, Virginia. Those lieutenants checked in, drew equipment, and went to the field, all in twenty-four hours. Their arrival shock must have been one of stunned amazement. Since I had been assigned by Captain Tolleson as the aggressor-force commander, it was off to the races for me as well. With only the six young officers, a single experienced infantry staff sergeant, the two strong corporals who had already been seriously overworked, and 480 Marine privates, we departed to the field to fight. Also allocated to our force were a few communicators carrying marginal radios and an operator team equipped with one tired, old AN/MRC 38 radio jeep. As that jeep ran down the road, the Marine sitting in the passenger seat could observe the roadbed through the rusted-out sections on the floor. Some of those holes were five or more inches across.

Since our side of the operation was going to be the military equivalent of pickup baseball, we struggled to establish some sort of self-created organization that might work. The 480 Marines were divided into two companies of 240 each, with three officers and one corporal designated to serve as the company command structure. To facilitate assignments requiring less than a full "company," each company was subdivided into three eighty-man units. The entire operation was obviously going to be chaotic, but the innate enthusiasm of the young officers and the very young Marines began to give the enterprise the look of a good time for all hands. We chose to call ourselves the "Baldomero Lopez Battalion," and "Freedom" was our battle cry.

The 5th Marine Regiment was slated to come ashore at dawn on the first day of the exercise, crossing Camp Pendleton's White Beach with two battalions abreast. The regiment's third battalion was listed as the reserve force. Since, in reality, the third battalion did not exist, it was noted as "constructive" in the operations orders. This made the landing force reserve a mythical entity, and it had no ability to work against the aggressor force in the operational scenario. On D day the Baldomeros were ordered to offer a token, harassing-type resistance on the landing beaches. There was to be no grand-standing defense-to-the-death on White Beach. After the assault landing by the attacking force was firmly ashore, the aggressors were to move inland for later combat. Beyond those simple mission-type inputs, we had little or no detailed instructions on what was wanted to work out the kinks in the 5th Marines.

After providing the desired light resistance to the assault, the Marines of the Baldomero force followed their orders and retired to the hill masses inland. It was in those inland hills that our later defensive efforts would be concentrated against the southernmost of the two assault battalions. Meanwhile, one of my aggressor lieutenants was set up, with eighty Marines, to harass and delay deployment of the northernmost of the two battalions and to hinder their movement inland by what-ever means he chose. My last two lieutenants were ordered to move south away from contact and north away from the first contacts inland from the coastal highway. That way, if the 5th Marines did not locate them and deal with them effectively, the lieutenants would find themselves well positioned on the flanks and, later, to the rear of the landing force. From there, each unit of eighty men had the potential to become a serious thorn in the side of the regiment conducting the amphibious assault.

Using typical youthful energy and a brash disregard for

conventional thinking, one of the lieutenants on the northern portion of the exercise area set a trap for the northernmost battalion, 2d Battalion, 5th Marines (2/5), commanded by Lt. Col. Joe Muir, a two-war Marine with a well-deserved reputation for employing an ultra-aggressive, high-energy, leadership style. Lt. Col. Joe Muir was a very well respected leader and a real tiger when on the move. As 2/5 dislodged the defending force near the beach, they moved quickly inland. Lieutenant Colonel Muir and his command element arrived ashore and moved into the hills in the northern portion of his battalion's area of responsibility. He, being curious of course, wanted to see for himself what was happening. In order to see what he wanted, he took his entire command group up onto the top of one of the low, but inviting, hills that lay just inland, across the coastal freeway, from the north end of White Beach.

Lieutenant Colonel Muir and his staff made a fatal mistake. They were not paying attention. Neither the command-post Marines, nor the supporting communicators of 2/5 were covered by any infantry force of significance. He had rifle companies east of the hill mass, but they were already moving inland—away from the hill on which their leader was standing. Muir's command element moved to the hilltop, and they bypassed more than twenty Baldomero Marines and their lieutenant. These aggressors were hiding in spider holes that they had dug into the side walls of two or three of the water-courses. With wood, brush, or canvas covers for camouflage, the spider holes went undiscovered. On command, the grinning Marines crawled out and captured Lieutenant Colonel Muir, his executive officer, his operations officer, most of his staff, and a flock of his communicators. Those not captured by the aggressors were ruled by the captain serving as the tactical exercise umpire to have been killed. Lieutenant Colonel Muir was taken prisoner when the lieutenant stepped up and placed the muzzle of his pistol in the battalion commander's ear and demanded that he surrender.

The aggressors were fortunate because the umpire control group for the entire exercise had an officer, a captain, on the hilltop when the command group was destroyed. That officer controlled the incident, from the very beginning, in accordance with the exercise rules. In a real war, 2/5 would have suffered a great loss. After the loss of the battalion commander and his staff, 2/5 would suddenly have been commanded by whomever among the rifle company captains was senior. In such a case, effective command and control might not have been reestablished for hours, and many Marines might have been killed in the confusion.

At my makeshift—one radio jeep—headquarters a mile or two inland, we exulted at the capture of the commanding officer of 2/5, and I made a very cheerful report of that fact to the chief umpire. That self-important, sneering individual, a newly minted lieutenant colonel, was not amused or even mildly complimentary! Instead, he was actively hostile, snarling his disapproval of the trick we had played on 2/5. The pickup team of aggressors had expected a hearty appreciation of the clever work done by the lieutenant who masterminded the capture. What was received over the air instead, was a hectoring, hostile, personally demeaning lecture. The chief umpire voided the actions of the umpire at the scene of the capture, which was fine, however, he also spent a great deal of time dressing me down as he did it, which stunk. He treated me in the most arrogant and hypercritical fashion. It was my first real contact of any substance with that officer, whom I had only met briefly once before, and it boded ill for the future. The new lieutenant colonel was a very difficult and unpleasant man to work for or with—in any context.

After he had berated me for several minutes on the radio, I was able to switch to the aggressor frequency and talk to my lieutenant, who at that time, was still holding the 2/5 Marines captive. I told him of the chief umpire's decision and told him to pull off the hill and let his prisoners get on with their war. The lieutenant, with good reason, was so mad he could hardly talk. Even an apology from the captain serving as the unit umpire with the 2/5 command group did not mollify that enthusiastic officer. He remained thoroughly pissed off about my ordering him to let those people go for almost every moment of the next two years that he and I served together in 2/7. While the young Marines abided by the umpire's decision, they quickly began to exercise their age-old right to bitch loud and long. For days after the incident, they complained to anyone who would listen.

By nightfall of the first day, the 5th Marines were solidly ashore, and it was our job as the aggressors to test their unit security, keep them awake and worried, and to see if we could destroy any of their command-and-control elements. Before going to the field, we had acquired, by midnight requisition, many boxes of large sticks of marking chalk. Each Marine assigned an infiltration or destruction mission was told to mark any equipment he could have destroyed with a large *B* and a large *L*. That would signify to the umpires that the Baldomero Lopez forces had penetrated the unit security. In the morning, the commanding officer of the 1st Battalion, 5th Marines, found his helmet marked with a "BL." It had been lying beside his sleeping bag and the mark meant that he would have been killed while he dozed. In addition, the umpires gave the teams of young aggressors credit for placing explosive devices in, or on, two tanks and four artillery pieces during the night. Of course they also got credit for a large number of small arms and machine guns marked with the dreaded *BL* while their 5th Marine owners slept.

Naturally, no operation ever runs smoothly. Our minor triumphs against the landing force were partially overshadowed by the fact that one of our lieutenants daringly overplayed his hand, gaining both a significant success and more hatred from the chief umpire. He did all this with one brazen act. Somehow, the young officer had decided to bring to the field one of our old World War II flamethrowers, an eighty-five-pound man-load when carried into the field. He filled the flamethrower fuel tanks with water and added packets of powdered red dye. Once inside the 5th Marines field headquarters area, he made permanent enemies out of two or three of their more senior officers by waking them from their slumber, as they lay snoozing in their "bunny bags," and hosing them down with the very, very red water. This surprise visitation soaked their sleeping bags and destroyed their good humor. Even with the support of the umpires for a job well done, the Baldomeros had an extremely difficult time recovering that lieutenant. The wet, red, embarrassed, and outclassed regimental staff officers wanted to string him up from the nearest tree, where they also predicted they would string me up as well. None of us was surprised to learn that the chief umpire was also very angry with us, and I received a torrent of criticism over the exercise control radio frequency. He deemed our actions to be unprofessional. I considered that to be nonsense and communicated my full support to the offending lieutenant, commending his superior performance of duty and my appreciation of his clever use of the flamethrower.

The exercise went on for three more days and nights. As planned in the exercise scenario, we were steadily forced to the east by the 5th Marines. The Baldomero Lopez Marines played by the rules, mostly, and lost engagements that in a real shooting war they would have won.

At night, we were most often the victors because of the energy level of the teenage Marines. Those inexperienced Marines thought nothing of crawling hundreds of yards through the brush to scrawl another *BL* on some truck or a radio jeep that was being used at the moment by a member of the landing force. For reasons that were unclear, these brand-new Marines were not at all sympathetic to the attitude shown by the more experienced, slightly jaded, members of the 5th Marines. It appeared that the landing force Marines just wanted to get the field exercise over with as soon as possible. At times they acted a little bit bored by the entire effort. With that sort of dangerous attitude in play, the landing force Marines were often surprised as they slept the night away in their defensive positions. Oddly enough, a few units were seen to be acting bored, displaying a slightly superior air, and being lax while in night defensive positions in early 1966 in the Republic of Vietnam. There, snoozing in foxholes caused body bags to be filled by the riddled corpses of young men who should have been awake and ready to fight.

When we returned to Camp Las Pulgas after our stint as aggressors, we found that more Marines had come from boot camp, and a smattering of NCOs was checking into 2/7. The four rifle companies of the battalion were filling up, and some of the 3/9 Marines came back early from leave to provide leavening to all of the units. Training had not started in earnest yet, but the communications section was busy getting ready, and the personnel section was humming as it struggled to keep the administration for the entire battalion from faltering. Also, down in the motor transport area, there was a frenzy of preparation under way. Staff Sergeant Allen and his men were fully committed to preparing for a year-long period of lock-on training to help the Marines 2/7 to get into shape for transplacement to Okinawa.

For a short period, we faced a very disconcerting and unpleasant prospect. Rumors flew indicating that the chief umpire of the recent exercise, earlier a major who was on the list for possible assignment as our battalion executive officer, might now be assigned as our new commanding officer. We were nearly paralyzed at the thought. However, fortune smiled on us, and he went away to be the commanding officer, 3d Battalion, 7th Marines (3/7). We heaved a sigh of relief when he left 2/7, then rejoiced. We hoped that we would never have to cross his path again.

Later, at Camp Pendleton and in the war in the Republic of Vietnam, we saw that all of our own fears had come true for the officers and men of 3/7. Those poor Marines worked bitterly and very unhappily for that man for a very long time. When he left 3/7 during the war, after sustaining fragmentation wounds from a mine, he stuck to his normal leadership style; he loudly blamed a lieutenant who was with his command group for stepping on the mine. One doubts that any lieutenant would seek to step on a mine, so that response reflects badly on the senior officer. The rumor later reached us that a large segment of the 3/7 Marines who were nearby actually cheered when they heard the news about the departure of their "leader."

In just a few more days, the rest of the officers, SNCOs, NCOs, and Marines of 3/9 came back from leave, and the battalion was formed. We had a new commanding officer, Lt.

Col. J. K. McCreight, and an executive officer, Maj. Ray Wilson. All of the rifle companies now had been assigned commanding officers. Company E belonged to the wily Captain Tolleson who openly gloated that he had "snookered" me into the S-4 shop.

It was our good fortune on the battalion staff that Tolleson's abrasive style would be toned down and tempered by the addition to Company E of a superlative executive officer, 1st Lt. Roswell Paige, IV. "Rosey" Paige was a true Virginia gentleman who had been raised properly. He was smooth, capable, cooperative, and professional to the highest standards. Company F was commanded by Capt. Mike Welty, a quieter officer than Tolleson. Mike Welty seemed better suited for staff work than for leadership of a rifle company, but he appeared to revel in the task, and his company prospered under his leadership. Also important to that company was the fact that Captain Welty was a reasonable officer who remained calm when adversity was the order of the day. Company G was commanded by Capt. William D. Seymour, a smart, capable, and energetic officer who took prodigious joy in his assignment to command. Captain Seymour was an unusually good athlete. He had taught himself to play golf, as an adult, at the "scratch" level by simply working hard enough to master all of the basic skills. Bill Seymour applied himself with equal vigor to learning how to run a rifle company. Company H was commanded by Capt. Martin E. O'Connor, a tough, quick-thinking, no-nonsense type of officer. He was viewed by many as the most capable captain in the battalion. It was gratifying in all respects to see the battalion rise from the confused mess that the transplacement system had inflicted on it to become a real battalion again. From nothing at all—other than some abandoned barracks and steel sheds—with the addition of good Marines organized for war in the historic fashion of the Corps, we had created something, something we came to be ever more proud of as time passed.

# 2

# TRAINING FOR WARS PAST

In September of 1964, the 2d Battalion, 7th Marines began a formal cycle of training for transplacement. The program was familiarly known to everyone as "Lock-on." The term was supposed to mean that we were locked to our task and were not to be disturbed. This was, of course, just a pitiful joke. Interference with our syllabus of training was a constant with which we were forced to live each and every day of the entire program.

Lock-on was defined as a period of intensive training set aside as a necessary portion of the process to be used in making the battalion fully ready for transplacement or deployment to war. While the published orders showed that we were to be trained in 1964 and early 1965 for a summer 1965 transplacement to Okinawa, most pondered on our possible movement to the steadily expanding war that was taking place in the Republic of Vietnam. Some Marine units had already been committed to operations in Laos for a short time, and others were already operating under fire in the Republic of Vietnam. One of those operations, the deployment into the Mekong River Delta of Marine Medium Helicopter Squadron 161, was covered in considerable detail in the *National Geographic* magazine. The famous journalist, Dickie Chapelle, flew with the Marines and took the striking photos printed in the magazine. Her color pictures in that magazine showed the terrain and vegetation of the Delta provinces and gave the reader a small insight about the way things appeared to be happening in the Republic of Vietnam. Dog-eared copies of that *Geographic* were passed hand to hand by officers and enlisted Marines of 2/7.

In 1965, service in a shooting war was obviously a real possibility. Meanwhile, there was a battalion to build back to readiness. The training schedule was going to be a very complex and demanding one! It was of considerable interest to those of us who were in the battalion to learn that there were many and varied views at command levels far above ours as to just what kind of war—and where it might be fought—2/7 was to be trained to fight. From on high, we did not sense any particular urgency about Vietnam. There were classes and discussions on the subject of counterinsurgency operations, but other kinds of war received far more priority in the training syllabus.

Most of our senior commanders had been present when the Marines stormed across the beaches of the various islands over which the Pacific campaigns were fought in World War II. From them came a strong emphasis on amphibious assault truths learned so many years past. They still believed in the need for large assault landings across hostile beaches, and that kind of operation was to be highlighted in our training. The exercises planned for the coming year contained several amphibious operations. One was to be a division-size landing, the first since 1960. When we were deemed well enough trained, we were going to be storming ashore in a landing exercise that would be very similar to a World War II assault.

Many of our other combat-experienced commanders, working far above us in the chain of command, were just twelve to thirteen years away from battles in the bitter cold and snow of the Korean Peninsula. The schedule for the coming year clearly illustrated their input. Our scheduled year of preparation contained an entire month of cold-weather work. In November 1964, we were going to be going north to Pickle Meadows to take part in mountain warfare and mountain leadership training in the snow-covered Sierras.

Of course, we also had some leaders at all levels with little or no experience, but that shortfall seldom stopped them from being the holders of strongly held and, sometimes, ill-informed opinions. Even at the very highest level within the Marine Corps, the decision makers had clearly not lost any appreciation for the lessons learned in all wars long past. That, at least, was obvious from the content of many of the orders and other guidance documents that wended their way down the long chain of leadership to the working level in 2/7. We trained hard for all manner of wars. Some of the training was professionally rewarding and enjoyable. But other aspects of the constant pressure to qualify the battalion for every possible alternative created, instead, a tiresome drain on our energy and our enthusiasm.

At the infantry battalion level, getting ready for combat does not depend entirely on what kind of war is expected, or, for that matter, where the war will be fought. The first steps in getting ready involve the individual Marines and are almost completely independent of the kind of war that the leaders expect to fight. Every battalion must always begin with basic individual skills training, starting with the Marines at the bottom of the command chain. Training schedules focus on each individual Marine and his ability to function under pressure. Can that man march great distances, swim, shoot his weapon, read a map, use a compass, and demonstrate to the satisfaction of his leaders a host of similar skills?

Later, individual capabilities are melded with those of the other members of a Marine's fire team, mortar squad, or machine-gun team. Nothing works very well until all of the individuals are fully schooled and proficient in the skills they will need to survive on the battlefield. Each Marine must become part of the team, a player in the bigger picture that involves his actions with those of his comrades. No infantry battalion can be expected to fight well as a unit until each frontline Marine is proficient enough to pull his own weight in the organization.

At Camp Pendleton, the training of individuals began for 2/7 in earnest during September 1964. Every day, and often the night as well, was filled to overflowing with movement to various ranges for weapons firing and the never-ending classroom work needed to bring the new Marines up to the skill levels required. Subjects covered the gamut, from simple personal field sanitation matters to the need for everyone to be fully capable of taking part in combat maneuvers across unfamiliar terrain. Every individual skill set forth in the *Guidebook for Marines* received close attention.

All of this training had to be conducted inexpensively (we were poor!) and with miserable materiel resources. Therefore, we had to be innovative, all the time, every day. The 1st Marine Division had very significant shortages of the things we needed to have if the training was to be of solid professional value to the Marines. Field support for operational infantry units (now characterized by the presence of computers and logistics specialists) was often known in those simpler days as the "three bees"—beans, bullets, and bandages. All three of the bees were in short supply. It was again an almost comedic situation. Marines of 2/7 were again asked, or more truthfully, told, to do more with less. This condition again resonates with some truth today in the late 1990s. Marines often speak today of having to do more with less—as a normal function of their day-to-day existence. In the fall of 1964, after all the shortages were identified, the battalion got on with the task of doing a great deal of complex training with far, far less than the desired level of support.

Field rations were stacked by the thousands in Camp Pendleton's warehouses; however, the newer rations stored there were set aside as part of the stocks held for a mount-out to war. The small number of the older field rations that were allocated for training was insufficient to feed the battalion's Marines deployed all over the base to dozens of field firing ranges and to the many small-unit tactical training areas. At times the Marines faced the fact that it would even be necessary to skip the midday meal and "simulate chow." Hot chow is, of course, always preferred by the troops. It gives them something to bitch about, and bitching loudly and at length is one of the few great pleasures open to privates and privates first class in the Corps.

Throughout this period, the available field rations were hardly any culinary bargain, being as they were, Korean-War-era production items. It is always easier to feed small units with field rations than with freshly cooked food. Regardless, the cooks and messmen of the battalion accepted the challenge and set up field ranges in from as few as three to as many as eleven places in one day, doing their best to cook fresh meals for the Marines on the old M-1937 field ranges that had survived both World War II and the Korean War.

While there were no difficulties in getting all the fresh food needed to feed one thousand one hundred or so Marines in the field, our fuel allocations were so meager that there was often very little fuel available to boil water for field mess-kit sterilization. Without plenty of boiling water, a battalion of Marines will quickly be immobilized with serious intestinal problems. It was not unusual for some of the messmen in the field to be designated to siphon a gallon or two out of the tanks of the trucks of the 1st Motor Transport Battalion that carried them to the field—while the drivers were distracted in some way. As the months of intensive training continued, the 2/7 food section got better and better at "acquiring" gasoline to augment the small ration we could obtain through normal supply channels, so our battalion never had a serious sanitation problem nor was there an outbreak of food-related illness. Our medical section worked closely with the food handlers to make sure that nothing unacceptable to the rules of good field sanitation occurred to endanger the health of the Marines.

The fuel shortages that merely bedeviled the Marine cooks had a devastating effect on the motor transport capability of the battalion. Many long and worried hours were spent in the S-4 shop where fuel availability was examined and balanced against the needs and desires of the operations officer, Captain Doublet, who was working to get the battalion war-ready by training it hard. Again, a certain larcenous bent emerged and the Marines from the motor transport section also became adept at obtaining a bit (actually a great amount) of extra fuel here and there—without requisition documents.

Almost every driver just "happened" to carry a long plastic or rubber hose in his vehicle. Owning that hose and an expeditionary gas can or two made the acquisition of additional gasoline a great deal simpler.

Being scheduled for deployment to Okinawa in 1965, we were going to be involved in larger and more complex training efforts as the year passed. Those efforts would require the use of more of our vehicles, and it was essential that we save enough gasoline and diesel fuel from our allocation to make those exercises meaningful. Every day of training in 1964 and 1965 was based on worrisome trade-offs with regard to fuel matters. The fuel shortage problem never did get any easier until we deployed for combat, and then worrying about getting enough gasoline was replaced by more significant, life-and-death concerns.

Training Marines for war requires that they shoot their weapons on live-fire ranges, and it requires that they have blank ammunition for use in the practice of the maneuvers used in combat. The battalion did get a fair allocation of live ordnance to use, about half of what we wanted, but enough to put to good use. It was the allocation of blank ammunition that frustrated our training. All the experienced Marines had heard of, or had taken part in, field training when the troops in the field had to shout, *"Bang, bang, bang,"* to simulate firing their weapons. Those days descended on 2/7 in the fall of 1964. No matter how clever we were at making do with small quantities of blank ordnance, no matter how sharply we traded with other units, and no matter what the NCOs handling blanks for their companies had squirreled away, we did not have enough to train as we should have to make it realistic. Almost every regulation in the books concerning the use, handling, and storage of blank ammunition was violated by the battalion at one time or another. Men from 2/7 begged, borrowed, and stole blank ammunition from anyone and everyone. Sergeants who hid away blanks and booby-trap simulators under their bunks were ignored because to do otherwise would hamper training. Even in the S-4 office, there was always an illegal, "emergency," cache of blanks hidden out so that it would be handy. It was the logistics section policy to occasionally help out a company commander who had no ammo and who was desperate to impart realism into his training. As with gasoline, once we left Camp Pendleton for war, we had no ammunition shortages, none.

As the training was expanded from individual skills, through small-unit- and rifle-company-level skills, to training that involved the entire battalion, things became even more hectic. When the snow flew in the high Sierras, we were off to the Mountain Warfare Training Camp at Pickle Meadows. In the 1970s, long after 2/7 had gone to the war in the Republic of Vietnam, the Camp Pendleton infantry battalions that were heading for cold weather training would board C-141 Starlifters from the U.S. Air Force and fly north to the air station in Fallon, Nevada. From there, they would quickly bus over to the mountain training camp. In 1964, that same trip took us two miserable days on chartered buses. At the small town of Lone Pine, the bus convoy parked on a dark street, and the drivers went to a motel for some regulation-mandated rest. The forty Marines in each bus were left behind to sleep in their seats, where they would sit, shivering and shaking, until morning. Despite the body heat created by the packed-in Marines, the bus would chill down thoroughly, long before the drivers returned. In the morning the tired, sore, and angry Marines were transported the rest of the way up into the high country to begin what some called, "Can you survive with a frozen ass?"

At first, the mountain warfare training returned the battalion to an emphasis on individual skills. Obviously, we had to get to work to establish the proper foundation of skills for another war in the Korea of 1952. The fact that it was then 1964 and everything in Korea was quiet, or the fact that a jungle war was heating up in the Republic of Vietnam instead, seemed to be lost in the shuffle. Marines learned to climb on icy rocks, to do the slide-for-life across ice-cold streams, and to deal with the cold while worrying in their minds about a war far different in character from the one for which they were practicing. Marines are resilient, but that exercise in mild futility was very hard on the entire unit. There was a great deal of discontented grousing among the troops who just did not want to believe that the Marine Corps wanted to bury them in the snow for a month while everyone fully expected to be sent west to a war in a hot, dark green jungle.

Morale and attitude in an infantry unit are extremely fragile things. In any Marine unit that is being placed under considerable stress, small matters can have great impact on how the individual Marines feel about themselves and about their unit. At Pickle Meadows, the Marines of 2/7 were constantly chilled to the bone because their cold-weather gear, which was not very good in the first place, was worn and battered well past its normal service life. They were annoyed because they had to trek across the mountainsides to eat freshly cooked food at the central mess area because of the shortage in field rations. It was not that they hated the food, it was the march in the morning darkness and the evening darkness that annoyed them greatly. Most of them just wanted to drop into their sleeping bags at the end of each hard training day. Once a bit thawed and settled in their shelter tents, they would have preferred to open a ration to eat. Instead, they had to walk a mile or so, stand in line in the cold, eat out in the cold, and then walk back to their tents.

In the middle of the hardest snowfall that the battalion experienced during its weeks in the mountains, a morale-killing event took place. For some it was a watershed event that caused them to be resentful and utterly dissatisfied with the battalion and the Marine Corps from that day forward for many months. The thing that happened that night took place in front of about three hundred Marines and at least twenty-five offended officers and SNCOs.

It is a rock-hard tradition in the Marine Corps that privates eat first, privates first class eat next, and so on up to the officers, who eat after all enlisted men of any rank have been provided their meal. Because of this, the captains who commanded the rifle companies and their lieutenants would often gather near the logistics section tent, where we kept a fire burning, and wait there in conversation until their units had gone completely through the chow line. After their last man had been served, the second lieutenants would lead and the captain would be last to eat. That traditional way of life in the field dates back to the very first days of the Marine Corps. All troops know this Junior Men Eat First Rule, and they sometimes get to enjoy it. Troops have been known to suppress many a low-level chuckle when their officers have to eat scraps from the bottom of the kettle or their colonel finds nothing left for his meal.

On that particular night, it was snowing steadily and the troops from Company F and Company G were lined up in the dark to get their evening meal. The tired Marines were steadily stamping their feet to ward off frostbite and bitching among themselves. As the Marines slowly moved toward the chow line, a sergeant came down from the commanding officer's tent. That sergeant, the battalion commander's driver, had been ordered to bust into the chow line of the rifle companies to get dinner for Lieutenant Colonel McCreight. The embarrassed Marine NCO was challenged by the mess sergeant who knew the rules, but the driver had his orders. Our colonel was not going to come out in the snow and stand in line behind his deeply chilled troops. The shock was instantaneous. Several lieutenants threw their mess kits on the ground, grabbed them back up, and stamped away without eating. One, 1st Lt. James Lau, was so angry that there were tears in his eyes. He vowed that someday he would find a way to get back at the colonel for his contemptuous treatment of the troops. Of course, with so many privy to the event, it was only a matter of hours before every man in the battalion knew what had happened. For many of the Marines, it was only a small matter, one that would provide something to bitch about, not something that would disrupt their progress toward readiness to any great degree. However, for the officers and SNCOs, it was an utter betrayal of the long-proven standards relating to the relationship between seniors and juniors in the Marine Corps. The action was very destructive to morale and to the overall attitude we maintained toward that commanding officer and his desires for the battalion.

Once the battalion had suffered through its snowy preparation for possible return to the undulating terrain of the Korean Peninsula, we had our Christmas holiday break and then began training in earnest again. By February of 1965, we had a well-trained battalion of Marines, and it was time to practice the conduct of our trade with larger exercises. Captain Doublet and his S-3 section created many and varied scenarios, and the battalion worked through them. Some were defensive, and others mirrored the opening tactics of an amphibious assault, tactics that would be used beginning at the water's edge after an amphibious assault.

While that training was going on, it was clear that Company H, commanded by Capt. Martin E. O'Connor, was far outperforming the other rifle companies. Competition always exists within a rifle battalion. The companies are vying for the attention of the battalion commander, and each will do so in its own fashion; each rifle company in an infantry battalion reflects a bit of the personality of the commanding officer in the way it does business. That was exceptionally true in 2/7, wherein Company E was always complaining about something; Company F was quiet, extremely capable, but less demanding; Company G was calmly professional, and Company H had the honor of being the best at almost any task. Captain O'Connor and his executive officer, 1st Lt. James Lau, had fashioned a top quality organization.

As winter faded away, we continued the expansion of our training by getting ready to make a World War II amphibious assault. Our task in the spring of 1965 was to be a participant in the largest Marine Corps landing exercise since 1960, when the 2d Marine Division had taken part in a large exercise in Spain. To prepare, we did all the normal things that Marines must do prior to going aboard amphibious shipping. We started with individual aspects of shipboard life and moved on to teach all the skills needed to safely debark into landing craft from the attack-transport rails.

This very large operation was given the title Operation Silver Lance. The entire 1st Marine Division was to come ashore across three landing beaches on the coast of Camp

Pendleton. The operation was based on a mission of assistance to a third-world nation that was being menaced by an insurgency that was fomented and supported by its evil neighbors. As the figurehead for the nation we were to help, the division installed a gunnery sergeant Woodall as the president. Woodall was perfect in the part. He was a very large man with a great booming voice that, when in character, he used to berate those cast as his subordinates in the government of the friendly land. He had thick black hair that he was allowed to grow long for the part, and he slicked it straight back with enough grease to make it shine in the sun. He played his role with gusto, swaggering about, hectoring the officers of the division, and portraying to perfection a petty tyrant of the kind we were to meet later in the Far East.

The landing phase of Operation Silver Lance was very difficult. When the troops boarded the landing craft and amphibious tractors for the assault, the weather was marginal, and many fearful lessons were imparted to the Marine participants by the heavy surf on the landing beaches. Some of the landing craft were broached in the surf, and overturned, and others were driven so far up the beach by the waves that they were stuck fast. On the night of D day, under the lights used by the shore party and the beachmasters, the beaches actually looked as if a disaster were in the making. It was fortunate that no Marines were killed or maimed during the landings.

While 2/7 was aboard ship for Operation Silver Lance, the rumor mill was roaring at full power. Everyone seemed to have a theory about when California-based Marines would be off to fight in Vietnam. Many suggested that the ships would not return to Camp Pendleton at all and would, instead, sail west to deliver the battalion to war. Of course, that was impossible as none of the division units in the operation had more than a minute portion of their total equipment and materiel stocks. Also, there were no platforms in the ship's hold containing the mortar, machine-gun, rifle, and pistol ammunition that the troops would take ashore if committed to war.

By the end of April 1965, the battalion had been well trained for all manner of wars except the one that looked most likely. Courses had been taught on counterinsurgency and guerrilla warfare, but not with the intensity of our other training. The Marines of 2/7 could perform an amphibious assault, they could scale steep mountain heights in the snow, and they were ready for almost any kind of scuffle in between. As a battalion, 2/7 was ready, willing, and able. Even training for wars long past has value, and the Marines of 2/7 had gained valuable personnel cohesiveness during the high-stress training process. As deployment continued to be rumored, everyone in the battalion was comfortable with that possibility. We felt that 2/7 was fully trained and capable of working together at a level of professionalism that made our battalion fully ready to go anywhere to do whatever we might be asked to do. The hard work of the operations section had paid off grandly, as the battalion was obviously ready for the long-planned overseas deployment, whether to Okinawa for peacetime readiness duty or to the war in the Republic of Vietnam. It all depended on whether the dithering leadership in Washington would see fit to send us west.

# 3

# PACK IT UP—NOW!

Not very long after Operation Silver Lance, in the middle of May 1965, all of our questions were answered by one message. The 7th Marine Regiment was ordered to deploy to the war in the Republic of Vietnam. After all the myriad rumors and all the constant concern expressed in the press about the fact that the United States was building up its forces in the Republic of Vietnam, it was almost a relief to know we were actually going. The nonsense would cease—or so we thought—and a realistic focus on doing those things for which we trained as Marines would finally be a valid possibility.

We were told that we would be deploying from California to add our combat power to that of the already deployed infantry units from the 3d Marine Division. Maj. Gen. Lewis W. Walt was already in Vietnam, and he commanded all deployed elements of the Marine Corps, air and ground, through his 3d Marine Division headquarters.

We 2/7 Marines would deploy to the Republic of Vietnam as a unit of Regimental Landing Team 7 (RLT 7). RLT 7 was to be based upon the structure of our parent regiment, which would separate from the 1st Marine Division. Of course, the regiment was to be very heavily reinforced by other elements of the 1st Marine Division, Force Troops, and the 3d Marine Aircraft Wing, all of whom would be attached prior to sailing. We were told that on arrival in the Far East, we would drop our 1st Marine Division title and would be redesignated as units under the operational control of the 3d Marine Division. We would still be 2/7, but we would be a 3d Marine Division battalion as soon as we checked in for duty. The shorthand used in the message traffic contained terms like OPCON (operational control); ADCON (administrative control); and RLT 7 was directed to be prepared to "chop to," i.e., report in to work for the commanding general, 3d Marine Division. While this sounds more than slightly confusing, it was really fairly clear to those of us who were going. Using all this shorthand jargon helped to establish for everyone in RLT 7—including the Marines down in 2/7—a simpler and more efficient way for General Walt to exercise his control over our activities when we got to the war.

Now the fretting was over! We were going to stop playing games and actually go to war. No more getting ready to maybe, possibly, perhaps, deploy to "someplace," instead we were now going to be entering the "real" world. No more shouting bang, bang. As the word of our immediate deployment became known to everyone in the battalion, it caused a frenzy of work for every part of the unit.

All of the staff sections in the battalion headquarters of 2/7 were suddenly placed under great stress. For the operations section, the stress was extraordinary. They had far too much to do, and too little time to do it. Yet, it is always that way for any operations section in peacetime or wartime—they don't ever seem to have the number of people needed to do the job, and the entire section is constantly overworked. When a unit is ordered to conduct an amphibious assault, there is almost as much stress in the logistics section as well. Because 2/7 had very little time until its sailing date, doing the job required an around-the-clock effort, with lots of people sleeping on the deck next to their desks. Our headquarters building continued to be one of the most dismal places in the world to work; it was simply a horrible dump. But now, still struggling in the gloom and dust, all of the staff sections had some really complex and difficult things to accomplish in short order. There was damn little time left to us if we were going to do what was required to comply with the directive sending us to war.

When the executive officer, Major Wilson, called me to his office the morning of 18 May, he revealed to me that we were going to go to war. Our battalion had received the official orders, and we would be sailing, on the morning of 24 May, from the naval station in San Diego. We would embark and sail to the Republic of Vietnam as Battalion Landing Team 2/7 (BLT 2/7), a part of RLT 7. As I listened to Major Wilson's calm recitation, it was immediately clear that 2/7 was in need of many things before we could meet that sailing date. It would be a mind-crunching time during the following five days if the S-4 section was to meet even the most basic needs of the battalion. Every single materiel aspect of the battalion had to be reviewed, items that were beyond saving had to be immediately replaced, and items that could not be replaced had to be repaired. Since the entire regiment was going, we could not borrow from a sister battalion; we had to find things both through the system and/or through the back channels in double-quick time. Our sailing date was almost on top of us, and everything had to be ordered, allocated, and included in the embarkation planning.

Every kind of thing that we required had to be obtained from outside sources who were normally very slow to react to our needs. At first look, nothing about the effort appeared to be easy. Requisition priorities suddenly went from "routine," which meant a response at some indefinite time in the future, to "emergency," which meant that there must be an immediate response from all supply sources. All of the emergency requisitions would be signed personally by the commanding officer. With the flick of a pen, each of those documents would have the power to provide an important improvement to the battalion's materiel readiness status. Going to war looks deceptively easy in the movies. In real life, it can be a rough ride. Getting ready to go for real is not simple!

When he first asked me to come into his office and shut the door, Major Wilson was very emphatic in directing me to keep the information about deployment secure. He pointed out that the S-3, Captain Doublet, and I were the only officers to whom, at that time, he was revealing the information that we were departing. He asked that we in the S-4 keep our knowledge to ourselves while we got busy on the planning. When I asked, as I thought appropriate, if he wanted me to go next to the office of Lieutenant Colonel McCreight for his commander's guidance, there was a pause. Major Wilson then chuckled a bit and dryly explained that I would not need to plan on doing so at this time. He stated, to my surprise, that he was no long the executive officer, he was now the acting commanding officer, and that the previous commanding officer had departed. The operations officer from the regimental staff, Lt. Col. Leon N. Utter, would be joining us aboard ship as the new commanding officer, 2d Battalion, 7th Marines.

For all hands, the command change was a very great surprise, though hardly an unwelcome one. Learning in this fashion that the old commander had virtually vanished into thin air was both unusual and intriguing. His instantaneous departure, without fanfare, illustrated to all of us at the working level, that the higher commanders were aware of the fact that 2/7 needed new leadership if the battalion was to be ready for actual combat. Both the commanding general of the 1st Marine Division and the commanding officer of the 7th Marine Regiment had direct, personal involvement in the selection of Lieutenant Colonel Utter to take us to war. As a matter of fact, Lieutenant Colonel Utter had been well known by both of those senior officers for the majority of his adult life, in peace and war. It was clear that both the general and the regimental commander reposed a great deal of that "special trust and confidence," that is mentioned in a Marine Corps officer's commission, in Utter's leadership abilities. In the battalion, we didn't even have time to ponder this shift in our fortunes. There was just too much to do and too little time to do it all.

Our classified order to deploy for war was not some silly little kid's playground secret that could be kept under close wraps for very long. Marines are alert, and unusual activities catch their attention quickly. When a unit's S-4 shop starts unrolling the plans of ship decks, and stacks of ammunition and explosive requisitions, all marked at the highest possible priority, are piling up, the conclusion is quickly reached by passersby and casual observers that the activity is no drill. It took less than a hour for all the troops who passed our office to sense what was about to take place. Minute by minute, the number of deeply serious faces multiplied, and the officers and SNCOs got busy with the myriad details that fell into their areas of responsibility. In just a few hours, everyone knew full well that the battalion was going to war, and it was going to be leaving very soon. All of 2/7 was humming with extraordinary activity. None of it was the usual peacetime make-work nonsense.

From an equipment standpoint, the battalion was in miserable condition. Problems ranged from the duplicating machine in the S-3 shop that was on its last legs, to jeeps and other vehicles that were truly unfit for peacetime or combat use. It was a very gratifying surprise to all in the headquarters when a new duplicating machine, a top quality product of the A. B. Dick Company, arrived in the dark hours the first night. It came in a special truck, along with a myriad of other essential items, from the Marine Corps supply depot in Barstow, California. These were items from our very first priority-one requisitions. The duplicating machine and the items that arrived with it had been requested during the afternoon of 18 May on an emergency basis. For once, it appeared that we might be able to obtain all the gear we needed to do what we were expected to do. Captain Doublet and his section would, at least, be able to print readable briefing documents, planning guidance, and orders needed to keep all elements of the BLT functioning.

Not only did we get a new duplicating machine but we immediately began to receive visitors from the 1st Marine Division staff, all of whom came to help us cope with our more pressing problems. They had the rank and the authority to press other units for help, to facilitate rapid response of all elements of the division, and to order anyone who was not cooperative to become so. Those were valuable skills that made our lives far easier amid the chaos. All of the tired, worn, old vehicles of Staff Sergeant Allen's motor transport section were examined by experts, and some disappeared to be replaced by used but serviceable rolling stock. Because the other division units had not yet been ordered to go west, the staff officers were willing to shift tired, worn equipment to units staying behind. That would, at least partially, solve many of our most important motor transport difficulties. For those wheeled vehicles that could not be swapped, we submitted, and had immediately filled, requisitions for critical parts. The mechanics assigned to the motor pool worked there, and they ate there, and they slept there as well. Truckloads of parts and supplies began arriving at all hours of the day and night, and when a critical item arrived, a 2/7 mechanic was there, ready to install it no matter what time the load was dropped.

One problem was nearly unsolvable. The Marine Corps of the 1960s had a jeep, known as a Mighty Mite, that was an absolute horror to keep operational. The Mighty Mite (actually the miserable thing was officially designated as, Truck, 1/4 ton, M-422) was made of magnesium and other light metals throughout. These metals had been chosen because it had to be very light in order for it to be lifted by the helicopters used by the Marine Corps. When the design team created the vehicle, our helicopters had been smaller and the Mighty Mite's light weight essential. After a few years, helicopter lift capabilities had greatly improved. Alas, we still had the ugly little darling in all of the Marine battalions. Mighty Mites ran poorly (the designers had skimped on the power plant, too) and their suspensions, transmissions, and transfer cases were not as sturdy as one needed in a military vehicle. Getting together enough of those substandard pieces of equipment and getting them as deployable as possible was an enormous task. Staff Sergeant Allen, the old pro who ran the motor pool, used every legal and illegal technique he could muster to get his section ready. He succeeded grandly. Perhaps the motor pool equipment was not very well designed for use in a war, but that hardworking Marine SNCO made sure that what he had worked as well as it could. Through diligence and close supervision, he made the 2/7 Motor Transport Section fully ready for deployment.

On occasion, there were minor flaps that actually provided humor to the tense and demanding situation. Among the many hundreds of items that were requisitioned were fifty replacement recoil springs for the battalion M-60 machine guns. Recoil springs are important. They can, and do, break at the most inopportune times. Every gunner should have a spare recoil spring in his gear if he is going to be in the field doing much firing. Because we expected our machine gunners to fire a great deal in a shooting war, we wanted to have a stock of recoil springs on hand. All emergency requisitions, for anything, required the commanding officer's signature, but when that requisition went in, it was considered to be just another one of the huge pile of standard requests for spare parts so the recoil spring paperwork was not taken to Major Wilson for signature. The error was mine, as I had a lapse of judgment, thinking that things like parts for machine guns should just come with everything else when asked for by the battalion.

About an hour later, the supply sergeant who had gone to pick up a truckload of items requested earlier that day, hand carrying the recoil spring requisition, came back looking very sheepish. He had returned with everything requested—except the machine-gun recoil springs. That requisition had been denied by the supply mavens and was stamped, in red, "No AMRD." Here was a code, new to me, one that I had not seen before on any document. Nobody standing nearby in the S-4 happened to speak the exotic language of supply so I picked up the phone. After a few minor, rather loud and rather profane, shouting matches with division supply, I finally got an explanation of the code. The four letters, it turned out, meant that 2/7 had no "average monthly recurring demand" for recoil springs, and the supply weenies had no intention or interest in giving us anything that we had not been using at a manual-prescribed or previously proven use rate. My reaction was volcanic, but there was no time to go to division supply to kick their asses as the troops desired. Once we had Major

Wilson's signature, we went back. This time, two battalion SNCOs, each over six feet four inches in height, were hand carrying the emergency requisition, and the supply folks just backed down as meek as lambs. They handed over fifty of the desired recoil springs to the large, glowering representatives of 2/7. Another glitch had been overcome at some cost in time, energy, and enthusiasm.

Getting all of the recoilless rifles and the mortars ready to leave Camp Pendleton required a great deal of energy from the battalion armory team. Some of our weapons were just worn out. Others were in the shops at division being rebuilt. Before sailing, 2/7 had to have a complete set of ordnance inspections on items in hand and some sort of replacement policy for items that could not be repaired and returned before we sailed. It was lucky that the division commander and his staff made the effort to assist us in this important area of responsibility. Once we had set forth our needs and our problems, the division ordnance officer took over and just buried anyone who did not want to assist us in getting ready. Many of our battalion rifles had to be shipped out and replaced, just as we were doing with the larger, crew-served weapons. All in all, the ordnance support we received prior to deployment was of the very highest quality. With only minor exceptions, the battalion weapons would be fully ready for use when we finally got across the Pacific Ocean.

In the Communications Platoon, commanded by 1st Lt. Al Kehn, we had some of the worst problems that any element of the battalion encountered during the preparation for deployment. To begin with, all of the radio equipment of the battalion was marginal—even when it was working well. Our gear was not up to the latest standards, and there was little or nothing we could do about it. Every unit in the division had the same tired old radios. Swapping would be of little use, except that we could trade off those items that were listed as "inoperative, awaiting parts." Those we sent away to other units, using a paper transfer of ownership. In the same fashion, we traded away radios that were in the hands of the supporting maintenance facilities, gaining replacement items as directed by the division communications officer. Regardless of our efforts, and those of all the senior division communications officers, we had to sail with radio equipment that was only slightly better than that which was used fourteen years before in the Korean War. In fact, many of the jeep-mounted radio sets had been used in that war. Not even the best efforts of everyone involved could improve our communications equipment, and there were times in 1965 and 1966 when that substandard equipment let us down in combat.

Every staff section was buried in details, all of which had to be coordinated by Captain Doublet and his S-3 crew. Since 2/7 was going to war in amphibious-assault shipping combat-loaded in preparation for an amphibious-assault across an unknown beach, he had to plan every single thing in an inverse order. Doing that required the development, by the S-3, of a very flexible plan for landing on any hostile beach that might be assigned to the battalion. His basic plan for the landing would include all of the unit assignments and a set of detailed scheduling sequences for these units to go ashore during the assault phase. When that rough plan was initiated, the loading sequence for the assault shipping would begin to firm up.

In addition to all the weapons and equipment, our battalion was going to be taking men to combat. This salient fact was made evident by the enormous workload of the personnel section (S-1) of 2/7. Even being in lock-on for a planned deployment did not mean that we had all the people we needed. All shortfalls in manpower had to be made up from other units, and there were going to be some severances as well. The S-1, 1st Lt. Nate Jolley, had his hands full. He had to examine every Marine in the battalion to ascertain his deployment status, transfer out those whom the law prohibited from being assigned to combat duty, and join the flood of arriving Marines that would bring the battalion up to 106 percent of its normal Table of Organization (T/O) mandated strength. Marines who were sole-surviving-sons and other nondeployables often complained bitterly and made every effort to circumvent Lieutenant Jolley's orders, but he stuck to his guns and made the battalion personnel legal for deployment within three days of receiving the word that we were going with RLT 7.

Closely allied with the hardworking personnel section was the battalion chaplain, Lt. (chaplain corps) Walter Hiskett, USN. Chaplain Hiskett had been a Marine infantryman in Company F of 2/7 in 1950 during the famous battle of the Tok Tong Pass in Korea. The story told about him by the battalion Marines is that he made a deal with his God, promising to become a minister if he survived the bitter battle in the snow. After the Korean War, he left the Marine Corps to complete his education. He lived up to his promise to become a minister, returning to active duty as a navy chaplain. Stationed in San Diego, where he learned that the Seventh Marines were going to war, he begged his superiors for the privilege of serving a second time in combat with his old battalion. As we prepared for deployment to war in May 1965, he returned "home" again to 2/7. His work with the troops, individually and in groups, as a calm, resolute source of firm counsel on how to prepare for service in wartime, went far to ease their minds. Every Marine could look at him and see a man who had survived the most trying conditions possible. Chaplain Hiskett was also of great value to all the unit commanders in the BLT; he turned away anyone who even appeared to be a whiner or a complainer in search of a soft shoulder to cry on with a very firm admonition to pay attention to what his leaders told him and to get on with doing his job. Chaplain Hiskett stood tall for all as an example of how a man should be ready to face service in combat. That wonderful, tough, and caring man went on in his military career, rising to serve as the chaplain for the entire Marine Corps, an assignment for which he was supremely well qualified.

Combat loading of an assault transport begins by identification of the vehicles or pieces of equipment that will be wanted on the beach absolutely last. Those items will follow ashore behind every other vehicle or piece of equipment assigned to the battalion landing team. Thus, they become the first to be positioned on the schematics and the first to be loaded in the ship's hold or on the vehicle platforms below decks. Once that final item is assigned a spot, the embarkation planning begins to become a reality. If the whole task is done right, the key vehicle or piece of equipment that is wanted first on the beach can be found, ready to go, on the highest equipment deck of the assault transport. It should be sitting there, all ready to go ashore with the assault elements—precisely on time and with the unit that needs to have that item when it crosses the beach.

The entire process of embarkation, fully combat-loaded for war, is quite similar to solving a very complex, three-dimensional puzzle. Neither ship hulls nor military hardware can be easily warped, shortened, contorted, or compressed, therefore, the proper use of the available space is critical to doing things right. In many instances, the various items must be fitted into spaces with only an inch or two of clearance. Combat-loading a ship, even one configured for amphibious-assault use, is not an easy task for a peacetime practice landing. For a full-on deployment to war, with very heavy loads on the vehicles, with all manner of extra items lashed on the outside of vehicles, and with some attached units that arrive bringing an extra trailer or two, the Marines working on the embarkation planning can be buried under a gigantic load of nearly impossible problems. All of this complexity fell on S.Sgt. R. D. Tackett who worked almost without a rest from the word "go" until the moment our assigned ship, the amphibious attack transport, USS *Pickaway* (APA-222), stood out to sea from San Diego. It was a tribute to Staff Sergeant Tackett's competence that when our BLT sailed, the staging areas where we had prepared for loading were empty. All of the equipment and vehicles for our huge battalion landing team had been successfully moved aboard the shipping, carefully tied down for sea transport, and properly accounted for on all of the embarkation documents.

Now that the word from Washington, D.C., was official and preparation for embarkation was set in motion, the BLT began to take form. The parent commands of the units that would be attached to 2/7 began to bring in their vehicles and equipment. Often they would send the drivers who were going with the battalion to stay with 2/7 instead of having them deliver the vehicles and go back to their own billeting areas. That cooperative spirit made convoy movement of all of the BLT 2/7 vehicles to the ammunition pickup site and to the port of embarkation an easier and more flexible effort.

A totally positive spirit within RLT 7 was facilitated by a meeting personally conducted by the regimental commander. After much speculation and rumor, Col. Oscar F. Peatross, who previously had been issued orders for a late June 1965 transfer to another duty station, the Marine Barracks at the naval training base at Guantanamo Bay in Cuba, was permitted to remain in command of the 7th Marines. Had he not been given special relief from those orders, we were anticipating the arrival of Col. Louis H. Wilson, a very respected recipient of the Medal of Honor during World War II and future commandant of the Marine Corps, to take RLT 7 to war.

Once firmly sure of his job, Colonel Peatross called all the attached and supporting element commanders, and a good portion of their staffs, to a meeting at Camp Las Pulgas, near the 7th Marines headquarters area. He delivered a very serious and very impressive speech to all hands, covering the points he wanted us all to consider as we put his enormous, task-organized combat team together. Colonel Peatross was a very calm and dignified southern gentleman of the old school. He never raised his voice; instead, he made his points clear by the force of his intellect and his professional personality. That, and the fact that we all knew full well that Vietnam was going to be his third war as a Marine officer, made us all feel both proud to serve under him and comfortable as members of his command.

As RLT 7 became clearer in its organization and the size of the attachments that were being made to the RLT became known, it was obvious that ours would be one of the largest such task-organized units ever assembled by the Marine Corps. More than eight thousand Marines and their medical support personnel would be placed under the command of Colonel Peatross. The RLT was assigned an amazing amount of artillery firepower. This was very impressive, as was the remainder of the list of units that was to accompany us to Southeast Asia. RLT 7 was going to be taking along far more than would be found in a normal unit and equipment list for a reinforced regiment. That was pleasing, as we all hoped that the artillery and other combat support units would always be there when we needed them. We expected to need them in any serious fight, and it was good to know that when we got overseas those cannons would not be left behind at home, sitting unused in the gun parks at Camp Pendleton.

At least initially, Colonel Peatross would also be placed in command of some aviation elements attached to the RLT. This surprised many at the time, but in the light of knowledge gained from books written by military historians thirty plus years later, it was an obvious way of getting more fixed-wing and rotary-wing assets into aviation units already operating in the Republic of Vietnam. Getting there, without declaring them openly or as separate deployments, bypassed some of the idiotic wrangling and internal battles being waged in Washington. Doing it this way was better than getting some staff officer to break the news to Robert MacNamara or President Lyndon Johnson that the Marines wanted to deploy more aviation. Such a remark might provide enough energy for the secretary of defense to force another long-winded, statistical, extremely nonoperational study of the matter. More air power went to the Republic of Vietnam, and the matter was not mentioned in great detail to those who might want to analyze it, mess with it, or deny that it would be allowed to happen.

Every ship that was going to take RLT 7 to war already had on board a large load of ammunition and other supplies. This storehouse was called the L-Form, for reasons unknown to me then and unknown to me now. Each ship in the amphibious force always carried its assigned loads of L-Form in order to be ready for deployment without the delay and danger of embarking tons of explosives prior to sailing. Loading of explosives in these huge quantities takes many, many hours. It was fortunate that all the expert planners had done their job correctly because that amount of additional loading time would not have been available to BLT 2/7 if we were to depart as ordered on 24 May 1965.

L-Form munitions were embarked in various quantities and types as the result of careful calculation by high level, naval amphibious force, embarkation specialists who were tasked to create, revise, and update for the amphibious force a thirty-day quantity of ammunition for various-size Marine deployments. Since deployments could range from a battalion-size operation to deployment to war of a full strength Marine division, that meant the ships must have something like a "variety pack" aboard. On an attack cargo ship, an AKA, one might find tons of eight-inch ammunition stowed below, even if the eight-inch guns were not scheduled to go with the particular unit that was embarked in the accompanying attack transports. However, since the ships always kept stowed in their holds a wide variety of ordnance, the shipping could support almost any deployment. To face the access problem head-on, the war stocks on each ship were stowed vertically in the holds. Vertical stowage allows the disembarking Marine unit to get at any one kind of required munitions without first being forced to move ammunition of another kind and stack it somewhere.

Two days after receipt of the order to go to war, the battalion parade ground began to fill with vehicles—ours and those of the attached units making up the BLT. From the S-3's landing plan, a detailed embarkation plan had been created that "staged" (a shorthand word that means lining them up in sequence) the vehicles we were taking with us. There were staging assignments set forth for each of the several activities that were going to be taking place as the BLT was getting ready. The first such evolution was the simple staging of the vehicles on our parade deck. That permitted a detailed and careful check to see that we knew all the things that we had to know about the vehicles. Nobody wanted a surprise when the cranes began lifting gear aboard ship. Surprises can hamper or halt embarkation, and since everything was on a time sequence that ended with the absolute finality of the chosen sailing hour, we had to pay close attention. Some of the vehicles would go to San Diego under their own power, and some would be transported to the port of embarkation on flatbed trailers. Regardless of how they were to get to San Diego, both types of vehicles would first have to be loaded with their prescribed loads of ammunition.

Once the BLT had control of all the vehicles and they had been inspected and staged in sequence, the next step was the publishing of a full plan for loading every vehicle with its particular load of munitions. Loading of all the ammunition and explosives would require the second staging evolution, with every vehicle in its proper sequence. The second staging of vehicles took place near the portion of Camp Pendleton where the 1st Motor Transport Battalion trained its drivers, a flat area large enough for staging of all the BLT 2/7 vehicles, in a long column. At the same time, other columns from BLT 1/7 and BLT 3/7 would also be moving through the site. Handling of the columns would be fairly easy because the ground was hard, and there were several wide entry and exit points. All of this was to take place just off Basilone Road, where all the trucks could be seen by anyone, military or civilian. So much for secrecy! The trucks would stage, enter the loading site in convoy, load, and depart for Camp Las Pulgas where they would be restaged, exactly in the sequence they had been assigned previously, on the 2/7 parade deck.

The area where the loading took place was selected because it was large enough to suit the ammunition handling Marines, and it was far, far away from any of the Camp Pendleton billeting areas. Many tons of explosives, ammunition, and pyrotechnics were being loaded, and everyone wanted lots of space in case all and sundry suddenly went away in a blinding flash. Military ammunition is designed to be safe as it is being handled, but we could see no harm in worrying.

Vehicle load planning is complicated by the rules of ammunition handling, the limited space available on some vehicles, and the likes and dislikes of the particular commander who owns the vehicle. As an example, one of the rifle company commanders wanted both white phosphorous and fragmentation grenades in his jeep trailer. It was his view that he wanted them close at hand to issue when needed by his Marines. The captain could not have his way because that load mix was not going to be permitted at Camp Pendleton or aboard ship. The U.S. Navy has safety rules that are very precise and very stringent, and when we Marines load one of their ships, we must always find a way to comply with the detailed safety rules. At the same time, we tried to ensure the commanders had immediate access to the items they thought necessary when they went ashore. The yelling and confrontations often lasted for extended periods, but there was almost always a way to satisfy most of the petitioners for special treatment, and the plan was set for execution. The amphibious navy of the 1960s was always very cooperative, and it energetically tried to help the Marine units get embarkation loading completed with minimum fuss. However, "Gator Navy" sailors have some tough rules to follow, and they enforce them to the maximum.

On the morning of the fourth day after our receipt of orders, at the appointed loading hour, all of the BLT 2/7 vehicles began driving, in a very slow and sedate column, to the loading site. Huge stacks of every sort of ammunition awaited us, and the loading began. Forklifts loaded artillery ammunition and other heavy items. Young Marines assigned by nondeploying units to working parties, loaded the rest by hand. Checklists had been used to set out the precise and specific amounts of each kind of ammunition prescribed for each vehicle. The process took several hours, but at the end, the ammunition sergeant and his team could look across the loading site and see only empty boxes and other debris. It was a rewarding sight that meant that the vehicles, by then staged again on the 2/7 parade deck, had all of the ordnance items set down in the plan for loading aboard ship.

Everything we had requisitioned via the division ammunition section had been delivered. Ammunition had moved from the dump on the day requested, at the time desired. Every vehicle was carrying the prescribed load for its first movement ashore. An impressive amount of combat power had been shifted from those who kept it safe during peacetime to the hands of those who were trained to use it under fire. It was also impressive to look at the trucks and see just how heavily laden they were and to watch how very different the attitude of the drivers was toward their job when they were driving vehicles with tons of high explosives aboard.

With the ammunition loading completed, the vehicles were ready for the trip south to the Naval Station, San Diego. Once they arrived, all of the vehicles were again parked—nose to tail—in their planned loading sequence. All of our wheeled and tracked vehicles were fully staged at the port of embarkation for loading aboard the assigned shipping.

When a reinforced battalion embarks, some portions may travel to the objective area on other shipping. For example, trucks that are to carry tank ammunition for the tank company supporting BLT 2/7 would naturally be staged in another site. From there they would be loaded on an AKA where the tanks would ride to war. While it was our job at the BLT to load and manage those trucks, as part of our task-organized unit, the realities of space and capability would place those trucks on another ship.

At the San Diego Naval Station, with all of the RLT vehicles lined up to suit the beachmasters from the navy who were on scene, everything was ready. Loading began in earnest and the "last needed" vehicles and supplies disappeared into the deep dark holds of the ships. Loading never goes terribly smoothly, as something always breaks or something does not fit where the plans say it should fit with inches to spare. Nevertheless, BLT 2/7 had a remarkably easy embarkation load-out aboard USS *Pickaway*. Each vehicle was swung up and over the ship's side by the winch booms and then carefully lowered into the correct level, moved into its assigned place, and chained down with great care.

The final major evolution for the embarkation was the establishment of the munitions for the D-1 platforms aboard all the shipping. That stock of ammunition, grenades, explosives, pyrotechnics, mortar rounds, and other items needed by the infantrymen in the assault, are all stowed for direct issue to the troops on D-1, the night before the landing. Calculating all of the amounts to be placed on that platform, aboard each ship, includes everything from the twenty-one rounds of .45-caliber pistol ammunition set aside for each Marine or corpsman carrying a pistol to the first day's allowance of TNT blocks for the attached engineer platoon.

By nightfall on the last day permitted to us, the Marines of the BLT 2/7 were aboard ship. Everything belonging to the BLT was stowed as ordered, and it was possible to report to Major Wilson that the battalion and its reinforcement were ready to sail. We were set to go. The BLT had met its responsibilities, and it was now up to the U. S. Navy to transport the battalion and all its attachments across the Pacific Ocean to war.

# 4

# TRANSIT TO WAR, THE OLD WAY!

Embarked Marines are always somewhat nervous and slightly antsy at sailing time. The Marines of BLT 2/7 aboard the USS *Pickaway* in May of 1965 were no exception. Everyone was aware that our movement was not a drill and that his future was up to the fates. Our departure from the naval station at San Diego held within it the seeds of fear for every one of us. The concern was not so much a personal fear as it was an inner, basic concern about the unknown and the unexplained. Our departure was not a World War II sailing where we Marines were clearly off to do battle on hostile beachheads against a well-recognized enemy. Instead, being sent to the war in Southeast Asia was more like stepping off a cliff into a dark abyss. Nothing given to us, from any source, served to provide us with a clear idea of the missions that the BLT was going to be asked to perform. For that matter, we had almost no information about just what kind of war it was that awaited us eight thousand miles from home. Those things that we read in the newspapers and saw on television made it look like the Viet Cong were just a bunch of kids in black pajamas who only won when they blew some unwary American military advisers apart while they slept in their beds. That kind of attitude could have led to all manner of serious and misguided overconfidence. Such ideas would have to be countered with training designed to make the 2/7 Marines respect the Viet Cong as potentially formidable foes.

Basically, all of the conversations and training given to us about counterinsurgency actions in Malaya and the counterguerrilla warfare against the Huk-Bala-Hap in the Philippines actually combined to add to the confusion. Studying the war against Ch'in Peng in Malaya only served to produce information that would never be used by the troops of the battalion or most of their officers. As to what a guerrilla war was actually like, there had been no clear clues passed down to us. None of the well-meant training in California could make shit-dipped punji spikes sticking up from a ditch, or the ballistic crack of bullets slashing through the bamboo, real, clearly understood aspects of life in the battalion. Such things would remain just theoretical concepts, until they were actually encountered. Of course, we had classes on the war and on the "enemy," something that was open to fretful imaginations, our own overwrought internal demons, and lots and lots of confusion. Yes, the Marines were antsy, and they had good reason!

Loading aboard the attack transport that would take us to war consumed the period 19 May to 23 May, 1965. On 24 May 1965, Lieutenant Colonel Utter took command of the battalion. That afternoon, all of the Marines and U.S. Navy medical personnel of the 2d Battalion became the personal, life-and-death responsibility of that thirty-nine-year-old combat Marine. The ship stood away from the pier, and we sailed west.

Our first order from Lieutenant Colonel Utter was for all hands to muster on the weather decks as the USS *Pickaway* stood down the channel of San Diego Harbor and made for the open sea. His order included everyone, even the mess cooks and those unlucky Marines who had been assigned to wash dishes and clean up the mess decks. The new colonel was emphatic about what he wanted, and he made sure that every officer knew that he was serious. He made it clear that he wanted *all* of the mess cooks, *all* of the working parties, and any other BLT 2/7 Marines and corpsmen who might be assigned below decks for any reason, on deck to watch as the United States of America was left behind in our wake.

Our new commander, who was obviously a fantastic improvement over the previous one, was going to be leading us in the third large-scale war to be fought by the Marine Corps in his life of service to Corps and country. Lieutenant Colonel Utter was calm, resolute, attentive, impressive, and absolutely professional in every single thing he did during his initial hours as the new commanding officer of the battalion. He was a tough, dynamic leader, who clearly would brook no "half-steppers." Lieutenant Colonel Utter was not a stranger, but he had only been known to us before, from a considerable distance, as the regimental operations officer. During our training at Camp Las Pulgas, we had learned that this tough, rugged individual was famous for getting to the point in very few words. As we jumped smartly, to be sure that his order was followed to the letter, the rails of the attack transport were packed with the 1,836 men of the BLT. Every last one of us was Utter's responsibility. It was his job to take us to the unknown.

As the USS *Pickaway* rounded slowly to port and began to pass up the channel, headed for sea, with Point Loma on the starboard side and the ammunition piers at the North Island Naval Air Station on the port, Lieutenant Colonel Utter began to speak to us on the ship's booming loudspeaker system. He pointed out the ammunition bunkers on the port side and spoke of standing guard there as a private first class, early in World War II. As the colonel continued speaking, everyone on the weather decks looked quietly out from the ship. There was hardly a murmur from the serious young men leaving their country, perhaps for the last time. The nature of their inner thoughts was mirrored on the faces of the older, Korean-War veteran SNCOs and the few officers who had seen combat. Only a few of the men present on that ship had ever served in combat, either in Korea or in World War II, but all had thought about it a great deal. For some, that was the first time they actually understood that the cost of being a Marine is, potentially, payment of the supreme price. Death was a real possibility, and we understood that fact.

As the colonel spoke, the long column of heavily laden

ships pushed steadily toward the open seas and a war not yet understood in any form. Our leader concluded his remarks with, "I want each of you to look to your right and look to your left. Look directly at the men on either side of you. Remember their faces. Remember that we are going to war, and one of those men will probably not come back. It is not easy being a Marine. That is the truth. Good Luck. God Speed! You may secure."

Some drifted below decks immediately. Others stood at the rail and watched as the coast of California dropped farther and farther behind. A few Marines, having skipped their evening meal to stand there while night fell on the wind-whipped and choppy sea, could be found at the rails long after dark. After all the ships of the convoy cleared the channel and took up their steaming stations in the task-force formation, the movement west began. It began relatively slowly at first. The sea was growing fairly rough, and it felt as if the ships were moving with care as, free of the constraints of the land, they began getting comfortable again.

Some Marines quickly began to succumb to seasickness as our formation began the long journey into a quartering sea that made the ships roll and pitch dramatically. The speed of the formation was really determined by the need to rendezvous with shipping that had sailed that afternoon from Long Beach with other elements of RLT 7. There were ammunition ships in that task force element as well as some amphibious shipping that was bringing men and equipment from the Marine Corps air station at El Toro. Additionally, the speed of movement was affected by the sheer weight of our materiel and munitions. Every ship carrying any component of RLT 7 was loaded with the enormous stocks of ammunition. The ammunition loaded in San Diego had come to us from the bunkers in Fallbrook Naval Ammunition Depot. Amazing amounts of other munitions had been taken aboard ships sailing from the Long Beach Naval Station. Those supplies had come from the bunkers at Los Alimitos Naval Ammunition Depot and had joined all the El Toro based equipment and supplies in the staging areas on the docks of the Long Beach Naval Station.

Just looking at the ships as they steamed westward brought home the reality of what we were doing with great clarity. In all training exercises the Plimsoll mark, which is a line that is painted on a vessel's hull to denote the expected depth of its draft when the vessel is loaded to match design calculations, stood well above the surface of the sea. We were now sailing for a real war, and the Plimsoll marks on all of the amphibious shipping in our convoy lay well below the surface. Our RLT was the largest regimental landing team ever deployed by the United States Marine Corps, and the ships of the task force were settled deeply into the sea by the weight of our materiel and explosives.

The first morning at sea was characterized by an effort by everyone in the battalion to get acquainted with the ship. There was an enormous amount of simple roaming about as the young Marines learned where everything that they believed to be important was located and how to get there. Besides getting the troops settled, it was essential to check every vehicle and every piece of equipment stowed on the weather decks and in the holds below. Tie-downs were checked and rechecked, load lashing was checked, the batteries were checked, and the ammunition loaded on all vehicles was carefully examined to see that it had not shifted in the pitching and rolling that started when we went to sea. The checking of vehicles and equipment at least twice every day was soon to become habitual, just an automatic response to the arrival of another day.

Of course, as always, the navy had plans for the embarked Marines, too! We had the requisite drills for man overboard, battle stations, and abandon ship that every embarked Marine finds to be completely mind numbing—even while admitting freely that all such drills are obviously necessary. Petty officers on board USS *Pickaway* quickly went to work training the BLT Marines on proper shipboard movements during drills, emphasizing efficient traffic in the passageways and on the ladders throughout the ship. Anyone on the starboard side of the ship was to go either forward or up, and anyone on the port side would only be permitted to go aft or down. Any Marine who did not want to cooperate would find that he was grabbed by the master-at-arms and firmly, often physically, corrected by both the senior petty officers of the ship and by the SNCOs of the BLT.

Between working at various assigned tasks and the simple act of settling in by just looking around the ship, it still did not take long before all the embarked Marines began to acclimate themselves to life at sea. They could find their way to desired locations, and that made them feel that they now belonged on the ship. Marines love going to sea so that they can visit the ship's store to buy cheap cigarettes. At the "geedunk" they can buy cheap ice cream and cold sodas. The USS *Pickaway* was a very sharp ship with every evidence of good leadership from the top down. The crewmen were very positive and friendly toward the embarked Marines and appeared motivated to do their best to make the long transit of the Pacific Ocean as pleasant as possible. At times in training, we had encountered units of the navy's amphibious shipping, which treated us as an enemy. That made for difficult times, fistfights, and navy gear "gone astray" when the Marines left the ship. On the USS *Pickaway*, we did not encounter one individual who was other than professional in his dealing with the embarked troops.

From his BLT staff, the new commanding officer began requiring a series of long and detailed briefings. He wanted to be fully educated by every staff section and by the attached element commanders. Lieutenant Colonel Utter was determined to gather to himself all of the information about the battalion and its attachments that he would need to make command decisions. The colonel was gentlemanly as he posed his questions, and briefing him was a breeze. He was a senior Marine officer who clearly respected those who worked for him. As the commanding officer, he was willing to defer to the expertise of his subordinates in their particular fields, while at the same time forcing careful discussion and explanation of the things he needed to know. A true westerner with a residual twang in his speech, Lieutenant Colonel Utter was very good at camouflage, hiding his superior intellect behind a facade of "old-country-boy" low-key humor. The more we came to know him during those initial briefings and discussions, the more impressed we became with our new boss. We began to feel that we had been far more than just fortunate to be assigned to work for this man. This feeling came to us because his entire personal and professional approach to those who served him was an immeasurable improvement over his predecessor. We found him to be a man we respected, a man with whom we felt comfortable. His knowledge and his common-sense approach to anything and everything was of great value in helping us to settle into a professional mind-set.

In the day-to-day operation of the battalion, the executive officer, Maj. Ray Wilson, proved to be the perfect man to work with Lieutenant Colonel Utter. Major Wilson was also a Marine who dated back to the grim days of World War II, and he was totally unflappable. Nothing that happened seemed to upset him. Problems were encountered, but Major Wilson's view was that each was merely another item to be worked through. He never lost his cool, nor did he ever berate those junior to him who may have created the problem in the first place. His working relationship with our new colonel seemed to all of us to be an absolutely superb melding of abilities and attitude.

Each day, as we transited, first toward the Hawaiian Islands, where it turned out that we would make a short stop, and later when we left the islands for the northern Pacific Ocean, life aboard ship began to look more and more like a World War II movie. The weather quickly began to grow warmer, and on the weather decks there were constant physical fitness drills by unit commanders who sought to keep all the troops in top shape. Everywhere, Marines were cleaning and working with their weapons. Both the individual weapons and the crew-served weapons were cleaned, oiled, and reoiled. The officers and SNCOs held inspections and reinspections at all hours of the day. Every aspect of our days at sea came almost verbatim from the training texts that were used to prepare Marines for the shipboard phase of the amphibious warfare world. In garrison, Marines have always been given instruction in "Troop Life Aboard Ship," using the lessons learned in the island-hopping Pacific War. Our BLT 2/7 Marines were actually living their lives aboard ship exactly the way the officers and men of another generation had lived their lives as they rode ships like the USS *Pickaway* to Iwo Jima in February 1945, or to Okinawa on April Fools' Day of that year. The passing of twenty full years seemed to reflect no changes, none.

Each day after the weapons had all been inspected, the classes endured, and the long chow lines braved, the Marines got busy. They swapped rumors, played cards, looked quietly out to sea, and some even wrote letters home to be posted from Honolulu. As one might expect, there were a few John Wayne types who were always strutting around with something to prove. They could be found daily in the gun tubs or other small, secluded spots, honing big, ugly knives and talking out of the sides of their mouths. Many just had to tell anyone who would listen just how "bad" they were going to be when we got to combat. Oddly, while they took themselves very seriously, most of the other Marines just chuckled and got ready to do whatever was next on the day's agenda. Those who talked of winning the Medal of Honor or made other fatuous remarks were mostly scorned as acting very much like little boys whistling as they walked past a graveyard at midnight.

As one would expect on an overcrowded ship, hot water for bathing was in short supply, and many Marines just lazed away their evenings waiting for a chance to take a quick navy-type shower. The navy shower requires that you get wet quickly, turn off the shower, soap up quickly, turn the shower back on, and rinse quickly. You are to get out of the shower as fast as you can accomplish the necessary steps. These steps must all happen in a matter of moments, but despite the inconvenience, these were hot showers, a very important aspect of life. Later in 1965 and in 1966, as Marines and corpsmen dug into the mud and waited out their sweat-drenched nights in the Republic of Vietnam, there would be long, very nostalgic discussions about the pleasure of those short showers.

By that time, the concept of being clean was almost an impossible dream. Like dry socks for jungle-rotted feet, warm showers became part of a lovingly remembered past.

The enlisted men of BLT 2/7 lived rough and hard aboard ship; their crowded accommodations were not dissimilar to those in World War II amphibious shipping. The USS *Pickaway* actually was a World War II attack transport that had delivered troops to Iwo and Okinawa, but it had been refitted and improved over the years. Regardless, personal comfort for the embarked troops was no more part of the deal than it had been twenty years before. There was some minor-league air-conditioning, and the troop spaces were a bit more habitable, but life in the troop billeting spaces was definitely not comfortable, nor was it easy. Troop bunks were still too narrow, too short, and too hard to permit anyone to sleep comfortably as the ship worked in the swells. Of course, in all the berthing spaces, space requirements determined that the bunks would always be stacked three or four or five high. Each group of bunks stood very close to the next group of bunks, so close that most everyone had been stepped on by his neighbor a hundred times and/or had banged his head on the bunk above him a hundred times before we got to Hawaii.

For the SNCOs and officers, things were a bit better, but nothing like life at the Ritz. For the lieutenants and most of the captains there was the "bullpen" in officers' country, where thirty-nine young officers shared a space with bunks three high, gear piled in every conceivable corner, and a total of two tables and ten or twelve chairs standing about in the small open area that was available. For a few of the more senior captains there were a couple of staterooms—tiny places where gear could be stowed, and we could revel in the fact that we had only two bunk levels instead of three. Of course, the colonel and the major had more comfortable quarters as befitted their status and their responsibilities.

Life at sea quickly became a steady drumbeat of hard work with mealtime serving as the only real period of relaxation during the day. At the wardroom table, hungry young officers relaxed by all manner of pranks, unlimited teasing, and the worst ribald humor imaginable. There were silly things such as a few "free-style eating contests"—particularly on Thursday night when the wardroom was served curry—and long quotations from a book about the French Foreign Legion. This book about the history of the Legion was passed from hand to hand throughout the voyage. Many were heard to loudly intone, "There is no mother! There is no father! There is only the Legion! March or die!" Joking around and playing poker late into the night were just ways to ease the tension. We had little or no idea about events outside the ship—other than the limited news flashes found in the ship's daily bulletins. We were almost completely cut off from the world, so we retreated into ourselves and accepted that our personal worlds, just like the worlds of those who had been hauled to the Pacific War battles before us, had become exceptionally circumscribed.

Those officers who did not gamble at the evening poker game, shoot dice, or play hearts, would read or sleep away the evening hours. Of course there were the wardroom movies, but those were usually a less than exciting way to spend two hours in the evening. Even the frequent swapping of movies with other ships of the task force did not produce much, and it was not long before the movie lovers had seen everything even slightly worthwhile that was available.

Entertainment for the Marines of the battalion was also severely limited, just as it had been aboard ship twenty years before. There were the few movies (same set of films that the wardroom watched) that were shown on the weather decks, and there were some activities conducted by the chaplains and the education officer. With little else to do, many of the troops gathered in small groups on the decks at night and played hearts.

One of the events that really typified our almost complete reliving of the World War II experience at sea was the organization of a BLT Boxing Smoker. The sporting event took place in a ring fabricated on one of the main cargo hatches. These hatches were the entryway into the holds where our equipment was chained down to the various storage platforms that lay above the ammunition holds near the keel. Just as men did on the way to Guadalcanal, Tarawa, and all the other landings in World War II, our Marines took part in an evening of cheering and shouting while a few brave souls pummeled and pounded each other as they careened around the ring. A few scores were settled, some noses got broken, but most of the fights just wound down to a decision as the men who took part learned just how wearing it is to keep up a boxer's pace during three rounds of hard boxing. Because of the ship's working in the sea, the footing was sometimes precarious, and a few of the fighters fell without taking very hard punches. Others went down hard when they found that they were matched against a "real" fighter who could knock them silly in the first minute or two of the first round. The BLT Smoker was deemed a success at relieving tension, even if it did look as if we were players in a movie about Marines set in 1944 or 1945.

Arrival at Pearl Harbor was a thrilling moment. Every man who could be there crowded onto the weather decks at dawn when we steamed into that famous harbor. Honors were rendered to the port side as we passed the USS *Arizona* Memorial. All hands could feel the aura of history in that harbor. The USS *Pickaway* was assigned to berth at the Mike docks across the southern arm of the harbor from the *Arizona* Memorial. As we steamed by, it was hard not to think with a sad reverence of the men lying trapped for twenty-four years in the hull. As we turned to go alongside our pier, many of us looked back across the open water at their tomb and remembered. In a very few minutes, the lines were made fast to the bollards by working parties of Pearl Harbor sailors, and BLT 2/7 had officially arrived in Hawaii.

Shortly, we learned that RLT 7 would be granted liberty ashore. What a surprise! Everyone thought it odd. In San Diego, our move had been treated as a highly classified matter, not to be discussed with anyone. Yet in Hawaii, our arrival was in all the local papers, and our troops would soon be on liberty ashore, openly illustrating the presence of a Camp Pendleton unit on the way to the western Pacific. Regardless, there were no sad faces among those who were going to get ashore for a day or so. The men of the liberty party piled gleefully off the ship and vanished into the warm Hawaiian sun to be treated like tourists and fleeced of their money in the process.

For some, the visit to Hawaii was a time for more work. The operations and intelligence sections had to make coordinating and information collection visits to the Fleet Marine Forces, Pacific, (FMFPAC) headquarters on the hill overlooking Pearl Harbor. The personnel section had to work as they were going to be required to send a few Marines ashore, men leaving the battalion and/or its attached units for disciplinary or administrative reasons. They also would be joining some new men who had, for one reason or another, missed our sailing date or had been sent out by air to add to our strength. Of course, the communicators and the classified material clerks would be joining the operations and intelligence folks up on the hill at FMFPAC, sorting out all manner of equipment and classified communications matters. This important work would include obtaining the codes and ciphers that we would need when we arrived in the Republic of Vietnam.

In the area of logistics, there were many things to sort out and much checking and rechecking would be required before liberty call for drivers, mechanics, and the embarkation section could be sounded. Every single vehicle, every tank, jeep, mechanical mule, bulldozer, forklift, or amphibious tractor embarked on any of the shipping had to be started and run up to operating temperature. Other pieces of equipment, such as generators and air compressors, would also be started and their ability to function properly evaluated. The colonel did not want any surprises when we tried to get those machines to work after the sea voyage.

Of course, starting all those engines in the holds of the ship posed a very significant threat to every man who was involved. Poisoning by exhaust gases was a very serious possibility. To help us, the sailors on every ship rigged blowers and fans to move the carbon monoxide out of the holds so the Marines could work. All of that took several hours, but in the end BLT 2/7 was able report to Major Johnson, the RLT's S-4, that all vehicles and equipment were ready. With great shouts, whoops, and loud hollering, the men who had been sweating in the holds to get all that equipment checked out, left the ship and took off for the pleasures shoreside.

Many are the tales told and retold about that thirty-six-hour liberty in Hawaii. Every beach, every bar, and every alleyway on Waikiki was teeming with familiar faces and our trademark high-and-tight haircuts. Some of the Marines had friends who were stationed in Hawaii and made quick use of their cars and their patio furniture as they relaxed with a few beers after the dry transit from California. However, most of the Marines preferred to be on the streets with the rest of the RLT, taking part in the last day and evening of free association and laughter they might ever spend on the soil of the United States of America. Everyone played hard, swam hard, drank hard, and as the hours before the end of the liberty grew short, most tended to be fretful and a bit nervous about getting back to the ship on time.

Some probably already missed the shipboard routines and wanted to get back into that familiar mode of life. Some almost certainly felt a bit out of place among those ashore who were not going to be part of the "great adventure." Both the civilians and the shoreside military that we encountered seemed to be part of some other life, one in which it did not appear that we belonged. Many of the Marines and corpsmen of the BLT felt that alienation and chose to come back to the ship early. Even those who waited until liberty was expiring, quickly kissed their dates good-bye and climbed rapidly, with the rolling gait of true swashbucklers come home, up the gangplank. They appeared to sense the finality of their return aboard ship. Those last few boarded, to vociferous catcalls from their friends, under the watchful eye of Lieutenant Colonel Utter. At midnight, all of the BLT was back aboard and ready to go to war. For the BLT Marines, the die had already been cast, and our number had come up. Even the pleasures of the liberty time ashore seemed almost an improper intrusion on our lives, an intrusion that took time from more important matters.

The next morning, the USS *Pickaway* and all the other ships of the amphibious task force sounded their horns and stood away from their moorings, again forming a long line as they made for the harbor entrance. A few friends from local commands came down to the docks to wave, and a band played some of the old martial tunes. As it had been in San Diego, that sailing, too, was suddenly very serious business. We were gone, perhaps forever, from our land and we were now embarked for the purpose of doing our nation's business. It is sad to know now, more than thirty-three years after that sun-dappled morning, that the powerful men in Washington, D.C., who had set the effort in motion did so without knowing a damn thing about what they were doing. The Marines of BLT 2/7 had already been betrayed, and many of them would die because of the arrogance and inexplicable actions of others at the highest levels of our nation's government.

At sea, we were once again whole. We no longer had ties with those outside the BLT, those with whom we did not fit. We were at ease, knowing that everyone in our midst belonged with us. It was comforting to be back among our own kind. With practiced ease the Marines slipped back into the routines established on the first leg of our journey. Weapons were again lovingly checked and rechecked, and time was again measured by the length of the chow lines and the time remaining before the next meal. Navy showers were laughingly compared with showers taken in hotel bathrooms ashore that had lasted for extended, almost sinfully extended, periods. Those long, wondrous showers with the steam roiling around the room, may or may not—depending on the truthfulness of the teller of the tale—have included passionate female companionship. Truly told or not, the showers taken in Hawaii were grist for the tale-tellers and a matter of fond memory for many of us for the next thirteen months.

A few days out of Hawaii, the amphibious task force hove to and stopped steaming toward the west. It was disconcerting to be sitting still in the middle of the North Pacific Ocean. The reduction almost to silence of the constant familiar noises made by the ship caused the whole thing to seem almost unreal. The USS *Pickaway* lay to, with its bow pointing to the west, rolling gently and quietly. The ship was being lifted and caressed on the starboard side by long rolling swells that were heading south from the arctic toward the north-facing shores of the Hawaiian Islands. Boats were put over the side and shark-guards with M-1 rifles were posted on both the ship and aboard the circling small boats. We were amazed to learn that it was time for a "swim call." The bottom, which many swimmers would like to touch from time to time, lay seven thousand feet below the smoothly rounded swells. A huge cargo net, of the kind used to debark troops into landing craft, was hung over the side, and anyone who wished to do so could dive or climb down into the deep blue sea and take a saltwater swim.

Some of the Marines were glad to take part, but others were so terrified by the thought of more than a mile of water between them and the sea floor that they could not force themselves to go for the refreshing swim. Every shark-guard, Marines and sailors alike, was ready and willing to shoot any shark that came near, but the swim was conducted without a single fin's being sighted. Looking across the water at the men swimming alongside each ship it was easy to think that when it was over the Marines might be back on deck learning from their leaders the layout of the beaches of Saipan or Tinian.

While the Marines were swimming, the RLT was busy planning. Its efforts had to encompass almost every sort of mission assignment because those who had sent us west were not sure just what it was that they had in mind. The RLT staff was forced to prepare for tasks as diverse as "administrative landings" across a pier and full-on assault landings on a beach held by a determined enemy. Of course, none of our confusion would have been necessary had there been any clarity to the national intent of the United States vis-à-vis the Republic of Vietnam.

At our level, we all felt painful frustration, almost anger, at the fact that we had so little information with which to plan. Marines are habitually the most willing of creatures when faced with hard or dangerous tasks. However, when they are treated contemptuously, they tend to develop long-term ill will toward their tormentors. We were beginning to feel exceptionally put upon as we steamed west without so much as a landing site having been divulged to us. Where were we going? We did not have a clue.

In the days following the Hawaii liberty, we steamed steadily westward on what we assumed to be the great-circle route across the sea. Expecting to unload soon in the Republic of Vietnam, the men of the BLT worked hard in order to be ready for anything. Everything was checked over and over and over. The D-1 platform on the ship where the ammunition was stacked for preassault issue to the troops was inspected and the ammunition counted and recounted so often that we laughed about wearing it out. It was from that time that a certain cynicism began to grow. And out of that time of cynical consideration evolved the attitude that was later spelled out in our battalion motto: "Ready for anything—Counting on nothing." All through the time we served together in the Republic of Vietnam our motto held true. It was prophetic, and a most appropriate way for every man to look at the battalion's life during 1965–1966. We got many helpings of "nothing" while we tried to be ready for anything.

One day during the long transit, our amphibious task force suddenly altered course and steamed to the northwest, toward Okinawa. We did not understand why such a thing was being done to us. But there we were, a few days later, 18 June 1965, anchored off White Beach, Okinawa, with orders to unload. We were furious, but we followed our orders, and unloading began immediately. The battalion command post and all the troops were moved to Camp Schwab on the island. Only the logistics section and those working parties directly involved in the unloading remained aboard ship.

For sixty-eight hours the Marines of BLT 2/7 sweated, strained, and cursed, working without sleep, as every vehicle was put ashore, every crate of ammunition sent ashore, and all but the working parties who were cleaning out the ship's holds, moved to shoreside billeting. At the end of that backbreaking effort, the logistics section was able to report to

Lieutenant Colonel Utter that every item of ammunition and pyrotechnics had been safely moved ashore to the ammunition dumps; that all vehicles had been safely moved ashore and returned to their units; that the entire evolution had been conducted without any loss of life or serious injury to a single Marine; and that the BLT working parties, known as the Ship's Platoon, had left the USS *Pickaway* clean and fully squared away when they departed the ship for the last time.

In the early morning gloom, it was still rather dark as I related all of the above to our leader in his room. The colonel's face was tired, and the stress he was feeling was evident as he looked up at me. Without comment, he handed me a message sheet directing RLT 7 to reembark—on different shipping— and proceed to the Republic of Vietnam. Of all possible outcomes, that was the most unexpected. Of course, it also meant that everything we had done at Camp Pendleton to prepare for embarkation—everything—had to be redone immediately, without an office and without any rest.

Staff Sergeant Tackett the unflappable logistics chief, was in the main, a pretty cool, self-contained customer. However, when he was told that we had to create new loading plans and reembark the BLT on a different ship, he blew up. He cursed those on high who could not make up their minds, those who enjoyed screwing-over all of the Marines who worked for a living, and just about everyone else who came to his mind. It was impossible to disagree with his view, and we all vented our anger at those who farted around in Washington when they should be paying attention to what was happening in the world. Once past his understandable explosion, Tackett grabbed the plan-form layout for the new ship we would use, the USS *Okanogan*, and began creating a new loading plan. Since none of us had been asleep for most of the last seventy-two hours, Lieutenant McElwain, the clerks, and I served as detail checkers for Tackett as he created the first layouts on each page of the loading plan. Our job was to make sure that Tackett's plan did not leave out any vehicles, that it again matched the operations officer's plan for landing, and that we again recalculated the ammunition loads for all vehicles to match their location in the planned movement ashore.

The logistics section set up a field site, where it was expected that it would be possible to control the reloading of BLT 2/7. Our choice was to set up camp right in the middle of White Beach. It was desirable to be near, but not too near, the tower manned by the shore-party people who had the mistaken idea that they, "somehow," were in charge of all of White Beach. We chose to live and work in a large hole that some bulldozer operator had seen fit to dig for purposes unknown.

On the beach with BLT 2/7 were going to be the other battalions of the RLT, the rear elements of Regimental Landing Team 9, and at least elements of eight or nine other units of the 3d Marine Division. In addition, there were all manner of stray elements, known simply as "the cats and dogs," present on the beach. Some of those tag-along units would be added to our load or the load of one of the other BLTs. They would be tucked in wherever they could be fitted into the available shipping headed for Vietnam.

When our vehicles began to arrive, they were again loaded down with their ammunition, and they sat staged in long rows on the packed sand to await loading in the inverse order of their planned use during the landing in the objective area. Everywhere I looked on White Beach, there were rows and rows of parked vehicles and hordes of moving vehicles—the traffic control effort made by the military police (MPs) was utterly overwhelmed. Every unit had to pitch in from time to time with officers and Marines to help the overworked MPs get some balled-up traffic mess unscrambled. After a few very difficult hours of shouting and shoving, it was pleasant to see things actually working the way they should work. Once the beach traffic was under control, the vehicular portion of the back-load finally became a manageable act.

The next major hurdle for BLT 2/7 was the vast array of palletized gear that was going to be moved across the beach. In San Diego that part of the load was easy. Big trucks moved to the side of the ship and the ship's booms lifted the pallets and placed them in the holds. Across a sandy beach, moving all the materiel was a different matter. Forklifts moved the pallets to the water's edge, the shore-party cranes lifted them into the shuttling landing craft, and then, out they went into the anchorage where the pallets were lifted from the landing craft by the ship's cranes for stowage below.

One pier was available. Some of the ships were slated to come alongside the pier for cargo loading. However, the vast majority of the RLT gear was going to move across the flat sandy beach. It quickly became obvious that the key to all things on the beach was control of the big, all-terrain forklifts. Many Marine units are equipped with those multipurpose wonders. The big, rough, and powerful machines can work all day on a sandy beach without getting stuck. It was Staff Sergeant Tackett's view that whoever had control of the forklifts would, in reality, control White Beach. Jointly, he and I decided that we would establish our own forklift control plan, one in which all forklifts we could get our hands on would be working hard. We planned to see that they would be primarily working hard for BLT 2/7.

The section clerk was sent, in a jeep with a trailer, to the nearest Okinawan village. He went there with a handful of money. He was not to return until he had obtained a jeep-trailer-load of good Japanese beer and a remarkable pile of ice. On his return, we opened all the beer cases and piled the mixed Kirin and Asahi beer into a big pit in the middle of our working area. We covered the beer with ice and went out to speak kindly, soothingly, convincingly with forklift drivers wherever we might find them on White Beach. The BLT 2/7 pitch was a simple one. We told every forklift driver that if he would come work for us for an hour or two or three or four he would get some very cold beer for his trouble. We also had available an open pallet of rations to counter the fact that some of the units had not seen fit to feed their forklift drivers either a morning or a noonday meal. The offer of both food and cold beer was overwhelmingly acceptable to the forklift drivers. Suddenly, without fanfare, BLT 2/7 was running an "incentive-based" embarkation.

With the good sense that one would expect of Marines doing a difficult task, to a man, the forklift drivers rallied to BLT 2/7. One corporal even downed his beer and offered to crown me "God of the Beach!" Since humor makes almost any situation better, I accepted the title with laughter. Meanwhile, the work we needed to do began progressing with ease, and the loading of the USS *Okanogan* was ahead of any schedule we had thought possible. That permitted us a moment of calm, so we began to work the beach to see just what we could scrounge from the materiel assets that were staged for movement aboard ship by other units—particularly items not well guarded.

Improving materiel by collecting items belonging to others is a Marine Corps art form. With help from a team of willing engineers, we obtained pallets of concertina wire that nobody was watching. Parked all alone we found an "unloved" water trailer that had been left behind by its prime mover. On some pallets sitting at the back of the beach, we located three gas operated refrigerators that might be useful for storing medical supplies. All in all, we made ourselves quite useful. We also got some items that unnamed units had probably found difficult to fit into their combat loading plans. By the end of the loading of the USS *Okanogan*, BLT 2/7 had been enriched with considerably more useful gear than we had taken with us from Camp Pendleton.

In the middle of the second day of our working the beach, we looked up and realized that we were about to receive a helicopter lift of troops. Flights of CH-34 helicopters were bringing elements of BLT 3/7 to the beach by air. Sadly, no coordination of any kind had been attempted. There were no helicopter support team (HST) troops from the shore-party battalion available. Since our "contracted" forklift drivers were busy working happily for us, the logistics section took time out to act as the HST for the arriving troops. Each of us stood at a quickly selected landing site, signaling to each arriving helicopter that it was his touchdown point. Some of the time our signals were obeyed, and at other times, the CH-34 would just land anywhere the pilot damn well chose to set his machine down. Of course, all of us had to make do without eye protection or dust masks. Once the third wave of the transport helicopters was down, we grabbed some 3/7 Marines and had them take over the HST function. Then we dashed back to our hole in the ground, wiped out our eyes, and had a cold, cold beer to clear out the dust and sand from our throats.

Because those of us on the beach managing the back-load were so tired and spaced out from the three days of unloading, we needed some help to keep us functional. The battalion medical officer handed over a full bottle of magic white pills to keep us fired up. Without those amphetamines, we might not have stayed awake long enough to get the BLT onto the ship. Of course, depending on "speed" is not the best way to work, but it did the job for us for the two critical days. After the logistics section was done and had moved from White Beach to our billeting areas aboard USS *Okanogan*, we all crashed into sleep without even loosening our bootlaces.

At the very last moment, after all the loading of all the ships was completed and the USS *Okanogan* was about to sail, the word changed again. Capt. Al Doublet, 1st Lt. Al Kehn, and I were to return to shore. They wanted the operations officer, the communications officer, and the logistics officer to fly to Da Nang in the Republic of Vietnam. It was at Da Nang that Major General Walt had his interim headquarters, and someone, someplace, felt that we three ought to fly there and talk with the 3d Marine Division staff. It took five to ten tries, violently rough tries at that, for First Lieutenant McElwain to get me up. I was not really present for duty as I had just gone into a very deep sleep. Once he had me standing, I stumbled—rather than walked—to the rail to return ashore. In a way, the three of us felt cheated. We were to fly down to the Republic of Vietnam and await the arrival of BLT 2/7 on shore. After all our work and effort, we would not be with our unit when it began its combat tour in Vietnam. That seemed bitterly unfair, and it made for a deeply felt disappointment.

We three got some bunks in a barracks, assigned by someone ashore who was awake, and collected a night's sleep.

Other than the liberty time in Hawaii, it was our first moment away from BLT 2/7 since we had sailed from San Diego a month before. We were uneasy and somewhat lost in a detached sort of way. It felt as if our actions were happening to someone else. In the morning, someone in the 3d Division rear command post got the three of us some high priority orders, and we departed Okinawa around midday. We flew south on a Marine C-130 that was lifting priority cargo to Da Nang. The highlight of that noisy and uncomfortable trip was the sight of three crated popcorn machines that were tied down in the center of the aircraft cargo deck. All three popcorn machines were marked "Red Ball Cargo," i.e., the popcorn machines had priority over any and all cargo shipments being made from Okinawa to the war. The sight was both annoying and depressing. There, just two or three feet from our faces, was another indicator that something about that war might already be out of kilter.

After what seemed an interminable flight, we arrived in the Da Nang area. Using a very steep approach to the field to avoid possible enemy fire, the pilot delivered us quickly to the runway where he landed the aircraft without incident. The first thing we saw on the field was another C-130, a forlorn sight as it was badly damaged. One wing was hanging down, one of its four engines was blown completely off as a result of an explosion that had nearly destroyed the aircraft. A day or two before, the Viet Cong had rather successfully carried out a sapper attack. Several aircraft were destroyed, and the entire facility was in an uproar as security was being tightened while the cleanup of debris continued. The three of us left the airfield with the impression that the enemy we were going to be fighting was both a capable fellow and one who understood how to target the weak points in security.

In Da Nang, we visited with the 3d Marine Division headquarters where we got to talk to the various staff sections without learning very much that would help us.

At Major General Walt's headquarters we were told that BLT 2/7 was to land at a town known as Qui Nhon in the II Corps Tactical Zone (IICTZ, "Two Corps"). That was a considerable distance south down the coast from either the Da Nang enclave or the Chu Lai enclave in ICTZ*—both of which were being populated with Marines. Qui Nhon was an area that had presented a difficult problem, one that was held to be of grave importance by the Military Assistance Command–Vietnam (MAC-V). The commanding general of MAC-V was reportedly annoyed because the city had been the site of a very successful Viet Cong sapper attack during February 1965. Part of that attack had targeted a hotel where American officers and senior NCOs were billeted and more than thirty Americans had been blown up and killed. At levels far above MAC-V, it was postulated that BLT 2/7 should be sent to the area, in part, for the purpose of retaliation against those who had blown up the American soldiers. Of course, it also made sense to send a Marine landing team into such an area to provide security for the arrival of large, follow-on formations. However, it is important to point out that it was the retaliation aspect of the landing that first caught Washington's interest in ordering 2/7 into Qui Nhon.

Plainly, the passage of more than four months made any idea of retaliation less than credible, but the arrival of fresh troops, from whatever source, seemed to feed into such logic at the MAC-V headquarters in Saigon and with MacNamara and the other silly men in Washington. BLT 2/7 was going to be sent south to land at Qui Nhon. We Marines would be working for a new Field Force headquarters that was going to be set up by the U.S. Army farther south in the coastal city of Nha Trang. All the rest of the RLT 7 would be together in the Chu Lai enclave, but BLT 2/7 would be detached and forced to operate far from our kind.

After a night spent in a dank and gloomy old barracks building in Da Nang, one that undoubtedly had housed French troops during their turn in the Indo-Chinese battle, we three 2/7 Marines were ready to fly on to Qui Nhon. The barracks buildings where we had been billeted were dark, shabby, old concrete structures that smelled of mildew, urine,

*"First Corps Tactical Zone" soon foreshortened, forever, to "Eye Corps."

and rot. Any time spent in those miserable surroundings was truly depressing. Outside, the summer night was lit and relit by heat lightning shimmering around the clouds. At first it seemed as if we were looking at the muzzle flashes of artillery pieces, but shortly it was clear that—old newsreels showing thousands of huge, white artillery muzzle flashes, to the contrary—Da Nang had no artillery fire going out. What we were seeing was just plain old tropical heat lightning flickering away in the night sky.

Movement within the Republic of Vietnam appeared to be quite informal. We told the Marine transportation NCOs at the air terminal where we wanted to go, and they just yelled out which C-123 aircraft we ought to run over to. Once we were on board, the crew chief confirmed that the bird was, indeed, going where we wanted. Then, without ceremony, the pilot taxied out, and we were flying to Qui Nhon just minutes after asking the Marine in the terminal. Our flight was without incident, and we landed on a red, dusty airstrip lying just inland from the city of Qui Nhon late in the afternoon of 6 July 1965.

# 5

# AMPHIBIOUS ASSAULT?

At dawn on 7 July 1965, Capt. Al Doublet, 1st Lt. Al Kehn, and I stood on the beach at Qui Nhon, watching the amphibious ships carrying BLT 2/7 and all of its reinforcements steaming slowly along a short distance off the coast. Capt. Jim Nolan, now serving as the intelligence officer (S-2) for BLT 2/7, was also in Qui Nhon, having flown ashore the night before to seek intelligence information and maps. He was not with us and was probably busy with the local army staff officers, away from the beach, when the first troops came ashore. As we watched, we could see that there was much activity visible on the decks of the ships, and Marine CH-34 helicopters were maneuvering overhead. Waiting in utter amazement on the shore were several hundred Vietnamese, civilians of all ages and a few military men carrying rifles, rushing up and down the beach chattering in their singsong voices about the armada that was about to invade their country.

Aboard the ships at sea, none of the Marines and sailors could have had any idea of the effect that their presence was having on the locals. Everyone we saw, men, women, and children, was agitated, most fluttering about in a state of great excitement. They ran hither, thither, and yon; they climbed up into the trees to see better, and they shouted continuously.

We on the shore, unable to influence that action in any way, were, with good reason, also very worried. All three of us were seriously concerned that enemy forces might be present.

None of us felt confident enough to ignore the fact that Viet Cong elements that might be present that morning were sitting up on the jungle-covered hillsides with a much better view of the landing than we had from the beach area.

Since the U.S. Army engineer, supply, and motor transport elements in Qui Nhon had no infantry troops assigned to protect them, every American stationed there had, for months, been living in a certain amount of danger. Few, if any, infantry patrols were being conducted by the Army of Vietnam anywhere on the hillsides that dominated Qui Nhon and its beaches. If the enemy wanted to, he could use beat-up old mortars to fire on the beach, an act that could cause extensive casualties among the Marines moving inland and the civilians who were milling around them like flies on garbage. Incoming mortar rounds, arriving as the troops came ashore, would have increased an already mind-shattering level of confusion.

However, it is important to explain to the reader that, in our unbelievable ignorance, we voiced the opinion that should the Viet Cong choose to take offensive action, they would be hammered flat by Marine combat power once the BLT was ashore. While the army support elements were not fighters by trade and we had next to no information of Vietnamese military presence in the area, we were very overconfident because in our view the BLT was ready to unleash power the likes of which Viet Cong local force and regional force guerrillas had never encountered. Of course, we were gravely uninformed; we had not yet grasped the limitations that regular forces face in the conduct of guerrilla warfare. Nor, for that matter, had we any understanding of the limitations imposed on our forces by outside agencies, which were empowered to issue operational edicts without the slightest level of operational knowledge.

When the first wave of the "amphibious assault" roared ashore in the LVTP-5 amphibious tractors, the Marines deployed quickly from the tractor ramps, prepared to fight if necessary. The troops were astounded to find the milling throng of Vietnamese citizens watching their every move.

There they stood, Marines in full combat gear, flak jackets zipped tightly, weapons locked and loaded for combat, with no enemy to fight. Instead, the Marines found themselves amid hundreds of laughing and shouting women and children. Their shock was obvious, and their hesitation could have been fatal had the enemy had strong forces in the area prepared to attack the first elements of the BLT at the high-water mark. We were fortunate that BLT 2/7 received no fire of any kind that day.

For many of the Marines making the landing, the very first aspect of combat service in the Republic of Vietnam, one which definitely impressed them, was the presence of an extremely large volume of human feces on the beach. For some reason, the locals had chosen to use the white sand of the curving, attractive beach as a communal toilet. The leavings of hundreds of people lay on the sand where much of it got stuck to the combat boots of the arriving infantrymen and in the tracks of the amphibious tractors. The smell of the feces along the otherwise pleasant shore was strong enough to induce nausea.

To escape the confusion, the commanding officer and his S-3 immediately began moving all of the combat elements of the BLT inland. The rifle companies, and their supporting armor and engineers, were moved out of the city as quickly as possible. The Marines were deployed into areas Captain Doublet selected as possibly secure locations from which the city could be provided some degree of protection against infiltration. His basic concept was for the careful establishment of a battalion defensive area outside Qui Nhon. The battalion commander wanted an area where the four rifle companies, and later the headquarters, could live while the BLT got sorted out and organized for operations. At first, the BLT headquarters, the artillery firing battery, and the combat service support units would be colocated with the logistics section near the airstrip. Later, after the battalion commander was more comfortable with the terrain and situation, the command post and the artillery would be moved out into the countryside. A site was needed that would permit the command group to more efficiently control and support the anticipated infantry combat operations.

Therefore, based on all the relevant considerations, the initial positions selected by the commander of BLT 2/7 kept its command post and its artillery near the Qui Nhon airfield for a short time. Command was exercised from Qui Nhon from the day of landing, 7 July, until the morning of the tenth, when both the artillery and the headquarters were moved inland, away from the busy airfield construction area. On the morning of 10 July, everyone moving inland was very, very glad to leave the confusion and chaos of Qui Nhon behind.

The location selected for development as the inland headquarters for BLT 2/7 was within the Phu Thanh Valley, a small valley tucked into the hills quite near, but not astride, National Route 1. Captain Doublet established the site off the main north-south thoroughfare serving the entire country for a reason. He did not want the BLT headquarters area inundated by civilian vehicular and foot traffic. We all agreed with his choice—nobody in his right mind would want that heavily traveled roadway bisecting the command post.

National Route 1 was the battered, partially paved, generally rutted coastal roadway that had been made infamous by the French author, Bernard Fall, but when he movingly wrote about the highway, calling it *The Street Without Joy*, he was actually referring to the part of National Route 1 that paralleled the coast in the most northern province of the Republic of Vietnam. In BLT 2/7 we began to see our miserable section of National Route 1 in his terms very soon after we had established ourselves ashore. As a highway, National Route 1 was not even equal to a backwoods road in Alabama. However, the narrow disaster of a roadway was filled daily with the most amazing quantity of people moving north and south for purposes unknown.

The first order of business for the BLT was to set up checkpoints and begin exerting some sort of control over this chaotic movement. At first, our Marines felt threatened by *all* of the people, any one of whom could be a Viet Cong or a carrier of arms and equipment for them.

For the individual Marines of the BLT, the first few days after they began acting as policemen at roadblocks and checkpoints were a time of confusion. There were no clear and easily understood rules. Much of what had been taught about guerrilla warfare had, perhaps, led to a form of overkill. Constant emphasis in training and discussion had leaned heavily on the idea that guerrillas were "everywhere" and that no area was ever really safe. That kind of training had plainly worked against efficiency and, instead, had made the troops more nervous than they should have been. Worse, no one had ever mentioned anything, ever, about rock apes. Often the checkpoints on the highway were established in choke points where rock outcroppings made it easy to channel ground movement to the road. At night, when a rock ape would fling a stone or some feces at the American intruders, the Marines would leap to a high state of alert. Everyone would be ready to repel an attack, but rock apes do not attack, they just annoy. Like little boys who had cried "Wolf," the night security detachments soon feared that they would not be believed when they reported that a real Viet Cong attack was being mounted against the positions. They correctly reasoned that if a rock ape could toss a stone or a handful of shit, any passing Viet Cong could just as easily toss in a hand grenade. The nervousness of the riflemen was thus increased.

Another wonderful surprise for the troops was the presence in the area of a large number of very hungry, very nasty lizards which, of course, had not been mentioned in any training. Like the rock apes, the lizards worked best at night as they foraged for food among the sleeping Marines. As the lizard claws scratched and scraped on the men, their weapons, and their supplies, much-needed sleep was lost. In fact, there was a great deal of shouting, some shooting, and much upset after every lizard contact. Those lizards were not cute, quick little reptiles, horny toads and the like, familiar to those who live in the American west. They were formidable and worthy opponents. Counting the tail, a full-grown lizard would reach three to four feet in length. Several Marines, including first lieutenants Joe Lloyd and Hank Ketchem, as I recall, had themselves photographed holding a lizard tail at shoulder height while the head of the recently killed reptile was lying on the ground by their feet.

While Captain Doublet had his hands full from a tactical and operational standpoint, BLT 2/7 had other pressing problems. The battalion needed to get all its supplies and equipment off the ships and onto the beach. Navy amphibious shipping could not be expected to hang around Qui Nhon any longer than necessary, so the Marines had to get cracking. This work took time, sweat, and an unanticipated level of patience on the part of the troops doing the work. Every vehicle that unloaded from a Mike boat (LCM-6 landing craft) was impeded on the beach by a throng of civilians, primarily children, who begged for rations, begged for candy, begged for rides, and tried their very best to steal anything and everything that came within reach.

The busy S-2, Capt. Jim Nolan, was ably assisted by the intelligence chief, Gunnery Sergeant Kerr. This was another fantastic SNCO who, like Staff Sergeant Tackett, was a superior, workaholic performer. Neither would have been welcome at the Eighth & I evening parade* in Washington. He was not pretty in any recruiting poster sense, but he was worth far more than his weight in gold to BLT 2/7. The task of the S-2 was a monumental one, and the section had attacked it with gusto while enroute to the Qui Nhon area. Since all preparations that had been made for intelligence support of the battalion in the I Corps Tactical Zone (ICTZ) of the Republic of Vietnam were knocked into a cocked hat by the shift in landing site and area of operations, new maps and new data had to be acquired. From the USS *Okanogan*, Captain Nolan and Gunnery Sergeant Kerr had initiated voluminous message traffic asking for an enormous number of maps. It was the view of the captain and Gunnery Sergeant Kerr that every squad leader in the battalion should have his own maps so the squads could operate independently. That view was often contrary to the opinions of those in high places, but Captain

*Location of the Marine barracks in Washington, D.C.

Nolan's crew pressed on. To the surprise of everyone, when BLT 2/7 came ashore, a refrigerator-size carton of maps was waiting on the beach. The carton was marked to the attention of Captain Nolan's section; the small-unit leaders throughout the BLT were going to get enough maps to do their job right.

Another function of the S-2 section was to administer the use of Vietnamese interpreters at the headquarters and in the rifle companies. During the afternoon of the second day ashore, nine young Vietnamese soldiers were brought to Captain Nolan. They had been ordered to be the interpreters for the BLT. Almost immediately after the group arrived, eight of them deserted. Some came back later, with military police assistance, and other Vietnamese soldiers arrived to replace the deserters who were never found. Only one of those first nine men, Sgt. Nguyen Van Luan, did not desert. He stayed with the battalion for years. He was there during our tour of duty and during the tours of duty of thousands of other Marines who called the 2d Battalion, 7th Marines home in the Republic of Vietnam.

The logistics section's job was a reversal of the role we had played on White Beach in Okinawa. Now 1st Lt. Al McElwain and I were moving everything from the ships to the shore and trying desperately to locate places where the locals could not steal our materiel out from under our very noses. We had to be ready to bring the enormous stocks of ammunition to our dump sites; we had to get control of all the palletized cargo; and we had to do it all with insufficient assets. We pined in sadness for the large, rough-terrain forklifts and the cheerful, easily motivated men who manned them in Okinawa. During the unloading of BLT 2/7, the logistics section was forced to make do with less than one-tenth the materials-handling support needed, and the unloading seemed to take forever.

BLT 2/7 also had the task of getting the combat support and combat service support elements ashore and established on the western side of Qui Nhon, near the airfield. Eventually these units were all assembled in a dry, dusty, sun-baked area that had been pointed out to us as ours, with a wave of the hand, by the senior army officer in Qui Nhon. The soil we stood upon was, in every direction, reddish in color and very dry. On the surface was a film of powder with a consistency like that of bath talcum. This dust film had a soft red cast to it. We learned from our army contacts that this variety of dirt was known to the busy army engineers as a red laterite soil. That red soil was exceptionally pleasing to the engineer types, who happily were pushing it to and fro as they made roads and parking areas.

Engineers loved the red soil because it was easy to work, compacted well, and stood up fairly well to rain when a little oil was added to the mix. The same soil was used, with steel planking overlaid, to create runways and helicopter landing pads. While the engineers took great pleasure from the presence of the red laterite, it was a far different matter for the infantrymen. Red laterite soils provided another horrible entry on the great list of difficult matters affecting men and weapons in the Republic of Vietnam. No description of the soils present in Vietnam had been part of our briefing or training. We Marines were doomed to continue learning more things the hardest of hard ways.

Everyone was affected adversely by the red dust. Each afternoon, no later than 1330, the winds would begin to rise, and clouds of the powdery dust would be blown into the eyes, mouth, nose, clothing, and the very pores of the skin. Our field uniforms were quickly ruined by the accumulation of the red dust, which when it was mixed with sweat, permeated the fabric. Thus began the rotting process of our field uniforms, known to Marines as utilities or "utes."

The Marine Corps utility uniform of 1964–65 was manufactured entirely of a cheap type of cloth known as cotton-sateen. That worthless cloth had been chosen for the Marine Corps by the U.S. Army as it complied with Robert MacNamara's "Single Manager Program." Under that program, each of the major services would be assigned responsibility to procure certain materiel items for themselves and *all* of the other branches of the military. Hence, the army procured all items made of cloth, tentage and the like, and all forms of clothing. They did that for everyone from the frontline Marine private to the general officers in the Pentagon. Utility uniforms made from that cloth were very quickly rendered virtually useless. The huge volume of sweat produced by the BLT Marines, the salt from the salt tablets that were liberally prescribed to everyone, and the growing load of red laterite dirt that we each carried, combined to destroy our utility uniforms at an amazing rate. About fifteen days after the BLT came ashore, it was not unusual to see a Marine stretch his back muscles and, in the process, rip the back of his utility jacket from the neckline to the belt. Worse, many of the cotton-sateen cloth trousers shredded in the crotch. The Marines—who had learned quickly to avoid crotch rot by never wearing under-wear during the hot humid days as they busted their humps in the jungle—marched along with their private parts exposed in the sunlight for all to see.

As our clothing was actually rotting off our backs, every-one soon was involved in trying to scrounge uniform clothing from army units. Most of the army troops working the Qui Nhon area were already wearing clothing made of synthetic cloth. I suppose the clothing was manufactured from some variations of nylon or rayon, but whatever it was, the Marines wanted that kind of clothing. A few of the army troops even had new test uniforms that were made with nylon reinforcing threads embedded in the fabric to discourage ripping. By the end of the war, everyone was wearing nylon rip-stop clothing, but none was available to Marines in the Republic of Vietnam in 1965. A particularly wonderful thing about any of the syn-thetic uniform clothing available at the time was the fact that it was actually possible to get the dirt out of that material when the garment was washed in a stream. No one ever got very much of the red laterite muck out of the cotton-sateen clothing, and it was the universal desire of all to get their hands on some of the army clothing as quickly as possible. This created a marvelous black market opportunity, and soldiers traded uniforms to the Marines for all manner of items, as well as conducting a multitude of plain old cash transactions for items from their uniform allowance.

All weapons, individual and crew-served, were being destroyed by the red dust. Cleaning them and oiling them for later use became a very difficult chore, one that was virtually continuous. Weapons cleaning was a boring, essential, and repetitive task that took an enormous amount of the available time of every Marine. A clean and ready weapon was the only kind of weapon to have, yet, just as soon as the weapon was clean and ready, all the work was defeated by the arrival of another load of the damn dust. Not only did the dust affect the weapons, but it also affected the health of the Marines. Much like Beijing, China, where everyone coughs all the time from breathing the dust-and-ash-laden air, the Marines at Qui Nhon hacked and coughed steadily because the red laterite dust was filling their breathing passages in the same manner as it clogged their rifles.

When night was approaching, the early evening dusk was very soon abuzz with the sound of hordes of hungry mosquitoes. Being hungry and very persistent, the mosquitoes spent most of the hours of darkness biting BLT Marines from one end to the other. The flying bloodsuckers were impressive, being able to bite effectively right through the utility shirts and trousers of sleeping Marines. In the morning light, it was not unusual to see large numbers of Marines with puffed and swollen faces. The puffy, moon-faced Marines reminded one of the pictures of the similarly round, stolid faces of the Mongol horsemen who rode the Asian steppes in the time Genghis Khan.

For staff officers and civilians far from the combat zone, things like swarms of mosquitoes pose no threat and are not considered important. Those folks live far too well to believe that operational units are bothered by mosquitoes. For the men of BLT 2/7, the vicious mosquitoes were a major irritant, one that affected every aspect of their ability to fight. Night ambush patrols and listening posts set out for security could not function as they should because the Marines were being devoured while waiting for the enemy. The military-issue mosquito repellent was marginal at best, and it could never be used on security duty or in ambush patrolling because the Viet Cong could pick up the acrid smell of the repellent as quickly as could the mosquitoes. Anyone who was stupid enough to let the enemy smell him hiding in the bushes could very quickly find himself a dead or wounded Marine.

As the days passed, everyone in the BLT began to betray signs of sleep deprivation. Obviously, the mosquito problem was one factor, among many, that contributed to the condition. Marines who were not on watch, on patrol, or out on an ambush could sleep, but the mosquitoes did not allow them to get enough "good" sleep. Tired Marines quickly became prone to making mistakes when they were pushed hard by the operational situation.

We in the logistics section were overbusy and overstressed as we developed a logistics support area (LSA) for the BLT. To leaven a difficult situation with some humor, I reprised my role as God of the Beach, and the troops began taking over space on the ground that was not ours, borrowing (most of the time forgetting to return) equipment that was not ours, and obtaining assistance from people not assigned to have anything to do with BLT 2/7 or any of its components. The job of creating an LSA for the BLT, one that would be ready to provide whatever Lieutenant Colonel Utter might ask, was made slightly easier by the total lack of any viable senior headquarters that might interfere with anything that we decided was needed at that moment.

Often it seems that the primary role of senior headquarters is to find reasons why something cannot be done rather than finding ways to make things happen. Without the slightest identifiable need to clear our activities with anyone in particular, the BLT soon had enough space to set up our logistic elements and to get them started doing the things that needed doing. Extra space was obtained by the simple flexing of muscles by Marine NCOs and the erection of our worn tents in spots that appealed to us. We had lots of Marines; we had guns; and we acted as if we owned whatever it was that we wanted at that moment.

Lieutenant Colonel Utter was laughingly dubbed by Staff Sergeant Tackett as "God of the Mountains"—he for whom the God of the Beach toiled. The colonel was amused and in return dubbed me the "hairless Mexican bandit." Lieutenant Colonel Utter could get away with calling me that because I really had no hair, and I was acting like a greedy, freely wandering Mexican *pistolero* who could always be found squatting happily precisely in the middle of property claimed by others. He accused me of trying to steal every single thing in the Qui Nhon area that was not nailed down. Since this was a fair approximation of the truth, his remark was accepted with a cheery, "Yes, sir." Of course, since he was a realist, the colonel also told me to keep right on being pushy, arrogant, difficult, and acquisitive on behalf of the BLT. He even took a moment to slyly suggest that we up the ante in our search for "other people's" gear. Such gear being defined as anything else that might be useful to the troops. One item that he happened to mention in passing was water trailers, and a team went to work on that project immediately. Once a water trailer had been obtained, a little Marine paint and a Marine serial number made it part of the BLT. That sort of collection effort was always completed without need of the colonel's notice. That way, he would never be required to lie to anyone.

All of the hard work to establish our combat support and combat service support domain took place amid constant harassment by the loudest children ever heard on this planet. At the airstrip, the army engineer units operating the earthmoving equipment seemed to have a very large number of soldiers from the states of New York and New Jersey. The hard, nasal accents from their home states had obviously reached everyone. From the children came an unending stream of American-Vietnamese words and Vietnamese-American words. Most were so butchered as to be without meaning. But, all the words came out in the harsh tones known to anyone who has heard taxi drivers screaming on the streets of New York, Jersey City, and other urban areas of the eastern seaboard. About one-half the din from the children were requests for us to give them something and one-half suggestions that, "GI, you number ten thousand!" The children also invited all who would listen to perform various carnal acts upon themselves, almost always acts that happen to be anatomically impossible. The bawdy suggestions were repeated over and over and over amid great laughter from the kids. Another often heard phrase, shouted at the very top of their lungs, was "Geehhdda yeerrr azzzz ouddhaaa hyeer." It was their version of what the U.S. Army engineers working on the airfield had probably been yelling at them, to no avail, for months.

A bit behind the children, came a few adults. Other than men with an arm or a leg missing, few military-age males were hanging around. The majority of the Vietnamese adults who approached us were women. There were also a few elderly men with wispy white beards among the throng. At first the adults spent the days just watching us as the logistics section set up and began to operate LSA which contained the ration dump, the ammunition dump, the fuel pits, and the other supply and support-type entities that the BLT needed in the rear area. We later learned that those people wanted to do our wash, to cut our hair, to haul away our trash, to give massages, and to perform various other "personal" services often obtainable for a price in the red-light districts of the world. Initially the silent adults were far less pushy than the children. Later, after they grew more comfortable in our presence, the adults became louder, ruder, and much more aggressive.

Adult Vietnamese posed a significant risk factor. For all we knew at the time, they might well have been the enemy. They might be members of the *Du Kich*—the local-force troops who were farmers or laborers by day and Viet Cong fighters by night. They might also be members of the *Dia Phoung*, the provincial-level Viet Cong. The fact that the provincial fighters supposedly lived in the jungle full-time and conducted operations in all parts of their province would not prohibit their walking among us, in civilian garb, just to see what they could see.

*Dia Phoung* troops infiltrating our visitors would look no different to us than any other Vietnamese, but they would be dangerous, full-time guerrilla fighting men who could kill Marines. The army and the Marine Corps were in agreement that the *Du Kich* forces posed only minor problems to line units—the local-boy guerrillas just did not have access to the firepower needed to fight effectively against American infantrymen. On the other hand, the regional Viet Cong lived up to their billing. Those forces turned out to be made up of very capable fighting men. They were often well led and were as tough and well trained a force as anyone would want to face in combat.

All of the confusion and difficulty we faced with the local people would never have occurred in a real amphibious assault. Obviously, the civilian population and the confusion they caused would have vanished when the preassault naval bombardment began to pour into the beach area. As the landing force crashed ashore and drove the enemy fighting men off the beach and back into the hinterlands, the local civilians would have been forced to take cover or die. No such relief was ever possible in the Qui Nhon area. Every one of the BLT rear area dumps and supply sites was surrounded, at all times, by the locals. The Marines just had to get used to the constant civilian interference.

On any day, we knew that it was possible that the commanding officer of the local Viet Cong unit might be walking around the barbed wire surrounding our tents and storage sites, taking notes. He could have done that without our knowing that anything was out of the ordinary. For that matter, the Army of Vietnam (ARVN) soldiers who were present might have been enemy troops in disguise. Pairs of ARVN troops wandered in and out of our area with rifles slung over their shoulders or pistols on their belts. They would saunter in and out, holding hands and looking bored. For many of the Marine sentries guarding our gear, it was a terrible cultural shock to see men with rifles slung over their backs holding hands like lovers as they ambled along.

Many events that took place during this period were humorous, some were tragic. We all had a wonderful chuckle when one of the loudest braggarts in the battalion, a bellicose staff sergeant who had spent most of the voyage west telling all of us, in great detail, just how he was going to be getting a Medal of Honor in Vietnam, fell victim to his own stupidity.

Incapable of logical, rational thought, he happened to come down with a case of the really "stupid-stupids," when he was forced to make a quick decision. While on patrol for the intelligence section, he had mistakenly gone out of his way to irritate a farmer's water buffalo, an almost fatal error. Every water buffalo we ever met in the countryside reacted badly to the smell of American troops. That particular beast was no exception. When the animal charged him, our idiot-hero tripped and fell flat on his ass. As he fell backwards, firing in panic, he shot himself in the foot with his personal "status symbol," a .45-caliber M-3 submachine gun (the "grease gun" of World War II).

Within the battalion, the amused reaction to the self-inflicted wound was slightly muted by the fact that the braggart had damaged his foot badly enough to require evacuation to Japan. Behind the scenes, the Marines laughed and said that being "dry-gulched" by a water buffalo was a fine come-uppance after all the sergeant's talk of the Medal of Honor and being, in his own words, "No stranger to danger." The pointless nature of the self-inflicted casualty and the reality of where we were serving combined to ensure that after the first few days of our tour in the Republic of Vietnam, the number of Marines bragging about their planned heroic performance quickly dropped to zero.

In the support area, there were also constant chuckles among the ammunition NCOs about which rifle company was going to request various kinds of resupply. Basically, it was an easy call. One company commander would arrive each morning and regale us with hairy tales of enemy mortar rounds falling on his company. After impressing us all, he would depart with several new cases of hand grenades bouncing around in his jeep trailer. While it was possible that the local Viet Cong had available to them some 61mm Chinese mortars, everyone knew that it was very unlikely that anyone had been mortared. The explosions that the captain heard each night were grenades being thrown into the dark by jittery young Marines. There were also some rumors that his troops were not under firm control and that their night defense positions were not being supervised properly. While the captain's tales were entertaining, mortar shells explode on impact and leave behind a distinctive crater. Near the crater you will always find the tail-fin assembly of the mortar projectile. The tail fins survive undamaged because they are blown off in one piece, not fragmented by the detonation of the mortar round. Neither the captain nor any other member of his company ever turned in a single tail-fin assembly. The commanders of the other three rifle companies did not tell tales of mortar attack nor did they have to stop by for cases of replacement grenades.

Our awareness that we were always being watched by enemy troops was quickly reinforced by an unusual event. Moving inland from Qui Nhon, one of the tanks from the attached tank platoon became mired when the tank driver was directed to cross a small stream. An aggressive young officer looked at the crossing site and declared it safe and hard enough for the tank to traverse. When ordered to cross, the tank driver tried to power his tank quickly through the stream and up onto the far bank. The idea was an absolute nonstarter. Speed just did not work for the 120,000-pound monster. The mushy bottom of the stream would not support the weight of the tank, and momentum was quickly lost. Our tank, from which the crew emerged without injury, was soon mired so deeply in midstream that it began sinking quietly into the muck while the Marines watched.

Tank recovery from a muddy stream is not child's play, and a great deal of effort was expended before the beast was again on dry land. To pull the tank out of the slop required three other tanks, some help from our attached motor-transport wrecker, and the winches on some two-and-one-half-ton trucks belonging to the artillery. Also present to struggle with the tank were a number of 1st Lt. John Rivers's engineers from the platoon attached to the BLT. Getting the tank loose from the mud took several hours of time that could have been more productively used by everyone involved in the recovery. In the process, the tank was ruined by the water. All of the various components of the tank's communications and fire-control equipment were so badly damaged that the entire sixty-ton monster would have to be sent back to the United States for a rebuild at the repair shops of the Marine Corps Supply Center, Barstow, California. The loss of the tank, which was essentially gone forever, underscored the reality of our eight-thousand-plus-mile supply line.

During the evening of that eventful day—less than ten hours after the tank was driven into the stream—the English language radio program beamed from Hanoi to Americans serving in the Republic of Vietnam could be heard by those who had transistor radios. With the soft voiced, English speaking "Hanoi Hannah" acting as hostess, the broadcast welcomed the 2d Battalion, 7th Marines, to Vietnam. She suggested with quiet urgency that we all leave immediately to avoid a horrible fate. About halfway through her broadcast, she made laughing reference to the tank stuck in the muddy streambed and all the work it took to get it out. Needless to say, the troops were impressed. In fact, we were all a little spooked by the speed with which the story had been reported by our enemy to their leaders in Hanoi.

As the battalion began to establish a headquarters site in the Phu Thanh Valley, another of the worries held by the Marines about life in that land was confirmed. We had been told that there were going to be many poisonous snakes living among us. To that point, we had seen none, but concern about deadly reptiles remained foremost in the minds of many who greatly feared snakes of all kinds. Confirmation of the presence of dangerous snakes living nearby did not take long. First Lieutenant Nicholas Groz, by then the commanding officer of H & S Company, was clearing brush out of an old French trench about forty feet south of the S-4 area when he shouted a warning. He had scared a snake out of a hole in the wall of the trench. The four or five foot snake he had disturbed was banded along its body with rings of yellow and black. And it was one very, very quick snake! Lieutenant Groz swung his machete, missed the snake, and watched as it slithered into the underbrush between his part of the trench and the logistics section.

The snake was no laughing matter; its markings meant that it was probably a yellow-banded krait, a killer whose venom is both neurotoxic and hemotoxic. Our new neighbor had the ability to kill almost anyone it decided to bite. Death might come in less than an hour, and there was no antivenom available in the BLT for a yellow-banded krait. We had one very badass snake wandering about the new command post.

Lieutenant Groz, who had made a trip to Vietnam during 1964 for orientation while stationed in Okinawa, remained utterly unimpressed. Once the snake had left his part of the trench, grinning broadly, he bellowed, "Yours for action; the enemy is now in your tactical area of responsibility!" First Lieutenant McElwain and I, assisted by the rest of the logistic section, looked for the damn snake. Looking long and hard produced no further sightings, and the black and yellow snake was never seen again. But everyone knew that he and his kin were nearby, waiting.

Besides operating roadblocks and checkpoints on National Route 1, the battalion began to send its infantry companies farther and farther into the local valleys. Our moving inland was part of the real reason that BLT 2/7 had been sent to the Qui Nhon area. Our real mission, despite the need to cover National Route 1, was to provide security for the buildup of larger forces that the U.S. Army was going to deploy through the port of Qui Nhon. Our going into the hills would make that effort safer and less subject to interruption by the Viet Cong. Snooping in and around in the hills and valleys was also our first attempt to find and fight the local force and regional force Viet Cong units. Intelligence as to the Viet Cong location, strength, and/or intentions was scanty, but the BLT began expanded patrolling as a technique to broaden the field experience of the troops and to show the enemy how far we could reach out if they attempted to attack the city.

Thus, after only a few days of deployment in the Qui Nhon area, BLT 2/7 was functioning ashore and was prepared to get out into the hinterlands where we could fight the enemy—if we could find him.

# 6

# LOCAL OPERATIONS

As the expansion of U.S. forces in the Republic of Vietnam continued in the II Corps Tactical Zone and elsewhere, our battalion was busy consolidating its hold on the flatlands and some of the low, rolling hills lying inland from Qui Nhon. By late July 1965, the rifle company efforts at controlling civilian traffic on the major coastal highway had become far more successful. Although it was a matter of some surprise, a few of the Marine checkpoints were beginning to produce bits of useful intelligence on the local Viet Cong.

With the enthusiastic blessing of the controlling II Field Force headquarters in Nha Trang, BLT 2/7 continued to press inland. Despite limited contact with the enemy, there was a growing sense that all of the battalion Marines were, at least, becoming more comfortable in the environment. This comfort level included both living in the physical environment of the tropical landscape and coping with the psychological environment of combat against an enemy that was elusive at best and simply invisible most of the time.

Obviously, there remained a lot to learn. Nothing in any training program had really prepared the Marines for the chaos of the Asian mainland. Moving from place to place were pedestrians, buses, handcarts, motorcycles, taxis, cyclos (three-wheeled motorized carts), ancient trucks, wheelbarrows, and even the occasional rickshaw pulled by an old man. All of the people and their chosen forms of transportation had to be examined and either detained or passed on down the road. Just to the south, not more than two or three miles from the 2/7 checkpoints, one of the Viet Cong commanders was running his own checkpoint, where all those traveling civilians would leave our area then be checked into the enemy-dominated countryside. If that had not been a serious, life-and-death situation, it would have been easy to bill all this frenzied activity on National Route 1 as simply a farce.

Mistakes in handling the traffic often were made by Marines who were doing their best to do an unfamiliar job. Mistakes were logical offshoots of the language difficulty and the semihostile nature of civilians who clearly distrusted our intentions. The Marines were already growing tired from working in the baking heat and dust. They worked for long hours during the day, and then got limited rest, or no rest at all, during the tension-filled nights. The troops never got a real break because of the constant need for them to take part in essential night-security duties. They stood sentry duty in the headquarters; they stood watch on the defensive perimeter; they manned outposts and listening posts; they guarded bridges and overpasses; and they spent long dark nights waiting in ambush sites. Every one of those duties was essential to our survival. Working all day at the checkpoints was never, ever, followed by more than one-half night of sleep—on any night. In addition, there were just too many bags, bundles, boxes, crates, and other containers being moved on the highway to permit an effective search of every passing person. At some level, every Marine knew that the Viet Cong were probably passing among us from time to time. That was not a reassuring idea, but it was one that generated some energetic action by two of the more self-motivated members of the battalion.

Late one afternoon, a busload of civilians was stopped for interrogation. When it pulled out, two of the more innovative officers, 1st Lt. James Lau (Chinese-American) and 1st Lt. Herbert Yoshida (Japanese-American), decided that they would do something about the Viet Cong checkpoint to the south. They removed their helmets and flak jackets, put on straw hats, and, carrying their weapons, climbed aboard the bus. Without telling anyone what they had in mind, the two officers were traveling south with the Vietnamese passengers, right down the road to the Viet Cong checkpoint. Probably they believed that, on arrival at the Viet Cong checkpoint, it would be possible for them to shoot all of the troops assigned there. And it is possible that the arrival of two lieutenants actually might have discomforted the Viet Cong, causing them to flee; a more probable result would have been two very dead Marine officers.

Fortunately, as the bus moved south an alert Marine private yelled out to his sergeant, "Hey! There are gooks with guns on the bus!" Hearing that, the sergeant and all his Marines jumped into their fighting holes, alerted everyone nearby, and then positioned themselves to fire on the civilian bus. Only the common sense of that rifle squad leader saved the two lieutenants. The sergeant looked into the bus and saw Yoshida—a big man, six feet or more tall—and concluded that the guys carrying guns on the bus were not Viet Cong soldiers at all. The bus halted when the driver was aware of the many, many guns pointed his way. No shots were fired. The two lieutenants were quickly and undiplomatically removed— at gunpoint—from the bus. They were embarrassed and had to face a significant ass chewing about the matter from their very, very angry company commander, Capt. Martin O'Connor. As an incident, the silly behavior of the lieutenants was only humorous after the situation had been defused. Despite everyone's effort to take it seriously, it did seem a bit funny after the fact. It remained so because the foolhardy act highlighted a disconnect that lay between reality and our almost romanticized view of what was going to be possible during our tour of combat. Even after a month of operations and a number of combat casualties, there were still those who felt themselves to be almost immortal. Not unlike children playing war, the two lieutenants failed to think of the consequences that were certain now that the battalion was playing the game of war for "keeps."

Young Americans are normally, by nature, quite friendly and easygoing. They tend to be polite to strangers and avoid rude, brusque behavior that would give affront. Those traits were especially on display when the Marines were dealing with the aged and the infirm at the highway checkpoints. Operation of the roadblocks on National Route 1 and on some of the other roads in the area resulted in many unplanned contacts between the infantry Marines and elderly and handicapped Vietnamese. That was natural because most of the able-bodied men were away—either in the Army of the Republic of Vietnam or serving with the opposition, the Viet Cong. Many old women were on the roads, and crippled males were frequently encountered, mostly older men with one arm or one leg missing. To avoid seeming cruel, the troops often let up a little and the items carried by them were usually less thoroughly searched. That kind of courtesy dispensation came to an end one day when Captain Seymour, the Company G commander, grew suspicious about an old woman carrying two large, heavy tins suspended from a shoulder pole. She told the interpreter that there was cooking oil in the tins. The old woman's load consisted of big square cans with plastic covers secured firmly across their open tops. Normally the Marines would have passed an old lady like that on down the road. But before that could happen, the captain acted on his suspicions and would not allow her to depart. A decision which caused her to complain loudly.

When the captain, growing exasperated by loud protests and shouting from the old woman, kicked over the can nearest to him, its contents spilled out on the dirt. As she had claimed, it was cooking oil, but five packages wrapped in plastic had been submerged in the oil. Each package contained a fragmentation grenade. The second can contained five more fragmentation grenades. There in front of the troops was proof that in a guerrilla war almost anyone can be a member of the enemy—even old women with the wrinkles of seventy plus years on their faces. Lesson number one.

A second learning experience of great value took place at the same moment. The grenades carried by the old woman were not manufactured by the Russians or by the Chinese. The grenades packed in the old woman's oil tins had been made in the United States of America. That is, they were identical to the grenades carried on the cartridge belts of the men of BLT 2/7. A possible source for these grenades could have been a successful Viet Cong attack on an American unit or an ARVN unit—with the grenades taken from the dead. Or, more likely, the grenades had come from corrupt members of the ARVN, many of whom profited by diverting munitions and selling them to the Viet Cong. Throughout the war our enemy was innovative in acquiring and using our own munitions against us. One old lady with ten grenades had become a valuable training aid. She made us completely aware, for the first time, just how seriously the enemy's ability to innovate could affect the survival of each and every member of the battalion.

The elderly grenade transporter, and several others traveling with her, were quickly taken into custody and turned over to the Vietnamese National Police. Every Vietnamese we met in the Qhi Nhon area, and the old lady was no exception, seemed to fear the National Police. Those hardcase policemen, the "White Mice," were far more feared by the populace than were either the Marines or the ARVN. While many of those professional policemen were good, solid, dependable men, the old lady's apprehension still made very good sense. Several of us had already seen less professional National Policemen very happily beating suspects and kicking them from place to place as they worked hard to produce whatever they wanted in the way of "voluntary confessions."

Briefings and other warnings had made many teaching points about being aware of the danger, but the training emphasis had not created much more than a minor increase in vigilance. Discovery of the grenades lying in the cooking oil was a perfect way to actually make Marines understand that the danger was *real*! Word about how the grenades had been found whipped through the battalion in nothing flat. Needless to say, from that day onward, examination at checkpoints of the old and the infirm, as well as everyone else who was on the move, was intensified. We now had proof that the Viet Cong were all around us all the time, and the discovery made many of the battalion Marines far more wary than they had been.

News from the north during late August of 1965 caused the men of BLT 2/7 some bitter feelings. From the *Stars and Stripes* newspaper, we learned about our being left out of the war being fought by the other battalions of our parent regiment, the 7th Marines. During August, a large Marine Corps formation, one that included our two sister battalions, 1/7 and 3/7, conducted Operation Starlight on the Batangan Peninsula in Quang Ngai Province to the south of the Chu Lai enclave. Reports came to us, perhaps greatly enhanced before their arrival, that six or seven Marine battalions had been committed and that more than one thousand Viet Cong had been killed by the Marines who had taken part in Starlight. The operation was hyped in some elements of the press as a great victory and as a proof that the tide was turning in the war. Our officers and enlisted Marines were still naive enough to be a bit sad when they learned that the units to the north were getting solid contacts with the Viet Cong. BLT 2/7 Marines were somewhat disheartened to find that when a large, tough operation had been conducted, we had been left, under army command, to languish as guardians of our little area around Qui Nhon.

Two basic reasons made it absolutely essential that BLT 2/7 expand its area of operations. First, we needed to begin opening the coastal portion of National Route 19, the main east-west highway leading to the Central Highlands. That was necessary because the highway was going to be the land lifeline for the U.S. Army's 1st Air Cavalry Division, which was already beginning to stage its advance party and lead elements ashore. Second, the city of Qui Nhon was overrun with refugees, who were sleeping in the streets by the hundreds and the thousands. From their homes in the countryside, the refugees had fled to the city to escape the depredations of the Viet Cong. The refugees were simple farmers who had been forced to contend with both local-force and regional-force

Viet Cong units—units that demanded rice and other support from the villages throughout the fertile rice- and manioc-producing lowlands. The Viet Cong forces were always there, in the hills or in the jungle, ready to prowl into a village at night and terrorize the inhabitants. To avoid the justly feared terrorism as well as the real possibility of a sudden "gun-point" conscription into the Viet Cong, most of the farmers from the villages had deserted their homes and fled, with their families, to the city to await developments. In all of the soft green valleys, the fields lay fallow, and the rice and manioc crops were going unharvested. Farmers are tough people, but they had no guns to defend themselves against the Viet Cong, so they ran for whatever safety lay in the city of Qui Nhon.

Every time BLT 2/7 moved a rifle company into one of the deserted farming areas, the troops would find the empty homes and the untended fields serving as silent witness to the strength of our invisible enemy. Yet, within hours of our starting to maneuver in a valley, the residents would learn, by some unknown means, where the Marines were conducting operations. The village and hamlet residents would start back on foot to their homes. In what seemed to us to be an amazingly short time after we came to an empty valley, there would be farmers in the rice or manioc fields with hoes or plows. They arrived at their homes ready to work. Of course, they brought along their skittish water buffaloes to pull those essential plows—the design of which had not changed in three thousand years. With the farmers came smiling women and the energetic children who were again playing in and around the houses. The only thing that those rural farm people wanted out of life was to be left alone to plant their crops, to harvest those crops, and to live out their lives where they and their families had lived for generations. It was a sad situation for us because we knew that the moment that the Marines moved out to another valley the enemy would return to terrorize those farmers and their families.

The goals of the power elite in North Vietnam and the goals of the power elite in the United States made sure that the desires of those hardworking people had no effect on their fate;

zero value was placed on the hopes of the villagers by both sides. The war in the Republic of Vietnam was often utterly disastrous for the families who lived in the agricultural villages and hamlets. Both sides were feared—almost equally—because it did not matter who was operating in their area, the villages always suffered. The terror campaign against the farmers had begun long before BLT 2/7 arrived. In 1963 alone, the Viet Cong cadre units, under the direction of Le Duan, the chairman of the Lao Dong (Communist) Workers Party in Hanoi, had killed more than three thousand priests, teachers, and village headmen to demonstrate their power in the countryside.

By 1965, the Viet Cong had well-organized regional forces that were an even greater danger to individual Vietnamese farm families than the cadre units of earlier years. The increased danger was based on the fact that these *Dia Phoung* units were always there, a hostile presence in the jungle, dangerous at all times. Marines of BLT 2/7 or the troops of the ARVN would come and go, so the fluid tactics of our military forces failed to protect the farmers for very long. All of the villagers knew what to expect, and they tried very hard to keep themselves out of the whole horrible mess.

As BLT 2/7 maneuvered inland along National Route 19, the rifle companies began to have a few heavy firefights with small units of the Viet Cong. Occasionally, one of our offensive maneuvers would catch a Viet Cong unit off guard, and it would be forced to fight a rearguard action. As predicted by those who had tried to train the battalion to fight a guerrilla war, the Viet Cong always tried their best to escape rather than to fight. Our enemy was very logical from a military standpoint, and he made it a policy to avoid any form of stand-up fight against our better equipped and very aggressive Marines. The Viet Cong wanted to fight, but only on their terms, only on ground of their own choosing, only at a time of their choosing.

During one small, inconclusive firefight, a few of our Marines learned a very painful lesson about construction practices in the Republic of Vietnam. A rifle platoon had been fired upon as they approached a small hamlet, and the riflemen reacted by moving swiftly forward under the protective fire of their attached section of two M-60 machine guns. Because of the speed of advance by the Marines, some of the Viet Cong fighting men found themselves unable to escape the hamlet by running into the jungle to hide. The two elements began a small, violent firefight at a very close range. Both sides were dodging back and forth among the small huts of the hamlet. As the shooting continued, several energetic riflemen dashed up and pressed their bodies closely against the walls of the houses on the Marine side of the hamlet, using the walls as cover. Once there, they prepared to make an assault into the buildings. Using the tried-and-true tactics that they had learned in Combat Town at Camp Pendleton, they pulled the pins on their grenades and tossed them through the windows into the buildings against which they were sheltering. When the grenades detonated, several of the Marines learned—to their everlasting embarrassment—that in the rural farming areas, the Vietnamese build their houses out of sticks and mud. None of those walls was concrete, even though a white-washed mud wall does look very much like a concrete wall. Sticks, mud, and whitewash are no match for grenade fragments moving at high speed. Blazing hot chunks of steel from the fragmentation grenades flew through the walls as if they were paper. The immediate result was that some violently surprised Marines were wounded by fragmentation from their own grenades. Their embarrassment was made even worse by the fact that that the wounds were most frequently sustained in the rump. Instantly, the newly wounded troops had learned another awful lesson about the war, one that might be very difficult to recount truthfully to their grandchildren in the far, far future.

During an operational maneuver down the long axis of one valley, Company E came under sporadic fire from the low eastern hills that overlooked the rice-paddy land. As the Company E commander at the time—"personnel turbulence" was a dominant current in our lives in Vietnam—I attempted to maneuver a platoon, supported by fire from four machine guns, quickly to engage and destroy the enemy riflemen. In the process, some of the farmers and their cattle in the paddy land found themselves between the two infantry forces, with bullets flying back and forth over their heads. The firefight was of short duration, but fate was unkind to one of the cows. The poor scrawny animal had been hit two or three times, and one of the wounds was clearly mortal. A 1st Platoon fire-team leader went up to the wounded animal and used his M-14 rifle to put it out of its misery in short order. Within minutes, the farmer who had owned the creature came forward issuing forth great wails and lamentations. Through the interpreter, I worked out an agreement and paid him for the animal in the coin of barter. He went away, quite happy, with some Marine Corps clothing, with about twenty gallons of cooking oil that we had found in the hills, and a rather fine stack of field rations. We kept the carcass of the cow.

Every Marine rifle company that ever formed up for service in far-off lands has had in it a number of "good old country boys." Company E was no exception. As the day waned, the cow was rapidly butchered by troops who knew exactly how to do such things. No one wasted time asking me or any of the other officers if we wanted the meat butchered, they just began cutting it up. Those Marines were sick of eating field rations and saw a providential way to supplement their diet. The job was done without delay, and it was completed right out in the field where the animal had been mortally wounded. All of the edible meat taken from the carcass was packed to the village where Company E had its command post. By the time the maneuver elements arrived, proudly bearing their bloody booty, a large fire was blazing. This fire had appeared immediately after the cow was killed, and it was the product of the communicators and the command post security-squad Marines, all of whom knew that fresh meat was on the way. Our country boys roasted the meat in large chunks that were hacked into individual servings with dirty bayonets and K-bar knives. That wonderful meat was the first fresh food the infantrymen had eaten in more than three months.

I drafted a message report to battalion and mentioned in the text that, "subsequent to the demise of the Charley Oscar Whiskey, we ate same." The message was sent off to battalion via a radio-relay site that was operating on a hill mass from which they could talk to battalion in its valley and to us in our valley. The necessity for that difficult and dangerous relay for a ten-mile transmission of information was another commentary on our miserable radio sets. After the message was sent, no further thought of the evening meal passed through our consciousness. Instead, we were busy setting out the night ambushes, listening posts, and village patrols that were to be conducted by Company E between 2200 and morning. Once that was completed, I dozed in the command post, lying on the ground between the company-tactical-net radioman and the battalion-tactical-net radioman, awaiting the night's developments. At about 2330, the company gunnery sergeant awakened me and told me that the radio-relay communicators wanted to talk to the "actual" on the battalion tactical net. The term used meant that they wanted me, not my radioman. When, muttering curses, I returned the radio call, I found that I was talking directly to Capt. Jim Nolan, the intelligence officer. The hardworking S-2 was taking his turn in the S-3 as a night-watch officer, a job he had to do because there were not enough officers in the S-3 to man the battalion command center all night, every night.

When I came up on the net and identified myself, it turned out that Captain Nolan had climbed to the top of the hill mass to ask me, "What the hell is a Charley Oscar Whiskey?" In reading my message he had not made the connection between the mention of livestock that got in the way of the firefight and the international-phonetic words that I had used to spell out the word cow. Yawning and chuckling at the mix-up, I pressed the push-to-talk switch and said very firmly with careful diction, "A Charley Oscar Whiskey is a cow, you idiot! We ate the damn thing. Over." There was a very long pause, then Captain Nolan came back laughing nearly hard enough to choke. "Oh. Now I see. Roger that. Out." He had bravely climbed the radio-relay hill, going out in enemy territory without anyone covering him, to ask me the question. By rights, he should have been gravely offended. However, Captain Nolan was a far better man than most, and he just chuckled and took no personal offense at my snotty response.

While 2/7 was working in the coastal area, the 1st Brigade of the 101st Airborne Division arrived with much fanfare and fuss. They were brought to the Qui Nhon area to clear the Viet Cong from areas farther inland, to the west along National Route 19. This combined effort to open National Route 19 for safe use by the 1st Air Cavalry Division was dubbed Operation Ramrod. Some of the airborne soldiers were to fly in and begin operating eastward out of An Khe, clearing the route as they maneuvered. Other brigade units would work with the Marines to clear the road westward from Qui Nhon.

An Khe was site of a base camp area chosen for the 1st Air Cavalry Division, some components of which were already arriving in our area on the coast. Even before we arrived at Qui Nhon in July, hordes of engineers were being delivered to An Khe. Those engineers, sent in by the MAC-V headquarters in Saigon, were busy creating a major camp with landing strips and parking hardstands for the hundreds of helicopters that the Air Cavalry was going to be operating. The men of the 1st Brigade of the 101st Airborne were to make the road trip up to that camp safe for the cavalry soldiers and their logistical tail. Before the 1st Air Cavalry's arrival, it was a real crapshoot for anyone who wanted to use National Route 19 to travel inland to the central part of the country. The highway led, via An Khe, across the mountains to cities like Pleiku and Da Lat in the Central Highlands. In July 1965, when BLT 2/7 arrived in the area, the road was still designated as unsafe for travel by anyone, American or Vietnamese. Nevertheless, many civilians seemed to pass back and forth between the coast and the Central Highlands without difficulty and without attack by our enemy.

The 1st Brigade of the 101st Airborne had a far more difficult task than that which BLT 2/7 faced. The country inland was nasty, with steep slopes and all the double- and triple-canopy jungle anyone could ever want. Often, because of the thick undergrowth, road-clearing actions would sometimes be limited to a one- or two-man frontage. There was a very good chance that any unit trying to clear the road would be badly hurt by Viet Cong forces fighting on terrain very favorable to them. During the 1950–1954 French war in Indochina, a unit known as Mobile Groupment 100 had been badly mauled in those same steep canyons by guerrilla forces of the Viet Minh. The guerrillas ambushed the column in many places, killed very many French and Foreign Legion soldiers, then melted away into the trees to strike again another day. Mobile Groupment 100 lost most of its vehicles to mines, rocket-propelled grenades, and hand-carried satchel charges. Engagements along the jungle roadbed took place at ranges of less than twenty meters, with Viet Minh soldiers destroying the armored vehicles and killing their crews almost before the French soldiers knew they were there. In 1965, the rusted and corroded hulks of the dead armored vehicles still lay at the roadside or on the jungle fringes. They were a disturbing sight.

Having the 1st Brigade of the 101st Airborne Division arrive among us was a bit of a thrill for common mud-Marines. That famous airborne division possesses a great and glorious battle record from World War II. Their deeds in Europe, from D day until the end of hostilities, earned them, forever, the respect of other fighting men. The brigade was an interesting unit to outsiders as it was filled to brim with "characters." There were men like the very well known, and controversial, Col. David Hackworth, then a major. He, and an amazing number of others, all seemed to be different. They were all drawn a little larger than life, and they strode around and about with what would be known today as an attitude. Not that it was bad, because the attitude was one of tough, aggressive fighting men who had their heads up and their weapons ready. The unit was clearly very well prepared to fight an aggressive and energetic war against anyone they might be pitted against. The airborne soldiers were always civil to us lesser mortals, but it was clear that they held themselves in great esteem.

One character, among the many present in the brigade, impressed us greatly. He was Lt. Col. Hank Emerson. That ferocious officer commanded one of the brigade's airborne infantry battalions and was the utter epitome of the aggressive, fighting leader. Hank Emerson wanted kills, and he wanted them quickly, spurring on his sky soldiers with promises of hatchets to carry on their fighting load for every confirmed kill. Of course, his airborne infantry battalion quickly became known as "Hank's Hatchets." While Emerson may not have said it directly, the less-than-subtle hint given by this move could only be construed to mean that the airborne soldiers were to chop off the heads of any Viet Cong fighting men they ran into in the jungle. As might be expected, all the fatuous little journalists, who were constantly hanging about and getting in the way, got a bit wide-eyed and fretful when the hatchets were discussed. From the perspective of today's sad, political-correctness-dominated military it is clear that men like Emerson would probably be cashiered for such an idea in this decade. Regardless, the hatchets motivated his men, and that battalion was a proud and very superior unit. The men of his battalion worked hard to live up to the pride their commander had in them. Those soldiers wanted to earn their hatchets by fighting ferociously and winning. From all that we Marines could see, they did so, with gusto!

Being around the army is always interesting to Marines. The army has such a vast array of gear, so many people, and so much flexibility that we look at them and see scant resemblance to ourselves. The 1st Brigade of the 101st Airborne had so many jeeps and radio vehicles that we became quite envious. They had the new field radios, the AN/PRC-25s, while we Marines made do with the long-obsolete AN/PRC-10s. The "Prick Ten" radios worked poorly at best and not at all a considerable portion of the time. The army brigade also had a personnel luxury never available to Marine units: many, many extra officers available to help get things done and to fill in for losses. We were even made privy to a rumor, by a grumpy, overage army major in a support unit that there were twenty-three sons of army general officers present. The major assumed that those young men had been quickly added to the brigade so they would be sure to get a chance to earn the coveted Combat Infantryman Badge, early, before the war "petered out."

One afternoon, several of us were sitting, a bit in awe of what was happening, while on a coordination visit to the brigade, as a tall, thin, twenty-three-year-old Captain of the United States Army stood casually by his radio jeep and simultaneously controlled his three platoons in three separate search operations. He actually had available to him three separate radio nets to control their activities. He did that while surrounded by an artillery representative, a spare captain observer from brigade headquarters, his mortar-unit leader, and a couple of field-grade officer observers from II Field Forces headquarters in Nha Trang. In contrast, Marine captains in the BLT 2/7 rifle companies had to make do with one ratty AN/PRC-10 and a magnificent young man to carry it. They did have, however, the distinct advantage of having a Gunnery Sergeant of Marines to advise them as each day wore on. That, we thought, responding in the way Marines always react to adversity, meant a great deal more than the simple addition of extra equipment. However, when Marines watch the United States Army at work, there is always room for a little envy, and it was clearly both present and justified in that case. Just looking at the airborne brigade was enough to cause us to feel neglected and mistreated. The men of BLT 2/7 could easily argue from the position that we Marines were, as usual, the bastard stepchildren.

Another illuminating aspect of working closely with the army is the wonderfully professional attitude of their top-line, or more well-known units. From the top of the command heap, all the way to the last soldier, a fierce and aggressive attitude was obvious in that brigade of the 101st Airborne. These were all fighting men who had come to the Republic of Vietnam on purpose. The nation may have had masses of draftees floating around in the army in 1965, but it seemed doubtful to us that there were any unwilling draftees in that brigade. Throughout, the brigade was a solid, professional, and competent representation of the best that the U.S. Army had to offer in 1965.

Even the army communications mavens had a fighting spirit and an aggressive attitude. They assigned call signs with verve. Names like "Striker" and "Stiletto" and "Savage" were assigned to task-organized units, while our battalion made do with its tried-and-true call sign, "Dixie Diner." I happened to be in the 1st Brigade's tactical operations center (TOC) one afternoon listening on the loudspeakers to a unit commander, Savage Six, as he was describing an ongoing firefight. The action was hot and heavy, and the Savage commander was busy living up to his call sign as his soldiers knocked hell out of the Viet Cong unit through the use of maneuver and artillery firepower. In some way, his unit seemed able to accept the persona of his call sign—those soldiers were savage to the core.

Obviously, it was hard to take much pride in being known as Dixie Diner, or the comical call sign, "Fat Stuff." That silly title was an actual call sign that was dumped on 2/7 about eight months later, in the spring of 1966. None of this call-sign activity ever, ever fooled anyone on the enemy side. All one had to do was dial up the frequency 36.00 MHz (known as "VC Common") on the backpack radios, shout a few obscene remarks about Ho Chi Minh, and you would soon hear something on the order of, "Death to 2/7 Marines!" or "God-damn 2/7 Marines numbah ten." The Viet Cong, and later the North Vietnamese Army, were never at a loss as to who it was that they were facing in the field. Neither cute call signs nor formidable ones ever fooled anybody on the enemy side during the war in the Republic of Vietnam.

Being around the 1st Brigade of the 101st Airborne Division hardly represented our greatest involvement with the United States Army. Bringing us their shouted warnings that "The Cav is coming. The Cav is coming!", the 1st Air Cavalry Division representatives of the division advance party poured into the Qui Nhon area. That new airmobile division was the result of long and careful testing by the army. A very astute general officer, Lt. Gen. Hamilton Howze, had controlled the creation of the division, and it was his study, the Howze Board Report, that resulted in the army's establishing the 1st Air Cavalry, an organization that had its own massive aviation assets. That was one impressive outfit! The Air Cav came to the war in the Republic of Vietnam with 467 helicopters of its own. Even with those enormous assets, the division commander immediately requested reinforcement by more helicopter units. The added helicopters were to be made available by detaching them from army aviation elements that had preceded the division to the Republic of Vietnam. The Air Cav did not have small requests to make of MAC-V. What was wanted was not just a few extra helicopters for some special purposes. They wanted, and had assigned to them, more than one hundred extra helicopters. Most of those additions were the large CH-47s, but some of the units reporting to the Air Cav also operated UH-1 Hueys as gunships, "slicks" (troop-lift helicopters), and medical evacuation helicopters, known as "Dustoff."

As the Air Cav's massive aviation assets poured ashore, they quickly overloaded every bit of the available space on the airstrip at Qui Nhon. There was a terrible shortage of space on the parking ramps for all the helicopters to use during their "sleep-in" at night. It was a complex mess, one that grew worse every hour. The Air Cav aviation components assembled helicopters aboard ship, flew them ashore, and began to use them. Once helicopters were up and ready for use, the various commanders wanted to put them to work so they did just that. Of course, when the helicopters were parked side by side at night, lined up row upon row, they were very vulnerable to any kind of activity initiated by the enemy. As a target, the airfield at Qui Nhon was an absolutely golden opportunity that was missed by the Viet Cong during August, September, and October of 1965. The enemy never penetrated with sappers, and they did not mortar the field. Had they done so, the firestorm from the burning helicopters would likely have been visible from the hillside headquarters of Fleet Marine Forces, Pacific, in Hawaii. Since An Khe was not then ready to be home to all those flying machines, some way to disperse the aircraft was deemed essential.

Simple solutions are sometimes the best of solutions, or so most of us would prefer to believe. Plainly, that simplistic statement is often completely false because what is simple to one man is often a disaster to another. To solve the helicopter night-parking problem, someone created a solution that would make it possible for a large number of the helicopters to spread out each night into the local countryside. He sold the general the idea that the helicopters could spend the night with infantry units deployed inland to protect Qui Nhon. Thus, each evening, a flock of the noisy birds would be sent out to bunk down with one of the Marine or army rifle companies. The usual load imposed on a company was about three or four of the really big ones, the CH-47s, and about six to eight of the smaller UH-1s. For the aviators it was no big deal. They just had to take off as evening approached, find the assigned unit, and land amid some dusty tired-looking people in a field or on a ridgeline somewhere west of the city. The pilots and enlisted crewmen would bunk in, or under, their aircraft and pass the evening making noise, smoking, playing cards, showing lights, and otherwise compromising the security of the rifle unit. None of the aviators was required to survive much more than simple inconvenience. However, every infantry unit that hosted them suffered a great deal. The helicopters would be moved into the field just at the end of daylight, just as the troops were settling in for the night defense. The violent rotor downwash, created by even the smaller helicopters, would strip the troops of their tarps, their camouflage, and most of their other amenities. A man-made whirlwind would scatter dirt into everyone's eyes, ears, noses, throats, and into weapons of all kinds. The dust clouds also served almost as fingers from the heavens pinpointing the location of the infantry unit to any Viet Cong with a pair of eyes. Nothing about that simple solution was good for the infantry, but it did spread out the helicopters, taking them out of the potential assault area at the airstrip where the enemy sappers might hope

to conduct a night attack as they had so effectively done earlier in 1965 at the Da Nang airfield.

Although BLT 2/7 was providing sorely needed security
for the coastal region during September 1965, it was impossible to fully cover the city of Qui Nhon from penetration by
individual members of the enemy forces. Our intelligence
collection effort was steadily improving, and soon it began to
tell us that, just as we feared, the Viet Cong were still coming
into and going out of the city with virtual impunity. While
they never challenged the BLT directly, the fact that we knew
that enemy troops were able to move between the jungle and
city, as they chose, was irritating and extremely frustrating.

All of the fighting done during the first months of BLT 2/7's
combat tour took place as rifle-company or smaller-unit contacts. By the end of August 1965, all of the rifle companies
had been in numerous firefights with the enemy, but most of
them had taken place at the squad and platoon level. Very
often, our night ambush teams would have contact with a
moving Viet Cong unit, and a firefight would ensue. Some
combat patrols went out and made short, violent contact for a
few moments before the enemy forces withdrew. There were
never set-piece battles of company or larger size, and the Viet
Cong never chose to stand and fight; they did not want solid
confrontation. The Marines in the rifle squads were frustrated. They got little or no satisfaction out of the dangerous
and often deadly give-and-take. No one seemed to win or lose
any big fights. Regardless, the battalion was clearly beginning to suffer a steady trickle of losses to both the enemy action and to the difficult terrain. Painful losses were being
suffered. A few new arrivals came and were evacuated before
they were even starting to become acclimated. Others, some
of those who had been in the battalion for almost three years,
were also being evacuated with grave injuries. It was only the
beginning of losses for us, but it was an evil portent of what
could happen as the war grew ever larger.

So far, in the fall of 1965, the BLT 2/7 involvement in the
war in the Republic of Vietnam had been strictly a "bullet
war." Because there were so few fragmentation weapons, other

than hand grenades and the occasional rocket-propelled grenade (RPG) in use by the Viet Cong, the troops began to question the edict from on high that they wear their flak jackets at all times. Infantry Marines are pragmatic men, and they have a considerable capacity to understand that they must bear up under things that they consider to be "bullshit from above." None of the Marines shared the high command's positive view of the flak jacket. It was too heavy and too hot, and they wanted to pitch it and take their chances. Marines always bitch profusely about the loads that they must carry, and they no longer wanted to carry their flak jackets. Since the infantrymen were already overburdened, the flak-jacket requirement, which rankled them greatly, was a perfect target for their discontent.

Worse, the flak jackets available to us in 1965 were well known by the troops to be an ineffective defense against direct bullet impact. The plates sewn within the body armor would only slow, not stop, a high-velocity rifle bullet. Since we were getting no mortar or artillery incoming fire, bullets were creating the majority of the casualties. It was, therefore, the loudly stated view of the infantrymen who were living in the bush, that they should stop sweating their asses off in the heavy, Korean-War-vintage flak jackets. That view was always overruled. However, Marines are ingenious, and the troops began very surreptitiously to remove a few of the plates from their flak jackets every few days. The result was that there were many, many of the fragmentation resistant plates lying about in the brush, and a large number of Marines were wearing truly useless body armor. The essential "stiff-look" of the flak jacket was re-created by the insertion of cardboard from C-ration cases. Everything looked proper, but the protection provided by the flak jackets was approaching zero in many of the rifle squads.

Another factor that degraded the ability of the BLT to effectively conduct combat operations was the increasingly frequent diagnosis among the riflemen of a life-threatening form of malaria, plasmodium falciparum, which was resistant to the antimalaria drugs being taken daily by all hands. Plasmodium falciparum was not just resistant, it overwhelmed the daily dosage. What the Marines were taking, under the very earnest supervision of the medical corpsmen, were synthetic drugs that had been designed to replace the tropical medicine standard, quinine. Quinine, made from chinchona bark harvested in Peru, had always been the means of fighting malaria and its painful fevers. We were told that if the big orange pill was taken every day, as prescribed for everyone, the chance of getting malaria would be minimal. The drug, chlorprimaquine, did provide protection against the less virulent form of the disease, plasmodium vivax, but it provided no protection at all against its far more potent and deadly relative, plasmodium falciparum.

Most of the initial cases of malaria were discounted within the battalion as an example that proved that some troops were ducking the daily dose of pills administered by the corpsmen. Marines would pass out while maneuvering in the field and be found to have a fever of more than 105 degrees from malaria, not from heat exhaustion. The deeper the battalion operated along National Route 19, the more malaria cases were sustained. It did not require a medical genius to conclude that the mosquitoes living in the jungle along that east-west route were the source of the expanding number of sick Marines. Later, when the reality of the danger was faced at the higher naval medical commands, another antimalaria drug known as dapsone was added to the daily issue for every member of BLT 2/7. Dapsone was far more effective than the other synthetic medication, but it was nowhere near 100 percent effective. Our losses to plasmodium falciparum continued at a very serious rate until the battalion departed the Qui Nhon area in November and returned north to Marine control.

Sadly, the ability of the medical services to deal with the falciparum strain of malaria was severely hampered by the powerful impact of that disease on the tired, worn, and sleep-deprived Marines. Some who took their pills with resolute regularity, and proved it by doing so with the corpsmen looking on, fell deathly ill anyway. Oddly, of those who came down with plasmodium falciparum, it was the younger Marines who did not recover with any ease. The older SNCOs and officers, usually in their thirties, were the ones who would return to the unit from their period of medical evacuation to the navy's hospital in Guam or Kue army hospital, Japan. Many of the younger men relapsed and relapsed in those hospitals. Their systems just did not seem to rally strongly enough to fight off the disease. Eventually the relapsing men were sent home to recover in places in the United States with cooler climates. The deadly nature of falciparum was horribly proven one sad night at the U.S. Army's 85th Evacuation Hospital, in Qui Nhon, when three soldiers, one from the 1st Brigade of the 101st Airborne Division and two from the 1st Air Cav Division, died of high fevers despite heroic efforts by the doctors and nurses of the medical staff to cool their bodies.

Life for the Marines of BLT 2/7 had begun to go downhill the day they arrived in the Republic of Vietnam. It grew quickly worse each day that we were deployed in the Qui Nhon area. Everyone was suffering from sores, insect bites, infected cuts, and the lack of proper clothing. The materiel status of the BLT was as marginal as the status of the men who were serving in it. We had worn, rotted tents, battered equipment, substandard communications, and tired old weaponry. The supply situation was so difficult that Marines who wanted dry socks and dark green T-shirts to wear under their flak jackets had to write home and have them sent west by caring relatives. Physically, we had problems because sleep deprivation was an everyday reality for everyone. There were not enough Marines in the rifle companies to conduct the night defense at less than 50 percent alert ratios, and the headquarters paper staffing did not support twenty-four-hour days with enough watch standers to do the job. Everyone worked in a fog of weariness, wearing tired old clothing, and coping with the intestinal joys of continued consumption of very old field rations.

Everyone, from the commanding officer to the very rearmost ranking private in BLT 2/7 was constantly overstressed, excessively tired, and badly underfed. Weight loss among the younger Marines was dramatic. After only two or three months in the field, some of the eighteen-year-old riflemen, machine gunners, and mortarmen began to look as if they were thirty or more years old. Some of the Marines and corpsmen who completed their tour without becoming casualties lost weight for the entire year. They, and thousands of others in later years, departed for home so gaunt that it was easy to count the teeth pressing against their cheeks when they clenched their jaws.

Living without any amenities at all, the men of the BLT retained an amazing level of morale. Most of their positive attitude was the result of the personal leadership style of Lieutenant Colonel Utter. He spent every moment he could find in his busy schedule being out in the field with his men. He was with them in the heat and in the rain, never sparing himself for an instant. Every Marine, no matter what his job in the BLT, knew that the commanding officer cared about him enough to be out there in the bushes and the jungle with him, sweating in the heat, shivering in the wet, and sharing in the danger, while asking his men for nothing more than steadfast performance of duty. The colonel had the knack of making every man feel that his job was important and that, as Marines doing the best we could, we would all survive that hard time by pulling together.

# 7

# OPERATION STOMP

Often, an adage to live by as a Marine is: When things can go terribly wrong, they usually will do so—in short order. Perhaps this is just a short form of the old and famous Murphy's Law, but in September 1965, the adage was proven to be a clear statement of the truth for BLT 2/7. It is always a startling revelation to those involved when efforts that were begun in good faith, with logic and rational thinking applied, create a response that is out of all reasonable proportion. Just two months after BLT 2/7 had arrived at Qui Nhon, a devastating event nearly destroyed the battalion. The entire event took place in two days. BLT 2/7 conducted a minor operation between 5 September and 7 September 1965, and that operation created a most unusual situation. What began as nothing more complex than an effort by Lieutenant Colonel Utter to increase the pressure on Viet Cong units operating near Qui Nhon became a watershed incident in the history of the battalion and of the Marine Corps.

Operation Stomp, which was a self-generated, local ground combat operation of the battalion, ended in a situation that was so far outside the understanding of anyone in the organization that the event almost defies description. The absolutely unexpected, violently abusive fallout from the use of a simple riot-control gas during the operation both puzzled and infuriated all of the Marines and corpsmen of the BLT. The outcry over Operation Stomp became an international wild-eyed flap

**139**

for the press, a move that we all felt went far beyond what was reasonable. Yet, the use of the basically harmless riot-control gas during Operation Stomp created a situation that was deadly serious. The loudly roaring media mess, which exploded in just a few days, could not be left as an unresolved issue. The word *gas,* it appeared, had the potential to ruin the lives of the battalion commander and many of the other officers of the battalion.

Outside the city of Qui Nhon lay farmlands where rice and manioc were raised by the local farmers. They sold those foodstuffs and other farm products to the city dwellers. In the Qui Nhon area, the coastal highway, National Route 1, had been built generally along the north-south coastal plain. It climbed out of the flatlands only to pass over those few hill masses that reached all the way to the shoreline. Among these finger ridges, the Marines would often find caves and dugouts where the local force units (*Du Kich*) of the Viet Cong hid their weapons when they returned to their villages. Both the *Du Kich* and the regional force units (*Dia Phoung*) were marvelous diggers, and they could, and did, create amazing, interconnected tunnel complexes. That was true in the farmlands as well as along the ridges. Those underground works were difficult for Americans to examine because they were dug for use by men and women who were tiny compared to American troops. Because of the amount of underground water and the proximity of the water to the surface, most of the tunnels were located in the slightly higher and drier manioc-growing areas and in the hills. The reason for this was obvious; those were areas that were infrequently flooded by the farmers irrigating their crops.

The jungle terrain inland from Qui Nhon was home to several known units of the Viet Cong forces. Some of those units were aggressive, others spent all their time avoiding us. As described by the II Field Force Headquarters in Nha Trang, it was part of the mission of BLT 2/7 to make contact with those units, to destroy their hideouts, to destroy all of the war materiel we could find, and to bring the Viet Cong to battle—if possible. All in all, that was a very difficult and ambitious concept. Most of the concept was rooted in a serious misunderstanding at the very highest levels of our government as to what was really possible and what was not possible in the war we were fighting. In the field, our options were few. Like a monkey on an organ grinder's leash, BLT 2/7 had little or no room to maneuver far from the party line. When Lieutenant Colonel Utter chose to expand the unit operations into tunnel busting, it was just another way of getting on with the assigned mission.

Lieutenant Colonel Utter decided to conduct a combat operation, which was given the formal title of Operation Stomp, along a ridge known to be infested with Viet Cong caves and hideouts. He prepared to apply an old Marine concept, the standard Marine Corps method of dealing with bunkers and other fortified positions: the "Three Bees." For years and years the Marine Corps had taught its infantry to "Blind them. Burn them. Blast them." This meant, at the rifle squad level, the use of smoke or white phosphorous to cover the move forward of a flamethrower, burning the enemy troops in their fortification, and hand delivery by a Marine of an explosive satchel charge to blast the bunker into gravel. These were the tried-and-true techniques that had worked in World War II and in Korea, and it was expected that the troops would follow the same three-step sequence when, and if, contact was made with the Viet Cong units in their tunnel complex.

Almost as a side issue, an alternative concept was suggested for Operation Stomp by a battalion ammunition sergeant. He pointed out that within the prescribed ammunition load for the BLT was a large number of tear-gas grenades, which had been included for possible use in riot control. The sergeant suggested that we might consider using the gas grenades to flush enemy troops out of the caves and tunnels. The idea sounded very good, and it created considerable discussion within the battalion staff. Lt. (chaplain corps) Walt Hiskett (now in retirement as a navy captain) recalled in 1998 that he was asked to sit in on one of those discussions and was asked about his view of the use of tear gas. He remembers giving as his opinion that the use of tear gas would surely save lives—lives of Marines and of our Vietnamese enemy—and would be a properly humane way to separate the armed enemy from civilians forced into the caves and tunnels. The views of the chaplain and others who supported the use of tear gas seemed to be logical and reasonable, so the decision was made to have the gas available. The softball-size tear-gas grenades were added to the equipment list for Operation Stomp. Once the decision was made, the rifle companies taking part in Operation Stomp issued the grenades to the riflemen.

There were two types of tear gas available in the 1965 Marine Corps inventory, CN gas, which is a mild form of the munition, and CS gas, which is a much stronger chemical agent. CS gas has a very significant effect on those who are exposed to large concentrations. CS gas is a riot-control agent that causes tearing, vomiting, and sensations of burning skin. The milder agent, CN gas, is used at Marine Corps boot camp to "toughen" recruits in the gas chamber where they must remove their masks and sing the "Marine Corps Hymn" before dashing out into the fresh gas-free air. In the operational units, CN gas is often used in training maneuvers to create a need for gas masks during field exercises. Neither of the gases is, by any stretch of the imagination, lethal. Both forms of the gas will disperse quickly on a windy day, and neither gas is persistent. In lay terms, that means that there is no long-term residue or contamination left on the ground or vegetation after either one of the riot-control agents has been employed. Both forms of tear gas will cause anyone who is not protected by a gas mask to cry grandly and, sometimes, to throw up with great energy. It was the ammunition sergeant's view, a view with which the battalion commander agreed, that using the gas made sense as a means of rousting everyone out of the caves so that, while they were partially incapacitated, those with weapons could be quickly sorted out and taken prisoner.

At the rifle-company level, the use of the tear gas as a means of causing armed men to appear for quick and easy capture was greeted with a very positive reaction. The troops shared the ammunition sergeant's view that it might well be a way to save some lives—theirs. The CS grenades are round, about the size of a softball, and they looked to the Marines to be a very cheap plastic or fiberboard imitation of a fighting-man's weapon. Regardless, the rifle companies had issued the grenades, and they were in the hands of the troops, ready for use if needed.

When you issue a Marine something that he might possibly use against his enemy, it creates a situation that almost forces him to go out of his way to try it out the very first time he gets a chance. It was, therefore, not surprising to anyone when Operation Stomp began and some of the riflemen at the point of contact with the enemy used the CS grenades. As a tunnel clearing method, the tear gas produced spectacular results. *Time* magazine wrote, the following week, that 390 men, women, and children, captives of the Viet Cong, along with twenty armed Viet Cong fighting men, were brought out of the caves by the gas. A total of forty-eight gas grenades were thrown, and the version of events that *Time* magazine published was, with obvious reportorial and editorial em-bellishment, roughly what took place. Captive civilians—noncombatants—were released, and armed enemy troops were taken prisoner without the need for heavy fighting. There was no need for a firefight, and the Marines were greatly pleased to be dealing with nothing more difficult than collection of weapons from incapacitated enemy soldiers.

In just a day or two, our little local effort, Operation Stomp, suddenly became a major international news story. In the *Time* magazine report, titled "Tears or Death," it was noted that an AP reporter latched onto the story, inferring that the Marines had used poison gas. The piece noted that, ". . . from the hue and cry that followed, one might have thought that the scene was Ypres and the weapon was that cloudy green fog of 1915 called chlorine." We were told in BLT 2/7 that the AP re-porter was a young man named Peter Arnett. This is the same reporter who, in 1998, was personally responsible for a bla-tantly false and stupid story alleging the use of lethal gas by American forces in Laos. Regardless of the truth of the matter, the brain-dead assertion that the gas the Marines used was lethal was accepted world-wide. The outcry continued, despite careful clarification by the secretary of defense and other highly placed spokesmen in Washington. Some of the world press seemed delighted to accept uncritically that a lieutenant colonel commanding a rifle battalion could, on his own, launch a poison gas attack.

As events unfolded, BLT 2/7 moved from being busy in a relative backwater place in the war to center stage. Anonymity was replaced by international notoriety. Newsmen of all kinds arrived in hordes. Both the BLT 2/7 headquarters and the II Field Force headquarters in Nha Trang were deluged with reporters and senior officers. At the Field Force headquarters, the commanding general sent a message to MAC-V in Saigon stating that he had not had prior notice about the use of tear gas, but that he supported the action fully. His message and his opinion were both disregarded and massive amounts of journalistic nonsense was written. Lies, half-truths, and wild-eyed fabrications were filed by the reporters as fact. As the foolishness went on around them, the Marines of the BLT remained well pleased by the results of the operation; the tear gas had worked. Marines who might have been killed in a firefight laughed and traded stories about things that happened to individuals in the tunnels when the gas was being put to use. Their stories did not make it into the papers.

In one of the few cases wherein the use of the gas was not spectacularly successful, Bob Gallaher, who was then a member of a Company F rifle squad, recounts that one of the grenades that he threw bounced through a short tunnel and went off among a group of Company F riflemen in another part of the complex. Normally, he would have tossed in a fragmentation grenade. Had he done so, six or seven dead Marines would have been going home in gray caskets. The gas completely ruined the day for those other Company F Marines, but at the end of the day all of them were still very much alive. Gallaher also recounts that the crying, choking, vomiting Marines he gassed in error were not particularly amused. Some of them even threatened Gallaher's future if he ever made that mistake again.

Within BLT 2/7, everyone was completely comfortable

with the use of the CS gas to solve another problem. We were thunderstruck by the media frenzy that took place. When both the secretary of state and the secretary of defense—not to mention the president of the United States—found that they were fighting a losing battle to bring out the true story of Operation Stomp, the Marines in the BLT were amazed and disgusted. It seemed as if nothing on earth could douse the fury of the press against the battalion's allegedly "inhumane" action. For some reason, we never felt that what had been done was the action of "barbarians."

From Hanoi came the loud claim, repeated everywhere, world-wide, that BLT 2/7 was using a "toxic" agent to murder Vietnamese people. That further inflamed the world press and provided dramatic aid and comfort to the antiwar, left-wing groups at home. Bad publicity of that kind for our Marines aided those groups as they began mounting extensive opposition to the policy of involvement in Vietnam, the policy set forth by the Lyndon Johnson White House.

With great aplomb, the senior officers who visited Lieutenant Colonel Utter were able to speak out of both sides of their mouths at the same time. With their visits came soothing remarks about the use of gas being original and effective. When with us, they would seemingly agree with the action of BLT 2/7 but then remark to the press about the possible need to relieve Lieutenant Colonel Utter of his command. The chaos lasted for days, and the colonel's status hung in the balance. Everything about our leader and his life as a Marine was at stake. Everything he had stood for during all the years that had passed since he was a "fresh-caught" private, was subject to a drumbeat of inane questions by those who had not been anywhere nearby when the decision was made to use the CS grenades. Career destruction in the form of relief from command loomed as a real possibility for the colonel, and the officers and men of the BLT grew steadily more angry at the thought. Many loud, almost mutinous, remarks were made about the higher commands and their failure to stand solidly behind Lieutenant Colonel Utter. It appeared that the entire world was against BLT 2/7, and it infuriated everyone who was a member of the command.

One afternoon, a very senior Marine Corps officer, a general officer not in our chain of command who had evidently just wandered in from Washington, visited BLT 2/7. In a short and condescending conversation with Lieutenant Colonel Utter, the officer pompously opined that Utter would probably be relieved of command by Major General Walt in Da Nang. The general's remarks did not reflect the proper support due an officer who had just successfully executed a difficult and dangerous combat operation in a legal manner and with minimum loss of life to either side. The general estimated that the relief from command would be officially announced by General Walt within a week or so. That gave everyone the clear signal that senior Marine leadership did not plan to stand behind our mistreated boss. Instead, the general's attitude proved that most of those on high were going to fume, fret, fuss, and then duck for cover. His statements, and the conclusions we were forced to draw from them, were a crushing disappointment to the men of BLT 2/7. We could not imagine a Marine Corps that failed to stand behind a battalion commander when that officer was being openly lied about in the world's press, every hour of every day.

In wars and in peacetime, it is often the pure luck of the draw that decides who wins and who loses. Oddly, it came to pass that it was really our good fortune to have been ordered to work for the II Field Force, not the 3d Marine Division. While we Marines were administrative members of the division, we were under the complete operational control of the U.S. Army. In Nha Trang, in the offices of the II Field Force commander, Lt. Gen. Stanley R. "Swede" Larsen, the entire Operation Stomp fiasco was finally laid to rest. While the Marine general from Washington, who had flown to Nha Trang from Qui Nhon, was making his remarks about the prospective relief from command of Lieutenant Colonel Utter, General Larsen expressed another viewpoint. He stated, with a rather firm tone of voice that would not accept any form of rebuttal, that the Marines in BLT 2/7 did not work for General

Walt. Rather, they worked directly for him, and that fact made moot any talk of relief from command for Lieutenant Colonel Utter.

Having once served with Marines in combat during World War II, the general not only spoke our language, he also clearly understood that loyalty must, always and forever, be a two-way street. General Larsen stated flatly that if anyone was going to try to relieve Lieutenant Colonel Utter, for whatever reason, they would have to go directly through him. Those who might want Utter's scalp would first have to convince the four-star general who commanded all U.S. forces in the Republic of Vietnam to fire General Larsen. Basically, that hard-nosed army general laid his stars right in the middle of the table and challenged anyone to try to get past him. That kind of supportive reaction was what we had always expected; the expected support did not come from our own leaders. It came, instead, from a tough, honorable, and decisive member of the United States Army. With the decision made and with General Larsen's support in place, BLT 2/7 could get on with the war, continuing its service under the capable command of Lieutenant Colonel Utter. We all heaved a deep sigh of joy at the prospect of our boss's surviving and remaining with us as the combat tour continued.

An interesting aside to that miniature nonevent that mushroomed into a huge firestorm of criticism, was the employment, later in the war, of large amounts of riot-control agents in the Republic of Vietnam. As the war expanded, both the army and the Marines very frequently employed CS gas in bulk, powdered form, as well as in hand grenades to flush the enemy out of tunnels and caves. When bags of powder were used, engineers would blow it into the tunnel complexes with small, powerful air blowers known as "Red Devils." The blowers moved vast amounts of air and vast amounts of the burning, tear-producing powder down into the ground where the Viet Cong were hiding. By then, the war had grown huge, and nothing outlining this aspect of combat operations was ever written and indignantly filed by the fatuous, weepy little journalistic fact manipulators. By then, the riot-control gases

CN and CS had been returned to the inventory as just two more weapons that were available to infantrymen for use when the situation dictated.

A few days after the Operation Stomp firestorm of publicity was over, our regimental commander, Col. Oscar Peatross dropped in for a visit. As he returned Lieutenant Colonel Utter's salute he said, half jokingly and half as a serious comment, "Well, Leon. You out of jail yet?"

# 8

# MONSOONS COME

We newcomers to the long coastline of Southeast Asia learned some serious lessons in October 1965. We learned very hard lessons about the tropical monsoon seasons that everyone who lived there already knew and understood. The BLT 2/7 Marines learned, the hard way, that in the Republic of Vietnam there are basically only two seasons. These vastly different seasons are the two variations of monsoon weather, the northeast monsoon and the southwest monsoon. When the winds blow from the southwest, it is pelting down rain in the far south of the Republic of Vietnam and very, very dry and hot on the central and northern coastline. The variation begins roughly in the Nha Trang area, moves north through Qui Nhon, and holds firmly on up the coast toward the Demilitarized Zone that divided the two Vietnams at the seventeenth parallel. When the northeast winds began whipping across the shallow South China Sea, large quantities of rain, far more than most Marines could imagine, began to pour down in the north in a virtually unending stream. At the same time, things dried out down south. Every aspect of combat operations was badly affected by the foul conditions. During the monsoon, both sides had to fight the weather as well as each other.

At some level, everyone in the BLT was aware of the fact that the monsoons could drastically shift weather conditions in the Republic of Vietnam. But for some reason, the reality of the approaching wet season very nearly escaped us. As September 1965 waned, the skies more frequently turned ominously dark, and the clouds hung low over the sea. Along the coast, the miserable high humidity continued, but at the same time, the fearsome daily temperatures did begin to drift downward. All it would have taken for us to deal effectively with that newest aspect of our operational life was the concerted exercise of simple memory. Everyone should have recognized that it was going to start raining soon, and if the stories about monsoons were accurate, it was going to rain an amazing amount. Also, we should have noted that the rain was not going to blow away in a day or so. Monsoon rains are tough, steady, and heavy. Moisture was going to be coming down on us for the next six months or more. Alas, the BLT was not ready when the winds completed their 180 degree shift. Everyone in 2/7 had continued to operate as if the blazing hot, torridly humid, and utterly debilitating dry weather was going to go on forever.

Our battalion was hardly alone in its startling ability to ignore the obvious. Inland from BLT 2/7, the 1st Brigade of the 101st Airborne Division continued its operations along National Route 19, and army engineers from units in Qui Nhon continued to improve that highway by grading it into a neatly sculptured roadway made of their preferred material, compacted red laterite soil. The 1st Air Cavalry Division was using that road from first light until the very end of evening twilight to move fuel, materiel, and explosives inland to their base at An Khe. Their operational site was known locally, for a reason unknown to us, as the "Golf Course." None of us who had frequent contact with the army units ever perceived that they were expecting anything out of the ordinary to take place when the monsoon rains finally arrived. All of the Americans in and around Qui Nhon were in receipt of a clear warning, but most ignored the warning and went on with what they were doing.

Over a period that did not exceed a week, everything changed. The monsoon was almost upon us, yet we did not respond to that fact by thinking of particularly heavy rainfall.

The weather began its full switch from moderate southwest winds to very strong northeast winds, and the dust was atrocious. All of the very nice, powdery red laterite lying on the roadways and all the other surrounding areas began to move. It looked as if the very earth was on the move. The winds created a pervasive, reddish, wind-driven haze that was difficult to fly in, difficult to drive in, and difficult to walk in. Clearly, Vietnam's lightweight dirt—a great deal of which we military types had disturbed—was going to move from place to place, no matter how anyone felt about the matter. In some areas, the fine red dust, which was flying nearly horizontally, made driving a vehicle a dangerously chancy venture. Even with the use of goggles, the jeep drivers could not see the road well enough to drive safely. The huge U.S. Army truck convoys heading inland to An Khe were slowed to a crawl, and the passage of the large fuel trucks and other heavy cargo haulers stirred up more of the loose laterite, which swirled and eddied about in the air.

Inland from the city of Qui Nhon, where the rifle companies were living like animals in holes in the ground in the hills and valleys that they had cleared, there was also plenty of dust. The troops, who had survived more than two months of cleaning the dust out of their skin, their clothing, and their weapons did not even remark on the wind shift, they just felt cheered by the drop in temperature. When it began to rain, the troops took time to wash their dirt-crusted uniforms and to sluice off some of the dirt that was almost impregnated into all of those areas of skin that were habitually exposed. Earlier, when it was blazing hot and the humidity had neared the 100 percent saturation level, washing up had seemed to be a pointless effort. No matter how well a Marine washed, the dirt, the heat, and the humidity combined to make it an unrewarding activity. Sweat began to pour again, just moments after washing, and the dirt that had been removed was almost instantly replaced by new filth that adhered firmly to every part of the body. With the advent of cooler dryer winds, washing of both bodies and clothing took on new meaning as one of the few measures that could improve any aspect of the comfort of the infantrymen.

Since mid-July, the command post for 2/7 had been situated in the Phu Thanh Valley, a little more than six kilometers inland from Qui Nhon. It was a very nice valley, one that put us slightly off the beaten track while we remained near enough to both the coastal highway and the main roadway inland to operate along those routes when necessary. The primary idea had been to get the battalion headquarters out of the hustle and bustle of the Qui Nhon area. The unit command post was comfortably arrayed and spread out across the bottom of the valley, a sitting duck for a flood.

Much of what was happening in the city of Qui Nhon and the nearby areas was unrelated to combat against the enemy. Things taking place in the city were more related to infrastructure development. The most formidable development was continued extensive expansion of the airstrip by the engineers. As troop strength in Qui Nhon increased, so did the steady expansion of the off-duty pursuit of beer and ladies of the night undertaken by the U.S. Army troops. The BLT Marines were not permitted any liberty in Qui Nhon, none at all. Had BLT 2/7 remained in or near Qui Nhon, and had the policy included liberty, there would soon have been an opportunity for a serious conflict between BLT Marines and the men of the army's various support units who were billeted within the enclave. All of the reasons for getting out of the city were reinforced by the increase in confusion and the serious overcrowding in the port and airstrip areas when the major elements of the 1st Air Cavalry Division began to come ashore.

The commanding officer had his command post situated in what he determined to be the best location for control of the battalion's rifle companies. All four of the rifle companies were operating well inland, away from the battalion headquarters. If needed to add to the local security, one company could be ordered to operate close to the headquarters. When operating inland, all of the companies were permitted to operate on their own, in basically separate, independent operational areas. While the rifle units maneuvered as the commanding officer felt necessary for the protection of the American force buildup that was taking place in the coastal enclave, they also worked on their own to clear the Viet Cong out of the valleys where the local farmers worked their land.

The only identified drawback to the Phu Thanh Valley was the difficulty the BLT had in communicating with the rifle companies. When a rifle company was deployed more than a few miles from the command post, a radio relay had to be used. The communications platoon established and operated a hilltop relay site, but there were moments when that led to great confusion. In theory, a message is drafted, signed off, and transmitted by a communicator to another communicator who writes it all down and hands it to the addressee. Using a manned relay site meant that two more communicators entered the loop and the possibility for confusion of word use, transposed map coordinates, and the reality of slow movement of message traffic made everything more difficult. The fact that we had continuous high-quality communications support for every activity attempted by BLT 2/7 is a tribute to the professionalism of 1st Lt. Al Kehn and his communications chief. Those two Marines saw only challenges, not difficulties, and their every hour was dedicated to ensuring that the battalion commander could exercise control over his battalion and that the subordinate units could communicate. No one worked harder to make BLT 2/7 a success than the communicators.

Although the command post—when not being flooded—was most efficiently established in the Phu Thanh Valley, operational necessity always required that a component of the battalion's supply and support elements continue to operate near the Qui Nhon airstrip. Being there at the airstrip and near the port, they could draw rations, draw ammunition, and accept delivery of shipments that were air delivered for forwarding to the battalion or those arriving for the BLT on ships that anchored off the city. If Marines were not ready and willing to handle the materiel as it came ashore, the supplies and equipment would disappear suddenly and forever.

Staying ahead of the multitude of thieves was a challenging occupation for the support troops.

Close inspection of the command post site chosen in the Phu Thanh Valley back in July had quickly proven that BLT 2/7 was not the first combat unit to settle in that particular valley. From the hilltops, where the communication platoon set up its antennas, to the valley floor where the command post was first established (before the rains), the Marines found extensive evidence of previous use. There were old foxholes and trenches everywhere, and the unwary could easily break an ankle in some long forgotten drainage ditch.

Preparation of the field headquarters for an infantry battalion requires a considerable amount of digging and ground preparation if any kind of extended stay is expected. There must be drainage plans, security plans, and layout plans for the tents. When that work was being done, the Headquarters and Service Company troops found many relics of prior conflicts in the old trench lines. The first diggers turned up some rusty French helmets, buttons and buckles from long rotted uniforms, roll upon roll of very old concertina wire, and several small minefields. The mines, which we encountered by chance in utterly unmarked, open grassy areas in the valley, were extremely dangerous. There were all varieties of nasty antipersonnel and antitank mines. These dangerous explosive devices were covered with rust. There were mines of all sizes lying here, there, and everywhere. Some were partially buried, and others were just lying in the open. It was obvious that years of erosion had stripped the ground down to leave the metal mines poking up in a hodgepodge, like so many carrot tops in an abandoned garden.

The mines were all of French or Soviet manufacture, every one in terrible condition. Mines were found with rusted steel cases, with bent triggering spikes, and with open ends where the explosive had either fallen out or had been chipped out by the Viet Cong. Every mine, large or small, was encrusted with the hard, red, ever-present dirt. Some of the mines had obviously been tumbled along the bed of the valley's main stream by water action. Others remained buried in the hard ground where the French soldiers or, perhaps, the men of the Foreign Legion had set them out ten or twelve years before.

Every mine should have been examined by the explosive ordnance disposal technicians and destroyed under their supervision. Because there were literally hundreds of the things on the ground, that was not possible. The mine-clearing work had to be done by whoever happened to find a mine in the area where he was digging. In most cases that worked quite well, however, there are always some very stupid people in any organization. Several Marines were foolish enough to dig the first mines they found right out of the ground. Then the idiots happily carried them to their platoon sergeants or their officers. Only dumb luck prevented several tragedies from occurring. One mine was examined by a private who tried to unscrew the fuse, which had been in place for twelve to fifteen years. He was, after much work, successful in getting the fuse out of the case, and when he did so, the fuse went off as he pulled it out of the mine body. He was frightened but unhurt by the *pop* that the fuse made. The explosive charge within the mine body did not explode. Everyone around him dropped to the earth, heaved a sigh of relief at not being blown to bits, and then threatened to kill that Marine if he ever did anything so dumb again. Another mine was actually tripped by a Marine's boot; the fuse clicked but did not fire, the mine remained inert when he removed his foot, and that terrified Marine—who was living a charmed life—survived unhurt for one more day. Three or four other Marines, who had happened to be within a few yards of the mine-stomping fool, also felt a deep rush of thanksgiving at being spared the maiming and agony that could have been theirs in a split second had that mine been functional.

As the battalion operated out of the Phu Thanh Valley, it moved units wherever needed in the assigned tactical area. As a secondary mission, one that was well down the priority list, BLT 2/7 continued to keep National Route 1 under surveillance and to operate roadblocks at various sites. The fact that the Viet Cong were also using the highway was accepted and became part of the daily life of suspicion and concern for

Marines operating the checkpoints. No one, in the field or along the coastal roadway, had any fear concerning the arrival of the rainy season. Happy in their ignorance, the Marines of the BLT frequently crossed and recrossed the various bridges on National Route 1 without a single thought about the vulnerability of those bridges to flooding.

Operationally, the interest of the BLT staff in the various bridges was with regard to the possibility that the Viet Cong might either mine the short bridges to kill Marines, or they might simply blow the bridges to bits in order to deny us an easy way to cross streams. Examination of what was happening on National Route 19, the route inland, only reinforced the tactical concern about bridges. To the west of the BLT area of operations, the army was operating huge truck convoys over hundreds of stream bridges as they hauled materiel to An Khe. Convoys went inland at every hour with twenty or thirty five-thousand-gallon fuel trucks and apparently endless herds of huge truck-trailer rigs. All of those vehicles were going up into the higher ground to supply the needs of the 1st Air Cavalry Division and returning, pellmell, back on the same route to the coast. Every one of these vehicles was vulnerable to a bridge being blown up by the Viet Cong.

We were, as Marines often are, amazed and impressed at the amount and diversity of the equipment available to the U.S. Army. Much of it was equipment that we did not have and did not want, but it was still very impressive. By chance, several of the BLT officers happened to meet the army officer who commanded the armada of fuel trucks. He had forty of the huge vehicles to keep track of, to maintain, and to keep moving. The same group of Marines also met a captain who commanded a sedan company! Since no Marine present had ever even fantasized about a company of sedans, a number of questions were raised. The captain graciously explained that, as the commanding officer, he was the one who kept all of the shiny sedans, used by general officers, up and running. Expanding on the subject, he noted that he had twelve sedans, eight of them in use at the huge headquarters in Saigon. He was in Qui Nhon to visit the sedans he had deployed to that city.

The existence of such a unit as a sedan company had a very adverse impact on the feelings of us poor-relation Marines. A company of big, fat sedans was not any Marine's idea of a favorable thing in a combat zone. To Marines, the company's existence was a very bad illustration of a poor American attitude toward the need for creature comforts in a combat zone, an attitude that would, as the war years passed, create far too much noncombat "tail" and too much softness in the deployed force. The whole idea bothered us. Thinking about air-conditioned sedans hauling ass on the highway that we spent blood opening was too Stateside. As politely as possible, we Marines thanked the owner of the sedans and pondered a bit on what kind of deployment to war we were seeing.

The danger posed by flooding was suddenly made evident when the rains began in earnest. Since there was seldom any slowing or letup in the rate of rainfall, the hillsides quickly were saturated. Water then began to run off into all of the valleys. In the command post, the flow overwhelmed the drainage ditches, roared into the living and working tents, and then began to take tents and materiel away into the streams. Chaos was king as every section tried to cope with sudden submersion of its working spaces in a sea of mud and water. Almost every section in the command post had to relocate under the most unpleasant conditions imaginable. At first the Marines found it amusing to joke about, "Welcome to the monsoons," but it was not long before the daily misery of living a dreary, mud-encrusted existence crushed any attempts at viewing the debacle with humor. By the second day of heavy rainfall, the command post was virtually washed away, and that portion of the headquarters that was not afloat was sinking into the mud. The commanding officer and his operations center had to be moved to higher ground. As it poured and poured, the move was accomplished, but not without enormous difficulty. Sodden clerks tried, with little success, to dry their equipment, to make the wet typewriters work, and to rescue their files from the mud.

The monsoon rains were a horror for anyone wanting to conduct a road movement; BLT vehicles bogged down and the resupply of food and other items for the rifle companies was seriously compromised. Each rifle company commander lost the personal battle to stay dry and, at the same time, learned that he was going to have serious difficulty keeping his men fed. Morale among the infantrymen, which had been raised by the falling temperatures, was smashed down again by the fact that dry socks, among many other things, had become an impossible dream.

Within days of the start of the northeast monsoon, several of the bridges were seen heading out to sea, and the road network became a sea of mud. An uncounted number of the short bridges over small streams just vanished. Only roadways where the army engineers had mixed fuel oil with the red laterite soil and had moved to install steel bridges survived to support transportation. In addition to slowing the movement of supplies to the rifle companies, the weather created so much mud that the tactical vehicles were virtually inoperable. As expected by anyone familiar with the brutes, the disgusting, underpowered little M-422 Mighty Mite ¼-ton vehicles foundered immediately. Those vehicles were universally hated, and they earned that hatred with extraordinarily poor performance. The Mighty Mite did not even have a spare tire, so if riding in one and it suffered a puncture from some stick buried in the mud, the passengers had to get out and walk.

Only the larger vehicles, the 2½-ton and 5-ton trucks of the truck platoon, the engineer platoon, and the artillery battery, made much headway in the mud. Despite their multi-wheel drive capabilities, most of those vehicles had to stop where the bridges were gone and previously shallow streams had become five to eight feet deep.

Another difficulty that came with the rains was a redoubling of the attacks on every Marine in the BLT by the hordes of mosquitoes. Medical evacuations for malaria infection became a daily occurrence as more and more of the Marines of the BLT were infected with the plasmodium falciparum form of malaria. The increase in nonbattle casualties was a matter of deep concern. Despite each man's being forced to dose himself daily, under supervision, with both the chlorpri-maquine and the dapsone pills, Marines were still getting the disease. To anyone looking across the sodden jungle at the steady rainfall, it was clear that serving out the next few months in the Republic of Vietnam was going to be a very tough piece of work.

In the rifle companies, the war continued to be waged in tiny little firefights and sudden, violent ambushes. The pre-vailing wisdom dispensed from Capt. Jim Nolan's intelli-gence section was that the Viet Cong were probably using the bad weather to infiltrate small units into the valleys where the Marine riflemen were operating. He, of course, was getting most of this sort of data from ARVN sources and from intelli-gence bulletins forwarded to him from higher headquarters. To stem any infiltration that might menace the farmers work-ing their land, all of the rifle companies were directed to es-tablish night ambush sites along potential routes of access to their particular valley.

In the Company E area of operations, a well-used trail climbed over the ridgeline that made up the north side of the valley where the company was established. At the top of the ridge were two or three small open meadows among the jungle trees. We felt that those meadows might well be used by the Viet Cong as staging areas for their gear before they began in-filtration into the valley. As the rain continued to pour down, a reinforced rifle squad, led by a sergeant named Crosswait, was directed to develop an ambush on that trail. Sergeant Crosswait had nine men, including himself, in his squad, and he was reinforced by three machine gunners who were bring-ing along an M-60 machine gun. Sergeant Crosswait devel-oped his ambush plan, and my executive officer, 1st Lt. John Clancy reviewed the work and signed off on the plan. Ser-geant Crosswait was going to set an ambush on a portion of the trail that lay just to the east of the open areas on the top of the ridge. He wanted to catch his enemy as they manned their loads and started down the slope heading east toward

Company E in the valley. Supporting fire plans were developed and the entire effort was approved by Captain Doublet at the BLT command post.

When the gloomy, rainy day ended, and it began to grow dark, the squad leader briefed his men again, covered them with camouflage paint, and made them jump up and down to be sure that they would not rattle or clank when moving in the bush. Just before 2100, the patrol moved out and headed toward the ridge. They had to use the suspect trail because there was no other way to get to the chosen ambush site. By 2200, Sergeant Crosswait and his men were in position, an ambush that was shaped like the letter L. Crosswait had the long axis of his unit pointing to the west, toward the expected route of entry for the Viet Cong. The short leg of the L lay across the trail, with the machine gun set up at the base of the L. The machine gun was prepared to fire a stream of bullets, about ten inches above the ground, down the trail parallel to the long axis of the L, which was made up of the squad's riflemen. That layout permitted seven riflemen to be on the long arm of the L and the squad leader and his machine gun to make up the short leg of the L. The killing zone was ready for Viet Cong who were heading toward the valley. One Marine from the rifle squad was placed on the trail with his back to the ambush site. His mission was to provide rear security.

Once the squad ambush was in place, total silence was ordered, and the Marines waited in the rain while being chewed to pieces by the mosquitoes. Making an effective night ambush of a wary enemy is very difficult because whenever you have a number of men trying to lie silently in the jungle, it is possible that one will cough, another will sneeze, and the dumbest man present will drop his rifle or his helmet. A worried enemy will hear these noises at incredible ranges and react by either shying away from the site selected by the ambush commander or sneaking up and killing the waiting Marines.

Sergeant Crosswait's Marines were well trained and very well disciplined. They held fast, even when the rear security Marine crept in with the word that someone was coming up the trail from the rear. Whoever was coming was moving westward out of the valley instead of heading to the east into the valley. Sergeant Crosswait added the security Marine to the short leg of his L-shaped ambush and held fast, awaiting developments. Soon every Marine could hear the sound of men moving on the trail on the slope below the ambush site. The moving men grunted and spoke in short sentences as they climbed slowly up the slippery trail in the dark. They were noisy, and their chatter proved that they had no idea that Marines were out in the jungle awaiting their arrival. The rain continued, keeping visibility down to five to ten feet at the maximum.

Suddenly, an armed Viet Cong soldier slogged his way through the short leg of the L-shaped ambush. Instead of moving on toward the meadows on the ridgeline, he moved almost exactly to the end of the long axis of the L-shaped ambush. Once there, he dropped his pack and stretched. He said something to the men following him, and shortly, sixteen armed and dangerous Viet Cong fighting men were dropping their packs within three or four feet of the men of Sergeant Crosswait's squad. The Viet Cong all dropped their gear on the ground, stretched, yawned, farted, talked in short sentences, and relieved themselves at the side of the trail. One of the enemy soldiers chose to do his pissing on the ground at the rear of his group. The stream of urine he produced happened to fall across the barrel of the M-60 machine gun, a machine gun that he never saw. Despite the drizzle of urine being added to the rain falling from the sky, the Marines did not move. The ambush remained silent and undetected.

After taking a break of about ten minutes, the Viet Cong unit was told by its leader to pick up their packs and start moving again. When the last man was on his feet and had slung his rifle sling over his shoulder, Sergeant Crosswait said in his loud, very American, voice, "Fire!" Instantly, the machine gunner began to fire down the long axis of the trail, and every rifleman opened fire across the trail. Caught in a hailstorm of bullets, the Viet Cong never had time to even unsling their rifles. Every one of the sixteen enemy troops was first hit in the legs and then hit over and over and over in the body as he fell. The entire unit was destroyed in a matter of seconds. Every Viet Cong soldier was dead by the time he hit the ground. Sergeant Crosswait calmly ordered his Marines to cease fire and reported to Company E that he had conducted a successful ambush.

In the morning, Sergeant Crosswait wanted to leave his area of operations and return to Company E. However, that was not possible at first light because various people wanted to pop in to visit and view the carnage. Three or four helicopter loads of interested observers flew out to see Sergeant Crosswait and look at the dead bodies. Once the curiosity seekers were satisfied, the weary Marines were permitted to return to the company where they received a cheering welcome and their backs were slapped over and over by their exuberant fellow riflemen. That morning, I wrote a recommendation for a Bronze Star for Sergeant Crosswait on a cardboard C-ration-case sleeve and sent it in to the BLT headquarters on the next available helicopter. Someone there put the words in the right form and the award recommendation went on up the chain to the decision makers. Eventually, Sergeant Crosswait did receive his well-earned Bronze Star.

At the fighting unit level, the battle-to-the-death of Sergeant Crosswait's rifle squad in its ambush site stands as an example of what was typical during most of the days and nights that BLT 2/7 operated in the hills and valleys west of Qui Nhon. Sometimes the conduct of the Marines in an ambush site was lax, and the enemy would be spooked away. At other times, the Viet Cong surprised Marines and wounded or killed them. It was a bullet war with constant pinprick losses and a few very favorable results. Most Marines in the rifle companies slept part of each day and spent long hours in listening posts, on combat patrols, and in ambush sites hoping to kill some Viet Cong.

Even when they could sleep part of the day, the Marines of the rifle companies quickly began to show the strain of combat operations in adverse weather. By mid-October, all the Marines were growing gaunt and cadaverous. They were losing weight almost every day. The meals skipped because resupply trucks got stuck in the mud added to their discomfort and increased the weight loss. In theory, a full set of rations provides sufficient calories to keep young men well fed and energetic. However, the exertion of combat appeared to drain the Marine riflemen totally. It appeared that they could easily have eaten a double ration every day to keep up with the pounds lost to sweat, strain, and fear. Even the broad-faced young eighteen-year-olds took on the hungry look of men who are operating at, or near, their limit.

Another pair of very dubious pleasures were encountered as the monsoons began soaking the BLT all day, every day. The tired young men of the entire BLT faced the beginning of terrible foot problems. In the aid station, the corpsmen began seeing cases of jungle rot and immersion foot. Jungle rot was bad, and immersion foot was worse. They are dangerous conditions that turned out to be almost impossible to treat in the steady rain. BLT Marines were, by October of 1965, suffering from the poor quality of their boots as well as from the weather. Their footwear was just falling apart. In one memorable instance, a U.S. Army major with whom Captain Nolan was conferring on intelligence matters, looked down in horror at the tattered boots—normal then in the BLT—worn by one of the S-2 scouts. That kind and generous army major stared at the boots for a moment, sat down on a stool, unlaced his own boots, and without any comment, handed that pair of boots across the table to the Marine corporal.

Fighting in the Republic of Vietnam was not easy, even when confined to small-unit actions. In fact, the weather alone was almost as much an enemy as anyone would want to fight. All the adversities combined had the ability to make the Marines of BLT 2/7 very different from the men who had embarked in San Diego. Just a few months of combat had worn all of the Marines down appreciably and, at the same time, had honed them professionally to make them aggressive, competent, and self-assured as fighting infantrymen. The BLT had been strengthened by the adversity. The unit integrity we had at the beginning of our tour of combat and the personnel stability we enjoyed combined to make the unit even better and more effective. We all felt that, disregarding the weather, the BLT was growing more professional with each passing month. We had arrived well trained, thanks to the never-ending efforts of the operations officer, Capt. Al Doublet. We may have started as green as grass, but the time in Qui Nhon had made BLT 2/7 far more professionally sound than it had been on arrival in the Republic of Vietnam.

# 9

# RETURN TO MARINE CONTROL

By October 1965, it was time for BLT 2/7 to leave the II Field Force area of operations and return to fight under the control of the 7th Marine Regiment. From its arrival in July onward, BLT 2/7 had been working to provide security for army activities in the Qui Nhon enclave. Actually, that effort was in keeping with standard doctrine that sends the Marine units into an operational area to clear and control the ground for follow-on forces of the army. While it is doubtful that our landing in Qui Nhon was ever seen in that light by the men in Washington who had sent us ashore, it turned out that BLT 2/7 had taken part in a rather standard deployment—serving as a small part of the far bigger plan for American and third-country military operations in the Republic of Vietnam. Now that the U.S. Army and elements of the Korean Tiger Division were fully deployed, in strength, near Qui Nhon and inland along National Route 19 to An Khe, it really was time for us to return to our own kind. To get that accomplished would require that BLT 2/7 be relieved of its operational mission. Once relieved, the BLT would have to be detached from the Qui Nhon enclave, where the army still controlled all 2/7 operations, and ordered north for service in that portion of the Republic of Vietnam assigned to Marine Corps units.

For more than a month, starting in September, all of our elements found that they were being squeezed for space by the enormous U.S. Army buildup. Our battalion rear area was steadily shrinking as new forces came ashore, and ground space became more difficult to retain near the Qui Nhon airfield because of the steady influx of army combat support and combat service support units. All of those units wanted to get themselves established in a rear area so they could support operations being conducted farther inland. When their support elements were up and running, both the army and the Koreans of the Tiger Division were fully capable of accepting any and all of the responsibilities assigned to BLT 2/7. With our support areas being squeezed closer and closer to zero ground space, it would not be long before the Marines of the BLT would have no place to keep supplies, equipment, or ammunition. It was time to leave before we were trampled into the dust.

Out in the field, the rifle companies were running out of assigned maneuver areas. The combination of frequent operational maneuvering by elements of the 1st Air Cavalry Division, the very active presence of the newly arrived Korean Division, and the aggressive actions of elements of the 1st Brigade of the 101st Airborne Division combined to make the presence of the BLT Marines less and less viable. We no longer were a necessary security aspect of the Qui Nhon enclave. American participation in the overall war was steadily increasing, with deployed units ashore in the Republic of Vietnam having reached 125,000 men. It was logical that the high-level planners desired that Marine units like ours return to Marine control where they could conduct operations in that portion of the Republic of Vietnam, I Corps Tactical Zone (ICTZ), selected by them for the planned deployment of two full Marine divisions.

Meanwhile, to the north in the southern portion of the I Corps Tactical Zone, the Marine Corps was expanding the Chu Lai airstrip and basing more and more aircraft there. A new pair of runways was under construction by civilian contractors, and it was obvious that the rapidly growing Chu Lai enclave was going to need more security. The 7th Marine Regiment needed 2/7 and its supporting elements back as quickly as that movement could be negotiated with the high command in Saigon. Even without the completion of the new runways, expansion in Chu Lai already included new units of both fixed-wing and rotary-wing aircraft newly deployed from the United States. Those squadrons settled in and began to operate from the pierced-steel planking (PSP) landing field known as Old Chu Lai. Because parked aircraft and helicopters were always a very juicy target for Viet Cong sappers, all of the combat power of BLT 2/7 was sorely needed by Col. Oscar Peatross, the commanding officer of the 7th Marine Regiment, who was tasked to protect the entire Chu Lai enclave—with emphasis on the air facilities.

The tour of duty in the Qui Nhon area was good for BLT 2/7. In four busy months under army control, the Marines of the BLT had become ever tighter and more effective. The efficient nature of the unit made it clear to everyone that unit integrity really meant something special in combat. At every level, the teamwork was exemplary, and the daily interactions needed in combat became easier and easier because of the personnel stability. BLT 2/7 had become a team that had jelled to perfection—a tribute to the never-ending hard work of the operations officer, Capt. Al Doublet. His powerfully positive impact on the unit and its capabilities had begun the very first day of 2/7 training at Camp Pendleton and had continued every day thereafter. By October 1965, it was obvious that Captain Doublet had created for Lieutenant Colonel Utter a superlative combat command.

There was another good reason for the BLT to look forward to being back with the major Marine elements. Subordinate components of the BLT, such as the artillery battery, the truck platoon, and the attached helicopter unit, needed the maintenance support and other ministrations of their parent commands. In particular, the eight helicopters commanded by Major Blakeman needed far more mechanical support than they were getting at Qui Nhon. Major Blakeman's aircraft were suffering both from heavy logistics support usage by the BLT and from combat damage. In particular, the aircraft had all been shot up to one degree or another by Viet Cong fire during lifts conducted for BLT 2/7 Marines and for the assault infantrymen of the 1st Brigade of the 101st Airborne. The airborne brigade had requested Marine helicopter assistance on several occasions when they could not get the needed support from their own assets or from the Air Cavalry. Major Blakeman's pilots and crewmen had served the BLT to the very best of their ability from the very first day ashore. Major Blakeman had once said, during an officers' class on the critical differences between emergency, priority, and routine medical evacuations, that he and his pilots would land one of their CH-34s in any landing zone where a ground Marine was willing to stand erect. He and his men did just that, time after time after time, risking their lives for the Marine riflemen they had sworn to support. Bravery can only go so far though, and it was time for the helicopters to be returned to their air group for some serious maintenance.

Working for the United States Army was very good for the BLT. We learned a great deal, suffered some pangs of envy, and received vast amounts of willing cooperation and support. The support by army units ranged across the board, from bread baked at night on extra shifts by army bakers, for airlift to the rifle companies, to repair of our weapons and equipment on a priority basis. In fact, some of that repair was accomplished by officers and sergeants of the army who saw to it that our beat-up old Marine gear was placed far ahead of equipment sent to maintenance support by army units. Lastly, the largesse of the army units with which men of the BLT had daily contact knew no boundary between their service and the Marines. We were given, gratis, without paperwork, almost anything we needed. BLT 2/7 was obviously held in great esteem by the U.S. Army commanders, and their officers and men went far beyond the norm in taking care of us. Our needs were respected as valid requests for assistance, and every army unit made cooperating and helping us a standard part of their daily routine. When we left Qui Nhon, the Marines of the BLT had learned to deeply respect the men of the other service—leaving behind forever the contempt for the U.S. Army that is often inserted into the vocabulary of Marines during boot camp. While none of us aspired to leave the

Corps and become soldiers, none could ever fault the U.S. Army for its support of BLT 2/7.

Instead of moving the battalion and its supporting elements north in an administrative manner, the decision was made to create an amphibious assault, Operation Blue Marlin, for BLT 2/7 on a section of the ICTZ coastline. Part training and part operational, the assault was to come ashore on the anniversary of the founding, in 1775, of the United States Marine Corps. D day was ordained for 10 November 1965, the 190th anniversary of the Corps. Setting the date of an assault landing in that fashion, for propaganda or showmanship, flies in the face of conventional operational thinking. However, the planning failure was never deemed to be particularly critical because little or no real opposition was expected on the beach. It was going to be a show, not a real amphibious assault to secure a contested beachhead.

In the coastal areas of the Republic of Vietnam, the beach gradients are all fairly shallow, and the tide ranges offer few problems. Landings across the beach by the amphibious tractors and up to the high-water mark by landing craft are seldom very difficult. However, in almost every case, the exits leading inland from the beaches are poor. These factors being the operational "givens," the only thing that might upset a preordained and predictable D day, one that was being conducted for publicity reasons, would be the Viet Cong's ability to counter the landing with one of their interprovincial force (*Chu Luc*) regiments. The *Chu Luc* were tough, and if they were deployed against us, they would possess the ability to inflict serious losses on the BLT as it came ashore.

While the *Chu Luc* forces might have the power to oppose the landing, the best guesses of all the intelligence mavens was that there was no chance that would happen. Regardless, it was a real concern to BLT planning because the intelligence on the *Chu Luc* was often faulty or just plain lousy—at best. It was not surprising that BLT 2/7 was woefully ignorant about the possibilities of intervention. Captain Nolan had a problem during the planning phase of the operation; there just wasn't any reliable data on Viet Cong intentions available to interpret. If the Viet Cong were going to be on the beach waiting, there was no one in the unit who might know that before going ashore to find out in person. Being left in the dark was no longer an unusual experience for the BLT staff. Based on our operations in the Qui Nhon enclave, being in the dark was just accepted as the norm. Planning for Operation Blue Marlin went forward, and amphibious shipping was made available. The show was set for 10 November 1965.

After being relieved of security responsibility for its areas of operations, the BLT enjoyed the first moment of "administrative" time since its arrival in the Republic of Vietnam. One afternoon and evening of liberty in Qui Nhon were authorized. Allowing his Marines to have their liberty time was a calculated risk by Lieutenant Colonel Utter. That decision could have destroyed him, yet he made it almost gleefully, laughing about the chance his men had to take their first real break since June. Had the liberty time gone badly, with drunken brawls erupting between Marines and soldiers, his rapport with his army bosses would have been shattered. His Marine bosses would, of course, be standing ready and willing to criticize him when he arrived under their command. In fact, the liberty went splendidly, with many tales told during the following years about the good times, the cold beer, the bartering, the language difficulties, and the laughter. For many of the Marines of BLT 2/7, the hours of liberty and laughter in Qui Nhon were the last sustained occasions of pleasure that they ever experienced.

In short order, the shipping was alongside the piers, and BLT 2/7 embarked to sail north, fully prepared to conduct the desired amphibious assault on the Marine birthday. Few if any Marines of the BLT were sad to leave Qui Nhon. They were proud of their unit and its performance, but some firmly held the opinion that a great deal of what they had been doing had been wasteful wheel spinning. Failing to retain ground that had been cleared of the enemy was not an idea that sat well with infantrymen who had sweated heavily and bled profusely to clear that terrain. As an example, a number of

Marines complained bitterly about abandoning a hilltop that had been the scene of a firefight that cost five casualties within the BLT. Marines of Company E were asked to clear the hilltop, and they did so. Then a disappointing thing was done. An Armed Forces Radio and Television Station (AFRTS) was erected on that high ground. Logic and common sense did not prevail. Our Marine infantrymen could see no value in AFRTS. Neither the radio station nor the television station appeared to them to have any particular value that might be equated to the Marine blood shed on that bleak hillside.

From the United States, the troops were beginning to get new and unsettling feelings. October 1965 brought to Vietnam the news of widespread disaffection at home, culminated with extensive tales of what had taken place during the Watts Riots in Los Angeles. News items of that sort always surfaced deep concern, and many of the troops chose to question their officers closely. One Marine, Cpl. George A. Ware, a black communicator in Company E, asked me, "Captain. Why would anyone burn down the part of town he lives in?" Since I had no answer, the corporal and I discussed the racial tensions that were having their effect on the nation and the fact that, under fire, bigotry had a way of disappearing as black Marines and white Marines shared the danger equally. Corporal Ware pondered that for a time and then asked my permission to write a letter to his hometown newspaper questioning the need for both the racial gulf and the need to burn down cities to prove anything at all. He wrote his letter, sent it off, and it was published in his hometown. His hometown turned out to be Chicago, and the response was sizable. A few weeks later he received a package from the newspaper containing many of the letters they had received in response to his remarks. There were a gratifying number of very positive letters praising Ware for his caring and for his patriotism as a serving Marine in a war far from home. One letter, less favorable, told him that he would ". . . not recognize parts of Chicago because they are sending the niggers to go to school there . . ." Since he had made no mention of his race in his letter to the paper, Corporal Ware was hurt very deeply by that vile commentary. Afterward, he and I had many long discussions about the fact that racially inspired hatred of that kind had to be destroyed if America was to continue to progress. Had I denied Corporal Ware's request, he would have been spared that particular unnecessary hurt. Thirty-three years later, I still wonder if I did the right thing when I told him to go ahead and write his letter. Corporal Ware was a magnificent Marine, a fine and decent man who always cheerfully performed every assigned task to the very best of his ability. Perhaps I failed to properly protect him.

The Operation Blue Marlin assault landing was made on 12 November, across a wide, white beach. D day did not occur on 10 November as had been planned. The assault was delayed and delayed by variations in the monsoon weather. There was heavy rain, then clearing, then heavy rain again. The BLT failed to make an anniversary landing on the tenth, and the publicity-driven event desired by higher headquarters did not take place. Regardless, on the twelfth the BLT 2/7 troops poured out of the LVT-P5 amphibious tractors, leaped from the landing craft, and prepared to move westward. The planning for the landing directed that the BLT conduct an immediate sweep through some villages lying north of the Chu Lai enclave and inland between the South China Sea and National Route 1. The maneuver contained in the orders from above turned out to be impossible.

Once ashore, without a shred of meaningful contact with enemy forces, the assault rifle companies found that they had not been landed on a beach from which they could egress inland. The sweep that had been ordered could not be executed because there was an expanse of water to their immediate front. The rifle companies were ashore on a wide, sand island, or sand spit, that was separated from the actual coast by a significant body of water. On a far grander scale, the situation was similar to crossing a beach in Florida and finding out that you have no way to get across the deep channel of the Inland Waterway that parallels the beach. It was an unpleasant surprise, and it created both confusion and anger among the troops who were trying to do their best to carry out their orders. Instead of a quick, hard-hitting assault, the effort by the BLT was viewed by many as another form of "make work" inflicted on the command by people far up the chain of command who just could not understand the reality of ground operations. All in all, no matter how it was examined, participation by the BLT in the Operation Blue Marlin assault was not considered by many to be one of the significant events of the year 1965.

Despite the slightly disappointing way that BLT 2/7 returned to Marine control, it was exciting to be back with the rest of the regiment. As for the various reinforcements that made the battalion a BLT, they were all returned to, and reunited with, their parent commands. Working for their parent commands did not alter their mission to support 2/7, it merely shifted them from "attached" elements that worked directly for the BLT commander, to "direct support" units that worked for their own boss while supporting the operations of our battalion. The same reconnaissance platoon, the same engineer platoon, the same artillery battery, the same amphibious tractor platoon would still give us a hand when needed. Additionally, all the other small elements that had been attached to 2/7 at Camp Pendleton were released by Lieutenant Colonel Utter. The colonel expressed his great appreciation for their hard work and superior professional performance during a difficult, and sometimes frustrating, four-month mission.

Col. Oscar Peatross, the regimental commander, also formally thanked the commanders of all of the combat and combat service support units for the magnificent manner in which their detached elements had supported 2/7. He also welcomed 2/7 back into the regimental fold with warmth and a great demonstration of his sense of humor. He gently teased the battalion commander about leading a "renegade" unit of criminals and ne'er-do-wells that had tried to defect from his regiment to join the army—without success.

While he often used humor to make his points, Colonel Peatross was never in the least unwilling to give credit to those who performed in an exemplary fashion. He made sure that everyone in 2/7 knew that he had received glowing commentary from Lt. Gen. Swede Larsen, the II Field Force commanding general, about the performance of Lieutenant Colonel Utter and his battalion. The regimental welcome was great for the troops, and it was with a deep feeling of comfort that 2/7 returned home. The Marines of 2/7 were proud to learn that their performance of duty in the Qui Nhon enclave had been appreciated and respected by those serving farther up the chain of command.

The 7th Marines assigned 2/7 a section of the security perimeter established along the hill masses to the west of our favorite highway, National Route 1. The battalion command post was tucked into a small valley, and the rifle companies were billeted—if the word applies in any way—in their fighting holes on the hills. On the right flank, Hill 49 was occupied because it overlooked about twelve hundred meters of rice-paddy land that lay between the security perimeter and edge of the heavy jungle. The Vietnamese who worked those paddy fields lived, for the most part, in a village that was a very short distance from the command post. It was a very friendly village, and the battalion quickly became involved in the life of the villagers. We provided them with medical supplies, medical support, some food supplies, and basic security from attack by the Viet Cong.

Near the battalion command post, the cooks and messmen established a central galley where hot meals, created from canned B rations, could be served to the rifle companies and to the H & S Company Marines on a rotating basis. To support that food-preparation-and-feeding area, a water tank was elevated atop a wooden tower to permit gravity to supply the water to the cleanup crews who scrubbed the pots and cleaned out the garbage cans. The tank was refilled each day by pumping water from the standard water trailers that were moved from place to place by the 2 ½-ton M-35 trucks. On the side of the heavy canvas water tank some wag had, using a broad sloppy brush, splashed on the words, "BEAT VC - CLASS OF 66." The Marine who painted that comment obviously shared,

Commanding officer, Second Battalion, Seventh Marines, Lt. Col. Leon N. Utter, USMC, outside his command post, spring 1966. (*First Marine Division in Vietnam*)

Lieutenant Colonel Utter (right) with the commanding general of Task Force Delta, Brig. Gen. Melvin D. Henderson, just prior to Operation Harvest Moon, December 1965. (Utter Collection)

Lieutenant Colonel Utter and Capt. Martin O'Connor confer in the rain during Operation Harvest Moon. (Utter Collection)

Memorial chapel for the dead members of Second Battalion, Seventh Marines, in the command post area, Chu Lai enclave. (Utter Collection)

Viet Cong suspect being tagged after his capture during Operation Harvest Moon. (Utter Collection)

Lieutenant Colonel Utter and Chaplain Walter Hiskitt during a memorial service for those lost during Operation Harvest Moon. (Utter Collection)

The "Beat VC Class of 66" water tank. Allen's Oasis was named for the motor transport chief, Staff Sergeant Allen. (*First Marine Division in Vietnam*)

PFC Leroy Slaughter shows off the bear trap he stepped into during an operation north of the Chu Lai enclave. (*First Marine Division in Vietnam*)

Cake presented to the executive officer of 2/7, Maj. Ray Wilson, honoring his twenty-one years of service to the Marine Corps, 1944–1965. (Utter Collection)

Weapons captured during Operation Hot Springs as displayed for journalists who arrived after the operation was over. (*First Marine Division in Vietnam*)

Actor Don DeFore visits 2/7 on a USO tour. Left to right: Mr. DeFore, Lt. Col. Utter, Maj. Al Smith, Lt. Joe Lloyd, and 81mm-mortar platoon leader Lt. Jack Archer. (*USMC photo in Utter Collection*)

Company F maneuvering on the left flank of the battalion during Operation Montgomery. Author and two radiomen are in midground center. Shortly after the photo was taken, the company came under heavy fire from the hills to the left. (*First Marine Division in Vietnam*)

Part of a Viet Cong propaganda wall erected in the village of Ky Phu. We blew it up on 27 Feb. 1966, after Operation Double Eagle, Phase II. (*First Marine Division in Vietnam*)

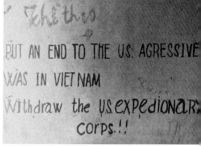

Interrogation of a Viet Cong suspect during a rare moment of sunshine, Operation Harvest Moon, December 1965. (Utter Collection)

Marines of 2/7 carefully check out an opening to one of the many Viet Cong caves and tunnel complexes they encountered. (*First Marine Division in Vietnam*)

Landing zone punji stakes encountered by the Marines of Company F on Operation Nevada. (*First Marine Division in Vietnam*)

Lts. Dan Flynn and Tom "Walrus" Riley during a break while rebuilding a school in Qui Nhon, September 1965. (Utter Collection)

An antitank weapon without discernible use during Operation Nevada, the ontos returned to Chu Lai after just one day in the field. (*First Marine Division in Vietnam*)

The author (lower right) checks his map as Company F moves through yet another village deserted by the hostile inhabitants of the Batangan Peninsula. (*First Marine Division in Vietnam*)

Sgt. Joseph Long (left) shows Staff Sergeant Kelly a diagram of the path of the bullet that entered his face next to his nose and stopped in the roof of his mouth. With just a few stitches, Long was back on duty in one day. (*First Marine Division in Vietnam*)

Badly wounded in the right leg on D day of Operation Montgomery, S.Sgt. L. Brown, machine-gun platoon leader of Company F, lies in a bomb crater. (*First Marine Division in Vietnam*)

Typical foot trap encountered by Marines of 2/7. (*First Marine Division in Vietnam*)

Sergeant Major Unger presents Lieutenant Colonel Utter with a plaque, listing 2/7's major operations during the colonel's tenure as battalion commander. (Utter Collection)

Change of command, 4 June 1966. Left to right: Colonel Roothoff, Maj. Roy Moss, Lieutenant Colonel Utter, and Major Stephens. (Utter Collection)

"Home is where you dig it!" Sgt. Bob Gellaher makes his home in the steady rain during Operation Harvest Moon. (Bob Gellaher Collection)

Col. Jim Nolan (center) at a Company F reunion in 1993. As a captain, Nolan commanded Company F during Operation Harvest Moon. (Nolan Collection)

with many others in the battalion and in the nation's capital, the hope that the entire war would be over by the end of 1966.

It was not long before all the elements of 2/7 were fully settled in their new areas. From the day of arrival, the battalion was busy operating all manner of local patrols, ambush sites, and listening posts forward of its assigned portion of the perimeter. The pouring rains continued, and the troops continued to suffer from the monsoon deluge. One Marine, who was a rifle squad leader in 1965, reflected in 1997 that his primary memory of Vietnam was being wet all year round. He was wet during the monsoon and had to deal with leeches and immersion foot. He was just as wet from sweat that poured from his body during the hot months, and he got jungle rot because he could never get clean. He said that for him, the entire experience of his tour in combat was the fact that he was never able to be dry and comfortable except when lying in the hospital with a gunshot wound.

After he had settled his battalion into a routine, Lieutenant Colonel Utter began to show the Marines just how a resolute commander can influence his battalion. He would stand near the chow line, close to the water tank with the cocky words splashed across it, and tell his men all of the latest news from the high command. The colonel did not sweat the security and classification nonsense at all. Secret and top secret messages were discussed as factually as the latest scoop from the *Stars and Stripes* newspaper. Lieutenant Colonel Utter wanted every Marine to know what he knew, and he took every opportunity to gather the troops around him in groups, where he told them the truth as he knew it at the time. Many 2/7 Marines cherish to this day the fact that their colonel would throw the security crap out the window and tell them what he had learned from the classified message traffic.

Another of Lieutenant Colonel Utter's tricks was a disappearing act. Often, in the early evening, our colonel would slip out of the command post with an M-14 rifle and a belt full of ammunition and attach himself to a rifle squad as it moved out in the dark to establish an ambush site or to conduct a combat patrol. The vanishing act left Maj. Ray

Wilson and Captain Doublet back in the command post with full responsibility for the battalion. Many outsiders, most of whom would have been too fearful to go themselves, were critical of our colonel for placing himself in such dangerous places. The 2/7 Marines had a view that was far more favorable. They respected the fact that Utter, even though he was a lieutenant colonel, did not hold himself to be above sharing, right down in the mud with the lowest private, the dangers of life in an infantry battalion. Lieutenant Colonel Utter always told those who asked that he went out in the dark because it was part of his job as a battalion commander.

The settling-in process for the battalion, with emphasis on local security operations, lasted about three weeks. At the end of the first week in December 1965, the battalion was alerted to take part in a large operation outside the Chu Lai enclave. Troops from combat support and combat service support units came forward and took over the 2/7 portion of the perimeter in order to free the battalion to assemble and move out to fight.

# 10

# OPERATION HARVEST MOON

On 5 December 1965, a high priority message containing an operational warning order was received by our battalion commander. The order formally alerted 2/7 for movement to combat operations in the field and established Operation Harvest Moon as the battalion's next large-scale effort. Operation Harvest Moon was to be a search-and-clear mission conducted mainly in the jungle-covered hills and valleys to the northwest of the Chu Lai enclave. The operational warning order was issued by the commanding officer, 7th Marines, and it formally directed that 2/7 was to be prepared to take part in a multibattalion combat operation. Lieutenant Colonel Utter was ordered to place himself and his battalion under the operational control of a new command organization known as Task Force Delta. This new task force was commanded by Brig. Gen. Melvin D. Henderson.

Operation Harvest Moon was planned from the very inception as a large and complicated undertaking. Making it work would be difficult, as the fighting infantry battalions would come from various regiments all operating at great distance from one another. At the start, two infantry battalions from the Chu Lai enclave and one battalion from the Da Nang enclave would be joined by the Special Landing Force (SLF). The SLF would be lifted ashore into the battle from the naval amphibious assault task force standing in readiness off the coast of the Republic of Vietnam. Face-to-face coordination

**177**

between all of the various unit commanders would, basically, be impossible until Operation Harvest Moon had begun and all units were busy conducting combat operations. The anticipated duration of the operation, which was created without any evident consideration of either the weather situation or the terrain faced by troops on the ground, was presented to 2/7 in the warning order as being about ten days.

Operation Harvest Moon was slated to commence on or about 9 December with a mission that included searching for, making contact with, fixing in place with combat power, and clearing out—if possible—major Viet Cong units in the Que Son Mountains and the Song Chang Valley region. While Brig. Gen. Melvin D. Henderson had been initially designated as the commanding general of Task Force Delta, he was replaced by Brig. Gen. Jonas Platt just as Operation Harvest Moon began. Brigadier General Platt remained in command of the task force, to which 2/7 was assigned, throughout the operation.

Operation Harvest Moon was to be the kind of operation that was covered, early in the war, by the broad-brush, utterly unrealistic title of "Search-and-Clear." Its operational goal directed the Marine units to sweep through the countryside, searching for the base camps used by units of the Viet Cong. Clearing of the enemy was to occur when all that wild tramping about eventually brought the Viet Cong to battle by flushing some of them from their hiding places. Any enemy units that chose to fight were to be destroyed. Those units that ran were to be chased down, attacked, and destroyed after they had abandoned their base camps.

Knowing the terrain to be virtually impassable in many areas, the troops were plainly skeptical about "searching and clearing" as an activity worthy of the title. As an aside, it was never explained to the troops doing the slogging, butt-busting work whether a Viet Cong unit that successfully avoided any contact with the sweeping Marines—by running their asses off—had been officially "cleared." All of the word magic appeared to the infantrymen as nothing more than high-level, pie-in-the-sky mental imagery. Any success during Operation

Harvest Moon would depend on three things. First, the task force must correctly forecast the expected combat actions by the enemy, otherwise the wily Viet Cong would elude the sweeping battalions. Second, the entire task force would be depending heavily on the superior mobility and firepower capabilities of Marine units. Of course, both firepower and mobility could be seriously hampered by foul weather, and the December weather was extremely foul—and getting worse. Third, and a slight oddity, the operation would be proceeding into the jungle with the fervent expectation that there would be a series of stupid responses made by the enemy commanders when faced with the major Marine deployment. Success is seldom achieved when so many factors combine to militate against our side's "capturing the flag."

In reality, any real searching and clearing was going to be a very difficult proposition. All of the terrain in the objective area was complex and difficult. The area contained some wide, flooded, flat ground, great numbers of small difficult hills, and a few steep hill masses that overlooked everything else. Between the hills, most of which were covered with trees and underbrush, were ravines and wider valleys filled with thick, thorny, intertwined brush and bamboo. All of the natural obstacles made foot movement anywhere off the established trails a very slow and difficult process. Every Marine infantry unit assigned to Operation Harvest Moon was always going to be in danger of being ambushed and badly hurt, even when they advanced with great care. Rifle squads and platoons in the brush could only present a one- or two-man front to the enemy, ensuring that the initial engagement with the Viet Cong would seldom favor the Marines. However, wider frontages would not be possible. The troops would be compelled to slip and slither along in the mud, dodging in and out between the bushes and trees as they tried to follow their orders. Just maneuvering combat units on the ground was going to be hard work, disregarding the fact that the orders tasked the Marines to conduct a thorough search.

Worse than the terrain limitations imposed on maneuver was the weather situation. The horrible state of the weather in

December was clearly a terrible factor with which all of the Marine air and ground commanders had to cope. A factual examination of the potentials for disaster should have shown that the well-intentioned plans for maneuvers carefully diagrammed on map boards were unlikely to be duplicated by Marine infantrymen plodding onward in the mud or creeping forward on hands and knees under the jungle canopy.

For aviator and infantryman alike, the visibility permitted by the weather was also a critical factor. At times, the ground visibility could be reduced to a meter or two by the heavy rainfall. That same heavy rain would preclude both fixed-wing air support and helicopter resupply by the aviation Marines. Operation Harvest Moon was an ambitious plan, one that had probably been sketched out on clean maps. Such plans are seldom so neatly replicated down in the muck and mire where the infantry battalion riflemen ply their trade.

Almost constant rain was expected for the duration of Operation Harvest Moon, so there would be heavy cloud cover in place most of the time. Low clouds always have a critical effect on the use of attack aircraft, and that limits the amount of close air support for the rifle companies when they blunder into a solid contact with the enemy. Another aspect of the miserable weather was the fact that constant rains might prohibit resupply and medical evacuation efforts for long periods of time. The Marine pilots who flew the 1st Marine Air Wing's workhorse CH-34 helicopters were willing, but they could not be asked to attempt support of the ground troops in weather that was outside the envelope of safe flight operations.

Another obvious addition to the equation was the horrible effect that continued foul weather would have on the physical condition of the Marines in the rifle companies. The fighting men were already living like animals in muddy foxholes, with little or no shelter whatsoever from the constant wetness. Once deployed on Operation Harvest Moon, their living conditions could only grow worse. In contrast, the enemy would be dry. Our Viet Cong adversaries could shelter in their caves or in any one of the friendly villages until their leaders felt like fighting the Marines or fleeing. Being dry at the start of any confrontation would be to the great advantage of our enemy.

The Task Force Delta staff, working at the 3d Marine Division Headquarters, conducted a preliminary briefing at 1000 on 6 December. The briefing was attended by the commanding officer of 2/7 and his operations officer, Capt. A. J. Doublet. To facilitate planning, Task Force Delta issued Lieutenant Colonel Utter an advance copy of the Task Force Delta Operation Order 1-65. As one can surmise from the numbering of the order, Operation Harvest Moon was Task Force Delta's first attempt at controlling and managing a multibattalion operation. That meant that the task force was always playing catch-up until its staff functioning could be improved sufficiently for it to keep current with events taking place in the field.

Of course, with the advance plan in hand, the 2/7 staff was quick to begin all of its own necessary planning actions. In order to be prepared for a major operation, the Marines of 2/7 had a great deal to accomplish. At Lieutenant Colonel Utter's direction, all decisions were based on the data received at the briefing and on the advance copy of the operation order. Not unexpectedly, the formal copy of Task Force Delta Operation Order 1-65 for Operation Harvest Moon was not received by the battalion until long after deployment had begun. The formal document arrived very late on the afternoon of D day. That was, of course, after the battalion was established in the field, preparing to execute the planned helicopter-borne assaults scheduled for D plus one. When the Task Force Delta order arrived, 2/7 had long since manned its loads and moved out. By the end of D day, the battalion was operating in the area of the provincial capital, Tam Ky, a small town a few miles to the north of the Chu Lai enclave.

Lieutenant Colonel Utter was also quick to alert his attached and supporting subordinate commanders as soon as he fully understood that a large-scale operation was in the making. He refused to wait for Task Force Delta to make up its mind, issuing his own Frag Order 14-65 for Operation Harvest Moon on 7 December, at midnight. That order prepared the battalion and the attached and supporting elements, to take part in the operation as it was then understood. Frag Order 14-65 was the result of enormous effort by Captain Doublet and his Marines in the operations section. They had to be quick to publish, as they were responding to the terrible time pressure imposed on them by the almost immediate D day that had been selected. Lieutenant Colonel Utter and his desperately overworked S-3 knew that anyone who waited for a senior headquarters to reach a set of conclusions and to issue orders to all hands would be overtaken by events. Delay would mean that the 2/7 Marines would be badly served by unnecessary confusion while they were making chaotic last-minute preparations. The view shared by Lieutenant Colonel Utter and Captain Doublet was that getting the word out quickly to everyone gave the subordinate units a bit of warning. They wanted every unit to have enough warning to ensure that all could more effectively and professionally prepare for the fight.

More important, it was the view of our commanding officer that those men at the bottom of the totem pole, the individual Marines who were going to be doing the fighting, deserved sufficient time to get ready. It was always Utter's firm policy that the riflemen and machine gunners who would meet the enemy head-on, be given as much of an early warning about pending deployments as was possible. He did so to make sure that those Marines could prepare themselves before the bullets began to fly.

With everyone already as fully warned as was possible, the battalion fragmentary order was released two days before the task force had finalized its plans. The 2/7 order was created out of sync with Task Force Delta, but it made sure that everyone would be ready to move out, on time, and with the least possible fuss and feathers.

Being properly prepared for a large operation, one postulated to last several days, meant immediately obtaining as much Class I supplies (food) and Class V supplies (ammunition) as the troops could be expected to carry. Failure to depart on the operation heavily laden with rations and munitions would place the battalion immediately at the mercy of daily helicopter resupply. Airlifting resupply of food and ammunition was going to be a chancy matter in the foul December weather, so it only made sense to be as prepared as possible. The northeast monsoon was in full cry, with heavy cloud cover, long periods of rain, and high winds battering the coastline. Everyone knew that continuous lousy weather could easily cause the deployed battalion to, in the very cynical terms of the riflemen in the field, "simulate chow!"

By the last days of 1965, the men of 2/7 had endured much, and they remained short of many items that they needed. Living constantly with shortages made the 2/7 Marines rather cynically skeptical of all things external to their own organization. It was their deeply held feeling that the powers above them did not see what they saw, nor did those far above them share in either the danger or the daily discomfort that they faced. In fact, the considered opinion of most Marines in the rifle companies was that the far-distant headquarters did not care very damn much at all about the welfare of those who were ducking the bullets. From their experience, based on the five months of combat behind them, the Marines of 2/7 would rather carry extra food and ammunition on their backs than depend on any outside supporting agency to feed or supply them. They did not trust any aircraft, truck, or mule skinner to get them what they needed when they needed it.

Of course, 2/7 really had no real choice in the matter. The battalion would quickly become dependent on others if the operation continued as long as the anticipated ten days or, possibly, beyond. If Harvest Moon was not aborted or shortened, the troops of 2/7 knew that they would be forced to wait in the rain, just like everyone else, for helicopter resupply. They expected that the wait would be made with an empty belly and empty ammunition pouches. It was not difficult for anyone to understand why the troops so often shook their heads and muttered the battalion motto—"Ready for anything, counting on nothing"—as a short and pungent commentary on their lives in combat in the Republic of Vietnam.

Operation Harvest Moon actually began earlier than

planned. The operation commenced at 1000 on 8 December 1965, not on the ninth as originally briefed. The reason for the rescheduling of D day was never made known to those who were to take part, but the change had no discernible effect on the overall results of Harvest Moon. For the Marine infantrymen, soaked to the skin by the steady rain, one day looked pretty much like any other.

On D day, 8 December, the battalion began its part with a motorized-mechanized movement from the Chu Lai enclave to the province headquarters at Tam Ky. Because the Marine Corps forces in the Republic of Vietnam did not have enough of the M-35 2 ½-ton-trucks needed, the battalion move had to be made in two separate tactical columns, using the same trucks and tracked vehicles for each trip. The lead element that was deployed consisted of Company E, Company F, and the battalion command group. Those battalion units arrived in Tam Ky late in the morning, and the commanding officer and his staff began coordination with the American Army officer assigned as the senior American adviser to the province. While the movement of the battalion was not accomplished over a great distance, roughly thirty miles, the last elements of the battalion, the rear command post and some attached Ontos vehicles—tracked, lightly armored, vehicles which mounted six recoilless rifles—did not close on Tam Ky until 1530. A large athletic field east of the Province Headquarters was designated by the army advisers as a "secure" night bivouac. Because that open field was no more secure than any other piece of real estate in the Republic of Vietnam, the battalion commander ordered Captain Doublet to establish a complete, 360 degree, defensive perimeter. Lieutenant Colonel Utter had no intention of being unpleasantly surprised, the first night out in the bush, by Viet Cong sapper squads.

From the province advisers, it was learned that within the area selected for the operation there were indications of as many as five battalions of interprovincial Viet Cong forces. The local intelligence section had fairly good data on the 60th, the 70th, the 80th, the 90th, and the 45th battalions (the

45th was also occasionally known as the 49th Bn). Also listed in the enemy order of battle was the regimental headquarters of the 1st Viet Cong Regiment. The army intelligence analysts felt that the enemy headquarters was possibly present in, or near, the Song Chang Valley. That important command headquarters was reportedly assigned to control and coordinate the actions of all of the units menacing Tam Ky and to oversee the other operations that had been steadily reducing the grip of the government of the Republic of Vietnam on the outlying portions of the province.

The level of actual menace to the provincial headquarters may well have been strongly overstated, for emphasis perhaps, by the advisers during their briefing. All of the intelligence that Marine analysts had examined indicated that the Viet Cong units in the Song Chang area were spending all their energy resting and refurbishing their units in preparation for later operations. The Viet Cong in the 2/7 area of the operation were expected to be relaxing a bit after returning from a major attack they had made against the ARVN units in the town of Hiep Duc. That attack, which took place on 18 November 1965, had been quite successful from the Viet Cong point of view. Unless provoked by either the Marines or the ARVN, the Viet Cong might well choose to stay quiet in the province, living comfortably (perhaps even remaining dry) in their base camps while they prepared to fight again another day. Operation Harvest Moon was designed by the general officers to provoke the Viet Cong to the absolute maximum degree possible. Our battalion, like all the other units committed to the operation, was expected to do its best to make those enemy soldiers run or to stand and fight after being cornered.

There were a few who held that another, more dangerous, outcome was possible for Operation Harvest Moon. A considerable amount of fairly good intelligence data tended to indicate a different possibility; some analysts expected the enemy to abandon his normal tactics and fight us tooth and nail in the Que Sons. Normally the enemy carefully avoided direct confrontation with, or opposition to, any major American military movement. But, because those particular Viet Cong battalions and their controlling headquarters were in an area that they felt was their own home base, some analysts opined that the 1st VC regimental headquarters might choose to stand and fight.

Acceptance of such a set-piece battle, except one that was fully on their terms, was very unusual for any Viet Cong unit. Our enemy was not stupid, and he knew that set-piece battles always favored the Marine forces and/or the joint Marine and ARVN operations. That view was based on a commonsense examination of the massive firepower of the Marines and the total domination by our side of the air over the battlefield. However, it was important for 2/7 to know that the Viet Cong in the Song Chang Valley were very strong. Their units had lived in the province for a long time, and they had many, many civilian supporters in the villages and hamlets. Our enemy habitually used the province for rest and relaxation, and the worried intelligence analysts felt that their commanders might possibly have become arrogant enough to be confrontational. The Viet Cong leaders were very much accustomed to having their own way everywhere in that part of the countryside. Some of the analysts even suggested that booting the enemy units out into the rain might anger them, and the resulting fight could produce far heavier combat than the Operation Harvest Moon planners were expecting.

The Song Chang Valley was about ten miles wide at its mouth, and it extended inland for about twenty miles. Flanking the valley were long finger ridges with elevations to as high as fifteen hundred feet. The area had been Viet Cong country for a long time—the government of the Republic of Vietnam was able to maintain only a few scattered outposts in the rural areas of the province. Almost all of the inland villages, the farming areas, the heavily forested portions of the valley floor, and the jungle-covered hill masses had been conceded to the control of the enemy. The battalion would not need to exercise very much concern about possible friendly civilian casualties during combat maneuvering in the field; no one expected to encounter any friendly civilians.

As a place to fight, the Que Son Mountains and the Song Chang Valley area was an absolutely miserable choice as a battleground for the Marine infantrymen. Most of the area contained a great deal of low, brushy, jungle-covered ground. The vegetation was thick and tangled. Both the thick undergrowth and the broken ground would hamper movement, reduce visibility, and permit sudden, unplanned contact with our enemy. Many contacts of the one-man-front variety would be a logical fallout from the choice of terrain. Poor visibility, caused by the jungle or by the weather, would also greatly inhibit any really effective use of close air support or the indirect fires of artillery and mortars. When supporting arms are hampered, the price is always paid by the men in the rifle companies. Everywhere in the lower elevations, the land was flooded or at least soaked enough to provide very difficult footing. There were few places where any Marine could ever expect to sleep, eat, patrol, fight, or stand security watch while even partially dry. Everything about the area of operations appeared to favor the enemy who lived and trained there most of the time. Worse, our enemy was going to be free to pick and choose his fights with 2/7 whenever and wherever he wanted them to occur.

The mission given to 2/7 was to establish, on D day, a secure helicopter loading zone near Tam Ky. From that zone, Task Force Delta planned to launch helicopter-borne assaults into areas suspected of sheltering some of the Viet Cong battalions that were to be brought to battle. The opening phase of the plan directed 2/7 to conduct, on D plus one, 9 December, a full-blown, battalion-size, helicopter assault into a landing zone (LZ) designated "LZ Spruce." The purpose of the lift was to quickly execute the first step in the Task Force Delta plan by moving without any delay at all into those areas where the Viet Cong were suspected to have established their base camps. Precise map locations were given formal names as Task Force Delta objectives and/or battalion objectives. The fragmentary order was issued, and the terrible game of infantry combat in the dark wet jungle was on.

Formal objective names never alter matters of concern to

the privates and privates first class in the rifle companies. To the normal infantryman, objectives assigned by higher headquarters all look alike, even if the generals do choose to give them fancy names. The Marines saw named objectives, such as LZ Spruce, as just being another dangerous, too small LZ where they could easily get themselves killed. The troops fully expected all landing zones selected from above to be surrounded by heavy dark jungle and to be too small for easy use. They also expected that most jungle landing zones would have in or near them some well-concealed bunker complexes where the enemy would have emplaced heavy machine guns. The troops also knew full well that in the beginning, after the helicopter-borne assault arrived in the LZ, the range of initial contact with the enemy was always going to be brutally short. Sudden, deadly firefights that are both violent and quickly decided often take place only a few meters from the edge of an LZ. Of course, in the jungle surrounding the landing zone there was also the fearful possibility of a solid contact with a superior enemy force. A contact like that would take place with absolutely no prior warning. The possibility that 2/7 might be in for a nose-to-nose fight against some heavy hitting Viet Cong units was considered by many to be rather high. That possibility was well known and thoroughly understood by the Marines in the rifle companies as they shouldered their heavy packs and tramped off across the mud to board the helicopters.

Within the mission statement for the D-plus-one operations, was a requirement for one platoon of 2/7 infantrymen to be left at Tam Ky to provide security for the supporting artillery. Initial fire support was to be provided by Battery M, 4th Battalion, 11th Marines, and they needed protection. Later, that unit was to move to Thang Binh where the artillerymen would be colocated with the support Marines of the logistical support area (LSA), and the 2/7 Marines assigned to the security force would be released for return to Lieutenant Colonel Utter. That security decision was typical for most major operations. Always, at the outset of extended combat, there would be an early bleeding-off of assets from the lead elements for security assignments of all sorts. The effect of that reduction in combat power was to ensure that the unit sent to fight during the opening stages of a battle was often growing more and more shorthanded—just when the heavy fighting began. In simple terms, this use of the lead elements as a source of security troops tended to arbitrarily strip combat power from the hands of the commanders on the ground. Lieutenant Colonel Utter appealed the decision to strip units from his command to no avail.

That same secondary-mission assignment concept, effectively an ill-considered reduction in the ability of the lead element to maneuver and engage the enemy, continued in use in the Vietnam War for years. Identical actions were still being used, to my personal knowledge, as late as the summer of 1969 when I observed a maneuvering battalion being bested in a brutal battle by elements of the North Vietnamese Army (NVA) in the Demilitarized Zone (DMZ). That Marine battalion was fighting for its life with four platoons of its infantry—25 percent of its riflemen— assigned away from the control of the battalion commander. They were sent elsewhere to provide security detachments for other units. Had not air power tipped the balance in favor of the infantry Marines on the ground, that battered, understrength, infantry battalion would eventually have been surrounded, defeated, and destroyed.

Sometimes the fighting battalions would go into the field only to find that as many as five or six security forces were to be extracted from their already thin ranks. The reductions in strength were a disaster because most Marine infantry units operating in combat, at any time between the summer of 1965 and the summer of 1970, were manned at a level that was far below the planned Table of Organization (T/O) fighting strength. The shortfall in manpower was a very serious business. Rifle companies with a planned T/O strength of 200 plus Marines and six officers were habitually fighting in the field with 130 to 145 fighting men and one or two officers. Every security element detached from those weakened units to guard someone else drastically harmed the ability of the infantry battalions to fight. As Operation Harvest Moon began, it was 2/7's good fortune to still have rather strong rifle companies. For example, Company F, commanded at the time by Capt. Jim Nolan (who left the S-2 position just before Operation Blue Marlin), started the operation with nearly two hundred Marines including the attachments of engineers, forward observers, and communicators. Captain Nolan was also unusually fortunate to have a full complement of six officers when he left the Chu Lai enclave for Tam Ky. The other 2/7 rifle companies all began the operation with fewer Marines than Company F.

Getting the security elements back, when there was no further need of their presence as guards, was also a difficult problem for any infantry unit. Only the higher headquarters that took the Marines away could return them to the unit. Those elements sent out to provide security for artillery firing sites, downed helicopters, or logistical support areas (LSAs) often were gone for extended periods. Sometimes there were delays because the security unit was tasked by energetic staff officers in the rear to accomplish some additional activity prior to being returned to its parent battalion. Meanwhile the riflemen of the parent unit, those who were in the field fighting the enemy, were forced to suffer more than their share of casualties. Again, using Company F as an example, Captain Nolan was forced to send 1st Lt. Bob Madeo and his reinforced platoon to guard a downed helicopter and the LSA, leaving Company F short one-third of its combat power until the last days of Operation Harvest Moon.

Most of the day of D plus one, 9 December, the battalion was involved in conducting the helicopter-borne assault, clearing the area around LZ Spruce, and attacking objectives set forth in the task force order. The landings began at 1040 with Company G, under the command of Capt. Bill Seymour, landing in LZ Spruce. On landing, Company G killed one Viet Cong female as she fled from the LZ carrying medical supplies. Company E, by then under the command of

Capt. Richard Theer,* and Company H, under Capt. Martin O'Connor followed Seymour's company into LZ Spruce. The command group followed. All three companies maneuvered to assigned objectives with little or no contact of significance.

Company F, reduced by one-third, was the last unit to arrive at LZ Spruce. Captain Nolan's company had been delayed by being assigned as landing zone security for another helicopter that was unflyable because of a damaged tail rotor. At 1640, a platoon from Company D, 1st Battalion, 7th Marines relieved Company F of responsibility for the landing zone and the downed helicopter. As the company moved out, it received thirty to fifty rounds of rifle fire from an unseen enemy force. Pursuit of the enemy firing on the company was denied to Captain Nolan because of the late hour and the colonel's desire to set his security perimeters for the night.

By early evening D plus one, the battalion, by then fully deployed, had established a pair of perimeter defenses (two rifle companies in each) on two unimportant jungle hills that had been given the pompous titles of Objective A and Objective B. First Lieutenant Jack Archer's 81mm mortar platoon and the 106mm recoilless rifle platoon were both in place and were prepared to provide close-in fire support. At 2200, the artillery support battery was asked to begin firing scheduled concentrations of harassing and interdiction fire (H & I) on possible routes of approach to the battalion defensive positions. During the very first H & I fire mission, one artillery round fell far short of its intended target, landed within the 2/7 perimeter, and wounded two headquarters Marines. No more H & I missions were permitted during the night.

The plan for D plus two, 10 December, was to consolidate the battalion with all four rifle companies prepared to move out to the east. Once consolidated, the battalion was to conduct a three-company sweep to flush out Viet Cong units. However, because of the intensity of the fighting elsewhere in

---

*I was in hospital on Guam at the time. After I was evacuated Company E was reassigned to Tolleson, then both were transferred to Fourth Marines! Capt. Theer's Company E is a new company, out of the mixmaster.

the objective area, that plan had to be scrapped by Task Force Delta. The 2d Battalion, 1st Marines (2/1) had landed near a hamlet known as Cam Lai (1); heavy fighting had ensued, and that battalion was pinned down by heavy enemy fire. Task Force Delta directed that a company from 2/7 be dispatched, at 1330, to help the heavily engaged 2/1 Marines break loose. Company E, commanded by Capt. Richard Theer, was selected for that dangerous mission. The company moved out in good order, reporting to the commanding officer of 2/1 who took operational control of Captain Theer and his Marines.

Since the planned sweep operation by 2/7 had been drastically modified, the 2/7 battalion command group stayed in place. After Company E departed, the command group continued operating in the area within the perimeter set up by Company G and Company F. On Objective B, Company H became responsible for its own, one-company, security perimeter. The arrival nearby of another infantry battalion, the 3d Battalion, 3d Marines (3/3), a Da Nang based unit, into the objective area required that Captain Doublet coordinate all of the night perimeter defensive fires and security patrolling with the newly arrived battalion.

Company E, maneuvering under the control of the commanding officer of 2/1, was ordered to press forward in the attack. Captain Theer was ordered to move toward a wooded area at the foot of Hill 407. The maneuver, conducted across the front of engaged rifle companies, was unorthodox and potentially disastrous if precise coordination was not carefully maintained. That the 2/1 commanding officer needed Company E to relieve the heavy enemy pressure on Company G and Company F of his own battalion was a given. But it quickly became clear that ordering an attack that moved across his front was an unfortunate choice. Poor communications were the rule of the day. When Company G of 2/1 stopped firing and fell back without telling Captain Theer, the result for the men of Company E of 2/7 was a bloodbath conducted in utter chaos. As Company E maneuvered across the 2/1 front, the company came under heavy enfilade fire, fire that had previously been suppressed by the Marines of 2/1's

Company G. Enfilade fire is defined as incoming enemy fire in which the heavy pattern of impacting rifle and machine-gun bullets lands in alignment with the long axis of the unit. Taking that sort of fire while moving in the open is the worst possible situation for a deployed rifle company. Company E was shredded and mercilessly battered. Wounded and dying Marines were scattered over a wide area and further movement became virtually impossible as more and more wounded men were immobilized and needed protection. Despite the heavy fire and the increasing number of casualties sustained, elements of Company E pressed forward trying their best to continue the attack. The bloody effort by Company E resulted in a partial success; Captain Theer's attack was strong enough to relieve the pressure on the two companies of 2/1, Companies F and G. Company F of 2/1 had been hardest hit, and the move by Captain Theer's company gave that unit the ability to collect its wounded and dead, withdraw, and break out of a desperate situation.

In attacking forward to assist 2/1, Company E paid a terrible price, crippling to the company. Company E lost seven Marines killed outright, two Marines who later died of their wounds, and twenty-seven other wounded Marines. Roughly 21 percent of Company E had became combat casualties in a very short time, and both the wounded and the dead had to be evacuated back to the Chu Lai enclave. In addition to the staggering battle loss, there were also a number of nonbattle casualties evacuated along with the wounded. Company E had been gravely, gravely harmed in the fight.

A disappointing fact was that only a few Viet Cong were known to have been killed or wounded by Company E or, for that matter, by 2/1, in that tragic and badly managed firefight. The transfer to control by 2/1 on 10 December was a painful and costly disaster for Company E. For the Viet Cong, it was obviously very profitable. At the end of D plus two, Captain Theer's Company E remained under the operating control of 2/1. During the night of D plus two, the surviving men of the company dug in as a component of the 2/1 defensive perimeter.

In the 2/7 area, Companies G and H did conduct an abbreviated sweep and collected about twenty-five individuals who were considered to be Viet Cong or Viet Cong sympathizers (VCS). The descriptor, VCS, was often used to designate those whom the line units sent to the rear to be interrogated and classified by Marine intelligence units, those of the ARVN, or those of the Vietnamese National Police. As far as 2/7 was concerned, a VCS was anyone in the Song Chang Valley since the enemy was known to control the whole area. It was almost an article of faith that they controlled all the people as well. Once the Marines turned the VCS over to the Vietnamese National Police, their fate was sealed; brutality was their watchword, and confessions of support for the Viet Cong were almost always the standard result of their interrogations. Most Americans worked hard to stay well clear of the National Police and their application of torture to any and all VCS.

While only a few rounds had been fired by either side during D plus two in the 2/7 operating area, one unique event took place that night, and it proved to the Marines lying in the mud that our enemy could be as confused as any Marine unit. The Marines learned that Viet Cong soldiers could also be found, wandering about, "semilost," in the jungle. At 2115, one enemy soldier stumbled into the battalion night perimeter, ran away when challenged, and was killed by an ambush when he tripped over a log and fell down in front of the waiting Marines. Despite all the noise of the battle that took place in the 2/1 area, and the noise of three separate Marine infantry battalions operating in fairly close proximity, that one man had remained totally confused.

During the late afternoon of D plus two, Company G had been stopped as it maneuvered on a sweep, and in accordance with orders from Task Force Delta, the company was dispatched to the operational control of 2/1. Now the commanding officer of 2/1 had two of Lieutenant Colonel Utter's four maneuver elements. The colonel was not pleased to see his battalion being pieced out a chunk at a time to other commanders. Capt. Bill Seymour's Company G completed its tactical move toward the 2/1 operational area without enemy interference. Moving carefully to the southwest, Company G arrived to take its place in the 2/1 night defensive perimeter at 2015.

On the morning of D plus three, 11 December, Task Force Delta directed the two battalions, 2/7 and 2/1, to consolidate their defensive positions and be prepared to attack assigned objectives, providing mutual support. A complex set of plans was developed for a helicopter lift to aid in consolidating the two battalions, but the helicopters lifted Captain Nolan's Company F of 2/7 to the wrong landing zone. Later, the weather closed in again and precluded further use of airlift. A helicopter-borne assault by Company F had been ordered to land it atop Hill 407, but it could not be made. Hill 407 was the high ground that lay beyond the wood line where Company E had taken so many casualties during the fighting on D plus two.

At 1005 on the morning of D plus three, Companies E and G of the battalion were unexpectedly returned to 2/7's operational control. Company E commenced battlefield salvage—finding all the rifles, machine guns, pistols, ammunition, packs, boots, helmets, flak jackets, etc., that the enemy might use—in the area where they had been fighting the day before. Company G was alerted to replace Company F as the assault element for the planned helicopter-borne attack of Hill 407. But that assault was also scratched because of the vile weather. At the same time, Company F, still missing Lieutenant Madeo's platoon, was virtually marooned by the rain. They were stuck at the wrong place from which to conduct planned operations, so they just stayed put. The company had no real choice other than to remain in its defensive perimeter and coordinate night defensive patrolling and the fires planned in and around its position with the commanding officer of 3/3. Captain Nolan went to a 3/3 briefing and found representatives from rifle companies from about four different battalions present, all attempting to coordinate their night defensive activities.

During the briefing at 3/3, Captain Nolan was told that the air force would be delivering an Arc Light during the night.

No one took the time to tell him what an Arc Light was or what it might mean to his company, and the briefing went on. Not having ever heard of an Arc Light, Captain Nolan stuck to the use of common sense and assumed that it must be some new kind of aerial flash bomb used for night photography. Settling himself against a boulder, he wrapped his too-small raincoat around his shoulders—the captain had no poncho because ponchos were also in short supply in 2/7, and he had given his to a rifleman—and tried to grab a little sleep. At about 0300, the boulder nearly leaped out of the earth. Captain Nolan was shocked to learn that Arc Light meant the thunderous explosion of three or four hundred five-hundred-pound bombs dropped from B-52s flying far above the rain clouds. The strike by the B-52s went in about three kilometers from Company F, and the concussion was magnified by the low cloud cover. The Marines of the company did little sleeping for the rest of the night.

Meanwhile, Company H had been very busy. Capt. Martin O'Connor's unit was directed to coordinate his maneuver with units of 2/1 and to make a feint across a rice paddy in an attempt to draw fire from the enemy occupying Hill 407. When nothing happened during the feint and no enemy fire was received, Captain O'Connor was authorized to attack the hill mass by ground assault. The company quickly captured the hill, arriving on top in the steady rain at 1830. On the crest of Hill 407, they found much evidence of the earlier presence of Viet Cong units. The ground was littered with debris, including cases of 12.7mm machine-gun ammunition, considerable amounts of explosives, grenades, and some articles of enemy uniform clothing. All of the ordnance was later destroyed by an engineer team. Also on the hill were Viet Cong fighting holes with blood and bandages lying about. The evidence provided a tiny fraction of the desired proof that our enemy was also getting hurt in this fight.

By 2000 on D plus three, Company H was in its defensive positions on Hill 407, Company F was dug in with 3/3, and the remaining elements of 2/7 were with the command group. None of the complex plans for the day had been executed as

designed. In fact, almost every minute of the day had featured
improvisation of a high order as units were forced to shift
from one task to another in an endless and nerve-racking
amount of confusion and difficulty. Most of the day had
been spent awaiting a break in the rain and a lifting of the
cloud cover—helicopter-borne operations were, for the most
part, impossible. That left the riflemen of the battalion down
in the mud with their enemy—on an almost equal footing.
That footing was horrible. Even as early as the evening of
D plus three, immersion foot, with its agonizing pain, was
rapidly becoming a leading reason for medical evacuation.

At 0900 on the morning of D plus four, 12 December, Task
Force Delta issued a grand overview plan. Lieutenant Colonel
Utter was to take 2/7 (less Company H), by helicopter-borne
assault at 1130, to the east and southeast, where he was to
conduct an assault landing and commence a search-and-clear
operation. All of his maneuvers were to be coordinated with
2/1 and 3/3. Elements of both of those battalions were deemed
by Task Force Delta to be near enough to the objective area to
provide a certain amount of mutual fire support, if needed.
But the weather on the twelfth was a rainy continuation of the
previous day, and there was no offensive helicopter lift for the
battalion. Later in the day, a substitute plan was created, and
the battalion began to move, on foot, to the southwest where it
was ordered to establish blocking positions on the slopes of
Hill 407. Late in the afternoon, when there was a momentary
clearing in the weather, Company F was returned, at 1550, to
the battalion by helicopter in an administrative lift.

The concept at the Task Force headquarters was that from
the slopes of Hill 407, 2/7 could possibly bring Viet Cong
units to battle as they moved away from the other Marine battalions. As a side issue, 2/7 would also be in position to possibly relieve Viet Cong pressure on an ARVN outpost at a
village known as Hien Loc (1). Overall, D plus four was not
particularly eventful. There was no definitive contact, but the
battalion did capture some VCS and two Viet Cong soldiers.
There was no need to be suspicious at all about the two soldiers; they were clearly Viet Cong who had been carrying

weapons when captured. They were transported as prisoners of war to the ARVN instead of as suspects to be interrogated in the rear by the National Police. Company H remained on Hill 407 all day. Captain O'Connor's Marines conducted local patrols and established other normal security measures without contact of any kind with the Viet Cong.

By the twelfth of December, the weather was having an accelerated, destructive effect on the sodden, muddy infantrymen. The constant wet, coming from both the steady rain and the normal ground water found in a rice growing area, was a very serious concern. The declining health of the troops overall, and of their feet in particular, was becoming a classic field medical problem not unlike those faced by medical personnel in World War I. Every movement ordered by the battalion was being accomplished in sodden boots by Marines who were soaked to the skin. In 2/7, Marines wore boots that were basically worn-out. Five months in the war had destroyed the Marine infantrymen's boots. For every man on the operation, there was a steadily increasing chance that he would become a nonbattle casualty from immersion foot. When a Marine had immersion foot, he was really experiencing a disintegration of his foot, with open sores, with splitting of the skin between the toes, and a breakdown of the skin on the sole of the foot. There was no quick cure for immersion foot when it was known as trench foot in 1917, and there was no quick cure in 1965. The serious nature of immersion foot was already, by D plus four, producing nonbattle casualties for all the battalions. Those Marines had to be lifted out by air or trucked out. Marines with immersion foot can no longer walk. Nonbattle damage to a Marine's foot stops that Marine as quickly as a bullet. By the morning of D plus five, more and more of the Marines in 2/7 were beginning to see the cracks between their toes and the mottled skin that meant they were developing immersion foot. Immersion foot, if not properly treated, with the affected area allowed to dry, will continue to grow worse. A few 2/7 Marines had already been evacuated with the problem, and many others were well on the way to being in serious trouble. The battalion could ill afford to lose many men to the elements, but the attrition had begun. Neither the best efforts of the battalion surgeon nor those of his magnificent medical corpsmen could stem the flow of combat Marines to the rear.

D plus five, 13 December, arrived with the same low clouds and more periods of steady rain. Task Force Delta was still trying to get 2/7 to conduct a helicopter-borne assault, but there was no opportunity to do so in a timely manner. Company H of the battalion was directed to pull off of Hill 407 to permit a B-52 strike to be made to the south of its positions. After the strike, the company was to reoccupy the hill. At that time, Captain O'Connor and his Marines were ordered to leave the control of Lieutenant Colonel Utter and to begin to operate under the direct control of Task Force Delta.

Around midday on D plus five, 13 December, Company E of 2/7 was relieved on the 2/7 perimeter by Company H of the 2d Battalion, 9th Marines, which had been ordered to report to 2/7 for operational control. Captain Theer's badly battered Company E was returned to the Chu Lai enclave. The commanding officer of Company H, 2/9, reported to Lieutenant Colonel Utter at 1210 on D plus five.

Immediately after Company H of 2/9 reported in, the battalion began a two-company sweep toward the village of Viet An to relieve pressure on the ARVN outpost. Companies F and G conducted the sweep astride a dirt road leading southwest toward the outpost, with the command group, covered by a Company G security platoon, moving closely behind. In trace, acting as the rear guard, was the newly arrived Company H of 2/9. Captain O'Connor's Company H of 2/7 remained on Hill 407 under the orders of Task Force Delta. The battalion closed on Viet An at 1940. At the outpost, the battalion commander and his staff obtained all of the latest enemy intelligence held by the ARVN. The Marines of 2/7 provided resupply to replace shortages and assisted in evacuation of the ARVN dead and wounded.

On the way to Viet An, the security platoon protecting the

command group was moving through the underbrush when they discovered a downed Marine helicopter with seven badly mutilated skeletons inside. The find was reported to Task Force Delta.

Other than some sniper fire encountered by Company F and Company G and the discovery of a Viet Cong minefield by Company G, there was little sign of the enemy on D plus five. The evening of D plus five was spent establishing a defensive perimeter. The night was quiet.

On D plus six, 14 December, the battalion was ordered to send a platoon back to the downed helicopter in order to provide security while Graves Registration recovered the human remains. This platoon had to be recovered early when the battalion actually had the opportunity to make the often-expected but never-accomplished, helicopter assault. The weather lifted slightly, and 2/7 actually conducted a two-company helicopter-borne attack beginning at 1125. The assault elements were landed after the LZ was prepped by fixed-wing aircraft, which delivered both high-explosive ordnance and napalm. Some Viet Cong troops seen escaping from the LZ vicinity were strafed by the aircraft after they had expended all of their HE ordnance on the target.

The two companies, Company F and Company G, that took part in the assault made light contact with the Viet Cong, and fire was exchanged for some time during the retreat of the enemy in the face of the arriving Marines. Before they departed, the Viet Cong fired on both the CH-34 helicopters and the ground troops with their heaviest machine gun, the dual-purpose 12.7mm antiaircraft weapon. Because the enemy quickly withdrew, only a few—about ten—Viet Cong could be confirmed as killed or captured during the assault landing. After the firing died down, the reserve company and the battalion headquarters were moved forward into the recently cleared LZ. A three-company perimeter (F, G, and H 2/9) was established, with the 81mm mortars prepared to fire H & I fires throughout the night. Adding to the fire support available to 2/7 was a section of 4.2-inch mortars that had been flown into the LZ. The huge mortars were appreciated because they could provide far heavier fire support than the weapons organic to the battalion.

When Company H of 2/9 first arrived in the LZ from Viet An, the company was directed to move to the south to establish control of the ground overlooking a suspected Viet Cong ferry crossing on the river. Heavy undergrowth slowed the movement of the company through the jungle, but by 1830, they had arrived at the assigned area. In the course of moving to their new position, Company H of 2/9 Marines captured one VCS. The company received sporadic sniper fire, which was returned without provable result as the Viet Cong broke contact. During the night of D plus six, a Viet Cong fighting man became confused and wandered into the Company H perimeter like a lost soul. By the light of the flare-dispensing aircraft that was keeping the sky well lighted for the Marines on the ground, he was taken prisoner.

The terrain in the operational area was made even more difficult by the heavy growth of elephant grass. When Company F was moving in the dark to set up its defensive positions, the lead platoon, led by First Lieutenant Kesslering, found the grass to be taller and taller. At first it was reported to be five feet tall, then eight feet tall, and finally twelve feet tall. The troops could barely press forward toward the hilltop through the heavy grass, and they were likely to lose their way in the process. Captain Nolan was concerned and called for mortar illumination. It was provided, but lighting up the hill for Lieutenant Kesslering's troops quickly exhausted the supply of 81mm illumination rounds so the battalion air officer, Capt. Jim Losse, got a flare ship, Snoopy 22, to help out.

The pilot of Snoopy Two-two called Captain Nolan on his company frequency and quickly moved to light the way for the company so it could find its way to the hilltop. Once he had helped solve the infantry maneuvering problem for Company F, Snoopy Two-two departed the area for a few hours, returning at about 0400 and requesting more work. Since the aircraft also had a Gatling gun on board, Captain Nolan asked him to light up the area for the troops so they could get their gear together and to prep the far bank of the river with the rapid-firing gun. When the pilot was offered thanks for his help, he replied, "Don't mention it, we want to do all we can for you young fellas." It was Captain Nolan's impression that the pilot was very possibly a senior colonel who cared enough to be out flying through the dark, dark night, trying to see what he could do for the infantrymen down in the mud.

On D plus seven, 15 December, the battalion sent patrols down along the north side of the river to confirm the presence of the ferry site. The actual crossing was located by Company F at 1630, but no boats were captured. Company F and Company H of 2/9 were assigned tactical areas of responsibility (TAORs) along the north side of the river. They were to conduct search-and-destroy operations in those TAORs to see what they could discover.

Earlier, at 1400, Captain O'Connor and his Company H had returned to Lieutenant Colonel Utter's control. They had been directed to conduct a reconnaissance of the area south of the river that had been struck by the B-52s on D plus five. The effort was directed from above by Task Force Delta, meaning that Lieutenant Colonel Utter had control of Company H in name only. Company H also had to coordinate its reconnaissance with a Vietnamese Regional Force (RF) company, a unit comparable to the National Guard in an American town. The RF company was supposedly familiar with the area, and its commander assigned a reinforced platoon to accompany Company H as the ground Marines maneuvered to see what had been hit by the high altitude bombers.

Being increasingly frustrated by the fact that 2/7 was not making solid contact, Lieutenant Colonel Utter proposed to Task Force Delta that he conduct a battalion-size patrol to the east toward the coast. The move would be made along the Song Chang Valley. He suggested that it begin on D plus eight, 16 December. The commanding general approved the plan, but he stipulated that the battalion must complete the operation and be back in the Chu Lai enclave within three and one-half days. He also stipulated that when Lieutenant Colonel

Utter began the maneuver, he was not to pull Company H from the company-size reconnaissance of the B-52 strike area. That stipulation reduced the 2/7's control of Company H to zero.

During all of the movements made during the day of D plus seven, Company G remained as the security force protecting the command group and the 81mm and the 4.2-inch mortars. On the night of D plus seven, there were a few minor contacts, and two Viet Cong were confirmed killed by Company H of 2/9. The only good news for the battalion was the return of First Lieutenant Madeo and his rifle platoon to Company F.

At 0730 on D plus eight, 16 December, 2/7 began its move to the east, with Company G in the lead acting as the advance guard. The command group entered the column next, followed by Company F, which moved from its night-security positions into the column as the main body. Company H of 2/9 joined the column behind the rear command group to act as the rear guard. A few long-range snipers occasionally fired on the column during 16 December, but for the most part, the Marines moved along the muddy trails and through the flooded streams without incident. It was, of course, still raining. Company H remained behind, its helicopter lift to the south side of the river for the reconnaissance canceled by the weather. Captain O'Connor's new mission was to provide security for the 4.2-inch mortar section and to conduct local security patrols. D plus eight was a day with limited, minor contact. At the village of Dai Trang, a massive cave complex was discovered, but it was unoccupied. The area was deemed to be a major Viet Cong staging and training area. One building appeared to have been an aid station, and there were vast amounts of blood and piles of soiled bandage material in evidence.

After moving a little less than seven kilometers, the battalion stopped at 1630 and established a night defensive perimeter. H & I fires were delivered by the 81mm mortars from the perimeter and by the 4.2-inch mortars from the old command-post site where Company H remained. The wet weather continued to leach at the manpower strength of the battalion. Every resupply helicopter that made it to the battalion was met by corpsmen from H & S Company and from the rifle companies sending Marines with immersion foot to the rear. During the dark hours, the rain continued to fall, and there were only a few shots fired by either side.

At dawn on D plus nine, 17 December, the battalion was directed to send one company to the northeast to link up with 2/1, pass through the positions of that battalion, and then loop south to rejoin 2/7 as it moved east. Company G was assigned the task and moved out to the northeast, but before the linkup could be accomplished, the order from Task Force Delta was canceled. However, this abortive move had, again, reduced the battalion to two maneuver elements, Company F and Company H of 2/9. Company G had already maneuvered away from the column, and Company H was going to remain with the 4.2-inch mortars. That left Lieutenant Colonel Utter, again, with a two-company battalion. As soon as Task Force Delta canceled its order, Company G was ordered to return to the moving column with utmost haste, however, the company did not close back with 2/7 until 1310 on the afternoon of D plus nine.

With only two maneuver elements left, the battalion's maneuver toward the east was halted for an hour and a half awaiting the return of Company G. For unit safety, at 1130, Lieutenant Colonel Utter ordered Company H of 2/9 to pass forward through Company F to secure a key pass on the trail leading east toward the coast. When Company G caught up with the battalion, the column resumed its movement under sporadic sniper fire. In each case, a heavy volume of return fire caused the Viet Cong to break contact. Heavy jungle and flooding streams prohibited any form of wide ranging flank guard, and the troops were essentially in a column most of the time.

A new aspect of the D plus nine fighting was the use of Chinese-type stick grenades by the enemy troops. In each case, the grenades would come flying out of the heavy undergrowth, and on detonation would produce more Marine casualties. Most of the casualties were minor, but like the cases of immersion foot, the injured Marines would eventually need to be evacuated. In one instance, a stick grenade fell into the middle of the Company F command group, detonated, and wounded every man there except Captain Nolan and the company gunny, Gunnery Sergeant Causey. The grenade had actually bounced off the radio operator's radio and dropped at his feet, where it exploded. Fortunately for Company F, the battalion surgeon, Lieutenant (medical corps, USN) Preda, was just ahead in the column, and he came immediately to the aid of the injured Marines. Looking at the fragments that had almost penetrated the radio operator's flak jacket at a point directly over his lungs, the doctor said, "Son, you are wearing a million-dollar vest."

Besides the steady loss rate of 2/7 Marines to wounds, the battalion medical officer continued to be very concerned about the increase in cases of immersion foot. He frequently conducted his own inspection of the troops' feet, and many men were ordered out of the field on the resupply helicopters. The number of fighting men available in the battalion was steadily shrinking.

The night of D plus nine found 2/7 another ten kilometers closer to the coast, where it established a 360-degree perimeter at 1810 in the evening. There was no contact with the enemy during the night of D plus nine. The rains continued, hampering medical evacuations and resupply.

On the morning of D plus ten, 18 December, the battalion assigned as a march objective the city of Thon Hai, ten or twelve kilometers to the east. Even before the column could move off, there was contact with the Viet Cong. The men of Company G were moving into position as the advance guard when they killed a Viet Cong carrying a stick grenade. The entire battalion column was held up until 1000 by the necessity for medical evacuation flights taking both wounded Marines and immersion-foot cases to Chu Lai. Once Company G was free to move on to the east, with the command group following closely, the sniping ceased. Company F followed Company G, with two platoons ahead of the rear command group and one following that group to provide it with security.

At 1335, the Viet Cong opened up on Company G with a heavy volume of fire, including machine guns and recoilless rifles. The fire was coming from one side of the narrow, slightly elevated track. The "road," which looked so fine on the maps, was more akin to a paddy dike or narrow causeway. Using their heads, the Company G Marines took cover behind it. This placed them on about a nine-hundred-meter line, sheltered behind the road and firing to the south and east as they returned fire. It was virtually the same as lying on a firing line back at Camp Pendleton, a wide frontage with a depth of one man.

As Company G was becoming heavily engaged, the rest of the battalion column began to receive significant sniper fire. The violent contact between the Viet Cong and the battalion advance guard continued for twenty to twenty-five minutes. The rear guard, Company H of 2/9, also reported a very heavy contact. As the fire ebbed, it appeared at the time that the fire of Captain Seymour's Company G Marines was driving the Viet Cong away to the south and west, reducing the fire impacting on the lead elements. However, the middle of the battalion column was taking more and more fire from the well-hidden, and often well-dug-in Viet Cong. Company G later received some incoming mortar rounds as it established a defensive position immediately to the east of the village Ky Phu.

Behind the command group in the column, Captain Nolan's Company F was taking some light fire as it moved east within the main body of the battalion column. Earlier, like all the other companies, Company F had lost some of its combat power during the stop at 1000 when they had to evacuate Marines with immersion foot. Of course, the injured Marines begged to continue on with the company, but they could no longer walk well enough to keep pace with the column. When Company G began its heavy contact at 1335, Company F was already well within the village of Ky Phu, and the company was, thus, partially protected from direct enemy fire. At about 1415, Lieutenant Colonel Utter ordered Company F to move forward as quickly as possible to help relieve pressure on the flank of Company G and to clear the way for the battalion to continue the column movement to the east. The colonel wanted his strength well forward in order to push aside what appeared to be a larger version of the delay-by-sniping tactics that had been employed by the Viet Cong during the previous days.

Captain Nolan took two platoons forward. He and his men passed through Company G in column by stepping, one at a time, over the hot rifle barrels of the Company G Marines who were engaging the enemy. The Company F commander reported meeting Capt. Bill Seymour and 1st Lt. Joe Lloyd along the way. The Company G captain and his barrel-chested lieutenant were walking calmly up and down the muddy road, issuing fire commands and encouragement to the Marines. They were strolling along amid the snapping sound of passing high-velocity bullets, acting as if they had nothing on their minds other than taking a nice walk in the rain. The rifle platoon commanded by Lieutenant Kesslering had been moving behind the battalion's rear command group, a location that made it impossible for those Marines to leave that area undefended. They did not go forward to catch up with the rest of the Company F Marines moving to the front of the column. Just as Company F, less Lieutenant Kesslering's platoon, had successfully completed passing forward of Company G, a very heavy volume of fire began to tear apart the middle of the column. The movement forward of Company F had left a very big hole within the column; that hole was just to the rear of Lieutenant Colonel Utter and his command group. Essentially, the move resulted in the fragmenting of the 2/7 column into two parts.

The portion of the 2/7 column that was suddenly hard-pressed by the Viet Cong attack did not have many riflemen. Fighting Marines were in short supply throughout the battalion, and that portion of the column had almost none available. It had, instead, the rear command post and a large portion of the administrative, medical, supply, and support personnel of the battalion. The executive officer of 2/7, Maj. George

Gentry,* who truly was a very big man, suddenly found himself trying to get his body, roughly the size of a National Football League tackle, down behind the very low dike on which the main trail to the east was established. He and 1st Lt. Nick Groz had bullets passing through their packs, and mud was being blown into their faces as the machine-gun fire directed their way was ricocheting off the trail.

The situation was critical! The Viet Cong attacked with fierce determination in an attempt to sever the battalion column. Several key radio operators became casualties, and the exercise of control by Lieutenant Colonel Utter was hampered. His ability to influence the action was degraded by both the lost communicators and the need to pass all his emergency air and artillery requests on the battalion tactical net. Because of the losses, none of the 2/7 emergency requests for supporting fires could be passed in the normal way on any of the conduct-of-fire networks. Without communications, the commanding officer was unable to learn what he had to know in a timely manner. All he knew for sure was that every part of 2/7 was in heavy contact with a very determined enemy.

This was the most advantageous moment the Viet Cong commander could have ever dreamed of as he maneuvered against 2/7. If the Viet Cong firing on the column were able to cut the battalion into two long, narrow elements, their soldiers could attack down the trail in either direction and effectively "roll-up" 2/7. The enemy might have had the strength to crush the long column of weary, trail-bound Marines by hitting them head-on, one or two at a time, with a far superior force. For 2/7 to survive, the column had to remain intact.

The fire on the west side of Ky Phu was so heavy that the only way for the battalion to deal with the problem was to turn Company F around and have it return to drive the Viet Cong back. While Lieutenant Colonel Utter did not yet know the grave nature of the situation, First Lieutenant Groz, on his own, had identified the only possible solution to this massive

---

*Major Wilson had been sent to Division because of his rotation date. The mixmaster struck again!

attack. He decided that he must get some riflemen to drive away the Viet Cong who were almost on top of the rear command group. Lieutenant Groz immediately grabbed the first Marine he could find and sent him forward to tell the colonel and/or Captain Nolan that Company F must come back to the west. That Marine was able to take only about ten steps before he fell, shot several times through the body, dead on the trail. Another young H & S Company Marine ran to Lieutenant Groz and offered to go forward. That Marine also was dead after a step or two, shot to rags and riddled by the heavy machine-gun and AK-47 fire pouring down on the trail.

Seeing that this moment was potentially the final hour for 2/7 as a combat unit, First Lieutenant Groz leaped up and set out running east along the trail himself. As he began to run, he was instantly ducking and dodging amid the Viet Cong tracers as he moved forward to find Captain Nolan or the battalion commander. Bullets ripped his clothing, a canteen was punctured pouring water down his legs, and the Viet Cong did their very best to kill the running officer with a storm of bullets. For 2/7, the action of First Lieutenant Groz provided another marvelous moment in the battalion's history. Because of his amazing good fortune, coupled with his personal courage, the lieutenant was successful. With his head ringing from the sound of passing bullets, Lieutenant Groz made it forward to Company F and got them to turn around. After telling the colonel what was happening, he accompanied Company F westward against the enemy that was shredding the battalion. Both he and Captain Nolan were shouting, "Fix bayonets," as the two platoons of Company F roared westward to take the fight to the Viet Cong. Later, 1st Lt. Nick Groz would receive the Navy Cross for his amazing example of personal performance under fire.

Now aware of the mortal danger to the battalion, Captain Nolan's Company F turned around and once again began jumping over the hot barrels of the Company G rifles as they dashed back to the west. They again crossed the nine hundred meters, running along the road under fire, with no time to take cover. Once again pausing briefly to exchange greetings with

Captain Seymour along the way, Captain Nolan placed his two platoons on line and ordered them to charge. With their bayonets fixed, first walking then running, the shouting Company F Marines smashed into the Viet Cong, blasting their leading troops and knocking them back. Nothing the enemy could do slowed this violent assault, and they fell back, leaving seventy-nine dead scattered throughout the battalion area.

Driving back the Viet Cong reduced the fire being taken by the beleaguered rear command post, the other support Marines, and medical personnel. Until the arrival of Company F, all those Marines had remained pinned down, taking casualties, at the trail edge as they popped away with their side arms. Major Gentry and the rest of the rear command group were almost down to the last rounds of ammunition for their personal weapons, ineffective .45-caliber pistols. The arrival of Company F brought them great relief. On the western edge of Ky Phu, several 12.7mm heavy machine guns had been firing almost directly down the trail. Company F continued its assault and maneuvered to knock those guns out of the war. Using flamethrowers and engineers with explosives, the company broke the back of the Viet Cong attack on the middle of the battalion column and caused the fire to ebb. Once again, 2/7 was free to maneuver to consolidate and establish defensive positions in the village of Ky Phu.

Captain Nolan, collecting Kesslering's rifle platoon as he arrived on the scene, crushed the enemy force. In his own words, the side trail down which 1st Lt. Bob Madeo's platoon of his company attacked, ". . . looked as if a gigantic bowling ball had run over the VC." He recalled in 1998 that he was amazed by the huge wounds that the M-14 rifle bullets had inflicted on the small-bodied Viet Cong who were lying dead all around him. The enemy retreat continued until a number of them had holed up in a bunker. The Viet Cong in the bunker were a tough bunch, and nothing that Sgt. Nguyen Van Luan, the interpreter, could say would bring them out. Even though Marines could get within a few feet of the bunker, the enemy would not come out and surrender. Facing the inevitable, Captain Nolan called up his attached flamethrower teams and burned them all to death. After the flamethrowers were through with their grisly task, the bunker burned, and there were occasional explosions almost all night.

By the end of this firefight, Captain Nolan's Company F was ready to gather its dead and its wounded. Three Company F Marines were killed and twenty-two wounded in the short time that all of this dashing forward and attacking back to the west took place. The fact that there were only three dead was astonishing. There were many tales about narrow escapes from certain death. Captain Nolan had a rifle bullet hit him in the side. The bullet hit the flak jacket hard, and then it rode around the plates under the nylon cover, exiting out the back without touching him. PFC James Clark was hit in the helmet, right dead center where the Marine Corps emblem is stenciled on the camouflage cover. Yet, all he got was a bad bump on the head. By the end of D plus ten of Operation Harvest Moon, all of the lieutenants in Company F had been wounded. First Lieutenant Bob Madeo was hit high on the leg, as he was crouching to fire on the enemy. The bullet exited his back less than an inch from the spine—a single inch to the side, and he would have been spending the rest of his days in a wheelchair. With all of his officers wounded, including 1st Lt. Bill Feille of the 1st Platoon, who was hobbled but not evacuated, Captain Nolan was dependent on his staff noncommissioned officers. Staff sergeants Duval, Young, and Best were his platoon commanders for the rest of his tour with the company. They served him admirably.

While the leading elements and the main body of the battalion column were battling for their lives, Company H of 2/9, the rear guard, was also taken under savage attack. At about 1350, only twenty minutes after the advance guard began its battle, Company H of 2/9 was heavily engaged in a violent battle with a major Viet Cong unit. The company was taking rifle fire, heavy machine-gun fire, recoilless-rifle fire, and mortar fire in huge quantities. The Marines suddenly found that they were completely pinned down, unable to maneuver in any direction. Control of the company by Lieutenant Colonel Utter was lost when the company commander and his radio operator were killed. For Company H of 2/9, the situation paralleled that of the battalion main body farther to the east. If something was not done quickly, the unit would be destroyed to the last man. The company officers did not rise to the occasion. Instead, a visiting artillery officer on temporary duty in the Republic of Vietnam from his normal duty station in Hawaii, Capt. Harvey Barnum took command. Captain Barnum was with 2/7 to learn, his visit being in keeping with the worries in the Marine Corps that the war might end before many officers could gain any combat time. The visiting captain acted magnificently. He rallied the stricken company, attacked the enemy troops with speed and violence, regained the initiative, and brought order out of chaos. Once he had driven the Viet Cong back, he medically evacuated his dead and wounded Marines and began moving Company H of 2/9 forward toward the village of Ky Phu, where Lieutenant Colonel Utter was establishing a battalion defensive position. The fighting had been violent and sustained, but the new company commander continued to press his Marines forward to the maximum. Company H of 2/9 had beaten the odds and had driven back a much larger force possessing far heavier weaponry. Although Captain Barnum had only come to Vietnam for ninety days of temporary duty orientation, he stepped in and saved the day for Company H of 2/9. After deliberations at the highest level in Washington, for his performance of duty on 18 December 1965, Capt. Harvey C. Barnum was awarded the Medal of Honor.

The battle in and around Ky Phu was a traumatic time for Lieutenant Colonel Utter. He had nothing left with which to influence the action, but he remained an island of calm in a time of chaos. Captain Nolan remembered him as quietly moving about among the troops, talking to them, and encouraging them. With bullets flying all around him, he was the perfect illustration of what a commanding officer must be during times of bitter crisis. Utter never lost his sense of humor either. As Captain Nolan was rushing his company back to the west to kick the Viet Cong off the main body, the colonel remarked to him, pointing toward where he had just seen First Lieutenant Madeo's attacking platoon moving into a side trail, "They went thataway!" No one who ever saw Lieutenant Colonel Utter under fire failed to understand that there was leadership, the kind of leadership that made the Marine Corps famous as a fighting force. The colonel personified to all who saw him the virtues of dignity and soldierly bearing, no matter what the adversity of the time.

Lieutenant Colonel Utter's most admired trait when under great stress was his ability to issue mission-type orders and then to allow those who served him to carry out, without interference, the jobs he had assigned. As an example, when he ordered Company F to return from the forward end of the column to attack the Viet Cong east of Ky Phu, he just told Captain Nolan to turn around and drive the enemy away. The key is, that the colonel did not tell the commanding officer of Company F how to do his job. Very few officers ever learn how to avoid interfering with their subordinates, very few.

For the night of D plus ten, 18 December, the battalion was consolidated in a perimeter around the small village of Ky Phu. Company F and Company G were astride the trail. Company F was facing west, and Company G was facing east toward the sea. Company H of 2/9 was integrated into the perimeter, taking positions on the north and south sides of Ky Phu. All units were tied in tightly, and a heavy attack was expected. No attack, other than sporadic mortar fire and some desultory sniping, took place.

During the afternoon of D plus ten, while the battle for Ky Phu had been unfolding, the battalion's organic Company H had been helicopter lifted, in an administrative lift, along with the mortar battery they had guarded, to Tam Ky. Company H took no part in the battle for Ky Phu and was later returned, again by administrative flight, to its normal defensive positions outside of the Chu Lai enclave on the nineteenth of December.

On the morning of D plus eleven, 19 December, the battalion began the day by initiating battlefield salvage. The enemy had left many dead and many weapons on the battlefield. That was significant, a prime indication that the Viet

Cong forces had been so hard hit that they abandoned their normal practice of taking all dead and wounded away to conceal their losses. Clothing, weapons, and equipment were scattered everywhere. These grim sights were of some solace to the Marines of 2/7 who were bone tired and filled with sorrow at their own losses.

When Lieutenant Colonel Utter ordered the movement east to begin again, Captain Seymour's Company G moved out. Immediately after starting, they began to receive fire. But armed helicopters were overhead, and the Viet Cong soldiers were killed as soon as they opened up. Angry Company G Marines fired a heavy volume of fire in response to each sniping Viet Cong, which when coupled with the helicopter machine guns, ensured that the enemy had no chance to impede the battalion movement.

After another day of sloshing through the muck while remaining constantly vigilant against Viet Cong attacks, the lead elements of 2/7 arrived at National Route 1 at 1830. Movement east had been assisted by a fifty-foot bridge erected by the engineers over a large stream and the constant cover of helicopters and artillery, ready and willing to fire on any Viet Cong who popped up his head. As the troops finished loading the trucks, mortar fire fell on the convoy. The 2/7 Marines and the helicopters returned a murderous level of fire, and the mortars ceased firing. After that bit of excitement, the convoy of trucks returned to the Chu Lai enclave without incident.

Instead of another night in the rain, the Marines of Company F were sent on board an LST, the USS *Kemper County*. On board the LST, which was commanded by Lt. Comdr. Bill Stockton, the Marines of Company F got a number of remarkable surprises. The sailors took their torn and muddy clothing and gave them dry clothes to wear while the torn field uniforms were washed and dried. The ship's cooks fed every Marine fresh food, all anyone could eat, the first fresh food the Marines had eaten since July. The sailors slept in the passageways, giving their bunks to the tired infantrymen. The senior medical corpsman of the *Kemper County* came to Captain Nolan the next morning and said, with tears in his eyes, "I'm sorry Captain, I put half of your company in the hospital with immersion foot last night." The unlimited good will of the men of the *Kemper County* has never been forgotten by the Company F Marines. As recently as a reunion in 1997, the men of Company F have feted the commanding officer of the *Kemper County* to offer their thanks for what he and his men did to renew the morale and physical well-being of the worn and weary infantry Marines and corpsmen. On the morning of 20 December, Captain Jim Nolan put his entire command, all the men of Company F and its attachments who could be returned to duty, on two trucks. The trucks were not crowded.

As an operation, the conduct of Operation Harvest Moon left a great deal to be desired. Marine backpack communications equipment was deemed to be utterly unsatisfactory in the monsoon weather, and the radiomen who carried the radios had clearly been the targets of the Viet Cong. Nine casualties—three dead and six wounded—were taken by the battalion communicators, a heavy toll. In the after-action report, Lieutenant Colonel Utter noted that nothing worked very well in the rain and that having the Marines carry three days of rations was unrealistic when they were constantly moving over arduous terrain in the driving rain. He also noted that the casualty reporting system was not adequate to the task, with some 2/7 casualties still not located seven days after the conclusion of the operation. All that was known about those men was that they had been lifted out of the battle; where they had been sent to recover could not be learned by 2/7.

Lieutenant Colonel Utter's battalion suffered heavy losses: In 2/7, the battle casualties totaled 115, 20 men dead, 95 wounded. To that must be added the enormous loss of combat power to nonbattle injuries and immersion foot. Precise totals were not kept as the situation was sometimes quite precarious. However, there was one day in which fifty-one men were airlifted out of the 2/7 area for nonbattle reasons. A loss rate like that is a horrible portent of what can happen during a war fought in monsoon rains. By the end of the eleven days of Harvest Moon, during which it had rained for all but a few

hours, 2/7 was a small shadow of a combat-ready Marine infantry battalion. The rifle companies were very shorthanded
with few fighting men present for duty. The H & S Company
would have had difficulty carrying out even a portion of
its normally assigned tasks in manning the battalion headquarters. The communications platoon, the platoon of 81mm
mortarmen, the flamethrower sections, and the antitank platoon of 106mm recoilless riflemen were all badly depleted.

The battalion had proof—walk-over and turn-over the
dead body type proof—of the death of 123 Viet Cong. This
was separate from estimates; it was a real count. In addition,
the battalion had, during its maneuvering, taken eighty-six
captives, either VCS or known Viet Cong soldiers. All in all,
the totals illustrated a lousy exchange for the terrible battle
and nonbattle casualties suffered by 2/7 in eleven days of
struggle through sodden countryside.

Interestingly, that battle in the rainy jungle was considered
to be of significance on the home front. Reports on Operation
Harvest Moon received extensive coverage on the front pages
of many newspapers. The *Miami Herald*, for one, had bold
headlines that stated that more than one thousand two hundred of the enemy had been killed in Operation Harvest Moon
and a similar size effort in the south of the Republic of
Vietnam by an army task force.

Perhaps the counts made after Operation Starlight in August
should have provided the first bad omen about body-count statistics, but the problem had not been clear. By December 1965,
seeing who won by totalling the dead on each side began to pre-
dominate as a measurement tool. From Operation Harvest
Moon in mid-December 1965, until the end of the war in the
Republic of Vietnam, the body-count game was the lead item in
almost every reporter's story. Body counting was a stupid way
to measure results. It did not work in 1965 to give meaning or
bring clarity to what was happening in the war, and it still did
not work to mean anything at all, to anyone, during the next five
long years of Marine Corps combat against the Viet Cong and
the North Vietnamese Army.

# 11

# OPERATION DOUBLE EAGLE

In a way that reminds one of the *Rocky* movies, the battalion occasionally was ordered to take part in sequels to operations that had gone before. Operation Double Eagle, Phase II, was one such. Since the brutal fighting during Operation Harvest Moon, during December, had not resulted in a significant overall reduction of the enemy activity in and around the Que Son Mountains and the Song Chang Valley, 2/7 was fated to revisit much of the same miserable terrain.

We were warned that an even tougher enemy was expected to be operating out of the jungle base camps. Intelligence indicated that the enemy was being made stronger by the presence of North Vietnamese regulars infiltrated into the Republic of South Vietnam to increase the combat power of the interprovincial units of the Viet Cong. Higher headquarters felt the need to confirm that intelligence by actual contact. Thus, we again received orders to go into the jungle to search-and-clear the area. That was a dangerous thing to do because the presence of NVA regulars could be expected to make the normally tough Viet Cong elements more dangerous. They would have greater firepower, better trained and more highly skilled fighting men, and more crew-served weapons. In particular, the heavy 12.7mm machine gun so favored in the Russian, Chinese, and North Vietnamese Armies would likely be in far greater use by reinforced Viet Cong.

Operation Double Eagle, Phase II, began with a briefing in

which the intelligence people estimated that more than 2,350 Viet Cong and NVA troops were in or near the anticipated operational area. The goal of the operation was to bring a Marine presence, again, into the area inland from Tam Ky and to bring the enemy forces there to battle—if they could be made to fight. The battalion was to conduct a search-and-destroy mission, starting at two inland landing zones and moving as before to the east toward the sea. Every effort was to be made to find and fix the enemy forces. The opposition was again postulated to be under the overall command of the 1st VC regimental headquarters, the same *Chu Luc* or main force interprovincial unit that had fought so hard during Operation Harvest Moon. The regiment still had the same four infantry battalions as its baseline force, but it was said to be supported by two or three new battalions. There were also reports of a new heavy weapons battalion and some independent company-size units of unknown strength and origin. Of grave concern to Marine aviation units was the addition to the enemy order of battle of the 195th Antiaircraft Battalion of the NVA. Without a doubt, if the Viet Cong chose to mass and stand their ground for a fight, 2/7 was going to have another expensive and difficult battle.

During the briefing by Col. Oscar Peatross, the regimental commander of the 7th Marines, I posed a question as to how long we might expect to be deployed. As I was then the 2/7 operations officer—Captain Doublet having been evacuated to Kue Hospital because of broken bones suffered in a fall—it deeply annoyed me to learn at the briefing that Task Force Delta was unwilling to tell those of us who were going to go out to fight how long they planned to leave us out there. We were not even provided with an estimate of the expected duration of the operation anywhere in the fragmentary orders. That made planning decisions unnecessarily difficult for me and for my commanding officer. Clearly sharing my concern, but hamstrung by orders from above, the regimental commander looked steadily at me for a long moment. As the silence lengthened, Colonel Peatross began to rummage in his desk. More time passed and the colonel was still sitting there without comment. After a bit more theatrical fumbles with small items in the drawer he produced a single roll of Charms hard candy. He tore open the wrapper and removed a candy or two. Colonel Peatross extended the moment even more by taking the candies he had pulled out and dropping them into the open drawer below his hands. After gazing my way for another few silent seconds, he chuckled and said, "Now, A. Lee, you worry too much. They tell me I'm not supposed to let you captains in on secret things like that. But, if you suck on one of these every day, starting now, you will be sucking up your last red Charm when you walk back through my door." Everyone laughed and took great pleasure in knowing that the colonel cared enough to show his disdain for those who would not treat us as grown-ups. Many who were there that day still grin at the slow, almost formal way that Colonel Peatross handled the candy and his soft, ever-so-courtly southern drawl. He knew our feelings, and he had a depth of professional concern for us that was a solid anchor in a sea of confusion. He, too, was often annoyed at the way his Marines were treated by higher headquarters.

D day for Operation Double Eagle, Phase II, was set for 19 February 1966. The Task Force Delta Frag Order 109-66 was received at 0230 on 18 February, however the battalion already had the gist of the plan in hand, and two days of operational preparations were nearly complete when the formal document arrived. The battalion Frag Order 1-66 was published at 1000 on 18 February. The overall plan was for the battalion to move out to the west. Two rifle companies and the command group would conduct helicopter-borne landings to secure landing zones deep in the Song Chang Valley, not far from the areas traversed in December. The remainder of the battalion was to make a motor march to Tam Ky and then prepare to be helicopter lifted into the secured areas occupied by Company E and Company H. The commanding officer and his command group would begin the operation from the landing zone cleared by Company E. The rear command group and H & S Company would be flown into the area cleared by Company H.

Again the battalion was going to war with half of its maneuver elements detached. The overall plan required Lieutenant Colonel Utter, on his departure for the field, to detach Company F to the operational control of the provisional artillery group for security duty. At the same time, Task Force Delta was going to take operational control of Company G for potential use as a reaction force. That organizational nightmare was another invitation to disaster; the Marines of 2/7 were going to enter a possible Viet Cong stronghold with no reserve element at all. The commanding officer would have no way to influence the action should a battle ensue. His hands were, essentially, tied.

On D day, 19 February, the assault elements of Company E and Company H lifted off at 0938. Each company had twenty-four helicopters available to it, and the lift moved swiftly into the closely adjacent landing zones. By 1005, the two companies had secured the initial zones against minimal resistance by isolated snipers who decamped quickly when fired upon. One Viet Cong was killed by Company H and an automatic rifle captured. Once the command group was functioning in the field and the helicopter lift was completed, the commanding officer ordered the two companies to establish physical contact and to move, on line, in a search-and-destroy effort to the southeast. During the slow, careful movement, several Viet Cong laborers were captured, and the Marines of the rifle companies exchanged some long-range fire with Viet Cong soldiers firing AK-47 rifles. There were no known casualties inflicted on the annoying snipers, but the Marines drove them away by quickly returning their few rounds with a great volume of rifle and machine-gun fire.

While Lieutenant Colonel Utter was maneuvering the battalion on the initial sweep, Company G was returned to 2/7 control. But we were ordered to make use of the company as a security force protecting a helicopter that was down in the landing zone used by Company H. The battalion had at least partial control of three of its four maneuver elements. That was an improvement, even if Company G was still doing things for the task force headquarters. Captain Seymour and his Marines were nearby, and they would potentially be available should 2/7 get into a large engagement.

The night defensive positions of the battalion were established by 1910 on evening of D day, the nineteenth, and everyone settled in, fully expecting an eventful night. The presence of enemy units was proven early in the evening when three Viet Cong tried to penetrate the defensive lines of Company E. One of the enemy soldiers was killed and one Marine was wounded in the action. An American .45-caliber pistol was recovered at the scene. The rest of the night passed without incident. Company G also passed a quiet night in its defensive perimeter.

On D plus one, 20 February, Companies E and H continued search-and-destroy maneuvering with minimal contact. Company G, although nominally under 2/7 control, was again given its orders by Task Force Delta. Captain Seymour's Company G was ordered to conduct a combat patrol to an area dominated by Hill 488. The company was to take that hill if Captain Seymour thought he could do it. If he could capture Hill 488, he was to set up a defensive position on the hill and await orders. As Company G moved, it received some fire and had several short, sharp exchanges with enemy troops. In one instance, the men of Company G cornered two Viet Cong in a cave and killed them. Shortly after that, they killed another enemy soldier, presumably from the same unit. For that operation, reconnaissance teams commanded by 1st Lt. Dal Williams, who had been part of the BLT, were operating on the high ground in support of all of our infantry movements. The teams often spotted the Viet Cong as they moved so the reconnaissance Marines could alert the rifle company commanders to any dangers posed to them by the enemy troops. No enemy soldiers were detected, and Hill 488 was taken without a shot. Once Company G was established in the defense on Hill 488, the operational control of the company was taken back by Task Force Delta.

On D plus two, 21 February, the 2/7 Marines arose after another night without contact. The lack of contact was eerie and made everyone nervous because it was so unexpected. Task

Force Delta decided that the contacts were so barren in the area occupied by 2/7 that another helicopter-borne assault would be needed to get the battalion involved in active combat. The objective of the assault was Hill 110 that lay to the northeast. Extraction of the battalion, after several delays, began at 1435, and the lift was conducted while the 2/7 Marines awaiting pickup were taking sporadic, long-range sniper fire. Hill 110 was not occupied by the Viet Cong, and the battalion landed without contact. A night defensive position was organized, patrols and ambush sites were established, and the two-company battalion settled in, fully prepared to defend against any attack. None came. Again the night remained quiet.

On D plus three, 22 February, the battalion moved out at 0815. A search-and-destroy operation to the south was initiated just to the east of the inland portion of the Song Chang Valley. Moving with care, Company E and Company H had little contact. At 1735, a squad of Marines from Company E engaged four to six Viet Cong in a firefight at fairly close range. The "overs" from the fight began landing in the battalion command group, and everyone had to scatter to take cover. Our 81mm mortars fired on the enemy positions in support of the Company E squad, and the firefight soon died out. There were no Marine casualties and the results of the contact on the Viet Cong side were never ascertained. The battalion again established a perimeter and prepared to repel any attack, but for a third successive night, there were no contacts.

On D plus four, 23 February, 2/7 was ordered by Task Force Delta to hold its position while other elements of the task force were maneuvering. The two rifle companies busied themselves by conducting platoon- and company-size search-and-destroy operations in the nearby terrain. Contact was minimal, and the command diary for that date contains only three entries. One speaks of morning sniper fire falling on Company H, another mentions two Viet Cong spotted by a Company E patrol at noon, and the third shows that one Marine was wounded in Company E by a sniper. While there was little fighting, a few VCS were taken captive, and amazingly, one of the males admitted to being a Viet Cong guerrilla.

On D plus five, 24 February, the battalion found that a fourth night without contact had passed into history. Those who were keeping a short-timer calendar could tick off one more day that had passed without their being killed or wounded. For many 2/7 Marines, that was considered to be the only real victory possible in the Republic of Vietnam.

Throughout the battalion, nerves were on edge. The terrain in which we were working was leading 2/7 back toward the sea, toward the village of Ky Phu, where so much Marine blood had been shed. It was clear that 2/7 would again be moving east along the same trail, the dangerous one that passed through the Song Chang Valley. If Task Force Delta did not change the apparent scheme of maneuver, it would very likely mean that we would mount another column to move through the bloody area around Ky Phu. For some of the Marines that called up some deeply pessimistic thoughts. The troops reasoned, quite logically, that with only two rifle companies present for duty, the battalion might get its ass thoroughly kicked if it went to Ky Phu again.

The battalion commander ordered Company E to move forward on the trail to the east as a security-on-the-march force. When the company reached an area about eight kilometers from its starting point, it was to establish a blocking position for Company H to drive against. The idea was to try to crush any Viet Cong units unearthed by Company H as it searched and destroyed to the eastward. The Viet Cong were to be pushed against the Company E blocking force and destroyed. All day on D plus five, Company H searched and sought the chance to destroy Viet Cong forces to no avail. The men searched through as much of the terrain as the vegetation would permit a unit to move through. No huge Viet Cong ammunition dumps or other storehouses were encountered; our enemy was not home. Other than one Marine wounded by sniper fire, there was no significant contact. When the battalion was again reassembled in one place, it settled into a perimeter, patrolled, and awaited attack. No attack came.

On D plus six, 25 February, the battalion commander ordered the continuation of the movement to the east. He set as his march objective for the day the small hamlet of Tu Cam (2) that was just under ten kilometers to the east. Company H led the column, again doing as much searching and destroying as it could accomplish and still continue the movement. There was frequent sniper activity throughout the day as the Marines burned huts that might contain Viet Cong supplies or searched for caves. Snipers were successful in wounding three Marines. Two men from Company H were hit as was one Marine from Company E.

As the movement continued, Company L of the 3d Battalion, 1st Marine Regiment, assisted by serving as a blocking force for 2/7 until Company H was in control of a pass in the hills through which the trail passed as it led toward Ky Phu. By 1910 on the evening of D plus six, the battalion had closed on the pass area and was established in its normal, exceptionally tense night perimeter. For the sixth night, preparations for close combat in the darkness went for nothing; the Viet Cong made no contact with 2/7 at all.

On D plus seven, 26 February, Lieutenant Colonel Utter ordered the movement eastward to begin, with the bitterly remembered village of Ky Phu as the day's march objective. The move began at 0945 with Company E in the lead. Until the afternoon, very little took place other than the steady drumbeat of long-range shots fired from the jungle at the moving Marines of 2/7. At 1500, Company E, which had been receiving sniper fire and automatic-weapons fire for some time, halted the column. Facing to the north, Company E took a thirty-man unit of Viet Cong under fire and swept through the area of contact. Six VCS were captured. A quick search of the area produced a pack, a map case, and some loaded AK-47 magazines. A few Chinese Communist ("Chicom") stick grenades were also turned up by the rapidly moving Marines.

Lieutenant Colonel Utter kept Company E to the north of Ky Phu, holding it to a total movement of no more than twenty-five hundred meters. From the battalion command group, an air strike was called. The artillery liaison officer, 1st Lt. Jim Miller made the mistake of asking me what he might do to be helpful. I told him, "Climb up on that roof and call us a fire mission of 155mm guns. Put it on that tree line where the Viet Cong are firing on Company E." He blanched, looking for me to change my mind. Instead, I pointed up at the roof, said, "Move," and walked away to be nearer the battalion commander who was watching the progress of Company E. Lieutenant Miller faced his demons, climbed onto the roof, called the fire mission, adjusted it twice, and then he tumbled down to the ground as AK-47 rounds peppered the rooftop where he had been lying seconds before, looking through his binoculars, adjusting the fall of artillery rounds. Lieutenant Miller was obviously frightened, but he was proud to have accomplished an audacious act that he had, moments before, thought of as both foolhardy and impossible. The move by Company E flushed many Viet Cong, and an aerial observer (AO), an artillery officer conducting fire missions from the rear seat of an aircraft, assisted in taking them under fire whenever they moved. The AO later reported several Viet Cong bodies on the ground in the areas struck by air and artillery missions. The bodies proved to be elusive. By the time Marines on the ground arrived at the sites, no bodies were left. In Company E one Marine was wounded during all of that rapid movement and continuous exchange of fire.

As Company E was rampaging to the north of Ky Phu, the remainder of the battalion began closing in on the village. The move was not without incident as everyone in the column was subject to occasional sniper fire. At one stream crossing, about sixty meters of open ground, the bullets could be heard snapping across the muddy path. Every Marine in the column had to cross that stream to get to the comparative safety of the overgrown terrain on the other side of the wide, flat watercourse. Each man in the column, including the colonel, was in danger. From Lieutenant Colonel Utter to the most rear-rank private, everyone had the opportunity to dash across that space while the Viet Cong soldier tried to make another kill. The terrain was so difficult that for the rifle companies to dig out the lone sniper would have taken the rest of the day. Therefore, everyone stepped up and took his chances. Some dashed across in company with others, seeking safety in numbers or hoping to make up a three or four man group that would confuse the sniper. Others waited until a larger group had been fired on, and then zipped across alone. Our tiger of a colonel, when it was his turn, just looked each Marine in the command group directly in the eye. He said nothing at all, his look said it all. He expected us to cross without comment, as professionals should. We, one by one, followed him out into the open with our heads up, moving in his wake as he crossed the streambed quickly, in a dignified trot, to the other side. Around us the ballistic *crack* of AK-47 bullets could not be ignored, but the command group was not going to show a trace of fear in the face of the danger. The colonel's example made that a sure thing. That sort of movement under fire was repeated again and again while the Viet Cong continued to harass the column at every open space but chose not to attack 2/7 at any point.

When Company H arrived in Ky Phu, the commanding officer sent it to the south of the village, ordering no more than one thousand meters of movement to clear the area. The company encountered scattered sniper fire, returning that fire without known results. At 1800, Company G, which had finally been returned to 2/7 control at 0730, arrived at Ky Phu. The company had spent the entire day trying to catch up. Being alone on the trail they had moved behind the rest of the battalion, using as much caution as possible, but without ever having the company column contested by the Viet Cong. In silence, without having a round fired at them, Captain Seymour and his Marines trudged along the same route of march taken by the rest of the Marines of 2/7, who had been getting shot at all day long. Company G was sent to outpost a hamlet, Tran Vinh (1), to the north as protection from an attack against the battalion's Ky Phu positions from that direction.

On D plus eight, 27 February, the battalion command post received a wake-up call, a mortar attack, which arrived at 0203 in the morning. Five to seven rounds of what sounded

like a 60mm mortar landed in the village of Ky Phu and
brought everyone to full alert. One Company H Marine was
wounded, and everyone was again reminded of the bloody
fight that had taken place in Ky Phu in December. Most of 2/7
remained awake and alert until dawn, waiting in the dark for a
possible Viet Cong assault. No more mortar rounds arrived,
and the ground assault never materialized.

One aspect of the mortar attack provided a small humorous
note to the day. Lieutenant Colonel Utter and I were sharing a
village house where we had drawn up the plans for the D plus
eight maneuvers. We had briefed the company commanders
on the next day's plans, constantly cross-checking each other
to ensure that we did not leave any loose ends. With us in the
house, of course, were the magnificent 2/7 radio operators
who worked long, horrible hours to keep the commander and
his staff in control of the situation. Just as it was when we
were on the move, it was less than two steps from the colonel's
hand to the communicator who monitored everything that
was happening on the tactical net. When sleep overcame us,
the colonel and I were lying side by side on a peasant's plain
wooden plank bed, snoring away on our backs and sleeping in
our flak jackets—with boots on! As the first mortar round hit,
we both roused and rolled off our respective sides of the bed.
Moving to be nearer the tactical net radio operator, I crawled
into and hit my head on some metal-frame piece of furniture
standing against the wall. Angry at the bump and busy checking the net for information on the incoming fire, I ignored the
table or whatever I had crashed into until all was settled down.
At that time, I lay back down on the floor and, with my flashlight, began to examine the metal frame of the oddly shaped
piece of furniture. Suddenly, all became clear. I had been
lying inside the cast-iron frame, and across a wide foot
treadle that was molded into the word *Singer*. There in the
middle of a war without end was a Singer sewing machine,
foot-powered like my grandmother's, that appeared to be
ready for immediate use. It was an amazing moment, and I
wonder if the woman whose home we invaded that night ever
returned to sew clothing for her family on that machine.

The maneuvers planned for D plus eight, 27 February, began at 0815 when the rifle companies positioned themselves to sweep across the hillsides as they moved east toward the sea. The area beyond the hills to be swept was known as the Pineapple Patch, and Task Force Delta wanted it swept clean. Company G and Company H were to sweep while Company E was to keep the rest of the battalion alive. Maneuver of the main body of 2/7 began at 1030. Any move off the road was made difficult by the heavy undergrowth. It was unlikely that the Marines of Company G and Company H could maintain physical contact for more than a few moments out of each hour. The distance to be covered made a deliberate search impossible, and the numerous snipers firing on the battalion made the entire effort very dangerous and extremely frustrating.

As Lieutenant Colonel Utter moved the command group out of Ky Phu, he made sure that the engineer lieutenant knew full well that he was to use as much explosive as he could spare on a monument that stood in the village. That monument said, in rough translation, that here, in this place, a great victory over the American Marines had been won by the heroic Viet Cong on 18 December 1965. On the other side, the enemy had painted, in English, something about getting the American aggressors out of Vietnam. For everyone in 2/7, it was a pleasant thing to hear the cracking roar when that piece of Viet Cong handiwork was reduced to tiny, tiny little pieces. The blast may have used ten times too much explosive, but for us that was just a proper response to the arrogance of the Viet Cong who had placed it in Ky Phu.

Moving eastward was not rewarding for the sweeping companies. Company G had one Marine wounded, and Company H had seven men hit during the move. In the rear, Company E had one Marine wounded on the road by some snipers who had infiltrated behind the units making the sweep.

Once 2/7 arrived at the ARVN outposts along the hills to the west of the railroad tracks that parallel National Highway 1, a standard administrative column with flanking security was ordered. The battalion moved to National Route 1 without any enemy response. The administrative column was used to avoid passing the deployed companies through a series of uncharted ARVN minefields. The battalion formed up on the highway and marched to the south, returning once again to Tam Ky, where it would spend the night in the same athletic field that was used during Operation Harvest Moon as a "secure" bivouac site.

At 0330 on D plus nine, 28 February, a Viet Cong sapper unit of about ten men tried to penetrate the battalion defensive perimeter. They were detected, and the Marines held their fire until the half-naked men, lugging their packs of explosives, were actually at the edge of the concertina wire. When the machine gunners opened up at about fifteen feet, it shredded the sappers and the threat to 2/7 from that quadrant of the supposedly secure bivouac area was terminated. Once daylight had come to D plus nine, 2/7 returned to the Chu Lai enclave, taking over its normal defensive positions on the 7th Marine frontage.

To examine Operation Double Eagle, Phase II, Lieutenant Colonel Utter commented in depth about the difference in the civilian population that 2/7 encountered. In December, all civilians had been hostile and exuded hatred. In February, they frequently seemed to be cheerful and positive when they interacted with the Marines. There seemed to be far more farmers working crops and more people inhabiting the villages than had been encountered in the December fighting.

With regard to the enemy he remarked, in his official report, that the Viet Cong in the area clearly did not want to confront the American Marines. Whether it was the additional availability of air power or some other factor, the enemy kept his distance. In fact, during the operation, the Viet Cong usually engaged us with fire at the very limit of the visibility from their positions. As an example of their desire to stay away from us, there were no instances of Viet Cong fighting men moving up to the trail and closing it by tossing stick grenades into the column of marching Marines.

Lastly in his summary, Lieutenant Colonel Utter flatly stated that, "Employment of a battalion with only two of its maneuver elements is disastrous to both flexibility and staying power in combat." Later he noted that with the rifle companies dwindling in manpower, a battalion could barely hope to put 250 fighting men in the field if it retained only two of its four companies under its operational control. Of course, nobody listened to our battalion commander, nor did things change in any way because of his carefully framed commentary.

# 12

## MIXMASTER

By the fall of 1965, a very serious personnel problem had become clear to the members of the battalion and to the various levels of command far, far above the mud-Marines: Every last one of the 8,008 men from the original Regimental Landing Team 7, which had been so carefully task-organized at Camp Pendleton, California, for service in the Republic of Vietnam, had the *same* overseas control date. That meant that everyone who sailed west to war in the RLT should—in theory—go home on the same day in the summer of 1966. Obviously, if all of us who survived the war in the Republic of Vietnam, both Marines and supporting medical personnel who had sailed with 2/7, were to leave at once, chaos would prevail. Nobody wanted their particular unit to be harmed by the establishment of an arbitrary rotation policy, nobody. Yet, it was quite evident that something had to be done. Unless the amphibious task force shipping came back to Vietnam to gather us up, the resources did not exist to move that many men home from the Republic of Vietnam in a single group. It was also important that everyone understood that there were no combat-ready units, at sea or undergoing training at home, prepared or trained to pile in and take over the combat missions and responsibilities of the 7th Marines.

The 2/7 Marines all had a feeling of loyalty to the unit and to the battalion's record in combat. All of the personnel people worried steadily, and there was a lot of speculation. At all levels, rumors flew as to just how the decision makers on high would deal with the matter. The rumors ranged from the wild and fanciful to more logical concepts. Everyone had a theory. Many were of the opinion that the entire regiment would be pulled out of combat, moved to Okinawa, and all the empty billets would be filled by replacements. That theory suggested that the 7th Marines would be retrained in Okinawa before being sent back into combat in the Republic of Vietnam. Others were gleeful about a supposed early rotation policy that would send a steady stream of Marines home in the spring of 1966, the last of the original RLT 7 Marines going home in June or July. Those slated to depart last would be leaving relatively close to the regular rotation date, the day when their prescribed thirteen months of combat service overseas would be completed.

Among those who had come to the battalion in 1964 and those few who had joined at the last moments prior to our sailing for war, the Marines held more fatalistic views. Marines who already had served the better portion of three continuous years in the battalion bitched and accepted the fact that they might get screwed—even if they were the first ones who joined together to be members of the unit. Those with the least time in the battalion took the view that since they were last to become part of the organization, they could plan on getting the "short end of the stick" when some "heavies" (i.e., colonels and generals on high level staffs who make decisions that affect troops, none of whom they have ever seen) up the chain of command made up their collective minds. The newcomers accepted that with reasonably good grace. Of course, they exercised their God-given right to bitch just as loudly as the old timers.

One group of young officers and some SNCOs firmly believed in what they saw as an eminently fair policy, one grounded on the basic fact that we were supposedly all grown-ups who should expect to be forced to accept a little bad news from time to time. This group expected us to be told that, because of the rotation date problem, everyone would be reassigned new rotation dates that would be spread out over six or seven months.

In their concept, Marines and medical corpsmen who had been in the battalion since its first cycle at Camp Pendleton would begin rotating in May of 1966. Some who had been wounded and had two or three Purple Hearts might also be allowed to leave during May. The rest of the battalion would be given the opportunity to, voluntarily, select a rotation slot in June, July, August, September, October, or November. As Marines who were proud of their battalion, they expected that would work to effectively spread the rotation dates across seven months of 1966. When coupled with combat attrition and nonbattle casualty losses, that approach would effectively make the problem disappear.

None of the theorists expected anything other than normal Marine-type bitching or similar low-key grumbling from any of those who would be asked to spend sixteen or seventeen months in combat in order to assure unit integrity. Essentially, unit integrity thus stabilized would make it far easier for those who would be joining 2/7 from the replacement drafts. Everyone seemed to feel that, if asked, such a necessary change in the word could easily be accepted as part of the reality that the members of 2/7 often had to do something difficult or dangerous to make the battalion successful. Expectation throughout 2/7, was of course, that we would just have to get on with the job at hand.

Horrible actions have horrible outcomes, and the rotation policy that came down from those on-high horrified everyone beyond all belief. Somewhere, a powerful someone decided that rotation dates would not be altered. Unit integrity be damned! Unit cohesiveness be damned! Instead of setting forth a rational policy, Marines and medical corpsmen would be subject to a "mixmaster" evolution designed to scatter the men of units like 2/7 throughout the entire two divisions of the III Marine Amphibious Force.

One entire rifle company of 2/7—along with a representative slice of the Headquarters and Service Company—would be transferred to some other battalion in another regiment. A similar element from some other regiment would join us in 2/7. At least three iterations of that horrible interchange were planned to effectively mix up the rotation dates. Needless to say, in that solution to the problem, the concept of unit integrity and cohesive interaction within the fighting units had clearly been assigned a value of zero merit.

Once the designated rifle company, and its attachments, had reported for duty to the new unit, it was to be broken up and the men of that company were to be scattered throughout the receiving battalion to "spread out" the June 1966 rotation dates. We in 2/7 were expected to do the same for the reinforced company that would be joining our battalion. We would thus be scattering their rotation dates throughout the command. This evil was to take place three times externally and once internally, thereby assuring the spread of all the men with June 1966 rotation dates in a roughly even distribution throughout all of the units of the III Marine Amphibious Force.

That utterly mindless madness appeared to us to be specifically designed to destroy our unit integrity and morale in a single motion. At first the whole idea was laughable, however, the laughter was hollow, and the pain was real. It was a formal order from above that no amount of appeal to the regimental commander, Col. Oscar F. Peatross, or his boss the division commander, could alter. While it was unbelievable on the face of it, it was real, and it was obeyed.

Company E of 2/7 was the first element shifted, on 19 November 1965, to another battalion. When E Company arrived it was renamed and part of the settling in process into that unit included being forced to immediately take part in a "little mixmaster" within that battalion. The bitterness was immediate. The rifle platoons were broken up, the rifle squads were broken up, and even the fire teams and machine-gun teams were shattered. Marines always know that to live another day, they must depend upon one another when the bullets fly. Confidence in your fellow Marines comes from working with them during trying times—times that permit the entire team to get to know one another and to bond. Nobody can walk into a new unit and be immediately at home and comfortable. It cannot be done!

Suddenly, after the mixmaster, the newly joined Marines were being called on by their new unit to be ready to fight together with a group of utter strangers. They were also expected to effectively and efficiently begin working under the supervision of another group of utter strangers, those who were their new leaders.

The men who had the "dreaded" June 1966 rotation dates were already tired and worn from being in combat for five hard months. This distressing upheaval, coupled with the daily stresses of combat operations in a war without clear objectives, combined cruelly to make life for the men of 2/7 even worse. Because the human aspect of combat operations had been ignored completely, the equations of life and death became even more unfair to the young men in the rifle platoons and squads where the fighting is actually done. Our senior staff officers, who operated from on high, appeared to have forgotten something that was very important. They forgot that, between individuals, it is the bonds of shared experiences and shared danger that make a fighting unit cohesive and successful. Being dragged out of their units and thrown in with strangers created much bitterness within the enlisted ranks and among the officers who were forced to leave 2/7 for assignment elsewhere.

While all those newly organized elements with nicely spread rotation dates might have been pleasing to the paper shufflers, it meant death to a number of the Marines and corpsmen who were among those shuffled in the mixmaster. As a particularly poignant example, one of the most popular staff sergeants in 2/7, S.Sgt. John Vergalitto of Company E, was killed almost immediately after being sent by the mixmaster to a new unit where he knew neither the officers over him nor the sergeants and corporals below him. He died, trying to do his duty in an absolutely pointless, minor-league firefight, standing up trying to find the NCOs he needed to control his platoon. He died as a result of the uncaring nature of someone far up the chain of command, someone who could not see fit to treat the men of 2/7 as professionals or grown men.

To this day, retired Col. Jon Rider, who was a lieutenant in Company E during this horror show and was shuffled himself, holds the personnel mixmaster order as the primary factor, the "real" cause, of John Vergalitto's death. Colonel Rider has held within himself for more than thirty years a bitterness toward those who cared so little as to sacrifice the lives of good and decent Marines to the god of organizational neatness and paperwork beauty. He shares the author's view that, on many occasions, the price paid by the Marines who were sent through the mixmaster was far, far too high. Men from our battalion, like S.Sgt. John Vergalitto, followed their orders and left Lieutenant Colonel Utter's command. They were forced out of a unit where cohesive personnel integrity was paramount and the strengths and weaknesses of their comrades were all well known—just to make the rotation books balance. Instead of being part of something larger than themselves, those men found that they were serving as lonely individuals, working with people they did not know or understand. How sad it is that some of the 2/7 Marines were dead when their rotation date arrived, dead as a direct result of that personnel tap dance.

In 2/7, Lieutenant Colonel Utter did not hold a little mixmaster. He did not agree with the mixmaster concept. He had always believed, and he trained us to believe, that unit integrity should almost possess the standing of a religion. The colonel directed that the new rifle company, commanded by Capt. Richard Theer, stay together as much as possible while he got to know them and they got to know 2/7. They had to become familiar with the way things were done in the battalion and that could best be accomplished by keeping them together. Over time the colonel might move some individuals into or out of the new unit and in that way increase their close interaction with the rest of the battalion. He was masterful in his ability to motivate those who worked for him, and by choosing to keep the new unit relatively intact, he allowed those Marines to retain more of their own internal unit spirit and integrity—for as long as possible.

In some cases it worked reasonably well. The new Company E arrived en masse from another battalion in late November (just in time for Operation Harvest Moon). It was complete with its internal structure and its commanding officer, Captain Theer. Instead of immediately ripping the rifle company apart, Lieutenant Colonel Utter left that structure in place. Before he was committed to combat operations, the commanding officer of the newly acquired Company E was able to get to know most of the various battalion staff officers and the other rifle company commanders. He and his Marines had only a few days to settle in so that they could learn the 2/7 way of doing things, but they worked at it. In addition, they had the opportunity to quickly become familiar with the other supporting elements that habitually worked with the battalion. These units included the 2d Platoon of Company C, 1st Reconnaissance Battalion, and our firing battery from the 11th Marines, the artillery unit that was almost always in direct support of our efforts. Those units had been working with 2/7 since the beginning.

In very late February 1966, Capt. James M. Nolan and his battle-proven Company F were dragged, kicking and screaming, away from the battalion. A new company arrived to take their place. That rifle company had been in 2/7 for only a day or two when the order that sent 2/7 to Operation Utah was issued. None of the officers and SNCOs of our battalion had more than a moment to learn anything more about the new Company F than the name of the company commander, Capt. Jerry Lindauer.

In a matter of hours the new company, an unknown, untried quantity to 2/7, had to be committed to a helicopter-borne assault against heavy, sustained resistance. Operation Utah began on 4 March, and the company could not be spared any time for acclimatization to 2/7 and its ways. There was no choice in the matter. Our battalion was committed on very short notice, and there was not one moment left for examination of the capabilities and strengths of the newly arrived rifle company. The fighting was heavy, and Company F was in the thick of it from the start. Casualties in Company F were very high. Perhaps those men died or were wounded because they were shuffled to us while Captain Nolan and his well-known and proven force of Marines were sent elsewhere to be disbanded and scattered throughout their new parent battalion.

The entire mixmaster effort turned out to be an agonizing failure and a pointless expenditure of energy. The supreme irony was that there was never a real need to destroy unit integrity; Operation Mixmaster was a total waste of time. This fact became obvious when the combination of the losses of 2/7 to battle deaths, combat wounds, nonbattle injuries, diseases, stress, emergency leaves, and miscellaneous other personnel losses was tallied: an actual count would have convinced anyone that by July 1966, there were going to be few, if any, of the original Marines and medical corpsmen of BLT 2/7 left on duty in the unit.

Obviously, the planners had addressed their paper-based concerns, but ground combat in a tropical paradise, when fighting a determined enemy, is destructive to personnel strength. The big-deal planners should have left things alone; the steady stream of replacements that joined 2/7 every couple of weeks was sufficient to ensure that the battalion would have in it all manner of rotation dates, spreading rotation across the coming months.

All the stress and strain inflicted by Operation Mixmaster, and all of the bitterness and sorrow created in the hearts of those forced to endure it, were nothing more than wasted effort. Also a waste, but one never dismissed from our minds, was our eternal anger at, and lifelong distrust of, those who foisted that stupidity on the 2d Battalion, 7th Marines.

Personnel turbulence is a natural and expected part of combat operations. That was something that we could all understand, and we could live with that fact as our combat tour unfolded. Fighting men of 2/7 were killed and wounded while others caught malaria, otherwise fell ill, broke their bones, had home emergencies, and, for whatever other reasons, could not continue to serve in the battalion. All of those sorts of problems were understandable. Infantry combat in the Republic of Vietnam was conducted in the jungle, most often across some of the most rugged terrain in the country. Marines of 2/7 were carrying heavy loads, and many fell and were seriously injured. Some of those injuries were permanent and meant a return to the Stateside Marine Corps. A portion of the Marines of 2/7 vanished for weeks with malaria, and some never returned because they could not fight off the disease while remaining in the tropical environment. No matter what the reason, if their loss made sense to us at the operational level, we could live with it and we could adjust. We never adjusted to Operation Mixmaster because it was an external solution to a problem, actually a fictitious problem, about which no Marine in 2/7 cared the most infinitesimal bit.

Flexibility was one of the keynotes of Lieutenant Colonel Utter's leadership style. As an example of that style, I would point out that the colonel had, in July 1965, responded to the need for liaison with the army's Second Field Force Headquarters by assigning me to do that task in addition to being the S-4. Of course, that required that I obtain a helicopter and a crew from the army and commute back and forth, like a yo-yo, to Nha Trang almost daily. While in Nha Trang, I worked under Major General Larsen's guidance—a fact that one weekend had me in Pleiku establishing transportation for the 173d Airborne Brigade as it flew in to fight on the Laotian border—and while in Qui Nhon I would be at Lieutenant Colonel Utter's disposal. As another example of his flexibility, the colonel was, in early 1966, running his battalion with about one-third of the officers he needed. He had, fit to fight, twelve Marine infantry officers; one aviation Marine officer for the Air Liaison Officer billet; four Navy officers; a Naval Gunfire Officer; two doctors; and a chaplain. All to fill more than forty officer slots. His way of coping with the very real problem was simple. He merely double-hatted and triple-hatted several people, and his battalion got on with the work of the day. At one time, while Major Doublet was in Japan recovering from a fall, I simultaneously served the colonel as his S-3, as the Assistant S-3, and as the S-4. When the executive officer had to be away for a few days, with a laugh, Lieutenant Colonel Utter told me to add the XO's job to my billet descriptions. Every officer in 2/7 could tell similar stories of shifting jobs to keep things going.

In 2/7 we faced the turbulence and worked it out with almost seamless ease because we were comfortable with our overall knowledge of the people with whom we had worked, daily, for more than a year. Operation Mixmaster came along and interfered with that comfort and made everything much harder than it needed to be.

Added to the personnel disasters caused by normal combat losses, noncombat losses, and Operation Mixmaster—which first harmed 2/7 in the fall of 1965 when the original Company E was taken away to the Fourth Marines—was the simple fact that higher headquarters began, in early 1966, to "screw around" with the battalions of the Seventh Marines. Tried and proven officers were identified as being needed at the division staff and some favorites of senior officers were assigned down into the regiment to get operational experience. Suffice it to say that some of the fair-haired favorites did not fit in particularly well in our battalion. Of course, at that time the already bloated division staff was in an explosive state of expansion that did not stop until the staff was at 250 percent to 300 percent of Table of Organization strength. Into its depths were dragged—sadly, a few went quite willingly—officers and SNCOs who should have been left to lead the platoons of the regiment's rifle companies.

During Lieutenant Colonel Utter's tour as the commanding officer of 2/7, he was served by three different executive officers and five different officers occupied the crucial S-3 billet. All the other battalion staff billets were equally subject to the constant debilitating turnover—a great deal of it avoidable—with new faces appearing and old faces disappearing far too often. This maddening kind of personnel turbulence was something that made combat operations more difficult and far more costly for 2/7.

# 13

## OPERATION UTAH

When a Marine simply does his job every day it is a sad but realistic fact that his diligence will often go unnoticed by his superiors. On March 2, 1966, a Marine of the Radio Battalion was doing his job, listening in on our enemy. He was doing so in a very responsible fashion. His diligent performance of duty was to make a difference to his superiors and to the men of the battalion. The impact went far beyond that young man's wildest dreams. By dint of his analysis of what he was hearing as he monitored the radio traffic of the Viet Cong and North Vietnamese Army communications, that Radio Battalion Marine began to develop an idea. In light of his suspicions, he carefully examined and cross-checked what he was hearing. Once he was sure that he was on the right track, he made a high-priority report up his chain of command to the intelligence staff (G-2). The operator reported to G-2 his educated guess that the enemy was concentrating forces in a particular portion of Quang Ngai Province. The Radio Battalion intercepts were the final, corroborating piece of "the enemy deployment puzzle," coming as they did at a time when the ARVN 2d Division was passing on a great deal of very similar data. The gist of all of the analysis was that our enemy, including the newly arrived 36th Infantry Regiment of the North Vietnamese Army's 308th Division, was massing to the west of Quang Ngai City.

The Marine who was doing his job did not possess any

actual code-breaking capability. There was no breakthrough, with "cracked ciphers," of the kind accomplished in World War II. What the Marine did could better be described as the application of careful attention to all the details he was hearing, combined with plain old common sense. While he listened to the enemy transmissions, he could not easily discern just *who* was going to be present when the concentration of forces was completed because the enemy always used code words and code numbers to cover unit designations. Regardless, the Marine applied common sense so well that he was able to accurately predict most of the designations of the units being ordered to move. He even developed a fairly good idea as to the time and place for the next scheduled meeting of the enemy commanders: he was absolutely sure that the enemy was gathering, in considerable strength, south of the Chu Lai enclave. His superiors in Radio Battalion understood his reasoning, and they backed his analysis with a strongly positive endorsement when the basic summation was forwarded up to the intelligence analysts.

When the decision makers examined the estimate created by the young Marine, they integrated that information with what they were being told by the 2d ARVN Division, what they were hearing from friendly local villagers, and items gleaned from the interrogation of enemy captives. The analysts also came to believe that the enemy was massing for possible offensive action. An attack was being planned for either Quang Ngai City or the Chu Lai enclave. That conclusion made things begin to happen, and happen fast. Whenever our enemy could be detected at the beginning of that sort of massing of his forces, the decision makers always tried to do something to disrupt his plans as early as possible. At the higher headquarters, it was always hoped by the general officers that it would be possible to bring the enemy force to battle, nose to nose with the superior firepower of our ground forces and combat-support units. The young Radio Battalion Marine's view became the view of the decision makers, and decisions began to pour forth with amazing speed—decisions that meant death for many on both sides of the equation.

Of course, the decision makers could never tell us down at the battalion level that some Marine sergeant or corporal had been listening to the radio and had concluded that our enemy was moving and massing. Instead, the whole process was disguised, a pointless exercise to permit the fiction that the Radio Battalion "did not exist." Any data from Radio Battalion became a "URS," "Usually Reliable Source," and by inserting the key word, *usually,* the decision makers covered their asses in those cases when the information was plain wrong. If the information was wrong, it would be the Radio Battalion Marine's fault for coming up with a bad hypothesis, not theirs for any action they might have taken based on that hypothesis.

While we at the battalion level were not to be trusted with the truth, or so the decision makers opined, our boss did not agree. Lieutenant Colonel Utter would leap onto the top of a water trailer and tell the troops in the chow line just what the decision makers above him were saying among themselves and in their message traffic. In doing so, he also took time to throw away the gobbledygook of military jargon and convert it, at the top of his lungs, into what this jabbering from above might mean to 2/7. He put it into the English language, ripping out all nonsense along the way.

Lieutenant Colonel Utter made it known that he would never conceal from the men who would do the majority of the dying any facts that might help them understand what was taking place and what the situation was that they would be asked to face. He was a colonel who cared deeply about the questions in the minds of his troops. No silly story concocted at higher levels was going to keep him from making sure that his Marines knew whatever he could find out from those above him in the long chain of command.

With our enemy massing, 2/7 was placed on immediate alert. We were informed—at 1720 on 3 March 1966—by the operations officer of the Seventh Marines that the battalion must prepare for an almost immediate departure on a major operation. We were told that it was the regimental commander's estimate that the operation would be initiated at first light the next day, on 4 March. The worn and weary souls of

2/7 were to be the lead battalion of a multibattalion force. The alert message made everything complicated beyond belief.

The battalion had just conducted a relief of lines at 0745 on 1 March, moving through Lt. Col. Paul X. Kelly's 2d Battalion, 4th Marines (2/4). The relief of lines had returned responsibility for the assigned battalion defensive positions to 2/7. In doing that, we had taken our home turf back from 2/4, who had been "watching the store" while we were occupied with Operation Double Eagle, Phase II. The battalion had only returned to Chu Lai at 1700 on 28 February from nine hard days in the bush, and with one night of rest, we were back on the defensive perimeter. Once again, Lieutenant Colonel Utter had full responsibility for the area—even though a portion of 2/7 would still be operating elsewhere for another headquarters. Elements of the battalion were also still involved in the last vestiges of Operation Double Eagle, Phase II. Final closure of the last units of 2/7 into our normal defensive area was far from complete, and some small detachments would arrive from Tam Ky well after 2/7 had gone to war again.

Operating directly under the control of Task Force Delta, to the north of the Chu Lai enclave near Tam Key, was Company F, stuck there with its rifle platoons performing security tasks in three separate places. That company did not return to 2/7 control until noon on 3 March, when it was released, then returned to the Chu Lai enclave from Tam Key by motor march. The placement of 2/7 on the short-notice operational alert for the morning of the fourth, left Company F less than twelve undisturbed hours to prepare for a major offensive action. The operation clearly could be expected to involve heavy contact with powerful units of the enemy's best troops, possibly including regular units of the NVA. The war in the Republic of Vietnam was heating up, and it began to appear that anything was possible.

It must be noted that Company F, which had been separated from the battalion for the first three days of March, was one of those suffering the bitter effects of Operation Mixmaster. Company F, commanded by Capt. Jerry Lindauer, had been

Company L of another battalion when it was uprooted in the middle of February and sent to replace Capt. James M. Nolan's original Company F of 2/7. With Operation Double Eagle, Phase II about to start, the new men of Company F had not had time even to learn the name of anyone in the battalion headquarters. Because the Marines of the new Company F and their unit capabilities were unknown quantities and because there was no time available for any form of indoctrination, the new Company F had been dispatched, when it arrived, to serve under the operational control of the provisional artillery element formed for Operation Double Eagle, Phase II. Their job was to protect the artillery while the battalion went into that operation with one-half of its combat power assigned to other commands. While Company F guarded artillery pieces, Company G was taken from Lieutenant Colonel Utter, and operational control was passed to Task Force Delta. Later, Company F was also ordered to work directly for Task Force Delta. While such a degradation of combat power at the rifle battalion level was obviously in violation of some of the key principles of war, no one upstairs seemed to give a damn. That sort of thing happened all the time. In the senseless helter-skelter of combat in early 1966, no one was surprised.

With Operation Double Eagle, Phase II wrapped up on the last day of February, Lieutenant Colonel Utter had, at that time, enthusiastic hopes of getting to know his new rifle company commander, Captain Lindauer, and meeting his new Marines. Those hopes were dashed and the "new" Marines of Company F were forced by the pace of events to spend their very few hours in the battalion area getting ready to go out on active operations in the bush. Coordination and preparation of any unit for a combat operation is facilitated by unit stability and personal interaction. Captain Lindauer and his Marines arrived as outsiders, and as outsiders, they would need some time to settle in and acclimate to 2/7. The new Company F never got any of that time. Operation Mixmaster was again causing unnecessary debilitating personnel turbulence, one that thrust Marines already under great stress into units where they knew no one and had no idea of the way that their new command functioned.

Once we had an alert message in hand telling 2/7 to be prepared to lift off at first light, another all-night session was required in the operations section. Captain Doublet, who was normally assigned as the 2/7 S-3, was just back from hospitalization. He actually arrived late on the afternoon of March 3. I had been filling in for him for several weeks as the S-3. Because Captain Doublet needed a moment or two to get up to speed, Lieutenant Colonel Utter ordered me to continue as the S-3 until the morning of March 4. I was to prepare the plans for the new operation, brief all of the subordinate and supporting commanders, and see to the publication of the battalion operation order. Once that was completed, I was to turn over the operations section to Captain Doublet. On the morning of 4 March 1966 when the battalion lifted off for the helicopter assault, Captain Doublet would again be the S-3. The colonel also ordered that, pending a later reassignment, I would remain in the operations section as the assistant battalion S-3 (S-3A) for the impending operation. In that slot I was assigned to move with Maj. George Gentry, the executive officer, as a member of the battalion rear command group.

Having a leader like Lieutenant Colonel Utter who habitually led from the front of his battalion, always in the area of grave danger where he might be killed and his command group destroyed, made life in the rear command group one that required everyone to pay close attention; the possibility always existed that Major Gentry would suddenly accede to command. If that happened, it was the mission of his team in the rear command post to assume control of the battalion, replacing the forward command group. A big, tough man, a wonderfully capable Marine, Maj. George Gentry was always ready for command if bad things happened to our great boss. It was our supreme good fortune that our leader led a charmed life—bullets and fragmentation often whistled past Lieutenant Colonel Utter on all sides, but none of the enemy's bullets seemed to have his name printed on them.

During the night of 3 March, coordination with 2/4 was

essential as 2/7 would again be relieved on the defensive perimeter by that battalion. Lt. Col. P. X. Kelly's 2/4 would be responsible for our area of defense of the Chu Lai enclave. To get the shift of responsibilities under way while under tremendous time pressure, I asked someone to request that the S-3 of 2/4 come to our command post. As the evening shadows lengthened, Maj. Sammy T. Adams arrived, growled at me, and broke his cigar in half, shoving one half forcefully into the corner of my mouth. He was "Captain Sam" of years past, happily taking part in his third war. Sam Adams had been my company commander and my deeply respected mentor when I had been a lieutenant in 2/4, eight years before. He charged into the 2/7 operations tent and bellowed his greetings. It was a very special moment. As a captain, Major Adams had been instrumental in teaching me many of the things about leadership under fire that he had learned in the Pacific War and in Korea. The things held dear by that tough, gruff, and sentimental man and passed on to me, were the personal aspects of soldiering in hard and dangerous times. As I grew more experienced in combat, each of Sam Adams's instructions was proven to have been the "real deal." As a leader, Sam Adams was one of the two finest men I ever served. Seeing him again was like a tonic. Meeting him there as an equal, not as a subordinate, was a tremendous boost to my morale, and his energy rooted from my soul a great deal of the crushing fatigue with which we all lived. His infectious love of his life's work as a true mud-Marine rekindled my spirit and fanned the flames of my inner enthusiasms. Captain Sam long ago departed this earth, dying too young from cancer for his tour in Valhalla, but he was a marvel while he lived, a treasure among Marines.

If 2/7 was going to meet its next-morning deadline, a battalion operations order had to be created and all units had to be assigned their missions for D day, which was not likely to be delayed. The quickly written and published order was known officially as 2/7 Fragmentary Order 2-66. It would begin with a helicopter assault into a paddy area to the northeast of a village known as Chau Ngai. Chau Ngai lay about fifteen kilometers northwest of Quang Ngai City. The village was made up of a number of subordinate hamlets, all of which were identified on the map with a number in parentheses after the village name. Because of the numbering system, we found that the primary landing zone selected for the 2/7 assault, Landing Zone Alfa, would be within two hundred meters of a hamlet known from the map as Chau Ngai (4).

The helicopter-borne assault sequence would begin with Company F, which, despite the fact that it was an untried and untested element in the battalion, was by far the strongest rifle company available to Lieutenant Colonel Utter; Company F could lift from the landing zone with just over 230 Marines, including attached engineers, forward air controllers, mortar forward observers, artillery forward observers, battalion scouts, and the necessary communicators. Captain Lindauer also had a full complement of officers, something none of the other rifle companies could match. Because Captain Lindauer's company was near its assigned manning level, it was clearly the proper choice to take a leading role in the assault mission. Companies E, G, and H were all operating with 120 to 150 able-bodied men. Instead of the six officers that those rifle companies rated, all were functioning with only two or three officers present, fit for duty. For 2/7, the paper strength—which included everyone on the battalion muster roll, the wounded, the sick, the lame, the lazy, the emergency-leave cases, and possibly a few who were unproven malingerers—was in no way an accurate reflection of the number of men who could actually be committed to battle. Fewer and fewer Marines were doing more and more fighting, and the wear on the battalion was evident.

The first 2/7 Marines to move out was the unit ordered to protect the artillery firing site. At 0700 on 4 March, Company E, under the command of Captain Theer, departed to rendezvous with Battery M of the 4th Battalion, 11th Marines, (M/4/11), on National Route 1. Company E, less one platoon of infantrymen, was tasked to escort the artillerymen to Binh Son where a firing position was to be established. Of course, the riflemen were to stay, providing security, at that firing site for an unknown period of time. Once again, the battalion would be shorthanded as it went out actively hunting trouble. The action would begin, as it always seemed to do, with 2/7 short one rifle company. That sort of assignment came down to the battalion from above, cast in stone. An appeal was useless; no protest was lodged with either regiment or Task Force Delta regarding this fateful reduction of combat power.

Company F assembled first on the landing zone, breaking down into heli-teams in the process. The lift was to begin at 0940, but the helicopters did not arrive until 1030, and only eight CH-34s were available at first. After a forty-five-minute delay, the lift continued, about twenty helicopters taking part. With the delays and with a certain amount of confusion among the pilots as to where the pickup zone was—despite both panels and ground controllers being present—the lift of 2/7 into the operation took more than three hours to complete. Not a very positive way to begin! The commanding officer and his command group did not get on the ground, where both his Company F and his Company G were already heavily engaged in life-or-death struggles, until 1210 in the afternoon.

A great deal of fire was encountered when the first helicopters arrived and landed the first wave of Company F Marines. Touchdown for the first wave took place at 1100 in LZ Alfa. One of the CH-34s in the initial lift was downed, and three of the remaining seven helicopters reported that they had been hit with small-arms fire. For forty-five minutes, there were no additional troops delivered to LZ Alfa, and the lead company was waiting—under heavy fire—for the remainder of its combat power to arrive on scene. Simultaneously, while fighting for survival, the company commander of Company F also had to see to the security of the area around the downed CH-34. He was greatly hampered by the fact that his company did not complete the helicopter lift until after 1145. For nearly an hour Company F was forced to remain tied to the LZ with far less than half its combat power available. It was a miracle that the enemy commander failed to react to the precarious situation of Company F and failed to destroy that small force while he had the opportunity.

Meanwhile, Company G was also being lifted into LZ Alfa, which would provide the battalion commander just two—rather than the four he rated—maneuver elements with which to begin the search-and-destroy effort to the southeast. Coordination with the local ARVN command was made by Lieutenant Colonel Utter when his command group closed into the LZ at 1210. At 1245 he pointed out to the ARVN and their American advisers that the enemy contact had already begun in earnest and he said that once the battalion was free of the landing-zone security problems, it was his intention to begin the planned movement to the southeast. However, both the advisers to the ARVN and the helicopter pilots pointed out that the majority of the enemy activity lay to the east of the LZ. Because of that, the colonel decided to shift his line of movement farther eastward than had been planned.

As that coordination was being made, Company G had a short firefight with a reported one-hundred-man unit of the enemy. Marines from the company killed at least four Viet Cong and wounded an unknown number. They also captured thirty packs and about one hundred rounds of the big, heavy 12.7mm ammunition of the kind fired by the Russian and Chinese dual-purpose antiaircraft machine gun that was so popular with the Viet Cong interprovincial units. The 12.7mm machine gun was devastating when used against the thin-skinned helicopters, and it was feared by everyone, air or ground, who had ever heard it thumping away in the jungle.

By 1340, with the command group pressing the battalion forward into the attack, Company G was operating on the right, and Company F was operating on the left. One platoon from each of the two leading companies had been siphoned off for other tasks so neither company had a reserve element left to influence the action. (Company G had a platoon guarding a helicopter, and Company F had to place its 3d Platoon on the far left flank for the purpose of contact with the ARVN units instead of placing it in reserve.) For that matter, Lieutenant Colonel Utter seldom was permitted the luxury of a reserve at battalion level either. That matter had been raised, with strong protest, after Operation Harvest Moon, but there had been no changes in the way things were done. Company H, which was to be the battalion reserve, had yet to be flown to the LZ when the orders came down from Task Force Delta to begin as quickly as possible.

As 2/7 advanced to the east, the left flank of Company F was supposed to be tied, by physical contact, with a unit of ARVN Rangers. Their adviser, Red Hat One, was a graduate of the Military Academy at West Point who gained national prominence as an end on the Academy's football team. He was, supposedly, to be available to 2/7, by radio, at all times for coordination of the movement of the two commands. Of course, realistic coordination of movement was impossible because the communication link was as illusory as the physical contact that never was maintained by the ranger force.

Company G, attacking forward on the right, was maneuvering with an open right flank. Captain Seymour's Marines were to be tied in by physical contact on the left with Company F. Shoulder to shoulder, both companies began to move forward. Both immediately reported heavy incoming fire from the front. Hills 85 and 97, which overlooked the battle from the right, appeared to be deserted, and the companies began their sweep eastward with those hills menacing the battalion from the open right flank.

Company H, which had finally reached LZ Alfa only ten minutes before the maneuver began, was to move in the rear of the battalion formation as the battalion reserve. Completion of the Company H lift resulted in another helicopter downed in the landing zone and several more CH-34s damaged by the intense small-arms fire. First Lieutenant James Lau (who replaced O'Connor when the latter became S-4) was forced to detail his 1st Platoon to guard the immobilized helicopter. The combat echelon of H & S Company would follow the command group as it moved behind the fighting, moving just ahead of Company H, which provided the commanding officer with a reserve force of only two rifle platoons. Those two platoons of infantrymen were all that was available should Lieutenant Colonel Utter need additional combat power to influence the action as it developed to his front.

By 1440, the heavy sniper and machine-gun fire directed against Company F and Company G began to intensify dramatically. Just ten minutes later at 1450, both of the companies reported that they were in solid contact and were heavily engaged with enemy forces. It was close-in fighting, ranging from hand-to-hand combat out to a distance of twenty meters at the maximum. The enemy troops were supported by a large number of the heavy 12.7mm antiaircraft machine guns and many of the lighter, bipod-mounted, Russian-made, 7.62mm RPD machine guns. Company F, which was under heavy fire from the front, also began receiving a large amount of plunging fire from the enemy occupying a ridgeline to its left. The enemy, who were supposed to have been ousted from that hillside by the ARVN Rangers, were still in place, and from their vantage point, they were able to fire downward on the Marines of Company F. The American Ranger adviser, Red Hat One, earlier had made an official report to 2/7 that the ridge had been cleared of the enemy by movement forward of two companies of the ARVN Rangers. That report was false, the maneuver never had taken place, otherwise there would have been no plunging fire possible from that hillside.

On the right flank, Company G was getting a heavy volume of fire from the front and was being threatened by the enemy who was trying to begin a movement to the company right flank. That was serious, because it would leave the open flank of the company subject to encirclement. Additionally, Capt. Bill Seymour and his Marines were getting a large number of what are called "overs," swarms of bullets fired at Company F that passed by and fell in among the Company G Marines. Everything that was happening appeared to be bad news for the battalion.

To counter any possible encirclement on the battalion right flank, Lieutenant Colonel Utter ordered Company H to attack forward on the right. He wanted First Lieutenant Lau to bring his company up alongside Company G, clear Hills 85 and 97, and broaden the battalion's attack. Company H would immediately assault the first small hill on the right, Hill 85, where enemy troops might be maneuvering to encircle. If the enemy was able to get up on the slopes of that hill, he would be able to look directly down on 2/7's maneuvering units. That position would allow them to bring plunging fire down on the Marines of Company G.

On the left flank, it was essential that the supposedly coordinated attack become, in truth, an actual cooperative effort. So far, the ARVN reports of movements had been proven fallacious. On the ridgeline across the rice paddy from Company F were at least five of the big, hard-hitting, heavy machine guns and a large number of AK-47s and RPDs firing down the slope into Company F as it maneuvered forward. Immediate contact was made with the adviser, our pal, Red Hat One. The colonel requested that the ARVN Rangers move forward, without delay, onto the ridge, attacking forward to the place on the ridge where they had already reported being located. He needed that movement for the purpose of outflanking the enemy firing down from the ridge into the paddy area where Company F was being battered. Red Hat One flatly refused the request and stated that his counterpart, the Ranger commander, did not intend to move forward at that time.

By then under fire from three sides, as the enemy did begin to occupy Hill 85, the battalion was in very serious trouble. By 1620, there were no additional elements with which the commanding officer could influence the action. With Company E assigned to the artillery and the other three rifle companies fully engaged, Lieutenant Colonel Utter could only worry, watch, and advise while the issue was being clarified by the Marines fighting and dying in the mud. Other than his H & S Company, mortarmen, clerks, and communicators, Utter had no one left to send forward to alter the balance of power anywhere along the line of contact. On his right, 1st Lt. Jim Lau and his two platoons of Marines were fully engaged in a violent firefight on the slopes of the first hill mass, Hill 85.

Suddenly, another serious problem had to be faced by the battalion commander. The Company F commander, Captain

Lindauer, was very badly wounded by one of the heavy machine guns firing down from the ridgeline into his company. Moment by moment, because of the high casualty rate, things in Company F appeared to be going very, very badly. Just before he was wounded, the captain had reported that he had lost contact with both of his attacking platoons. Shortly after reporting that the Company F captain was down, the company radio went silent, and no further information was received at the battalion command group. None of the fire-support personnel could be raised on their radio nets. The forward air controller, the mortar forward observers, and the artillery forward observers were all silent—unreachable for any one of a dozen reasons.

In the rearmost portion of the ground controlled by 2/7 lay the executive officer and his alternate command group. Everyone was staying down tight to the earth, as a steady flow of bullets was passing overhead, smacking off the tree limbs and impacting nearby. We were receiving some direct fire from enemy forces on both flanks and could hear a large number of overs passing by us from the fighting out front. This happened because a great deal of the fire that was directed at Company F and Company G passed over them, flew over the forward command group, and began zipping by our heads in the battalion rear area. Upright movement in any direction was unsafe. The radiomen and everyone else in the rear command group took cover in the ditches or other handy depressions—all of which we were scraping steadily as we tried to make them deeper. The mud and dirt were flying as everyone used helmet or entrenching tool to get lower. In particular, the communicators were laying low in order to decrease the chance that their antennae would draw more fire than we were already receiving.

Through constant monitoring of the tactical frequencies, Major Gentry's group was reasonably well aware of the status of events. Although the rear command group Marines had no immediate task to take up, the possibility of our being called forward at any minute was obvious. The volume of fire between the engaged elements was utterly astounding; bullets were flying everywhere! There were many who wondered whether our enemy might both outnumber us and outgun us. And the periodic crash of exploding rifle-propelled grenades to the east served to reinforce our fears about the commanding officer's longevity.

A sweaty and mud-covered Marine with obvious terror in his eyes arrived at the rear command group and shouted that I was to follow him to Lieutenant Colonel Utter. Running—crawling when the sound of bullets passing overhead was at its peak—the Marine runner and I arrived at the colonel's position. He and the S-3 had the battalion command group scattered in a depression behind a dirt bank. At one edge, the commander and his operations officer could stand and see out across the open rice paddies toward the east, the area in which both Company F and Company G were operating. To the right front of their vantage point lay the moderate hill mass, Hill 85, on which we initially believed there were neither Viet Cong nor Marines. Enemy troops had begun firing from that hill, and Company H was fighting its way to the top to make sure that control of the hill stayed out of the enemy's hands.

Ordered forward to find and assume command of Company F, I was launched out into the open by the colonel. The only advice he could offer was two admonitions. First, he emphasized that it was essential that the company not be permitted to become encircled. Second, he told me that it was imperative to the survival of the battalion that the Viet Cong not be allowed to split Company F away from Company G. If the two companies were split, the enemy could launch a drive on the battalion command group and possibly destroy 2/7 where it stood. With that, Lieutenant Colonel Utter clenched his teeth, slapped my helmet with a very solid blow, and sent me forward to find Company F.

Out in the open paddies and manioc fields, it felt as if the incoming fire was almost a wall that had to be penetrated. There were water splashes and mud eruptions from bullet impacts seemingly on all sides. Movement forward to Company F was going to be a difficult, if not impossible, assignment. The footing was lousy. There was thick slimy mud in the flooded rice paddies and soft, ankle busting soft dirt and muck in the manioc fields. But fully understanding what my colonel wanted, I set off. I had about 750 meters of open ground to cross, and if Company F was to be returned to 2/7 control, it appeared that I could only accomplish that by getting there as quickly as possible. But it was clear that there was a very good chance that I would never get to the company at all. What I had just agreed to accomplish was quickly turning out to be far from simple. Any positive thoughts about getting myself assigned another rifle company to command evaporated under the withering fire that was directed my way by people who could see me clearly as I jumped, rolled, dove, crept, crawled, and ran pell-mell from one promising depression to another more promising depression. Being, at that moment, the only Marine moving anywhere out in the open made the entire effort considerably more exciting.

After dashing in a crazy zigzag, rolling dance from paddy dike to paddy dike and from muddy bog to muddy bog, while people with all sorts of rifles and machine guns tried to figure out where their chosen target would next appear, I came to the first of the Company F Marines. He was lying, facedown on a small hump of ground in a manioc field. There was a huge hole in the back of his flak jacket, and the blood that had poured from him was pooled in a congealing, stinking mass beside his body. When I rolled him over to take his M-14 rifle, looking for a more powerful replacement for the pistol I was carrying, he gave a grunting sigh and flopped back in death, like a rag doll. The rifle that was under him had been destroyed, like the Marine himself, by a direct hit from one of the 12.7mm rounds—probably the same one that had gone on to exit from his back. With a sob in my heart for this dead young Marine, I moved forward again, trying not to think about vomiting or crying. As I got closer to the eastern edge of the open ground, I came across several more dead Marines. All had numerous wounds and were no longer fully human in appearance because of the destruction that the many impacts had had on their bodies. One wounded Marine lay in a ditch with a bandage on a chest wound and a morphine syrette bent down from the lapel of his utility jacket. He had obviously had the attention of a corpsman, but was unconscious as he lay panting, covered by his own blood, in the ditch just below the passing bullets. Two or three of the dead had been eviscerated or had huge chunks torn from their heads by the heavy machine-gun bullets. Ahead of me, the firing of M-14 rifles seemed to have quieted, and for a moment, it seemed possible to me that I might be the only live, unwounded Marine around. Maybe it was quiet because the Company F Marines were all dead.

As I entered the brushy area where Company F was supposed to be operating, I came across one Marine, by himself in a depression. He had his helmet off, he had shed his flak jacket, and he was looking very frightened and disoriented. It appeared that five to eight more of the Company F Marines had been killed and wounded in this area. Their helmets, packs, and weapons were scattered all around, and the bodies of the two or three who remained also bore the terrible ripping wounds made by multiple impacts of the heavy machine guns. One Marine was lying about five feet from his head which had been removed from his body by a tremendous impact on his neck. I surmised that he, too, had been hit by a 12.7mm round that had come down to kill him from the Red Hat One area of responsibility. Silently, I cursed Red Hat One.

There was nothing anyone could do for the dead. So, I turned and crawled over to the dazed and frightened Marine. At first he seemed so shaken that he acted like a man in a drunken stupor. He was very lethargic and could only answer in a slurred voice. Taking him by the arm, I asked that he move to my right and cover me with his rifle while we looked for the 2d Platoon of Company F. With a sad expression on his face, he put on his helmet and began putting on his flak jacket and web gear. He said nothing at all, just began to follow me as I moved forward. As we crossed another paddy and came to some stubby trees by a watercourse he came to life and shouted, "Captain, don't go up there. Ain't no Marines alive up there." Telling him to cover me, I pressed on, finding two more dead Marines just inside the brush line. They too had been virtually eviscerated by the machine-gun fire. Each had huge, expansive wounds with gaping exit holes. The skin of the two casualties was growing waxy, and it appeared that they had been dead for an hour or more. Since leaving the battalion commander, I had lost all track of the passage of time, so that fact made little impression on me, although I can remember it registering on my mind as I moved farther to the east.

Pausing behind a taller than usual paddy dike, my newly acquired bodyguard and I spotted a trail to our front. The trail was about three feet wide and had been pounded smooth by the passage of many feet. As I climbed over the bank, I could hear heavy firing to my immediate right where Capt. Bill Seymour's Company G was in heavy contact. It was easy to tell who was firing—the M-14 rifles and M-60 machine guns did not sound at all like the weapons used by the enemy. Feeling reassured by the sounds on my right, I elected to check out the trail up to the point where it disappeared around some large bushes. It might be possible that the remainder of the 2d Platoon had moved into the tree line. We had to find out.

Once again the Marine I had found sitting alone and confused was acting terrified at the thought of any more forward moves. He asked in a pleading voice for me to let him cover me from the dike. His thin, reedy, quavering voice made it very clear that he was close to the end of his resources. We paused together, just for a moment, to gather ourselves. Then, I whacked him on the helmet and said, "Hang on tight! I need you! Stay right here! If I come running back, shoot the Viet Cong, not me. We have to stick together." With terror in his eyes, he lay across the dike and placed his rifle to his shoulder. I hoped he was ready to provide covering fire if I needed it to get back in a hurry.

Rolling over the paddy dike onto the trail was a fearful experience. Bullets were cutting through the brush all around.

The source of that incoming stream of bullets was unclear. We were now well inside the brush line at the edge of the cultivated area, and the fire could have been coming at us from almost anywhere in a 270-degree arc. Even a moment of exposure could be fatal, but there was no other way to find out if any part of the right flank platoon of Company F was nearby. They could have gone to ground among the big bushes and short scrubby trees. The trail was dark brown, made up of hard-packed dirt. There were footprints, but only the bare outline of heel marks caught my eye. I did no tracking. As I was moving forward, I spent most of the time "strip-scanning" the brush for possible enemy troops who would kill me if they saw me first.

For about the one-zillionth time I drew my ineffectual little .45-caliber pistol. Cautiously I began moving ahead to see what could be seen. Being busy trying to stay alive by the use of intelligent movement had kept me from pausing a second time over any dead Marines. I had not gathered up an M-14 rifle. Feeling like an idiot, I was still wandering around a battlefield that was wall-to-wall fire, carrying only the stupid popgun of a pistol and twenty-one rounds of ammunition. That was a mistake that I did not repeat ever again! Captains are not supposed to be part of the firefight; they are repeatedly told that their job is to direct the fires of others. But there are times when a captain may need to shoot someone at a distance—if he wants to live. World War II officers had the .30-caliber M-2 carbine available for such purposes. In the Republic of Vietnam, where engagement ranges could be from close-in—two or three feet—to as much as three hundred meters, a similar multipurpose weapon would have made me a much happier man on 4 March.

As I neared the turn in the trail, it became clear that the turn was very sharp, making about a 120-degree turn to the right where it seemed to head off roughly to the southwest. Jutting up over the eight to ten foot tall lower vegetation were the thatch roofs of five or six small buildings that stood just around the turn. From my map, I reasoned that it might, possibly, be the hamlet of Chau Ngai (4). It could also be Chau

Ngai (6) if I had selected the wrong paddy area in my quick map study. But in either case, it was where the 2d Platoon of Company F was supposed to have been when radio contact with the platoon leader was lost by Captain Lindauer.

With my pistol leveled, I took one wide, leaping side step, moving out to my left where I could see around the corner. *Surprise!* Instead of the dark green uniforms of the Marines of 2d Platoon, there were ten or twelve tan-uniformed, very tough looking enemy troops. They were not alert, a fact that probably saved my life. They were sitting, hunkered down over their feet, smoking, and looking bored. Like many of the Marines on our side, those men were probably waiting, smoking and spitting, for orders from their leaders. The squatting position is often used by Vietnamese men, women, and children, and through long use it has become their position of choice. However, fortunately for me, it takes a man a moment to rise erect and take up his weapon from that comfortable squat. The two men nearest me, just five or six feet past the trail turn, were both hunched over 7.62mm RPD light machine guns. The weaponry carried by the others is unclear in my memory. I did not stop to observe them in any detail. The RPD machine gun has a very distinctive circular magazine on the top, and I found myself looking almost straight down on the two guns with great surprise. The muzzle of the nearest weapon, which was mounted on its bipod, was less than three feet from my right leg. All of the men squatting there were uniformed, booted, and had helmets, either tipped back on their heads or lying nearby; they were either regular fighters of the interprovincial force Viet Cong or regulars from the North Vietnamese Army.

Without any real pause, I shot the nearest enemy soldier, the closest one who had a light machine gun. The shock of the first round hitting his chest bowled him backward, and for a moment, the other Vietnamese froze as they looked at me. I kept trying to kill as many as possible and shouted to the Marine at the dike to shoot through the bushes at the trail corner. The enemy troops evidently had been fully relaxed, and I was able to shoot, at point-blank range, at least four of them before the first one fired back. The Marine fired his M-14, and the bullets passed within a foot or two of my head as they streaked toward the enemy soldiers. Running back to the paddy dike, I fired a final two or three shots with my pistol, then dove headfirst over the dike.

There, standing in about ten inches of water, was my previously frightened, hesitant Marine. He was standing up on his feet, cursing loudly, and trading fire with the enemy. He seemed wildly enthusiastic, and his lethargy had vanished. That Marine should have been very proud of himself for overcoming his fear; I know I was proud of him! It is a sad necessity to include here that the valiant young Marine was killed about an hour later, shot through the head while still doing his best to keep me from harm as I continued to scramble through the bushes and the rice paddies attempting to find and gain control of the rest of Company F.

An interesting aside with regard to that short firefight: Training does have long-duration effects on a Marine's behavior under fire. When firing on the pistol range it was always common practice, in the Marine Corps, to slip the empty magazine into the front of your shirt when magazines are changed during the rapid-fire stage of the qualification course. Lying on my back in the mud, after diving over the paddy dike like an Olympic Games contestant, I looked down and found a magazine carefully inserted into my shirtfront inside the unzipped flak jacket. It was empty. I pulled the magazine out of the pistol and found that it held only two rounds. There was one round in the chamber. I had, therefore, fired seven shots, swapped out the magazine for a fresh one, saved the empty magazine, and fired four more rounds—all without so much as a single thought process being involved. Good solid training, pounded into me so many years ago by those who had done that sort of thing before resulted in my survival that wild day.

Because my bodyguard and I knew that the enemy was just to our front in the trees, we began to move to our left, toward the center of the area that we hoped was occupied by Company F. After about thirty meters of crawling along a small drainage ditch, we came upon the 2d Platoon's command group, or what was left of it. The platoon leader was dead. The platoon sergeant was not present, as he had been away from the company for a day or two to take a test he needed to pass as he sought to move up the ladder to officer status. The company tactical net radioman was dead, and there were both lightly wounded and seriously wounded Marines lying scattered in the weeds in all directions. With my one-man backup, I moved into the platoon, tried to make the Marines understand who I was, and appointed the first NCO I came across, a corporal, as the new platoon leader. Using the platoon's radio, I spoke with Captain Doublet, telling him that we had some very serious problems, and that some solutions were in the making if my luck held out and I could find the rest of the company.

Learning from the Marines taking cover in the brush that up to about an hour before they had been the ones in contact with Company G, I had to backtrack to the company's right flank. Once there, the object would be to restore physical contact with Capt. Bill Seymour's gang. Only with physical contact could we be sure that the enemy would not slip between the two units and take both companies under fire from the flank. Taking four Marines along to act as the right flank connection with Company G, we maneuvered back to the same paddy dike where the young Marine and I had just had our wild-west shoot-out. As I again dived behind the dike, I ran headlong into Capt. Bill Seymour himself. After hearing the hornet's nest I had stirred up, he had just arrived to see what was happening to his left. Feeling vulnerable on both of his flanks, he was there to restore the physical contact between his company and Company F. Seeing him provided me with one hell of a morale improvement.

Captain Seymour and I lay behind the dike, flat as pancakes on our stomachs in eight or nine inches of muddy water, and exchanged information. He told me that, as far as he knew, everyone in Company F was to the left of the watercourse and trail that lay behind the earthen dike. His company, like Company F, had been hit hard. We both worried aloud about

medical evacuation possibilities under the heavy fire that 2/7
was receiving. Company G, like Company H, had begun the
day working one platoon short. Seymour was angry because
his 3d Platoon was still back in the landing zone guarding another downed helicopter. He also quickly told me that one of
his flamethrower teams had just knocked out two or three
heavy-weapons positions. He hoped that killing those weapons
might be of use in reducing some of the fire in the Company F
area. Our eye contact lasted only a few moments as we lay
there, but the discussion was almost too long. Our hiding
place behind the dike became of immediate interest to some
enemy machine gunners. Just as we agreed on how we would
keep in contact along the watercourse, a burst of 12.7mm
heavy machine-gun rounds slammed into the dike, about
eighteen inches from our heads. Some of the rounds plowed
right on through as if the dike were not there, passing directly
between the two of us. These bullets went westward, slapping
off the paddy water as ricochets, heading off some 750 meters
toward the battalion command group. Captain Seymour was
a solid citizen, an officer who could be counted upon at all
times. He more than proved it again when he looked me in the
eye and said, "You know what, Podner? There are some folks
out here who just don't like us. Keep your fool head down!"
With that we both dashed away.

To the rear of the center of the Company F area of operations, my lonely Marine bodyguard and I found the shattered
command group, including the severely wounded Captain
Lindauer. In the command group, one of the few Marines left
who was not dead or wounded was 1st Sgt. Gene Mills. First
Sergeant Mills was of great value because he had essential information at his fingertips. Every scrap of what he knew about
the men of Company F was pertinent to what I was doing because, other than Captain Lindauer, I had never even seen any
of the members of the new Company F. That fact was making
life quite difficult at that moment, and I was gratified to find
the company first sergeant alive in this chaotic mess. First
Sergeant Mills and I moved, with two radio operators, away
from the wounded Marines and settled into a ditch, which we

intended to use as a command post while we tried to sort out the question of who was where on the ground—doing what?

Prior to leaving for the operation, First Sergeant Mills had prepared lists, called two-line impressions, of the entire company. Lying in the mud of our drainage ditch, he used them to bring me up to speed on who he thought was dead and who he thought was wounded. His information was probably far from accurate, but it was given me as the best that he knew or could guess. He had many names identified and guessed at others from my description of casualties I had passed coming in from the battalion. The survivors were assessed by Mills because he knew them, and looking at their strengths and weaknesses, he began to advise me on reorganization of what was left of Company F. Of course, we did share some concern about our ever being able to reorganize. There were heavy casualties among the company leaders, the enemy was right on top of us, and the miserable to nonexistent communications capability of the few remaining radio sets in Company F did not bode well for any easy solutions.

In the company center, the area assigned to the 1st Platoon, as a direct result of a serious misjudgment on the part of the 1st Platoon leader, the maneuvering Marines had become separated into three groups. That aggressive young officer had taken himself, and four other Marines, about two hundred meters in front of his platoon. He was then—inadvertently and unsupported by any fires—acting as the point element of 2/7. One of the very basic truths about infantry combat is that aggressive action can create magnificent results, but being overly aggressive can lead the unwary straight into a trap. The lieutenant's well-meant, aggressive action resulted in his death, the death of two of his men, and the wounding of the other two Marines accompanying him. His separate element was spotted by the enemy as it charged forward, and the Marines paid the price. The two surviving members of the four men who accompanied him, both badly wounded and unable to walk, were completely cut off from the rest of their platoon but there was some hope for them because the two survivors were together, they had a radio, and the Viet Cong had not chosen to move out of their positions to overrun the ditch where they were hiding.

A second group of pinned-down Marines consisted of about a squad of the 1st Platoon that had moved forward, on its own, to help their lieutenant. Using all the firepower they could muster, the squad had been able to maneuver about half the distance to where the lieutenant lay dead; enemy fire was just too intense for them to continue, and they bogged down, went to ground, and stopped moving. Those men continued to be under heavy fire, and events quickly made it impossible for them to move forward or to the rear: they could not press forward because they had too little firepower; they could not come back because to do so would force them to abandon a number of badly wounded Marines. They were stuck. The rest of the 1st Platoon was settled into whatever cover the men could find; those who were unwounded were engaging the enemy with their M-14 rifles. This small firefight was taking place at ranges from ten meters to about a hundred meters. The leading man in that group, Sgt. August O. Miller, was playing sheepdog, dashing back and forth keeping everyone involved in firing back at the enemy.

Another group of Marines of Company F that remained immobilized was the left flank of the 3d Platoon, the Marines farthest left on the edge of 2/7's maneuver area. The platoon had been positioned toward the rear of the company to coordinate with the ARVN force that was supposedly supporting that flank of the battalion. Because of the formation used, they had fallen farther to the rear of the rest of Company F. Despite their best efforts, they had no contact with any friendly forces. The forces that were supposedly protecting their left flank, and that of 2/7, had disappeared. All 3d Platoon had was the steady drumbeat of machine-gun fire falling on it from the hill mass across the paddy fields. That finger ridge was exactly where the ARVN Rangers and their uncooperative adviser, Red Hat One, were supposed to be moving forward to stop the enemy fire. No one on the hills to the left of 2/7 moved an inch. Murderous plunging fire continued to fall around everyone in the 3d Platoon, pinning it.

The 3d Platoon was fortunate; part of it was fairly well located to shelter from most of the long-range machine-gun fire from the left because there were a number of earthen dikes in its area to hide behind and the men could return fire across the small, flat valley in a vain attempt to silence those machine guns. However, the platoon also had taken several casualties, and they could either maneuver or sit tight to protect the wounded men. Doing both was not an option.

Sgt. August Miller of the 1st Platoon reported to my command-post ditch and asked for another platoon to maneuver and help him get his Marines out of the terrible situation they faced. When he had time to take a breath, I told him that no reinforcements were available, none. I immediately appointed him platoon leader of the 1st Platoon, replacing the dead lieutenant. When he understood the overall situation of the company and the real possibility that, because it was fragmented, Company F might be overrun, his eyes grew wide, and he muttered something about doing what he could with whoever was left alive. Up he jumped and away he ran, with the dust from dozens of bullets striking around his feet as he dove for the next available cover. Soon it was possible to hear him shouting and to hear the increase in the fire of M-14 rifles over that of the enemy weapons. As he had said he would do, Sergeant Miller was doing the best he could with what he had left. The tough, driving way that Marine reacted to the chaos all around him was typical of those who survived the opening firefights of the operation. Sergeant Miller later earned a commission as an officer in the Marine Corps. Getting approval for him to be promoted was a slam dunk, because that was one Marine who had already proved that he could function under the gravest of stress.

Another group of Company F Marines that could not contribute anything to the fight was the command group—what little was left of it. Most of the communicators were dead or wounded, several of the critical fire-support radios had been destroyed, and no respite was possible from the plunging fire falling among the survivors. Since there were both dead Marines and severely wounded Marines scattered in all directions, the men of the original command group remained, stopped cold, in the area where they had taken the casualties from the heavy opening bursts of enemy fire. That placed them in the middle of a bloody mess. It was a very poor location, far too exposed to permit any form of command and control. Company F was in dire shape. Survival until the end of the day was very questionable. The battalion would need to send forward some form of help before Company F could maneuver forward, backward, or sideways.

Meanwhile, the volume of fire on the far right flank of the battalion was increasing steadily. Lt. James Lau's Company H was fighting a violent battle on the hillside in that area, and those Marines were having a very hard time. Company H had moved up and entered the firefight understrength. During the fighting on Hill 85, some of which was almost nose to nose, the enemy broke through a portion of Company H's assault formation. As soon as that happened, even more Viet Cong fire began to fall directly on Company F and Company G. Both companies were vulnerable due to the fact that they were fighting in the flatter rice and manioc fields and in the nearby undergrowth. For everyone in the lowland area, that meant they were being fired down on from both flanks of Lieutenant Colonel Utter's maneuvering battalion. Instantly, there were no safe, covered places left for anyone to hide; taking cover from the enemy rifle fire on one side of a dike exposed your back to machine-gun fire from the other side of the valley.

First Lieutenant James Lau reacted immediately to the break in his company by gathering up all the loose Marines he could find in his command group. He added them to those who had been forced back by the ferocious enemy assault and charged back up over the top of the hill. His quick, decisive action drove the enemy from their firing positions and saved the lives of dozens of the Marines of Company F and Company G.

During all the tumult, Lieutenant Colonel Utter could easily see that he had to intervene in some fashion to influence the action. Since he personally had no reserve company, only his H & S Company Marines, he had to be creative. First, at 1635, he sent the 1st Platoon of Company H, which had just returned from guarding the damaged helicopter—the CH-34 had been repaired and flown away—to help Company F get some control of their situation. The task for those Company H Marines was to break the deadlock on the left by driving the enemy back far enough to "unpin" the men of Company F's 3d Platoon and the left portion of the 1st Platoon. This they were able to do after a period of solid contact and heavy fighting. Also, the battalion commander made another move, a move that must be credited for the survival of Company F.

Lieutenant Colonel Utter sent for Capt. Martin O'Connor and told him to scrape up as many Marines as he could find and take them out to Company F to deliver ammunition and return to the battalion area with as many of the company wounded as could be brought back. The H & S Company 81mm mortar platoon had, by that time on D day, fired all of its available ammunition in support of the rifle companies. With nothing left to shoot, the Marine mortarmen volunteered to go forward with ammunition for Company F and to move the wounded to the rear.

By that time, Company F and Company G had been heavily engaged for three hours and twenty minutes. Everyone in those companies was scrounging ammunition and grenades from the cartridge belts and grenade pouches of the dead and wounded. Some Marines in each company were busy learning how to fire the Russian AK-47 rifles taken from dead enemy soldiers, most of whom were lying where they fell. Two of the 12.7mm heavy machine guns had been captured by a direct assault, led by Pvt. Gary Rood, in the area of the Company F right flank. Private Rood and the other Marines there had shot them dry against their previous owners. Efforts by the Viet Cong to maneuver around the right edge of Company F in order to surround it and to drive a wedge between the company and Bill Seymour's Company G had been driven back by use of those NVA machine guns. The situation was not a favorable one. I chose to issue the command, "Fix bayonets," as ammunition ran desperately short. Company F had neither the combat power to move forward in its widely spread formation, nor did it have the flexibility of movement to consolidate for further action. The wounded Marines could not be abandoned, and they had to be moved before any maneuver, in any direction, would be possible.

At the moment when Captain O'Connor arrived in the area of Company F, the enemy had just slackened his fire. Captain O'Connor and his men were fortunate to be able to move about gathering the wounded Marines without being heavily fired on from the hillside to the north. Just before he arrived, there had been another short downpour of 12.7mm fire, some of which had impacted among the members of the command group without hitting anyone. It was close though. One round had passed between the thumb and forefinger of First Sergeant Mills as he lay next to the company radio operator and another had hit an abandoned flak jacket lying nearby. The enemy evidently wanted to illustrate for the Marines that they were not going to be leaving any time soon. But with the fire slackening, Captain O'Connor and his volunteers were quick to get in and get out again before heavy firing resumed. They dropped off the ammunition boxes and cases of grenades, then dashed forward to the wounded who had been concentrated, as much as had been possible, during the fighting. Wherever possible, the wounded men had been moved into defilade in ditches or other low places where they would be partially sheltered from the enemy fire.

Once Captain O'Connor's men had the wounded under control, they moved westward toward the battalion command group. To move the more seriously injured Marines they would drop a poncho on the ground, lay the Marine on the poncho, and cross two corners of the cloth across the man's chest, drawing it tight under his armpits. The wounded man was then dragged by two of the mortarmen across the wet, muddy, paddy field toward safety. For the men who were being dragged it was obviously a painful journey, but there was no way that anyone, other than the most severely wounded men, could be carried back to the battalion. Speed was essential if the wounded or those who had come to save them were to survive. The feet and legs of the wounded men trailing behind as they were dragged looked much like the blanket-wrapped travois that Sioux Indians pulled behind their ponies as they moved their belongings from one camp to another.

At 1845, Lieutenant Colonel Utter decided to consolidate his battalion and utilize supporting arms to hammer the enemy forces facing his command. By that time, all but the superficially injured, the walking wounded, had been recovered. There were still dead Marines on the ground among the riflemen of the forward companies, but the colonel reached the painful decision that the bodies must be left for later recovery. He ordered the rifle companies to move back toward the command group and to be prepared to establish a night defensive perimeter when they arrived.

Leaving Marines behind, dead or wounded, is only done when there is no other choice. Marines seldom, if ever, discuss the possibility of leaving anyone behind, ever. The orders were clear, and the need to leave some dead men for later recovery was obvious, but the Marines of Company F were hurt and angry when they were ordered to pull back. In fact, some of them openly cursed me, cursed 2/7, and cursed the fates, when I moved from position to position ordering them to move back toward the rest of the 2/7 positions. Some ignored the order and, using their ponchos in the same way as the men who came forward with Captain O'Connor had moved the wounded, they dragged bodies along with us as we withdrew. One of the most terrible memories from the dying light of that evening is the sight of one young dead Marine who lost his pants as his corpse was dragged back. His wet, blood-soaked, naked, lower body bumped and bounced obscenely as he made his last rough journey across the rice paddy with his comrades of Company F pulling him like a sack of rice.

By 1930 on D day, the battalion had all of its units back under control and a perimeter established. Lieutenant Colonel Utter placed Company F along a paddy dike with a right-angle bend, and the eighty-three remaining effective Marines flopped themselves down in the mud to spend the night awaiting a possible assault by the tough enemy battalions they had been fighting for many hours. Firing by the enemy continued, and every helicopter that came near was driven off by the volume of tracers directed skyward. Despite numerous attempts by pilots of the CH-34 helicopters who tried to come to our aid, the wounded of 2/7 still could not be evacuated.

Down in all three rifle companies, the commanders went from man to man along their defensive positions to reassure their Marines that they were still part of a tough and capable outfit. In Company F, it was even more than that. As the colonel had stated when I reported my return to him at the ditch where he had his command group, "This is your chance to get to know who your Marines are." Prior to that slow crawl from firing position to firing position, most of those Marines and I had never met. While we had never even seen each other before, during the fourth of March 1966, those men and I had shared a day of terror, a day of numbing frustration, and a day that ended with a wrenching, soul-destroying sorrow when we had to leave Marines behind, dead, and so very alone in the dark paddies.

At 2115, the battalion landing zone was still too hot for evacuation of the wounded. The colonel pounded the enemy, using every supporting arm at his disposal to make them pay a price for holding their positions. At 2200, a flare ship, a twin-engine C-47 type aircraft, known as "Basketball," arrived on station. Basketball began to turn the night into day with a steady procession of parachute flares that hung over the valley. The constant light gave assurance to the defending Marines that they would be able to see the Viet Cong coming if an attack was delivered into our lines. Despite the light, the enemy continued to fire on us, and bullets snapped through the bushes and cracked overhead all night long. Fire was returned by every unit, often more as a morale booster than an attempt to inflict casualties on the enemy. In Company F, the 60mm mortar section and the company machine gunners took great delight in pounding away at suspected Viet Cong positions whenever a muzzle flash was spotted.

It was not until 2230 on D day that 2/7 could finally begin a steady series of medical evacuations. But even with the flares from Basketball lighting up the area, the enemy engaged every helicopter that arrived and departed with wounded Marines. On several occasions, it was obvious that the enemy machine guns found their targets, as a CH-34 was seen to shed sparks as the bullets hit the engine or some other metal part. Despite all the Viet Cong fire directed at the 2/7 defensive perimeter and at the landing zone, the helicopters kept coming. All night long the artillery kept firing protectively, the flares kept falling, and the evacuations continued steadily until 0530, when the last wounded Marine had been lifted out of the LZ.

On the morning of D plus one, 5 March, resupply helicopters were slated to arrive with much needed ammunition of all types. Instead, the first aircraft to land contained newsmen and cameramen. Since the LZ was right in the middle of the Company F perimeter, those outsiders leaped out of the helicopter and immediately got directly into my face. As I tried to avoid them, I noticed that one of the cameramen was pulling the ponchos off the dead Marines who had been dragged in when the company came back to the battalion perimeter. Those Marine casualties had not been evacuated because they were dead and the living had priority; the dead are given the priority rating "routine." Helicopter crews are not asked to risk their lives for routine evacuations.

As I watched, the cameraman reached down and snatched off the protective ponchos. He stepped back to film the eight dead faces. A violent rage ripped through us all at the thought that he would do such a thing. Physical violence followed within seconds, and both the cameraman and his camera were harmed. Death threats followed, issued directly by myself, at the top of his lungs by First Sergeant Mills, and with deadly intent by both of my radio operators. The incident could have quickly been followed by the murder of the cameraman had not Lieutenant Colonel Utter arrived. His hatred for the indignity being done to his dead Marines was obvious, but he held his blazing temper and within seconds had separated the un-hurt newsmen and cameramen from the out-of-control Company F command group. The colonel never mentioned the incident in any later conversation, but had he not stepped in when he did, he clearly knew that it would have been over, forever, for that cameraman.

Later during the war, farther to the north, a cameraman took close-up photos of a dead Marine being evacuated from a battle in the DMZ. His body lay, with others, on top of a tank. The mother of that dead Marine saw her son's face on national television before the paperwork had been completed in the personnel system that would result in the normal casualty call to her home. The actions of the cameraman on 5 March 1966 were disgusting, and he will always be remembered by those who saw him reaching down to uncover those dead faces, as a true representative of the scum of the earth.

In the very early hours of D plus one, Task Force Delta had ordered that 2/7 remain in its position as a blocking force while other battalions maneuvered. Both 3/1 and 2/4, the latter having been rooted out of the defensive positions at Chu Lai that they had taken over, were on the move, and we were to sit still and block for them. It was hoped that the major Viet Cong units that had been fighting so hard against 2/7 could be pinched out and brought to battle by the task force maneuvers. For 2/7 it would provide time to recover, distribute ammunition, and reorganize.

At 0915 in the morning on D plus one, the battalion received official notification that powers far above had determined that the fight was to be honored with an official name. The name, Operation Utah, was dutifully entered into the list of important events by the clerk in the operations section who was responsible for the command diary.

From the battalion perimeter on D plus one, each company was allowed to send elements forward to perform battlefield salvage and to recover dead Marines. Each maneuvering unit was carefully instructed that before any corpse was moved it must first be turned over, using wires or ropes, to check for booby traps. It was, already in 1966, evident that we were fighting an enemy who would stop at nothing to create more American casualties. Not even the dead were considered safe to handle if the enemy had possessed their remains for any length of time. At 1015, Company G swept its area of operation from the previous day, had a minor firefight, and recovered its dead. At 1100, Company H did the same, sweeping to the south in its area of D day operations and having minor contact with enemy snipers.

At 1400 on D plus one, Company F conducted a sweep to the northeast to work through the area of the D day fighting. Debris was abundant, flak jackets, helmets, cartridge belts, canteens, and spent cartridges scattered everywhere. The enemy had been there in force during the night, as evidenced by the removal of the many Viet Cong dead who had been there the previous afternoon. A total of forty-six dead enemy fighting men was located in one cave, but the majority of the 250 plus estimated enemy bodies had been taken from the field. The Viet Cong were almost always efficient in that matter, and they were frequently able to conceal the effects of our firepower by hiding both their dead and their wounded. Because those far away in Washington were increasingly measuring the progress in the Republic of Vietnam by body count, the enemy's ability to disguise his losses increased everyone's frustration. The dead Company F Marines were recovered, and two Viet Cong were killed during the sweep. The night of D plus one passed without enemy contact.

On 6 March, D plus two, the battalion was ordered to move from its location near Chau Ngai (4) and to relieve 2/4 in another blocking position. That was accomplished by 1215 when Company F, which was designated as the rear guard of the battalion tactical column, arrived at the assigned location. Other than one sniper round which did not hit anyone, there was no Viet Cong reaction to the battalion's movement. The lack of enemy contact continued into the evening, and the night of D plus two passed without contact.

On the morning of D plus three, 7 March, 2/7 was ordered to conduct search-and-destroy operations within the Task Force fire coordination line. Each of the three rifle companies was assigned a sector within one thousand meters of the command post. The maneuvers produced twelve VCS, some military clothing, some medical supplies, and a land mine. There was no significant contact in any of the sectors. At 1200, the battalion was to conduct a search-and-destroy operation to the east astride a small dirt road. The movement was to be conducted jointly with the ARVN forces north of the battalion. The ARVN units were going to be moving in the same direction, and it was hoped that the Viet Cong could be flushed out and killed during this maneuver. At 1200, the leading elements of 2/7 crossed the initial point and began the move to the east with Company F on the left and Company G on the right. The two rifle companies were to cover a one-thousand-meter frontage astride the road, with Company F being responsible for the road. Total strength of the two rifle companies when they departed from the initial point was 4 officers and 179 men. This was in sharp contrast to the complement of 12 officers and 424 men that two full-strength rifle companies would have had to do the job. No enemy contact was made during D plus three, and at 1710 a truck convoy began transporting 2/7 back to the Chu Lai enclave.

During Operation Utah, the 2d Battalion, 7th Marines and its attached support units suffered a loss of forty-four men killed in action and one man who died of his wounds. A total of 120 men were wounded, 79 of whom had to be evacuated out of the Republic of Vietnam for treatment. The brutal cost of 165 men was almost 25 percent of the entire force deployed by 2/7 on D day. There are military texts that state flatly that no infantry unit can be counted on to continue fighting when it has sustained more than 15 percent casualties, but the men who wrote such nonsense had not seen Lieutenant Colonel Utter's Marines pick themselves up and continue—no matter the adversity. For the second time in four months, 2/7 had sustained a brutal casualty rate, yet regardless of the losses, the battalion had continued to fight on in a cohesive and powerful manner. That kind of performance will stand forever as proof of the superior leadership by Lt. Col. Leon Utter.

In his commander's analysis in the Operation Utah after-action report, Lieutenant Colonel Utter strongly suggested that a joint field commander was essential if Marines and

ARVN units were going to maneuver together. He pointed out that the 2/7 assault of D day took the pressure off the ARVN command as they desired, but when the enemy reacted violently and nearly engulfed the 2/7 left flank, there was no supportive movement by the ARVN. He also noted that this failure was one that included the violation of one of the most sacrosanct principles of war, that of unity of command.

The after-action report also returned to comment strongly on the steady erosion of the battalion's combat power through assignment of downed helicopter security and artillery fire-support-site security missions. The colonel was forceful in pointing out to the higher headquarters that when his battalion was most heavily engaged with major elements of a powerful enemy force, locked into a life-or-death struggle, one of his companies was assigned elsewhere and a full 25 percent of his available riflemen, the fighting men in the field, were away from their units guarding helicopters. The description of an infantry battalion fighting with "hands tied" should have galvanized those who read Lieutenant Colonel Utter's words. Alas, no one at any level ever appeared to notice the blatant errors being perpetuated. Operation Utah was a horror show, one that would have been far less costly had 2/7 been allowed to retain the tools needed to fight its way out of trouble.

Humor can find its way into any aspect of combat, and Operation Utah was no exception. Of course, the reader must understand that the humor of those who see death and mutilation on a daily basis is often very macabre. Once the battalion had returned to its normal portion of the Chu Lai enclave, I sought out my personal gear, intending to put on some dry socks and some "cleaner" clothing from my miserable stock. When I went to get the things I wanted, I learned that all my gear had been collected by the battalion supply officer, 1st Lt. Jerry Cornelius.

I went to battalion supply, ready to kill the supply officer. When I roared into Cornelius's tent, I found him soaking a very swollen and inflamed foot in a huge pot of hot water. He had failed to follow the most simple command in a war, the one that tells everyone to look into their boots before putting them on! When I shouted at him for gathering my gear, he looked up, his face paled, and he said, "Shit, Captain. They told me you got your ass killed on D day, how the hell was I to know you were coming back?" Suddenly, we both laughed at the situation, and he reached out to hug me. Lieutenant Cornelius, who had been bitten by a bamboo viper that had chosen to stop by the supply area to establish residence in his size-12 boot, had gathered up my gear because he had been told by two Marines that I had been killed in action on 4 March. Since he'd never heard anything to refute that, he had collected my effects in preparation for stripping out the personal items, that would be sent to my next of kin, from the military items, that would stay in the Republic of Vietnam.

At the conclusion of Operation Utah, it was evident that everyone had learned a great deal from the bad experiences of Operation Harvest Moon. Our casualties were tracked when they left 2/7. We did not have to spend days wondering where various Marines had been sent when they were evacuated from the field. As a typical example, Sgt. John Condon of Company F had scoured the medical facilities and the Graves Registration, learning in the process the status of all of the members of the company who had been brought out during the fighting. That young NCO was typical in that he, and many like him, took this task upon himself, ran it with vigor, and provided a perfect accounting of who had gone where and in what condition. Sergeant Condon later qualified for the Naval Academy, fell in love with twelve-hundred-pound propulsion systems, graduated to a commission in the navy instead of the Marine Corps, and retired from that service after a distinguished career.

Knowing where the casualties had gone was a new experience for the personnel people of 2/7. However, it did not help much in getting the battalion back up to strength. Replacements arrived, but not in numbers sufficient to rebuild the rifle companies to operational strength. For the rest of our tour in the Republic of Vietnam, being shorthanded in the rifle companies was just the way it was going to be, and bitching would not help.

# 14

# THE DANCES OF SPRING 1966

In March, April, and May of 1966, the end of the combat tour for the original Marines of BLT 2/7, those who had landed in July of 1965, began to be visible in the far distance. Those who remained with the battalion actually began to expect that they might survive to rotate back to the United States. Many quietly believed that if things would go even remotely right, they would be able to make it to June, the month when everyone who came to Vietnam with RLT 7 in 1965 was slated to go home. In part, that optimistic viewpoint was based on the knowledge that all of our experiences had combined to make it very much more likely that we would be survivors. Survivors make very good decisions under fire and carefully avoid the sort of rookie mistakes that can get an infantryman killed. Combat had been both a frightening and a meaningful learning experience for all of us who remained alive, fit, and present for duty.

Of course, just because it was the spring of 1966, no one decided that we were home free. We were often reminded, in the most horrible manner, that without the slightest warning, both combat-experienced old hands and neophytes could, and did, get killed or grievously maimed. Death could arrive at any time, and it could happen anywhere. Your number might just be up, and it would be time to die or be butchered by one of those to-whom-it-may-concern munitions. Long abandoned and unmapped land mines, simple little booby traps, and the unexpected arrival of mortar or artillery projectiles could suddenly steal anyone's life or shred their limbs—with no warning.

With the arrival of the spring of 1966, there began to be some noticeable alterations in the overall attitude of the 2/7 Marines. Wisecracks by the troops began to have a hard and bitter, cynical edge. The Marines were obviously far less positive about their service in the Republic of Vietnam. Jokes we had enjoyed like the sign "Beat VC, Class of 1966" on the water tank seemed to be far less funny. Winning seemed unlikely. The ever-present daily bitching by the enlisted men, and the officers as well, began to reflect an implied understanding of the futility of our mission; even the most enthusiastic members of the battalion had grown both sadder and more cynical because they had met reality head-on. All of the original Marines of 2/7 had been greatly sobered by what they had endured since July 1965. The 2/7 Marines had already been deployed to combat long enough to be somewhat inured to the danger there when frightful events like the Watts riots took place at home. None of them had ever seen or marched in an antiwar demonstration. Most of them probably did not even know anyone who had. Yet, the fact that such things were happening at home was known to them, and their sotto voce commentary on life in the Corps reflected that knowledge.

By the late spring of 1966, a few of the Marines were concerned enough to openly question the future of the war. All sorts of disgusting and horrible things were happening at home, supposedly because of the war. The changes and the well-reported, noisy unrest in America was confusing to us all. The situation caused Marines to ask some very serious, very penetrating questions of their officers and their SNCO leaders. Most of their leaders were ill equipped to answer those questions because, from a distance of eight thousand miles, not one of us could comprehend the seditious evils being plotted and carried out at home. Our ignorance was a fortunate thing. Our morale would have plummeted had we known even a fraction of what was to befall the country.

Everywhere in the battalion, helmet covers and flak jackets

began to show slogans. A popular one was, "You and me God, Blood Type O+." Another favorite was some version of "Seventy-three days and a Wake-up!" This type of commentary, and other more foul, specific, vulgar remarks painted on both helmets and flak jackets, were the not-so-subtle means used by the troops to let their commanders know that they were no longer very positive about their lives in the Republic of Vietnam. That mild sort of commentary was in no way similar to the gibberish and drivel being spouted by the ignorant, antiwar mobs at home in the United States. It was, instead, the result of the 2/7 Marines carefully considering life in combat and knowing in their hearts that they had been illtreated, overworked, and asked to die—all to no real purpose. Taking part in infantry combat never has been an easy way to live, and it never will be. The Marines of 2/7 understood that fact, and they could accept the anguish with some pride, as long as they felt that their sacrifices were appreciated. When the perception of their being appreciated was steadily altered, it eventually became clear to the infantrymen that even if a major engagement was declared a "win" by the newsmen or the higher headquarters, nothing was ever going to change for the better at their level. Already, it was clear to the troops that a real win—of any kind—was never in the cards.

Down in the rifle squads, our battalion was melting away, and it was slowly being replaced by newcomers—strangers. The battalion was steadily losing Marines killed or wounded, a painful attrition that went on day after day after day. The casualties were often not replaced for weeks. From far above us in the chain of command, the pressure was on for more and grander reports filled with the statistics of the meaningless body count. As a concept, the number of enemy bodies found and reported to Washington after a fight proved nothing and stood for nothing of substance. It had no positive impact whatever on the lives led by the Marines and corpsmen who were doing the fighting on the ground. Every single fighting man, from the newest private to the battalion commander, knew that if a 2/7 rifle company had a firefight and killed eight Viet Cong, the final number cataloged in Washington and trumpeted to the press would probably contain a body count of forty-five to fifty enemy soldiers. The higher the head-quarters, the greater the lie.

Counting enemy bodies was an exercise that held value only for swivel-chair-bound folks swapping stories in our na-tion's capital. The point that must be understood is that it was our Marine bodies that were important to us, and the count of Marine dead bodies was growing far too high for us to ignore. No slogan-jabbering whiz kid could convince the combat-experienced Marines of 2/7 that *any* kind of "exchange ratio"—an often-used nonsense term that spoke of trading our dead bodies for dead Viet Cong bodies—had anything to do with reality.

After Operation Utah, no one in the battalion could deny that, through the use of air and artillery, coupled with effec-tive infantry maneuvering, a Marine infantry force could chase the Viet Cong or the North Vietnamese Army units off the battlefield. However, everyone also had learned, the very hardest of hard ways, that our elusive enemy could just melt silently away into the jungle or into Laos and return at a later time, a time of his choosing, to kill more of us. Land was cleared of the enemy soldiers, and then it was abandoned so that the Viet Cong and their leaders from the north could re-turn to live there again.

Of course, for every infantry Marine there always existed the additional, very real possibility that he would not die on a major operation. He could be killed or wounded while pulling one of the essential, day or night, local security missions. Death could come at night on an ambush patrol or while pulling duty on a listening post out in front of the defensive perimeter. During daylight hours, a sniper could down a man as he walked the defensive wire or while he stopped to take a piss next to a bush. The experienced, original 2/7 Marines were very confident of their own ability to perform under fire, but they were increasingly aware of the odds stacked against them. In their pride, those "salty" men swaggered a bit. They would rag the newcomers and tease them. But they also took care of them and tried to teach them all that they had learned in eight months or more of combat. Anyone who arrived demonstrating the least hint of a developing hotdog attitude was quickly disabused of that approach to life by those who recounted to them the tales of the operational bloodbaths Harvest Moon and Utah.

At that point in our combat tour, we were overjoyed to see the arrival in the Republic of Vietnam of more Marine infantrymen. The 5th Marine Regiment entered the Chu Lai enclave and was established to the north of 2/7. The nearest unit of the 5th Marines was dug in on a hill mass roughly eight hundred meters across rice-paddy land to the north of a small rise known as Hill 49. That hill was the right flank anchor point of the 2/7 line. Prior to the arrival of the 5th Marines, 2/7 had been responsible for the paddy land and had habitually covered that open area at night with listening posts and ambushes. In daylight hours, the fields were always under observation by Marines on Hill 49 who could watch the rice farmers at work for any sign of Viet Cong interference. The 5th Marines added their strength to an expanded portion of the defensive perimeter that was established inland from the inhabited portion of the Chu Lai enclave. They also had units dug in along the higher ground inland and to the north from the construction area containing the contractors of RMK-BRJ, the Seabees, and everyone else involved with the new airfield being built for Chu Lai.

At first, the newly arrived Marines of the 5th Regiment were jumpy, just as the 2/7 Marines had been in 1965. Now and again, their troops were frightened at night, and a few of them chose to fire their weapons in our direction. Incoming fire, whether friendly or enemy, gave us fits. All hands dove for cover. Squads of the 5th Marines had an intramural firefight or two out in the paddy land during the first dark nights, and the men of our battalion watched the tracers snapping back and forth with a bit of smugness. Being "old hands," the 2/7 Marines pointed out condescendingly to anyone who would listen, that the tracers were obviously all American made. At least half of the tracers streaking across the paddy were the wrong color to make what was happening into a real firefight. The tracers seen from Hill 49 did not match the streaks of fire left behind by the ammunition used by the Viet Cong. It did not take long for the 5th Marine commanders to get control of their few shaky-handed riflemen, and the firing toward the 2/7 positions stopped sending us tumbling down into our fighting holes. As the 2/7 Marines had discovered in Qui Nhon, the newly arrived infantrymen found out that the night terrors faded and security became something like a second skin that everyone had to wear if he wanted to live to see his home again.

Of course, as the expansion of American involvement in the Republic of Vietnam continued, the battalion avoided boredom by having new developments to contend with in its daily life. After many, many months of separation from the 1st Marine Division, the 7th Marine Regiment was reunited with its parent division. While all three of its infantry regiments were already committed by early 1966, the division commander and his headquarters had been kept out of the Republic of Vietnam because of nitpicky adherence to personnel number constraints imposed on the Marine Corps by the force-structure agreements of 1965 with the government of the Republic of Vietnam. The agreements had been developed during the initial buildup of forces and were quite complex and very restrictive. Once the expanded force levels agreed to for the year 1966 were being met, the 1st Division headquarters arrived in country and was established in the Chu Lai enclave.

At first, the division staff was content to remain busy seeing to its own comfort and establishing its own operational structure. That quiet time did not last long. Senior staffs can be supportive of the fighting units or the staff officers can prove their value to their generals by demonstrating their ability to find fault. The good ones assist, and the other kind spend their time enforcing regulations that are being ignored among the lesser mortals. Unfortunately, the first contacts that 2/7 had with the division staff were formal, frigid, and uniformly hostile. The friendly, helpful attitude of May 1965 had been replaced, as had those who had assisted the battalion during mount-out for war. While, in theory, the battalion should have been protected by the regimental staff, some division staff officers saw fit to just drive into the 2/7 area and begin to meddle—without so much as a courtesy call at the regimental command post.

One incident that had the potential for serious consequences was caused by a simple signboard. At the foot of Hill 49, where the jeep trail to the Company F positions on that hill branched off from the main road, there was a dark green sign. The sign had been hand painted, by a very talented corporal of 2d Platoon, an Eskimo no less, on a stolen chunk of plywood. The board was roughly two feet wide and three feet tall. On the board was a wild looking cartoon, an auburn fox with a long red, lolling tongue and big paws. In one paw, the cartoon fox held the symbol 2/7 in black, and in the other paw he held a Zippo lighter. The lighter-flame was tall and bright. The sign stated, through its symbolism, that this was the road to Company F of the 2d Battalion, 7th Marines. Along the bottom it also stated that the company was commanded by Captain A. Lee, known to the troops as "Captain Zippo." I'd earned the title because, at my direct order, haystacks and other thatch-covered structures were routinely set afire, during search-and-destroy operations. I ordered that to find and destroy hidden enemy explosive munitions. Because several of the haystacks that had been set afire had gone off in high-order explosions, leaving behind some very large craters, the Marines of Company F had taken the message to heart.

One afternoon, as he was passing along the road, a nice, clean, very well fed, prissy major from the division headquarters saw the Company F sign. Evidently, he was infuriated, both personally and professionally, by its presence in the combat zone. Whatever it was that bothered the major, it caused him to act in a risky, very ill-considered and precipitous manner. He had his driver drive the vehicle directly to the hilltop where he jumped from the jeep shouting loudly for the commanding officer to report to him immediately. Looking about, he found himself among what he must have thought to be a group of savages. During the daytime, I had ordered that all of the troops of Company F were to wear minimal clothing—the warm time was returning again to the Republic of Vietnam. We were trying to use the sunshine to dry out the jungle rot from between our toes, in our crotches, and on other parts of our bodies. In addition to being mostly nude, the rail-thin men on the hilltop were engaged in firing rifles, machine guns, antitank rockets, and their pistols at rock targets on a jungle hillside to the west. Unknown to the major, the firing was also in response to my orders and was a normal part of the company routine. The Marines were ridding themselves, through competitive target practice, of ammunition that had been out in the field on combat operations, where it might have been bent, dented, or contaminated with mud and water. It was strict company policy that the troops were to shoot up such ammunition and draw replacement ammunition before returning to the field for operations of any length. In carrying out my orders, training and recreation were being usefully combined at the moment the irate major arrived.

Jumping from his jeep, in his fresh, starched uniform with the shiny boots peeking out from his carefully bloused trousers, the major loudly demanded to know who was in charge. He was so mad he was bellowing. He was rude, he was immediately impolite, and he seemed to be personally hostile to me from the moment he first opened his mouth. When the major found that the short, ugly, bald, and very angry man standing quietly nearby, dressed only in a pair of ripped off trousers, with a cap jammed on the back of his head—a pistol in a shoulder holster on his bare chest—was the commanding officer, he became nearly apoplectic. He demanded that the "unauthorized" firing cease and wanted to know if anyone present was aware that Company F was in direct violation of division order 4400 something or other. From his comments, it seemed that the order must be one having to do with signs, their size, and the printing that goes on them. Since there was not one single person in the entire world that anyone on Hill 49 could even dream of who might give the slightest damn about division order 4400 something or other, the major was answered with a simple, rather bored

"No." The major then loudly told the assembled Marines that the field sign for a rifle company must be no more than eighteen inches long and no more than twelve inches high. Further, he rudely pointed out that these signs could only contain the company letter designation, the number of the battalion, and the number of the regiment. At first, no one responded in any way.

After an extended series of nasty remarks, remarks that cast Company F in rather poor light, the major's tirade wound down, and he appeared to have reached some sort of conclusion. He stood almost on top of me using the opportunity for some sort of weird, unwinnable power struggle. He insulted me on a personal basis and ordered in a hard cold voice that I must have the sign removed immediately or he would see that I was summarily relieved of duty as the company commander. The major seemed, for reasons unknown, to think that he had the necessary authority to make that threat. Seeing no real reason to argue the point with him I ordered the well-armed Company F Marines, who were gathering steadily closer in a mildly menacing fashion, to clear their weapons, to step back, and to allow the major to leave our area alive. The danger of his being shot to ribbons by pissed-off Marines having come suddenly evident to him, the major calmed down momentarily. I suggested quietly that he had erred gravely in coming up Hill 49. Pointing out that at that moment I had on the hill 137 Marines with weapons and lots of ammunition, I suggested, using the third person to refer to him at all times, that the major should go somewhere and get himself 137 folks with guns. Then we could play, "winner take all" to see about "my fucking sign!" He seemed startled and almost undone by the thought of having a firefight with Company F over the sign. Blanching, he seemed to lack an answer, and he stood speechless for several moments.

Seeing that he was confused, I then added that my Marines had made the sign as a present for me and that I had no intention of taking it down on that particular afternoon, or on any other afternoon—for anyone, including him. Appearing to realize that he was not doing well, the major recovered some of his bluster, cursed me viciously, and climbed into his jeep to leave. As soon as the major went down the jeep trail I called Lieutenant Colonel Utter on the landline. In describing the event, I remarked to my commanding officer that the division major had not sounded sane or in full control of himself when he shouted his final obscenities at me and jumped back into his jeep.

Once off the top of Hill 49—alive—the silly major from the division staff made another terrible mistake. He not only drove to Lieutenant Colonel Utter's location to order the colonel to relieve me of command, he had his driver ignore an armed Marine rifleman who was manning the dismount point outside the 2/7 command post. At the dismount point all vehicles are supposed to stop, the people in them are expected to dismount and proceed on foot to anyplace they need to go within the command post. The major's jeep swept up to the colonel's living tent, trailed by an irate Marine corporal carrying his M-14 rifle loaded, locked, and shouldered—he was ready to fire on the intruder. At the door of the tent, the major was met by a short barrel of a man wearing only torn-off trousers and a pistol in a shoulder holster. Here was our boss, backing one of his own, 100 percent, against all comers, whomever they might be representing. Not a moment passed before Lieutenant Colonel Utter identified himself and suggested to the major that in the nearby hills he had, present for duty, 967 men of 2/7 with guns. The colonel also noted that, if the major wished, he could go get himself 967 other folks with guns for the purpose of playing, "winner take all." With his hard twang at the fore the colonel ordered the major to get out of his command post and to never, ever return on pain of being shot on sight by the dismount guard. Once again, Lieutenant Colonel Utter proved that loyalty downward was his stock in trade. He hated to have anyone messing with his Marines!

In the spring of 1966, the battalion had another silly season to contend with in its daily life. In 1965, everyone had laughed when we were ordered, from on high, to "Challenge, illuminate, identify, and only fire when fired upon!" At the rifle company level, that had translated directly into a more realistic, "Kill everything that moves, and we will sort it out in the morning!" Reality required that the Marines in the fox-holes protect themselves, and they were going to be allowed to do so by rational leaders who wanted them to be alive in the morning. As anyone could see, Vietnam was primarily an agrarian society, one without electric lights, running water, or roads. Anyone who was out and about in the countryside after dark was not a farmer living his normal life. Farmers in such societies go to bed with the sun and rise with the sun. Those Vietnamese that the Marines might find moving here and there in the bush at night were, de facto, bad guys. But, common sense be damned, with the arrival of more high headquarters, we again experienced a number of silly inputs.

The most humorous of all the odd and unusual orders received by 2/7 was a very serious missive from on high, forwarded down to all hands, that said, "Dark of the moon. Go to 75 percent alert!" This was a well-meant effort by some high-level staff weenie to cause the infantry to be more prepared for attack than they would have been without his proving his value to the general by taking an action. Of course, the wide defensive frontages that spread the riflemen painfully thin on the ground and the long experience of the 2/7 Marines with night defensive security made the order a fatuous joke. Each of the infantrymen on watch at night had to share only a two-man foxhole, a foxhole that was also his home. The infantry-man lived deep in the muddy ground, sharing his joyless space with another bone-tired Marine. Standard practice at night was for every hole to have one man awake and one man asleep, alternating throughout the night. The Marines would swap back and forth in order to ensure that the man who was up on watch was as alert as his fatigue permitted.

A direct, very disrespectful response to the "75 percent alert" order was suggested, but the response was not sent up the chain of command. Lieutenant Colonel Utter was in agreement with the remark, "What the goddamn hell is 75 percent of two tired Marines in a hole?" But, he made sure that the message proposed by Company F was not sent up the chain to annoy and upset the "busy" division headquarters staff.

It was a joyful event in the spring of 1966 when the 2/7 Marines got some new clothing. A new utility uniform of dark green cloth arrived. It had big patch pockets on the jacket and the trousers had big thigh-level pockets of the type known in the hiker's world as cargo pockets. Anything was preferable to the torn and ripped remains of the disgusting cotton-sateen utility uniforms that had been rotting off our backs since July 1965. Of course, the unit of issue (a formal order setting out who gets issued what) sent forth from above was *three full sets* of the uniforms to the headquarters Marines at division and two jackets with one pair of trousers, to the infantrymen. Typical: unfair and stupid! The infantrymen needed the trousers to keep their butts covered. Yet, the inequity of such a distribution hardly caused any comment at all. The infantry Marines fully expected that they would get screwed over from above; they had that experience with disappointing frequency.

The new uniforms were a great improvement over the lousy material used for the old cotton-sateen clothing. Everyone was pleased with the pockets, and the mere fact that the uniforms had arrived made for a tremendous morale boost. Of course, there was one drawback. The trousers for the new utility uniform were subject, like the cotton-sateen trousers, to sudden failure in the crotch. A large stride made across a wide ditch or up a slope could create a tear. For the second time during the 2/7 tour of combat, Marines could be seen using communications wire to stitch closed the crotches of their trousers. The failures always seemed to occur at the most inopportune moments, and it was not unusual to see a large number of Marines in the field on an operation uncomfortably displaying their manhood for the enemy, or anyone else, to view.

Along with new uniforms came the news that the supply elements now had boots for issue. That was wonderful news! There was even a selection of footwear. The supply folks had available both the standard Marine Corps leather boots and the specially designed jungle boots. While most of the battalion Marines opted for the jungle boot, generally because of the propaganda about its value in the field, a few wanted only the old leather boots, either because the low arch on the jungle boot was painful for some, or it was just the Marine's simple personal choice. For those with odd, small, or large sizes, there were leather boots that dated from the Korean War. One pair of boots that I saw in size 6-EEEE arrived with clearly stamped manufacturing data printed in white ink inside the boot top: October 1951. I wore them anyway.

Fresh food was also a wonder that came to us in the spring. Fresh rations became available to the battalion, and the mess section was able to discontinue feeding the canned B rations that they had been using to prepare meals in the command-post area. Lieutenant Colonel Utter made sure that all of the company commanders understood that Marines were to be encouraged to make the trip to the battalion mess area as often as possible. He knew full well that a percentage of the troops would rather suffer another day eating field rations than use their energy walking from the perimeter to the chow line and back, but he wanted them to improve their health by eating the fresh food. An odd aspect of the first fresh food was the absence of any meat other than that derived from the slaughter of pigs. Pork chops were available, pork loin was available, pork steaks were available, and hams appeared. There was no chicken. The fact that the Marines were eating fresh food at all was enough to obviate any complaint, but it was odd that no beef or chicken appeared in the field until a month or more after the first fresh meals brightened our lives.

Replacements were arriving from the United States in dribs and drabs, and the battalion strength began to rise slightly. Even with the new Marines, and with the return of some of the wounded from Harvest Moon and Utah, there were not enough men available in 2/7 to let the battalion even approach its Table of Organization strength. The rifle companies would occasionally bulge to more than 150 men. However, that level of strength was not sustainable. Losses to combat and noncombat injuries quickly drove the rifle company strength back below the 150-man figure, and on occasion the rifle company commanders could only muster 120 to 125 Marines.

New men were always integrated into their assignments with the help of the old hands. It was the colonel's battalion policy that a new man was not to stand night security watches in a foxhole with another new arrival. Every new Marine was trained by experienced men who were to get him past his night terrors. The battalion commander hoped that pairing up the new men with old hands would help settle the new guys down to be productive members of 2/7. He wanted them to learn quickly as much as possible about how the war was being fought so that they would have as good a chance of survival as possible.

It is always very sad when things occur that should never have happened. One newly arrived Marine was killed the morning after he arrived. When he arrived he was assigned to bunk with a corporal who had been promoted to that rank for his performance as a lance corporal squad leader under fire. The corporal took charge of the man and tried to teach him as much as he could about survival on the defensive perimeter. For the first night, the platoon sergeant placed the new man in a foxhole with the corporal and a third man, an experienced private first class. The new man never had to spend one minute alone on watch his first night. At dawn, acting without saying a word, he stood up from his night position and walked away. He ignored the shouts of the other Marines to come back to the foxhole. The Marine went forward to the tactical wire, walking fully erect, and stopped to take a piss. He was a stationary target for just a moment, then from the dark jungle across the rice paddy came a dozen shots of automatic-rifle fire. The new Marine was hit dead center in the chest by at least two rounds and was dead before his agonized squad leader could crawl to where he lay. By going forward in the morning light, he had chosen to disobey the instructions he had been given, and to ignore both a warning and a direct order from the corporal with whom he had shared the night defensive foxhole. Why he flouted both orders and common sense will forever be unknown.

Integrating new men into the rifle squads of the battalion took place every day, but it was not always easy. The old hands were always worried when they had to take new men out into the nearby jungle for a night ambush or to establish listening posts. Of course, there was no other way for the new men to learn, but that fact did not make it any easier. Night work in the jungle is always very dangerous, and the ambush sites were no place for slow learners. In one sad instance, a new man, taking part in a Company F night ambush, became disoriented. He silently stood up, left his rear security position, circled around, and came striding directly along the trail into the open end of the designated ambush kill zone. His sudden arrival in the kill zone triggered the ambush and the young Marine was killed instantly when the firing started. Of course, the new Marine had no intention of causing his fellow squad members to fire on him, nor did they have any idea that it was another Marine out in front of their rifle muzzles. As tragic as this incident was, the reaction of the squad leader and his men to the sudden arrival in the dark of the new man in the place where a Viet Cong unit was expected could not be faulted. The ambush leader was bitterly saddened by the event. But, in support of his actions, that nineteen-year-old squad leader carried on his shoulders the mandate of life-and-death responsibility for the lives of the other eight men in his squad and the three attached machine gunners. Those Marines had followed their orders. Well disciplined, they had sat tight, silently waiting to spring their ambush on the Viet Cong. The squad leader had no acceptable choice. The man who came striding through the dark into the kill zone could have been the point of a fifty-man enemy force. Hesitation could have meant death to every Marine in his squad. The ambush reacted as planned; the result was another tragedy in the lives of the 2/7 Marines.

During March 1966, the two-week period after Operation Utah, which was completed on the seventh, was spent in relative quiet. The battalion conducted its normal security patrolling, and all of the other security activities continued around the clock. As new men arrived and some of the wounded returned from treatment, it was obvious that it would not be long before 2/7 was ordered out on another operation. The tempo of our operations resumed and continued at a steady pace.

## Operation Indiana—D day, 28 March 1966

The operational concept for Operation Indiana was briefed to the commanding officer of 2/7 and his operations officer at 1245 on 28 March by the commanding officer of the 7th Marines and his staff. The operation had originally been planned to be a 1/7 operation with very minor 2/7 participation. Initially, the only 2/7 mission was to provide D day escort units to protect the movement of artillery batteries from the Chu Lai enclave to Quang Ngai. This movement actually began fifteen minutes after the briefing started when a reinforced platoon of Company F traveled to Quang Ngai with the lead portion of the 3d Battalion, 11th Marines (3/11). At 1500 on D day, the remainder of Company F provided security for the main body of 3/11 as it moved south from the Chu Lai enclave to the Quang Ngai airfield, where the batteries established firing positions. On arrival, Company F was placed under the operational control of the 7th Marines for the purpose of providing continued security for the artillery units firing from the airfield area.

On 29 March, D plus one for Operation Indiana, the battalion commander was alerted at 0015 that he would be required to attend another briefing at the Quang Ngai airfield at 0630. At that briefing, Lieutenant Colonel Utter was given verbal orders to prepare his battalion for commitment in support of the maneuvering 1/7, which had made a solid contact with the enemy to the north of Quang Ngai City, inland from National Route 1. At 0930, the battalion began a helicopterborne assault into a landing zone near 1/7. Company G secured the landing zone without contact with any Viet Cong elements. The rest of 2/7 poured into the zone without enemy contact, and by 1030 all of 2/7 (less Company F) was established in the field and ready to support 1/7 as it maneuvered. At 1120 on D plus one, Lieutenant Colonel Utter started Company E and Company G moving abreast on a search-and-destroy operation directed to the south toward Quang Ngai City. Supporting armed helicopters spotted movement in a trench line and took the area under fire. Company E flushed out several VCS and fired on them as they ran to the east. At 1710, Company E found an extensive cave and tunnel complex where the men found an American 60mm mortar baseplate, a Chinese mortar sight, and a cache of small-arms ammunition. Company E flushed out two VCS and captured them without a fight. For the night of D plus one, the battalion established a perimeter defense around a small village and conducted local security patrols. The night of D plus one was reasonably quiet, with the calm broken only by the arrival of an 81mm incoming mortar round at 2010 and the impact of another 81mm round at 2033. H & I fires were intensified as a result of the incoming fire, and for the remainder of the night, the battalion was supported by Basketball, the flare-dispensing aircraft. Basketball circled overhead, making night into day, until morning.

On D plus two, 30 March, the battalion ordered Company E to blow up the caves and tunnels it had located. That was initiated at 0700 and was completed without incident. A helicopter-borne lift back to the Chu Lai enclave was ordered by the 7th Marines, and by 1040 the battalion, less Company F, had returned to its normal defensive positions. One rifle company was placed on standby to serve as a rapid-reaction force should Company F have a contact while covering the return of 3/11 to the Chu Lai enclave. By 1500 on D plus two, all elements of 2/7 were back in the Chu Lai enclave where they returned to their assigned defensive perimeter responsibilities.

One of the key aspects of the operation was the consistent use of fully coordinated air and artillery support for every movement. At no time were any vehicular convoys or maneuvering troops conducting movement without immediate availability of air support or artillery fire. Of particular note was the presence overhead, for the first time, of armed helicopters. These were UH-1E Models, Hueys that, when fully loaded with ordnance, had a difficult time getting off the ground. But once those helicopters were in the air, they were a magnificent sight for the infantrymen, who knew that, at last, accurate fire against the enemy could be called down fifteen to twenty meters in front of their own rifle muzzles—fire that would blow the Viet Cong out of their fighting holes.

## Operation Nevada—D day, 12 April 1966

Operation Nevada was a return by elements of the 7th Marines to the area on the Batangan Peninsula where the major battle of 1965, Operation Starlight, had taken place. The intelligence order of battle for the enemy listed a "confirmed" Viet Cong battalion in the area. There were also listed for the area two "probable" Viet Cong battalions and nine "possible" Viet Cong battalions. Those forces were reportedly a mix of regional force and interprovincial force units. The analysts also mentioned that some specialized units of the NVA might be present as well. Those units, deployed as reinforcements, were reportedly concentrated in heavy machine-gun and mortar companies attached to the interprovincial force battalions. As an aside, we also received the unconfirmed report that a secret Viet Cong base where American prisoners were being held was located somewhere in the 2/7 area of operations.

The primary mission of Operation Nevada directed Marine forces to conduct another search-and-destroy operation, a maneuver aimed at the destruction of Viet Cong units in the area and the confiscation or destruction of enemy supplies that were located by the maneuvering units. Almost as an if-you-have-time add-on to the search-and-destroy mission, we were told to search the operational area for the possible secret Viet Cong base. Even the rumor of Americans being held there did not seem to stir the order writers to give that search priority. That was an attitude that concerned us. In 2/7, everyone was highly charged with emotion at the thought of Americans being held in some cage in the jungle.

On D day, 12 April, Company E, by this time commanded

by Capt. Ted Gatchell, was dispatched to the control of the 7th Marines, so once again, Lieutenant Colonel Utter was starting an operation with one maneuver element missing. At 0639, Company F was helicopter lifted from the Chu Lai enclave to a landing zone in the Batangan Peninsula about five kilometers east of National Route 1. Using twenty-two CH-46 helicopters permitted the battalion to move the assault company in one lift. On landing, Company F received no fire, but the assaulting troops did locate some caves that contained a very large rice cache. The assault lift was covered by both armed helicopters and fixed-wing aircraft on station overhead. However, since there was no opposition, there was no need for fire in the landing zone.

In a very short while, by 0915 on D day, the entire helicopter lift was complete. The battalion headquarters, Company G, and Company H all arrived in the landing zone without incident. Immediately after his arrival in the field, the battalion commander dispatched Company G to search the nearby high ground: A number of caves were found, and at 0940, another large cave with a rice cache was located. The regimental operations officer directed that all of the rice be evacuated from the field to Chu Lai. By the time the regimental commander arrived on the scene at 1010 to look at the rice, the amount that had been located was estimated to exceed nine tons.

Since the enemy did not seem at all interested in defending against the movements of the battalion, Lieutenant Colonel Utter ordered that Captain Seymour's Company G and Company F begin moving toward the east. At 1200, Company F captured six VCS. The Company F Marines suspected them to be our enemy because of the fact that they just happened to be carrying a Viet Cong flag. Along with the VCS were thirty-six refugees who requested evacuation out of the area. At 1330, all maneuver toward the east was canceled. We could not move because of the enormity of the task of evacuating the rice found that morning in the caves and the additional rice located during the early afternoon in the first village through which Company G maneuvered. At 1615, the regimental commander again visited the battalion and confirmed his order that all the rice was to be evacuated. Because no further movement was going to be permitted, the battalion spent the night in defensive positions from which aggressive patrolling was conducted. Artillery H & I fires were used on likely Viet Cong occupied sites.

On D plus one, 13 April, Company F was ordered to conduct another helicopter lift to a landing zone to the east on Hill 100. This lift was initiated at 1000, and Hill 100 was taken without casualties. On the hill mass were found a very large number of punji stakes, some antipersonnel mines, and a few booby traps. All of the booby traps were of the most simple variety, and they were easily dismantled by the infantrymen. Just after noon an aerial observer, who had been orbiting overhead in an 0-1 Bird Dog during the helicopter lift, reported that thirty to forty Viet Cong soldiers were moving away to the north, just at the edge of the Company F area of operations. Not long after that report from the air, the enemy moved into an area where they were under direct observation by the Company F command group. An artillery fire mission was called, and the naval gunfire spot team requested a fire mission from the USS *St. Paul*, a cruiser that was visible at sea about three miles off the peninsula. Both fire support agencies responded with alacrity. The artillery fire caused the Viet Cong to change direction and move into a small triangular patch of trees. They did not appear to leave the trees, as they would have come under observation again had they done so. When the naval gunfire began, the fall of shot included both five-inch and eight-inch bombardment munitions. The accuracy attained by the cruiser was amazing. Within twenty minutes the triangular copse of trees was destroyed. There was nothing left to see other than churned earth and tree splinters. Physical examination by ground troops of the impact area was not allowed. However, the almost perfect coverage of the target was a most gratifying sight to the eyes of the Company F riflemen. Those Marines, sitting on our hillside, had a ringside seat for the entire performance, and they cheered as each volley of naval shells arrived to bring death to the Viet Cong.

While Company F was maneuvering on and around Hill 100, the other two rifle companies were engaged in the evacuation of captured rice by helicopter to Chu Lai. At 1530, Company G was ordered to send a platoon to National Route 1 to escort an antitank platoon of Ontos vehicles to the 2/7 area. The theory for the use of the odd, six-gun vehicles was the belief that the six 106mm recoilless rifles mounted externally on their chassis could be effectively used in the creation of very tough, hard-hitting, night defensive positions. With the dryer part of the year a reality at last, wheeled and tracked vehicles could once again be taken to the field and tasked to provide support to maneuvering or defending infantry formations. On the night of D plus one, 2/7 settled into a pair of night perimeters and sent out night defensive patrols and ambushes. There was no contact on the night of D plus one.

On D plus two, 14 April, the battalion was ordered to begin its move toward the east again. Villages and hamlets were to be searched and cleared. A difference in our orders for D plus two was that any rice that was discovered was to be turned over to the ARVN for collection and evacuation. It was a joyful change for the infantrymen, who were sick to death of hauling bags of rice out of caves or out from under houses, packing the heavy bags to the LZ, and sweating in the sun while loading those bags into helicopters. All of this they had been forced to accomplish while wearing their combat gear, their helmets, and the ever-present flak jackets. As the maneuvering rifle companies moved carefully to the east, every village that was entered contained more rice, and the locations were dutifully sent on to the ARVN. Every Marine stomping along in the brush was happy to allow our ARVN friends the pleasure of dealing with the problem of the heavy bags.

During the day on D plus two, the regimental commander permitted the return of the antitank platoon to National Route 1; once in the field, the vehicles had proved to be difficult to maneuver. Neither Lieutenant Colonel Utter, his operations officer, nor any of the rifle company commanders felt that the Ontos could keep up with the battalion tactical column as it moved east in the more difficult terrain nearer the coast. We all just wanted them to "go away."

The night of D plus two was eventful and clearly proved that the enemy was around even though he was avoiding confrontation with the battalion. At 0120 in the morning, a Company H ambush caught a Viet Cong unit on the move. A firefight ensued, after which the ambush unit returned to friendly lines. At first light, Company H moved into the ambush site and found two dead Viet Cong with weapons.

On D plus three, 15 April, the battalion continued its search-and-destroy operations, sweeping through villages and locating numerous rice caches. At 1215, Lieutenant Colonel Utter conferred with the commanding officer of 1/7 with regard to areas that still needed to be searched and rice caches that had to be turned over to the ARVN or destroyed before 1/7 pulled out of the area. At 1305, our battalion began a helicopter-borne return to the Chu Lai enclave. The lift was completed at 1645, and once again, the entire battalion, less Company E which remained with the 7th Marines, was back in its familiar defensive posture to the west of the Chu Lai airfield complex.

While Operation Nevada was over, the excitement continued nonstop for the battalion. At 2315 on the night of its return from the operation, Company G was alerted for a helicopter assault into a possibly hot LZ in the morning. The assault was to be made to evaluate an air strike that had taken place a day or two earlier. The presence of a reinforced interprovincial force Viet Cong company in the objective area was confirmed. Company F was alerted to back up Captain Seymour's Company G if they got into a heavy contact. At dawn, Company F and Company H took over the Company G defensive responsibilities, and the helicopter lift began. A total of twenty-four CH-46 helicopters was made available, and Company G completed its assault lift by 0822. The assault went perfectly and was completed without a shot being fired.

At 0905, Company G located some occupied tunnels and proceeded to smoke them with tear gas (CS) and regular smoke grenades. A woman was captured who claimed that the area was a way station for the Viet Cong collection of the rice that they demanded from the local farmers. She even produced a receipt for fifty kilograms of rice that she had turned over to the local Viet Cong regional force commander. She also said that there had been thirty or more Viet Cong in the area two days before. These troops reportedly had been uniformed in black, wore helmets, and had been armed with carbines and submachine guns.

At 1050, Captain Seymour suggested that a sweep of the nearby high ground to his east would be needed if he was to maneuver on a search-and-destroy operation. He was told by the operations officer to conduct the recommended sweep of the high ground himself. When the hills were searched by the sweeping Company G Marines there were no enemy troops left for them to fight. There was ample evidence that the enemy had been there, but all the fighting holes, caves, and trench lines were abandoned. In the nearby villages, the Marines learned that the Viet Cong had collected and stored about five thousand pounds of rice. Villagers stated that the rice now belonged to some "North Vietnamese" who collected it and transported it inland to feed the combat units based farther to the west. Acting on their information, Company G searched to the west, but did not contact the enemy, nor were any more caches located. At 1800 on the sixteenth, Captain Seymour briefed Lieutenant Colonel Utter, who had arrived on the resupply helicopter, then sent his company in for the night. At 2215, a night ambush from Company G saw several men about fifty meters north of their position and took them under fire. A search of the area revealed no evidence of enemy casualties.

At about the same time during the evening of 16 April, Company F on the battalion perimeter was also in a small fight when one of its ambush units took some incoming—twenty-five to thirty rounds of small-arms fire. This contact, too, was inconclusive. However, blood trails on the ground and booted footprints made by men dragging casualties proved that there had been some damage inflicted on the enemy's probing force.

On 17 April at 0845, Company E was returned to 2/7 control, and by 1600 Company G had closed back into the battalion defensive perimeter, returning from the field by another helicopter lift. Their company-size operation had been inconclusive, but in his after-action notes, the commanding officer of 2/7 stated emphatically that it had been an excellent exercise in the rapid, short-notice, deployment of a rifle company by helicopter. He also was of the opinion that such company-size operations would serve to give added spirit and cohesion to Company G or any other participating rifle company. In one of the oddest notes on the small operation, it was pointed out to the higher headquarters that the results of Company G's effort proved that the Viet Cong had moved toward—not away from—the Marine positions at Chu Lai. Whenever they avoided contact with the elements of the regiment that were deployed for Operation Nevada, they had also chosen to move toward, not away from, the enclave. Lieutenant Colonel Utter referred to that information as an "uncredited intelligence" finding.

## Company F Deployment—D day, 19 April 1996

All throughout the operations of 2/7 in the Republic of Vietnam, a platoon of the 1st Reconnaissance Battalion, the 2d Platoon of Company C, led by 1st Lt. Dal Williams, had remained in close contact with the men of the battalion. The reconnaissance Marines in that platoon had been part of the BLT at the start, and many still thought of themselves as being just more of "Utter's Marines." Often the teams from the reconnaissance platoon would spot Viet Cong moving into or out of villages a few thousand meters from the battalion defensive front, yet nothing seemed to happen to these enemy troops. Lieutenant Williams, the platoon leader, was annoyed by this fact and made a personal effort to keep 2/7 aware of what he and his men were seeing.

A specific instance of this type was brought to 2/7 in April by First Lieutenant Williams. He and his men had seen local force Viet Cong guerrillas steadily increase their coming and going, with impunity, from the village of Tho An, a nondescript little village with a few rice paddies on one side and the jungle nearby on the other. It lay a few thousand meters to the west of the Chu Lai enclave perimeter, sitting undisturbed in somewhat of an out-of-sight, out-of-mind situation. The village was beyond the nearest hills, yet it was still near enough to be within the fan of artillery of coverage. No artillery units would need to be moved in order to provide fire support if a mission was sent to bring the enemy forces in Tho An to battle. Based on Lieutenant Williams's information, the decision was made that Company F would be allowed to take action against those Viet Cong with an assault landing to clear the village of enemy fighting men and to destroy any enemy food or equipment that was located there. The supposition by higher level intelligence staff officers was that the Viet Cong were infiltrating more and more forces into Quang Ngai Province. In 2/7, we believed that the buildup in Tho An might be part of that increase in the Viet Cong and NVA forces.

To support the Company F operation, two separate reconnaissance insertions were made before D day, with Lieutenant Williams and his Marines establishing themselves in observation posts on high ground from which they could report any Viet Cong movements. They would be in position so that they could directly observe Tho An as the assault fire was followed by the Company F assault landing. They expected to also be of assistance as the company was maneuvering from the LZ into and through the village. One reconnaissance Marine, who had been observing the area on and on for months, was attached to Company F to serve as a guide into Tho An from the LZ. Other support that would be provided included armed helicopters overhead for all ground maneuvers. Fixed-wing support was supposed to be available at any time, that support being added to the air strike planned to protect the assault landing. This landing was going to be done right. The LZ preparation would include a napalm attack on the village just prior to the arrival of the Company F assault troops.

At 0955 on D day, 19 April, Company F departed by CH-34 helicopters for LZ Thrush. The LZ lay less than four hundred meters outside Tho An. Our operation began with an artillery preparation, and the air strike arrived precisely on time. A portion of the village was ablaze as the company conducted its assault into the LZ without opposition. One helicopter remained in the zone with engine trouble, and a security platoon had to be designated. Regardless of our being short-handed, the rest of Company F followed the artillery barrage and air strike right into the village. Both the reconnaissance teams and the armed-helicopter pilots reported that the UH-1E helicopters were being fired on from the village as the two-platoon assault moved forward. By 1245, the village had been taken, and an extensive array of tunnels and caves had been found. Both the villagers and the concealed reconnaissance Marines reported that fifteen or more armed Viet Cong had run into the jungle when the LZ preparation began. Company F now had control of Tho An and had captured more than 130 Vietnamese civilians, mostly women and children, with a few older men being present as well. The absolute absence of men of military age among the initial captives was an indicator that any men of that age group who lived in Tho An were probably Viet Cong. They had run from our assault and were hanging around nearby, hiding in the jungle. Immediately after we gained control of the civilians, the enemy took the attached interrogation team under fire as it questioned the captives. Several of the civilians took advantage of the interruption and fled. Choosing not to lose the rest of the captives, I moved them, and the interrogation team, back to the north of LZ Thrush where they could shelter behind a four-foot dike that surrounded a square field near the LZ.

Throughout the afternoon, Company F received sporadic, long-range sniper fire from several directions. All the fire seemed to be rifles or carbines firing one or two rounds each time. We quickly decided that the local folks were operating without machine guns to support an attack on the Marines searching their village. I then used 2d Platoon of Company F to drive the Viet Cong off the slightly higher ground from which most of the fire had been received. In the firefight, the platoon suffered one Marine wounded, and a medical evacuation was requested. Covered by the armed UH-1E helicopters, a helicopter arrived for the wounded Marine. After the medical evacuation, the 2d Platoon stayed quietly in Tho An.

Company F made a grand show of pulling back from Tho An, moving the command element and two platoons, including the one that had been released from helicopter security, into the square field where the civilians who had not run from the sniper fire were safe from any new flat-trajectory fire. Helicopters came and went taking the seventy-seven remaining civilians back to Chu Lai. The Company F Marines remaining in Tho An, under the command of S.Sgt. John Kelly, lay quietly waiting. Some very stupid Viet Cong soon arrived in Tho An to make the silent, sweaty waiting worth all the trouble. They probably thought that the helicopters were taking the Marines away, thus could have concluded that it would now be a safe time to come back home.

Walking into the village with their rifles slung over their shoulders, about twenty enemy troops walked directly into the Marine riflemen. A sharp, very short firefight followed, and another Company F Marine was wounded. The Viet Cong ran for their lives, dragging the eight to ten casualties they suffered in killed and wounded along with them. The wounded Marine, Sgt. Joseph Long, provided one of the year's most unusual stories. Bleeding profusely from a bullet hole in his face, right next to his nose, he was airlifted to the hospital ship off the coast. He returned to consciousness on the ship as a doctor was looking at him and probing the roof of his mouth with a scalpel. The doctor cut directly into the roof of his mouth and extracted a .45-caliber bullet. Other than a through-and-through wound of the front of his head, Sergeant Long had suffered no other injury. By some twist of fate, that most fortunate Marine had happily survived a direct hit in the face. The bullet, an American round that was probably fired from an M-3 submachine gun, must have been a ricochet that was traveling fairly slowly when it hit him in the face. Rather shaken by the close call, the ultrafortunate Sergeant Long was

released by the hospital ship to return to Company F the following afternoon.

Another Marine who had a close call during the firefight in
the village returned to the company command post with a
painful limp. When asked why he was limping he thought that
he had gotten a rock bruise while jumping over a wall to shoot
at a Viet Cong who had just appeared in front of him. The
corpsman made him sit down and take off his boots. The
bottom of his right foot did, in fact, have a serious bruise, but
it did not come from jumping over a wall. The Marine had, between two layers of his right boot sole, another .45-caliber
bullet. The bullet, perhaps fired from the same weapon that
wounded Sergeant Long, stopped suddenly in the stitching
that held the layers of the limping Marine's old-style boot together. It had peeled back the edge of the combination sole,
just forward of the boot heel, and moving toward his toes, the
bullet had stopped just under the ball of his foot.

In the spring of 1966, outsiders often requested permission
to accompany a rifle company into active operations, just to
see what there was to be seen. Sometimes the requester would
be one of the phony tax-dodging assholes from Okinawa,
self-important jerks who would arrive on the twenty-ninth of
one month and go back north on the second of the next. They
performed that farcical dance to get themselves two-months'
tax relief and two-months' combat pay although stationed outside the combat zone. Such fools were almost always denied
the opportunity by Lieutenant Colonel Utter, who despised
them. However, some exceptions were made by the boss for
more worthy individuals who really needed to understand
better what took place in the lives of the infantrymen in the
rifle companies.

For the Tho An operation, I had been asked to accept such
an exception, a lieutenant who worked his part of the war in
the direct air support center (DASC). He wanted to learn what
it was like in the field, and Lieutenant Colonel Utter decided
to allow him to go along with Company F. I told the lieutenant
that he could only come with us if he agreed to bring along a
radio and an operator and promised faithfully that he would

be of value to me if I needed him. He was told that he would be allowed just to follow along and learn unless I wanted some air support in a hurry. If nothing else, First Sergeant Mills and I felt that his presence would ensure that Company F would get quick support from the DASC if we needed air strikes to keep us alive.

Shortly after the last of the seventy-seven civilians had been flown out of the LZ, things in the square field behind the four-foot dike grew still. Troops and officers grabbed a quick meal, and many Marines were busy reloading magazines from boxes of cartridges pulled from their packs. Reports were made to battalion headquarters, and it was time to wait for the Viet Cong to make their move. I was cheerful and relaxed as I contentedly began heating a tin cup of instant coffee, using a few sticks and dry branches as a heat source. That was when the firefight between the 2d Platoon and the Viet Cong began. A lot of bullets began snapping overhead through the brush, and all the busy Marines stopped what they were doing and rolled over, flopping into their preselected firing positions, where they were able to face outboard, giving the company an instant 360-degree perimeter. For the infantrymen, it was business as usual, only this time they were behind a four-foot wall of dirt—safe as houses.

The lieutenant from the DASC was not at all aware that he was safe, and he shouted, "Somebody is shooting at us!" at the top of his lungs. At the same time, he threw himself down across my pitiful little fire, knocking the tin of coffee ten feet away and dropping my drying socks into the flames. More bullets snapped and snarled over the dirt bank, and the silence in the command group grew longer and longer. From a position of ease against the dirt bank, 1st Sgt. Gene Mills looked sadly down at the sprawled lieutenant and dryly remarked that he was right, someone really was shooting at us. Mills explained what cover meant and showed him that, unless he stood erect, no bullet would hit him. He was told, with emphasis, that what he was hearing was a Marine unit in a firefight and the overs were passing just above our dirt bank.

The first sergeant and I then assured the terrified lieutenant, with some profanity, and some not so quietly delivered references to his parentage, that the heavier reports among the firing that he was hearing was the Company F Marines of 2d Platoon firing back. It was also made very, very clear that spilling the only cup of coffee that I might get that entire day could get a clumsy lieutenant shot at sunrise, not to mention possible dismemberment for the destruction of the weary company commander's only good pair of socks. All in all, the trip to the field was a 100 percent win for that lieutenant. He would never serve another day in the Marine Corps without a much fuller and more complete understanding of what it was like to be an infantryman in the Republic of Vietnam. He might live safe and comfortable in air-conditioned comfort, but his mind had been cleared, and he would most likely think back to that afternoon with Company F when his job in the DASC forced him to get an air strike response for an infantry unit in heavy contact. Later in the war, few if any outsiders wanted to wander about in the field with the infantry.

Late in the day on D day, about twenty Viet Cong were observed at about fifteen hundred to eighteen hundred meters range as they climbed up the west side of a very steep hill mass known as Hill 671. The terrain was so steep that artillery fire could not be placed on the enemy troops; they had maneuvered into an area that was just behind the hill masses that overlooked Chu Lai, an area over which the artillery rounds would pass without impacting anywhere on what can best be described as the "shady" side of the hill. Company F fired its 60mm mortars at their maximum range and fired machine guns at maximum range, all to no avail. Our supporting helicopters were gone and the best fixed-wing response time we could get was quoted as being more than forty minutes out. The enemy troops reached the ridge and slowly disappeared onto the heavy jungle on the very top. That infuriated the Marine riflemen, who hated to see the Viet Cong getting away. Company F completed its first day of the operation with a night defensive perimeter and several squad- and fire-team-size trail ambushes. There was no contact.

On 20 April, D plus one, Company F reentered Tho An for

a second time and conducted a third search of the village. The area was deserted, and there was time to examine the caves and tunnels, which were far more complex than normally found in villages where the inhabitants dug in for personal survival. The reconnaissance platoon's view of Tho An was obviously correct; it was a Viet Cong village, all the way.

At 1010 in the morning, Company F sent the 2d Platoon off on a small search-and-destroy operation while the rest of the company moved to the west and established a company combat base. Once the company was stationary, the 3d Platoon and the reconnaissance Marine guide moved out to the south to conduct search-and-destroy operations in that direction. The reconnaissance platoon, with concurrence of the higher-headquarters intelligence elements, held that there was a Viet Cong base in the area and a prisoner reeducation facility. Third Platoon of Company F found the camp, but it was deserted. The camp consisted of several structures believed to be a prisoner holding facility, a mess hall, a classroom, and two buildings used for troop billeting. The buildings were burned and the nearby tunnel complex was gassed and blown shut.

At 1240, the Company F command group and the 1st Platoon, using binoculars, observed seven to ten Viet Cong moving up a hill mass to the west of the combat base. The artillery observer announced that the artillery had just moved some self-propelled 155mm guns to a new location from which they hoped to better support the Company F operation. These guns had been moved to the south of the Chu Lai enclave and would fire from along the Tra Bong River. A quick look at the map provided the information that the flight of the 155mm rounds would be directly over the company combat base—not necessarily a good thing. Understanding the possibility of danger, the fire mission was called, and the observer adjusted the impacting rounds. Each adjustment was made in the normal fashion, using one base gun in the battery. When that gun was on target the observer asked for permission to fire for effect, which was given. Shortly, he reported that a fire for effect was on the way with four rounds to be fired from each of the four 155mm self-propelled weapons. While he was grinning proudly over the speed and accuracy of the artillery response, the first four rounds arrived. Three impacted exactly on the area, a thousand meters or more to the west, where the Viet Cong had been seen. The fourth 155mm projectile arrived with a huge crash about two hundred meters to the east of the company combat base. That chilling pattern of impacts was repeated three more times. Because the order to cease fire could not even reach the guns before they had completed the four-round fire for effect that had been ordered, everyone just had to hope the impact spread remained unchanged and that no 155mm "hello!" dropped on top of the company. The Company F forward observer, a corporal serving in a lieutenant's billet, could not have felt more responsible. He was saddened beyond his ability to apologize. Of course, we knew that he had had nothing to do with the laying of the offending field piece. Even so, he felt that he had personally done something to endanger the men he was supporting. No one, from me to the lowest private, was even slightly angry with him, a fact that amazed him. The infantrymen of Company F just chalked up the whole event to "God in Her perverse wisdom," and calmly ignored it. While it was not an unimportant event, short rounds falling to earth during a long day in the field just had a way of happening when it was least expected or appreciated, and the Marines looked on that as a fact of life.

On D plus one, Company F spent a quiet night in its combat base. Seven ambush patrols were deployed without contact.

At 0040 on D plus two, 21 April, Company F was alerted to be prepared at dawn for immediate helicopter extraction. The ambush units were recalled, and movement was begun in the dark to an LZ for a first-light lift. Somewhere to the south, the rest of 2/7 was heavily engaged, and during the morning, the troops of Company F could hear the heavy, Soviet 12.7mm machine guns at work. A shortage of helicopters prevented movement of Company F until late afternoon. And instead of joining the rest of 2/7, the company was returned to the Chu Lai enclave without incident. In his commander's analysis of this operation, Lieutenant Colonel Utter recommended more company-size operations be mounted to keep the enemy off balance and to reduce the Viet Cong control over the populace living near the Chu Lai enclave.

## Operation Hot Springs—D day, 21 April 1966

While Company F was in the field hammering on the Viet Cong near Tho An, the battalion was again alerted for combat operations near Quang Ngai to the south of the Chu Lai enclave. The information that set Operation Hot Springs into motion was obtained by the ARVN 2d Division from a Viet Cong who defected on 20 April 1966. That information was provided to 2/7 at 2230 that same day, a feat unheard of in the normal processing of intelligence data in the Vietnam War. Lieutenant Colonel Utter was briefed at the same time by the commanding officer of the Seventh Marines and his staff. In the briefing, 2/7 was verbally directed to be ready to execute a helicopter assault to the north of Quang Ngai, followed, on order, by a search-and-destroy operation moving toward the east. The operation was to be conducted in conjunction with ARVN units already in and near Quang Ngai. The 2d Battalion, 7th Marine fragmentary order for Operation Hot Springs was issued verbally at 0010 on 21 April.

On D day, 21 April at 0840, the battalion, less the Marines of Company F who were sitting in an LZ waiting for extraction, was lifted out of LZ Carp at Chu Lai by twenty helicopters. First Lieutenant Jim Lau and his Company H led the way, followed by Company G and the rest of 2/7. In the LZ, the Marines of Company H were scattered far and wide, based on the choices made by the helicopter pilots. Each separate group of aircraft landed and unloaded its troops in whatever portion of the wide fields they decided looked appealing. That meant Company H was spread out in four or five small gatherings, some of which were more than nine hundred meters from their commanding officer. At 0915, the company killed one Viet Cong and suffered one Marine wounded in a short exchange of fire. In the vicinity of the firefight, Company H found three hundred rounds of 12.7mm machine-gun ammunition, a sight for an antiaircraft machine gun and some documents. Clearly, the Viet Cong had been in the area recently.

By 1115, the helicopter lift of 2/7 was complete, and the battalion began to move eastward with Company H and Company G abreast. The command group and Company E followed in trace. At 1230, Lt. Jim Lau's Company H came under heavy fire from several 12.7mm machine guns. One Marine was killed, and two were seriously wounded in the opening volley. It was an ironic fact that the volley of heavy machine-gun fire was easily heard by Company F as we waited patiently in our LZ for the helicopter lift that never came. Listening on the radio nets also permitted the command group of Company F to determine, by breaking the thrust-point code being used, exactly where the rest of 2/7 was fighting. To counter the 12.7mm fire, Lieutenant Lau called for immediate air strikes and had his mortar forward observer take the tree line under fire with the 81mm mortars. Even with all that firepower, the Viet Cong fired 12.7mm guns at the medical evacuation helicopter that came to take away wounded Marines. At the same time, the 3d Platoon of Company G was maneuvering to flank the enemy guns by moving onto higher ground to the north of the enemy gun positions.

Company H moved out a second time, at 1430, attacking the area from which the machine-gun fire had been received. Immediately the company was again pinned to the earth by a high volume of enemy fire. Another flight of fixed-wing aircraft struck the heavy machine-gun positions and the village nearby. Napalm was used, and the air strike was followed by a Company H frontal assault. This attack was supported by fire from the 3d Platoon of Company G firing down on the enemy, and spotting enemy movements that they reported to Company H. Their position on the higher ground to the enemy's right flank permitted them to see the Viet Cong withdrawal. This combination of firepower, maneuver, and enemy information permitted Company H to move forward and to destroy the Viet Cong unit in the village area.

At 1515, Company H had completed overrunning the

enemy positions and had driven any survivors out of the area. Within the area from which the 12.7mm fire had been received, the Marines of Lieutenant Lau's company found sixty-two dead Viet Cong and five destroyed 12.7mm heavy machine guns. For once the Viet Cong were beaten *and* unable to conceal losses by hiding their dead comrades. It was very gratifying for the 2/7 Marines to see the enemy lying dead on the battlefield. It was clear proof to the men of Company H that the coordination of firepower and infantry maneuver worked as advertised. That short, brutal fight cost Company H eight wounded Marines. In Company G, only one Marine had been hit. After the enemy positions had been searched, the remainder of 2/7 closed into the Company G area, planning to set up a night defensive position with a defensive perimeter surrounding the village. The night position was selected, and organization of the ground began at 1700. By 1845, Company H had maneuvered out of the enemy firing site and moved into its assigned portion in the night defensive perimeter.

At 1715 on D day, while 2/7 was busy properly positioning for the night, the commanding officer of 3/7 requested permission to inspect the area previously occupied by the enemy troops because 3/7 had also received heavy fire from that location, and he wanted his Marines to look it over. When 3/7 had finished inspecting the battlefield, they returned to their assigned area of operation. The night of D day passed without further contact.

On D plus one, 22 April, the 7th Marines ordered 2/7 to sweep east toward the railroad tracks and National Route 1. Before that maneuver was launched, Lieutenant Lau's Company H returned a third time to the battlefield and conducted a detailed search. Before entering the village a forty-round barrage of artillery fire was delivered to prepare the area. Some of the artillery rounds impacted far from the target and a Marine in Company G was wounded by fragmentation. Once in the village, the Company H Marines found another abandoned 12.7mm machine gun, complete with all of its equipment.

At 0900 on D plus one, the battalion began a sweep to the

east with Company E and Company G moving abreast and Company H following the command group in trace. Company G found more than seventy packs, plus other equipment, as it swept through one of the villages in its area of operations. As the morning progressed, several medical evacuations were required because of heat casualties sustained by the infantrymen. The battalion was going to see a repeat of the first months spent in Vietnam: too much heat, too much equipment to carry, and too much distance to cover—all combining to create heat casualties that would hamper all units maneuvering on the ground.

At 1535 on D plus one, the battalion was ordered to continue to the east, to National Route 1, where a vehicular lift back to Chu Lai was to be conducted. This maneuver was completed when the last elements of 2/7 arrived back in the Chu Lai enclave at 2015 on 22 April.

In his commander's analysis of Operation Hot Springs, Lieutenant Colonel Utter repeated his praise for the presence of armed helicopters in support of maneuvering infantry units. He also commented with a bit of wry humor that "Attacking on the gun-target line of artillery requires detailed coordination . . ." In plain English this meant that artillery weapons that lose rounds—either short of the target or long beyond the target—can kill Marines. He also noted that the Viet Cong fighting man was one very tough customer, one who resisted surrender in most cases, often at the cost of his life.

## Operation Montgomery—D day, 9 May 1966

The operational concept of Operation Montgomery was simple. The 2d Battalion, 7th Marines was going to maneuver again over the exact terrain that we fought during Operation Utah. The enemy order-of-battle intelligence contained the 21st NVA Regiment as a probable user of the area, adding that powerful unit to the long list of Viet Cong battalion-size units thought to be operating in the jungle area to the north of Quang Ngai. It appeared that if even a portion of those many units was present and ready to fight, 2/7 was in for another blood letting.

At 0600 on D day, 9 May, 2/7 moved by tactical motor march to the Quang Ngai airfield. The convoy made no contact with enemy forces, a fact that might have been influenced by the steady presence overhead of armed helicopters. On arrival, 2/7 detached Company H to the operational control of the regimental headquarters and began a two-company airlift into an LZ known as Blue. LZ Blue was just to the east of the LZ used on Operation Utah, and everyone in Company E and Company F lifted off for the assault with considerable concern. That concern was somewhat eased by the presence of air on station and armed helicopters covering the assault landings. By 1145, all units, including the battalion command group and the battalion reserve, Company G, were assembled on the ground.

Immediately after the battalion was consolidated, Lieutenant Colonel Utter ordered the two assault companies to begin a sweep to the northeast. Company F was on the left and Company E was on the right when, at 1315, Company E came under fire. Capt. Ted Gatchell's Marines reacted with a swift and violent attack that swept over the enemy position. The attack killed two Viet Cong and drove off the others. Three weapons, an M-1 rifle and two old carbines, were captured. Just five minutes later, Company F came under fire by seven to ten enemy troops firing on the company's left flank. Heavy fire was returned and the enemy force on that flank was also directly assaulted. In the fighting, four Viet Cong were killed and four were captured. Company F had one Marine wounded. At 1730, as the sweep continued to the northeast, Company E had another firefight. The company returned fire and killed two more Viet Cong. The rest of what the company estimated to be a squad of enemy soldiers, ran to the southeast of the village of An Hoa (1).

Starting as far back as Operation Double Eagle, Phase II, Lieutenant Colonel Utter had often chosen to set the battalion into its night defense around a village if a viable village was available. The reasoning behind this was twofold. First, the villages usually had a ditch or wall surrounding the structures, a feature that could easily provide a perimeter defense with good fields of fire for the night defense. Second, villages with structures provided the command group a sheltered site where the staff could prepare the required reports for submission up the chain of command and where plans could be formulated for the following day of operations. On the night of D day, 2/7 established a night defense encompassing the entire village of An Hoa (1), sent out ambush patrols, set listening posts, and spent the night without contact.

On the morning of D plus one, 10 May, the battalion remained in the village of An Hoa (1) and sent out three separate company operations. Company G conducted a helicopter assault and began a sweep along the Giang River before establishing a blocking position against which the Viet Cong were to be driven by other elements of the battalion. During its movement, Company G spotted enemy troops estimated to be two squads or more, but the Viet Cong avoided contact with the company and moved off to the east. An air strike was called, and the target area had good coverage. But maneuver into the target area did not produce any Viet Cong bodies.

While Company G was busy along the Giang River, Company F was ordered to conduct a sweep for two thousand meters back along its D day route of movement and then to return to An Hoa (1). Throughout the sweep, Company F had frequent contact with between four and six Viet Cong who would fire at an extended range and then retreat immediately. A well-concealed enemy firing position was found, probably one that had been occupied on D day. A dead Viet Cong soldier wrapped in a hammock lay nearby. During the search, another VCS was flushed from cover. When he failed to halt on command, he was killed. Company F continued the assigned maneuver and continued to exchange fire with the elusive snipers until the company returned to An Hoa (1) at 1815 and assumed its night defense positions.

Company H was returned to battalion control at 1130 on D plus one, and this freed Company E to begin its maneuver across the Giang River as the company swept eastward toward the Company G blocking positions. Company E made no contact, but a large cave and tunnel complex was located and blown closed. One masonry building containing a hidden room was located as the company moved toward Company G. Near the building, Company E captured a Viet Cong, some medical supplies, a pack, and two magazines for an automatic rifle.

During a mostly uneventful battalion night defense at An Hoa (1), Company F Marines on the perimeter took three to five Viet Cong under fire as they approached the 2/7 defensive positions. Two Viet Cong were killed, and an AK-47 and a bloody rocket propelled grenade launcher were captured.

On D plus two, 11 May, the battalion continued search-and-destroy operations in its assigned zone. Lieutenant Colonel Utter created a formation that resembled the letter H. The crossbar was the command group. The left leg was Company F in the lead and Company G following behind. On the right leg was Company E leading with Company H in trace. The formation moved toward the east, looking for trouble. Company F killed one Viet Cong and captured another as it moved eastward. During the movement, all of the rifle companies located and destroyed caves and small tunnel complexes. Otherwise, the day was tense, but without major contact. At night, Company H was sent out to establish a company-size perimeter, and 2/7 settled down in a perimeter for the night, which passed without contact.

On D plus three, 12 May, Company H began a sweep at 0630 that carried the company to the east and north of the battalion perimeter. Company H did not make any contact with the enemy, and at 0700, the rest of 2/7 began to maneuver with companies F and G sweeping abreast. The battalion command group followed, with Company E in trace. There were no real contacts during the day, but a few hand-grenade booby traps had been left in the villages to cause injury to the unwary. All the booby traps were very rudimentary, and all were successfully disarmed. For the second night, Company H was set into its own separate perimeter while the remainder of 2/7 created a battalion night defensive perimeter around a village. The village, Xuan Hoa (1) was obviously a Viet Cong area; extensive defensive positions were dug all around it, and every house had a deep bomb shelter. Along the edge of the village, there were extensive punji pits, and the fences behind the ditches were all made with the most thorny materials available. During the night of D plus three, at about 2230, a Viet Cong soldier was captured inside the battalion command post. He was not entering to do harm. Instead, he was trying to find his way out of the occupied village when he tripped and fell over a sleeping communicator. That Marine communicator and a few of his pals made quick work of trussing up the unfortunate young VC like a chicken going to market. The remainder of D plus three passed without contact.

On D plus four, 13 May, the battalion took part in another helicopter assault. Company F and Company H were lifted at 0710, with the battalion rear command post, into an LZ on Hill 97, the same hill that had dominated the right flank of the Operation Utah battlefield on 4 March. The two companies were placed under the command of the executive officer and were to establish a solid blocking position for the rest of 2/7 to drive against. A heavy artillery preparation preceded the landing, and the assault was delivered on time and without contact. At the same time as the air-lifted assault was completed, the remainder of 2/7 began to drive against the block in hopes of trapping Viet Cong units between the two forces. No contact was made, but at 1145, the commanding general of Fleet Marine Forces Pacific visited 2/7. He stood on the top of Hill 97 and received a briefing on the battles of Operation Utah and Operation Hot Springs, both of which had passed over much of the terrain that lay spread out below Hill 97.

At 1130, Company F and Company H were ordered to sweep to the northeast, again under the direction of the executive officer. It was the most eerie aspect of the year in Vietnam for many of the Marines in those two rifle companies. The ground they walked on was the same ground that they had crawled over, an inch at a time, during Operation Utah. The memories were deeply moving, almost haunting in the pain they inflicted. Out in one manioc field, where once lay scattered piles of helmets, flak jackets, and packs taken from dead and wounded Marines, only manioc was to be seen. Where heaps of empty cartridge cases had been left behind by Marine and Viet Cong machine gunners who had shot their weapons dry was just mud. The violence of the battles of Operation Utah and Operation Hot Springs had been real, and there were ample artillery and bomb craters present to attest to the ferocious fight that had taken place. But, there wasn't even any fragmentation left lying on the ground. Everything was gone. Only the pitiful fighting holes that had been clawed into the dikes by Marines trying to hide from plunging fire from the left and right of the battlefield were left to show that Marine infantrymen had fought and died on that ground. On the enemy side of the battlefield some bunkers were still to be seen, and there were many, many empty firing positions. All had been partially absorbed back into the earth, hammered almost back into the soil by the rains. There was no contact of any kind that day with the enemy, only the blood-memories of the Company F and Company H Marines. The troops moved slowly and carefully through the area in utter silence. Some stopped for a moment and looked down at the place they had been lying when ordered back to the battalion, leaving the dead until another day. Nothing earth-shattering was said, but the pain was evident in the expressions of those who reached down, let some earth slide through their fingers, and walked away to continue the mission. Some wept and moved on. First Sergeant Mills and I glanced at the pitiful ditch we had used as the company command post and shook our heads. Neither of us felt the urge to comment; the moment was far too painful.

The night of D plus four was spent in a perimeter defense, but the enemy stayed away, leaving us all to hear again in our minds the shattering sound of the enemy weapons of the fourth of March, the pounding of artillery, and the cries of the wounded and dying. I doubt if anyone who had been on Operation Utah slept at all.

Very early on the morning of D plus five, 14 May, the battalion continued to sweep north and east. Lieutenant Colonel Utter used all four rifle companies as he sought to bring the Viet Cong to battle. But no contact was made, and at 1000, an airlift began back to the Chu Lai enclave.

The return of 2/7 to the Operation Utah battleground was different because that time maneuvering there cost the battalion thirty-three heat casualties instead of scores of battle casualties. In his analysis, the colonel suggested that, in the heat, a six-hundred-meter movement was enough to cost an infantry battalion a great deal. Lieutenant Colonel Utter also noted, for the history books, that for once he'd had all four of his maneuver elements, and that gave him a flexibility in operational choices that had never been his before. It is sad to point out to the reader that higher headquarters paid no attention.

# 15

# RELIGIOUS RIOTS AND POLITICAL UPSET

The 2d Battalion, 7th Marines, continued to fight the Viet Cong throughout the first half of 1966. Taking part in operations large and small from our base area in the Chu Lai enclave, 2/7 went into the paddies and jungle to fight. As summer approached, it appeared that we might also have to fight the government of Vietnam or at least some of its elements. Terrible forces of dissent and rivalry had been set loose by fighting and other events in the Republic of Vietnam during the period from July 1965 to the spring of 1966.

As early as the end of March, rumors of conflict between factions within the government of the country were no longer rumors; they had become detailed reports of physical conflict, often accompanied by an exchange of fire. Civilians and religious elements were clashing with their government in the streets. Within the military, there was dissension that caused certain units of the ARVN to rally and to serve as "enforcers" for officers who had earned their loyalty. The vague and unsettled situation was hard on the Marines who still felt that they had come to Vietnam to be of help to a country that needed them. But if Vietnamese troops were going to fight for any officer who opposed the government that was in place, they might suddenly become our enemies as well, and we had to be prepared for that. For the Marine infantry units on the ground, it was clearly the start of a very confusing and difficult time. Safety was an elusive condition to predict. Cities and other areas that were provided security by deployed Marine forces suddenly had the potential to explode into civil war. Internal warfare among all the conflicting parties would have disastrous results for both American and Vietnamese interests. Only the Viet Cong and their leaders in Hanoi would profit if civil war broke out.

In many ways, conditions within the Republic of Vietnam in the spring of 1966 were reminiscent of the tumultuous period between 1961 and 1963. At that time, the country had been bitterly traumatized by the unending conflicts between the government and various of the numerous private armies. All of the private military forces had been engaged in pressing their own agendas on anyone who would listen. Almost every one of the factions had tried the use of armed force as a method of swaying opinion. Each wanted to ensure that its viewpoint, on whatever subject, was selected over the views of any opposing camp. In early 1966, just as they had in the early 1960s, the conflicting viewpoints reflected utterly selfish, personally specific, regionally focused, and local dominance issues. The fratricidal warfare was far from what was needed—it most assuredly was not a form of the essential national consensus necessary to fight the Viet Cong and their North Vietnamese bosses. Every military or civil action by the Americans, who had come to help the national government, was being quickly overshadowed. The gravest danger was the potential failure of the entire government of the Republic of Vietnam to focus on the war with the invader from the north and his effective local agents, the Viet Cong local forces, regional forces, and interprovincial forces.

In the very early 1960s, many of the most divisive factors stemmed from a religious rather than an ideological conflict. Each religion and each sect of that religion seemed to have its own views and its own gang of fighting men. One Catholic priest, Father Hua, operating far south of Saigon in the Ca Mau Peninsula, had a force of ethnic Chinese fighting men. Upon examination of his troops, it turned out that they were Taiwanese Marines operating covertly for him and gaining some combat experience in the process. The Catholics, the

Binh Xuyen Buddhists, the Hwa Hao Buddhists, the Cao Dai
Buddhists, plus all sorts of other groups, dueled for primacy
in the streets of Saigon while the nation crumbled. All sides
were fighting each other as well as the governmental troops of
Ngo Dinh Diem. It was no great surprise that the Viet Cong
units, who were so well controlled by Mr. Le Duan, from
Hanoi, prospered and grew in strength amid all the chaos. Mr.
Le Duan's Viet Cong were, in 1961, 1962, and 1963, the only
fighting force in the country, other than the Vietnamese Marine battalions, that was absolutely stone-cold sure about its
role and mission in the strife.

By April 1966, the Marine commanders throughout I Corps
began to have a new set of concerns about their ability to
function when and if the Republic of Vietnam fragmented
again into local power struggles or religious pushing and
shoving. If the anger of religious zealots was concentrated on
our presence, we might have murder, arson, and sabotage
problems at the airfields, at the docks, and in areas occupied
by civilians. Instead of being relatively safe areas, the major
coastal enclaves of the Republic of Vietnam had the potential
to become the center of armed struggle for control of the
country. That sort of thinking was logical and very much to
the point. The danger was a real one. However, the most important point was that the worry over civil unrest significantly
reduced the offensive mind-set that is always so important to
effective infantry combat.

After some major disturbances, including firing between
factions, in the Da Nang enclave, a process of consolidation
and redisposition of available Marine forces was begun. Our
battalion, which had been based for some months as a part of
the 7th Marine Regiment's defensive alignment to the west of
the Chu Lai airfield, was ordered to realign its defensive posture to give additional, very, very close-in protection to the
airfield. The Marine commanders needed every A-4 jet, every
CH-34 helicopter, and every CH-46 helicopter they had operating in the country. Protecting those assets from Viet Cong
sappers or disgruntled local folks bent on sabotage was
considered by everyone to be of very great importance. The

coming of the unrest to Chu Lai made it possible that we
might lose our air support aircraft to random destruction by
disaffected elements. If there was any serious loss of aircraft,
that would probably hamper the infantry Marines operating
against the Viet Cong in battles that took place far away from
the protected enclaves for months to come.

Lieutenant Colonel Utter ordered Company F to depart
Hill 49 and establish a system of close, tight, but flexible, security for the main Chu Lai airfield. As the company had not
approached its rated strength for many, many months, carrying out that order was not a very simple task. Close security
was what the colonel meant, security that was almost on top
of the aircraft. Company F moved and established its command post on the bleak, white sands less than two hundred
meters directly west of the expeditionary runway used by the
fixed-wing aircraft. Even after Company F had moved and
was based on the airfield, it just did not have the manpower to
create anything approaching the desired physical perimeter
for the airfield. The distance was daunting. The airfield was an
ever-growing complex with a big footprint on the ground.
Company F had available, including walking wounded, 147
effective Marines, four medical corpsmen, and two officers.
That little force was no more than a minute shadow of what
was needed for "real" security. The only approach that made
sense was the creation of a flexible, ever-changing, pattern-
less, framework of squad- and fire-team defenses. Through re-
liance on the skills of the squad leaders and fire-team leaders,
it might be possible to force Viet Cong troops to filter past our
defense, one at a time. Of course, we hoped that an enemy or
dissident unit of any appreciable size would have difficulty
maneuvering close to the airfield without being detected and
engaged.

There were many things about our new assignment that
made the task extremely difficult and particularly unrewarding.
Some of these things were challenging from a physical standpoint, things such as the great distances between positions, the
lack of cover from possible incoming fire, and the utter absence
of any concealment. Other difficulties were complex matters

that made being an eighteen-year-old rifleman in Company F a task that would have driven most of the saints stark raving mad. First, the Marines were forced to live, with minimal shelter, on the ground less than 250 meters from the very busy Chu Lai fixed-wing airstrip. Second, the heat radiating from the white sand was amazing! One morning at 1015, an aviation NCO working on the airfield passed to Company F the information that the air temperature, taken at four feet above the ground (the temperature at that height is important to air density calculations for jet aircraft takeoffs) was 137 degrees! Thus, the chance to sleep soundly during the daylight hours, in preparation for night patrolling, was almost totally nil. The combat-worn, bone-tired Marines had to learn to sleep a couple of hours in the early evening, before patrolling, and a couple of hours in the early morning after coming in from listening posts, ambush sites, or security patrols. Every squad leader was forced to worry constantly about his Marines because sleep-deprived men can create disasters for themselves on night security missions.

The third, and by far the worst, aspect of the assignment was the noise level to which it subjected the troops. Having been placed almost on top of the Marine air operations, the men of Company F had no protection from the deafening sound of Marine A-4 aircraft taking off at maximum throttle. Nor were landings and the necessary taxiing of aircraft very quiet activities. Since operations were always heavy for the attack squadrons at Chu Lai, many aircraft were taking off day and night. The infantrymen were blasted with the high-decibel roar of the jet blast hour after hour. Landing aircraft did not create as serious a problem, as they made arrested landings a considerable distance from the company area. However, while taxiing after landing, the Marine pilots operated their jets at a lower, but still very loud, power setting as they passed near the Company F Marines, turned around, then taxied off to park their aircraft.

Another of the more physical difficulties was the constant wind. Each day at the Chu Lai enclave, the same wind cycle that had made life difficult for 2/7 in Qui Nhon in July 1965 was repeated. By 1300, the winds would pick up drastically, and a steady flow of fine grit would move rapidly across the landscape. At Chu Lai, it was not the red laterite soils that were moving through the air. Instead, it was a very fine, very abrasive, and amazingly invasive volume of tiny sand particles. Within minutes of the increase in the winds, all the weapons in the hands of the troops were filled with sand; every weapon had to be recleaned within minutes of being exposed, otherwise the possibility of malfunctions was terribly high. The ever-inventive infantrymen cleaned their weapons early in the morning and used many and varied ways of wrapping them to make them more "sand proof." It was not unusual for the corpsmen of Company F to draw large numbers of condoms from the medical support supplies to be employed in clever ways to block the sand from the weapons. Although it was a terrible problem for the infantrymen, the sand must have been an almost intolerable problem for the aviation mechanics sweating over aircraft repairs during the sand-blown afternoons.

For Company F, the physical location of the company added to the danger of confusion that could result in the loss of life among friendly forces. Looking directly to the west from the company bivouac area, one came upon the huge engineering works of the civilian construction consortium known as RMK-BRJ. They and all of their contract personnel were working around the clock on a new, concrete, dual runway, Chu Lai airfield. No more than five hundred meters in front of the company positions, just across a few wide fields, lay the new airfield. All day and all night, it was a busy construction site. Working under huge floodlights, the earth movers rumbled, the bulldozers roared, and dozens of huge water-spraying vehicles settled the dust raised by all the commotion. Construction teams from the Seabees (navy construction battalions) and from the civilian contractors roamed all over the place whenever they damn well felt like it. There was no way that Company F Marines could give any of those people any security. In fact, we could not even be confident that we could protect them from being hit by Marine firepower. Should anyone, the Viet Cong or some dissident faction, attack the older airstrip that was still in use, the Company F Marines would be expected to return the enemy's fire. Such return fire would, naturally, impact directly into the area where civilians employed by RMK-BRJ and their Seabee associates lived and worked. Since the Chu Lai enclave had been created, there had never been a resolute attack launched by the Viet Cong against either the air elements or the civilian populace. Based on that, RMK-BRJ and the Seabees had not chosen to live in the protected areas behind sand-bagged bunkers; they lived in some comfort, with electric lights, air conditioners, and rumor had it, actual flush toilets. They lived in thin-skinned buildings that Marine or Viet Cong rifle and machine-gun bullets would penetrate without difficulty.

Not only were the Americans and the others living and working on the new airfield at risk, but there were literally hordes of civilians moving on the highway and among the villages that were situated nearby. Almost any firefight that might occur as Company F attempted to protect the Marine aviation assets on the airfield would result in extensive civilian casualties.

The conditions of the assignment made for an utterly unacceptable situation, but as Marines, we had no alternative. Without wasting any time or breath complaining, the company moved to do what it was ordered to do, in the place it was ordered to perform the task assigned. The infantrymen, who were always willing to do their duty, could easily see that if they got into a firefight, they would probably be responsible for killing many of their fellow Americans, many Vietnamese citizens, and probably some of the men that the huge contracting consortium called third-country nationals. The latter were construction men from all over the world who had flocked to Vietnam in 1966 to be part of the workforce on the myriad major engineering projects that were under way to support American participation in the war.

Once Company F was in place at the airstrip, two things

were clear. First, there were far too few Marines present for duty in the company to do even a pisspoor, substandard job. Unless ambush sites were to be manned with only one or two Marines and security patrols were conducted only by four-man fire teams, the task could not be accomplished. An absolutely minimum security network could not be manned during the critical hours of darkness. There was no obvious way that the level of security demanded by the higher authorities in Da Nang could ever be reached—short of deploying the entire 7th Marine Regiment to perform close-in airfield security. The area was too large, and the confusion and civilian freedom of movement would permit any truly determined enemy to penetrate to the airfield. All that could be held as realistic was that Company F could act as a trip wire for any major force that might be maneuvering to assault the airstrip. The infantry Marines might be sacrificed to warn aviation and other support elements in the enclave that the Viet Cong were on the way. Once any assault force was past Company F, the question of what it was that those noncombatant elements were to do when the enemy began to leap on top of them was inadequately addressed. What the clerks and mechanics would have, or could have, done to protect themselves, had there been an attack, remains just as hazy to this day.

Some relief from the manpower shortfall at the security perimeter was agreed to by the commanding officer of the 7th Marines. He permitted 2/7 to dispatch a second rifle company to the airfield security mission. He thereby accepted a thinner presence on the ground in the normal defensive perimeter of the battalion. That decision brought 1st Lt. Fred Fagan* and his Company E down from the hills with about 140 more Marines. On arrival, Lieutenant Fagan made it plain that he was more than willing to work in any fashion that made sense to the commanding officer of Company F. Lieutenant Fagan wanted to effectively coordinate everything he did. In an

*Gatchell was, by that time, at regiment, which needed a good captain, quickly.

effort to make sure that his company did its job, that exemplary officer was able to set his ego aside and allow his company to become fully integrated into plans that Company F had developed over the first day or two of local operations. Before full coordination could even begin to take place, a two platoon element of Company E had to be deployed to the highway. That was necessary because it appeared that there was going to be an armed confrontation between civilian demonstrators and some troops loyal to a particular general in Da Nang. Lieutenant Fagan went himself to calm that potential powder keg.

With more than two hundred Marines available to the security element, a realistic plan of night security patrols, ambush sites, and listening posts could be created. Once in place, that plan was made known to the unit commanders on the airfield and to the ARVN commanders in nearby units. All parties who were on the scene knew that it was far from a perfect security plan, but it was one that could be accomplished with the assets available. While it did not meet the "sealed-in" desires of higher headquarters, it was the best the infantry had to offer their brother Marines of the aviation units. Once the rough plan was approved and understood by all involved local commanders, the two-company security force went to work. The night was immediately turned into the infantry Marine's day. As soon as the sun went down, Marines began getting up to get on with the job. They ate a meal, cleaned their weapons, and by 2130 all of the approach routes to the Chu Lai airfield, including those through the RMK-BRJ compound and the villages nearby, were blanketed with small teams of armed and dangerous Marines looking for trouble. Before dawn, the troops would return to their shabby living sites at the runway's edge, clean their weapons again, eat another meal, and struggle to get some sleep to prepare themselves for the next night of waiting and watching. After a few days of that tiring activity, it, too, became a normal part of the infantryman's way of living through his tour of combat.

While they did their job, the troops bitched loudly because

now that they were ready, no Viet Cong or other disaffected forces came wandering by for them to kill.

For some reason, the security forces on the airfield drew very little attention from anyone on high. Neither Company E nor Company F was visited with any regularity by anyone from regiment or division. Lieutenant Colonel Utter said openly that we had enough troubles and that he did not want to bother us. In other words, he was comfortable leaving us to do our job as we saw fit. On the other hand, the new battalion executive officer preferred to send for either Lieutenant Fagan or me in the early morning or in the early evening while we were catching our short naps. Such naps were our lifeblood, with nights devoted to the long hours of waiting at the radios for something bad to happen to one of our small units. This new executive officer, a Major Moss, was an unknown quantity down at the rifle-company level. He was nothing like Major Wilson or Major Gentry, both of whom had been very interested in everything that was happening to the riflemen. That difference was really the only thing we knew for sure about the man. In the end, his effect on our morale was not good. Lieutenant Fagan and I were astounded to hear him explain in a briefing for someone from the 1st Division staff that he had been the one who had designed the flexible, small-unit security system that 2/7 had in place at the Chu Lai airfield. This did not brighten our day. Lieutenant Fagan and I were annoyed and offended, because, as far as we were aware, the major had only set foot in our area near the airfield once, ever. As well, neither of us could remember his having any input to discussions that Lieutenant Colonel Utter had with his two on-scene commanders.

Marines seldom, if ever, thrive on inactivity. With a rather boring, repetitive, and standardized routine in place, the pranksters, practical jokers, and complainers began to make themselves known. They created vulgar songs about Chu Lai, they cursed the wind, and they chalked new and more venomous remarks on their helmets and flak jackets. One sign that appeared in the night at the door of my tent summed it all up. Obviously hating what they were doing and choosing to blame their captain for their being sent to the airfield security job, they painted a slab of plywood with the comment, "Oh how happy we will be, When we are rid of Captain Lee." I did not take the comment personally—they had every right to bitch about anything that pissed them off, and Chu Lai airfield security was right at the top of the list of things they should have complained about.

Of course, the security duty at the airfield was still punctuated by the sudden deployments of the battalion to the field in response to various intelligence inputs. Therefore, the Marines of Companies E and F jumped without warning from mundane, boring, security duty to a quick airlift into combat in the jungle. The adrenaline rush from that mission would hardly have time to be appreciated before a return flight of helicopters would deposit the Marines back on the hot sand for more night-security work. After a time, there appeared to be a slight rise in the overall pride of the rifle-company Marines. They knew that the cooks, bakers, and candlestick makers who took over the airfield security could not do it as well as they did, nor could those rear-echelon Marines go into the jungle and face the enemy in his own domain. Minor-league increases in pride aside, the lack of appreciation for their work and the near futility of operating in a populated area began to wear on everyone.

The battalion was rapidly changing as many of the old hands were being slated for dates of departure. On 4 June, our leader left 2/7 forever. Lt. Col. Leon N. Utter was relieved by Lt. Col. John J. Roothoff. Lieutenant Colonel Utter had often said that the generals ought to understand that they should leave the lieutenant colonels and the captains in place—once they had good ones who could do the job in command—until one of three things happened: The officer was killed; the officer was wounded and could not return; or the officer turned to his boss and said, "Sir, I cannot go on!" He always told us that command continuity was essential, yet the Marine Corps did not agree. In fact, over the later years of the war, the battalion commanders were swapped out every four to five months like jigsaw-puzzle pieces.

Some of the original officers of 2/7 explored the possibility of an extension of their tour in the Republic of Vietnam. Tour extensions were permitted and were being approved. But, for some reason, the 1st Marine Division ruled that any officer who did extend would be shifted from combat command to the division staff. Since the only reason for extension would be for the benefit of the Marines in their platoons and companies, none of the officers of 2/7 officially submitted letters requesting the four-month extensions that were being offered. One captain that I knew well, in another battalion, did extend for four months. While he had been led to believe that he would be an exception and would stay with his rifle company, on the day his extension began he was taken out of the infantry battalion and sent to take charge of the transient center in Da Nang.

Late June of 1966 was the time for the last of the old hands to go home. The battalion that left Camp Pendleton was finally being fully converted. It would no longer be an organization devoted to strong unit integrity and personnel stability. It would no longer be unique. It would, instead, become another way station for the stream of replacements that would be passing through 2/7 and all of the other battalions of the III Marine Amphibious Force for the next five years. No one who was not present as a member of the 2d Battalion, 7th Marine Regiment, when it served in the Republic of Vietnam, can ever fully understand the difference. But rest assured that those who saw it done both ways, and who served in the war under both concepts, will always know which was a better way to do the business of war. And, they will always know why 2/7 was unique. In part, it was fate, but in the final analysis, the historical difference that made the battalion unique, were the policies that our leader applied to the fighting Marines, the absolute professional dedication of his performance under fire, and the daily personal leadership of Lt. Col. Leon N. Utter, United States Marine Corps.

They say that men go forward to the sound of the guns for love of Corps and Country. That may be true, but I did not see it during my time in the Republic of Vietnam. I saw that the

Marine infantryman more often goes forward out of love for his comrades and because of both his love and his respect for his leader. Our battalion commander was the kind of man that his Marines could respect beyond all his kind, he was that rarest of the rare, the kind of man that the Marines of the 2d Battalion, 7th Marines could follow through all the agony we faced during 1965 and 1966.

# 16

## COMMENTS

It took only a little more than a year of combat in the Republic of Vietnam to bring the battalion, as we knew it, to an end. Having weathered the very toughest of fights against an able enemy, it was not only losses but time and policy decisions from above that brought to an end the unit integrity and personnel stability of 2/7. Infantry combat is not akin to a street game of ball played for fun by a loose group of confederates. It is serious business and should have been treated as such. Heavy losses can be survived by a fighting unit if overall unit integrity and stability have not been compromised by irrational concepts pounded down from above.

Rifle-company Marines—the men who actually fight the enemy in the jungle—will bear almost any burden if their leaders are not changed every few weeks for one reason or another. Not every Marine field-grade officer needed to get his battalion command time at the expense of the lives of privates, privates first class, and lance corporals. Not every captain was even marginally qualified to lead a rifle company in combat. Long tours of leadership duty for those who proved themselves to be able commanders at the battalion level and at the company level should have been mandatory. Such a policy would have sharply reduced the overall loss rate for infantry Marines in the Republic of Vietnam. Fairness be damned! Professional fighting men given leadership roles should expect to be asked to keep on fighting as long as they are needed.

The bone-weary 2/7 Marines who slogged through the jungles and who sat, night after night in the dreary rain-filled foxholes, deserved leaders who could do the job as it had to be done. Men like Lt. Col. Leon Utter had the combat skills and the intellectual ability to learn from each experience in that war and improve their performance each and every time they were tested. Such men, and the subordinate officers and SNCOs under their control, should have been required to stay in command to provide vital leadership and guidance for those who came to the war after 1966. Instead, everyone rotated, and the unit integrity and personnel stability that had made 2/7 a unique organization were lost forever. No other unit began with such solid unit integrity, and by the summer of 1966, it was evident that no other battalion was to have such good fortune. The war in that jungle hell was not pickup basketball, and the stream of body bags on the C-141s flying east to the United States of America proved that beyond any doubt.

Another aspect of the battles through which 2/7 struggled was the utter contempt by the overall high command for some of the basic principles of warfare. Every infantry unit in the Republic of Vietnam experienced the meddling from on high that sapped combat power at the precise moment when it was most needed. Time after time, our battalion, and all the other infantry battalions with which I had contact, had rifle companies spirited away just as an operation was being initiated. This was a tragic mistake because it hampered every commander by taking from him his ability to influence the action in his area of responsibility. No senior headquarters that took away combat power ever took away terrain responsibility, nor did the weakened unit ever find that it was not asked to go forward to engage the enemy. Operation Utah was a prime example of that disregard for rational, common-sense-based principles. Lieutenant Colonel Utter had been stripped of his reserves. As a consequence, he had nothing with which to influence the action when he could see that his battalion was being steadily destroyed by large volumes of Viet Cong and NVA firepower. He had to sit, seething, in barely controlled anger as his Marines were dying, knowing that he could not help them—nor could he get anyone else to help them.

Those who served in the 2d Battalion, 7th Marines, in 1965 and 1966 were a varied lot. Most have been quite successful in their later lives. Many of the officers who worked for Lieutenant Colonel Utter rose to be lieutenant colonels and colonels themselves. As an example, 1st Lt. Nick Groz who earned the Navy Cross on Operation Harvest Moon, retired as a full colonel and was proud to have his son serve as a platoon leader in the 2d Battalion, 7th Marines during 1995 and 1996. Many of the SNCOs and NCOs of 2/7 stayed in the Marine Corps and prospered. Almost all of the officers and men who served on in the Corps did other tours in the Republic of Vietnam. Capt. Martin O'Connor, who was known to be the best of the captains, earned a Navy Cross for himself on a subsequent tour of duty.

Others who were in 2/7 left the Marine Corps and sought other careers. None, officer or enlisted Marine, with whom I have spoken about the battalion over the years, has ever expressed anything other than utmost pride in his service as one of Utter's Marines because for one short period in time, things were done right. They were done as they should have been done, and we were honored to have been part of it all.

Lieutenant Colonel Utter left the battalion and was assigned to be one of the speech writers for the commandant of the Marine Corps. He once spoke of that period of duty as being "Will Rogers writing speeches for Calvin Coolidge." His Oklahoma wit and his twang were not particularly well suited for the down-east commandant who then led the Marine Corps. Lieutenant Colonel Utter did not get to command an infantry regiment, and he was easily bypassed by more self-seeking and politically-minded Marine colonels for the rank of general officer. That was, and shall forever remain, a travesty.

The saddest aspect of all the painful things that happened in the 2d Battalion, 7th Marine Regiment, does not relate to anyone who was part of the transplacement planning of the Marine Corps; he was not part of 2/7 when it sailed off to war.

It is a sadness that springs from the Vietnamese side of the equation. In 1965, each of the rifle companies of 2/7 was assigned an interpreter, sometimes two, to help the company commander function in a land where few Americans could master the complicated tonal language. The interpreter for Company F was a brave and willing man, Sgt. Nguyen Van Luan, a full member of the company who was wounded twice in 1966 serving beside me. Each time, he chose to refuse evacuation. He did so, because, in his words, he might be separated by his government from all of his Marine friends who had come to help him. In May 1970, by pure chance, I found that same interpreter standing on the edge of a landing zone where both 1/7 and 2/7 were preparing to depart for a large helicopter-borne assault. The virtually indestructible man was still serving as the interpreter assigned to Company F! He had more stripes, but he was still doing the same job. His combat time with the company covered about fifty-nine consecutive months since he had come to work in Lt. Col. Leon Utter's battalion. The calm, dedicated Vietnamese had, by early May of 1970, been wounded eleven times and had survived more captains and lieutenants as his company commander than he could begin to name. Yet, he still smiled broadly when greeted, hugged me firmly in the American style, and proudly said, in flawless English, "I will always be a 2/7 Marine." It is men like Nguyen Van Luan, the Company F interpreter, who this nation failed when it turned its back on the Vietnamese people and left them to the bitter fate of bowing forever to the tyrants of Hanoi.

I SPARE NO CLASS, OR CULT, OR CREED.
MY COURSE IS ENDLESS THROUGH THE YEAR.
I BOW ALL HEADS, AND BREAK ALL HEARTS.
ALL OWE ME HOMAGE—I AM FEAR!

—Gen. George S. Patton, Jr.
November 1918


ON HIGH WE HEAR THEM SAY
THAT NOTHING IS TOO GOOD FOR THE TROOPS.
THAT IS EXACTLY WHAT THE
POOR BASTARDS OF 2/7 GOT
EVERY DAMN WEDNESDAY.
NOTHING!

—Capt. Alex Lee, USMC
June 23, 1966

# APPENDIX

## AWARDS AND DECORATIONS

The Navy Unit Citation:
Second Battalion, Seventh Marine Regiment

Medal of Honor:
Captain Harvey C. Barnum, Jr., USMC

Navy Cross:
First Lieutenant Nicholas V. Groz, Jr., USMC

**THE SECRETARY OF THE NAVY**
WASHINGTON, DC

The Secretary of the Navy takes pleasure in commending the

**SECOND BATTALION, SEVENTH MARINES
THIRD MARINE DIVISION (REINFORCED)
FLEET MARINE FORCE, PACIFIC**

for service as set forth in the following

CITATION:

For outstanding heroism in action against enemy Viet Cong forces during OPERATION HARVEST MOON in the Que Son area, Quang Nam Province, Vietnam, from 8 to 20 December 1965. As part of a regimental sized operation, the Second Battalion, Seventh Marines, was launched against major Viet Cong Units then in contact with friendly forces of the Republic of Vietnam. Seizing its initial objective, the battalion carried the battle to the enemy, overcoming successive objectives, destroying the enemy and capturing his weapons and supplies. In the most adverse weather conditions, with incessant rain, flooded valleys, and soaked jungle terrain, the officers and men conducted their attacks with unrelenting energy and will. In spite of the deterioration of weapons and equipment, the suffering from constant immersion in water and mud, the tenacious resistance of the enemy, and increasing casualties, the Second Battalion, Seventh Marines remained a superb fighting organization repeatedly forcing the enemy from his positions, assaulting steep jungled hills and inundated paddy-lands, and boldly carrying out helicopter borne assaults in the face of enemy antiaircraft fire. As the operation drew to its conclusion, and the defeated enemy attempted to withdraw from the battle area, the Second Battalion, Seventh Marines remained in the forefront of the battle, aggressively pursuing the enemy on foot across flooded lowlands. As a final act, on 18-19 December 1965, the battalion engaged, assaulted, and effectively destroyed a Viet Cong Company heavily reinforced with mortars, machine-guns, and 57MM recoilless rifles. After killing over 100 Viet Cong in this one engagement, the battalion was finally withdrawn after 13 days and nights of uninterrupted combat. The fighting spirit, unflagging aggressiveness, and countless acts of heroism reflected great credit upon the officers and men of the Second Battalion, Seventh Marines and upheld the highest traditions of the Marine Corps and the United States Naval Service.

All personnel attached to and serving with the following units of the
Second Battalion, Seventh Marines, during the period 8 to 20 December
1965 are hereby authorized to wear the NAVY UNIT COMMENDATION
Ribbon.

>   **2d Battalion, 7th Marines:**
>
>   >   Headquarters and Service Company
>   >
>   >   Company E
>   >
>   >   Company F
>   >
>   >   Company G
>   >
>   >   Company H
>
>   **Supporting Units:**
>
>   >   Company H, Second Battalion, 9th Marines
>   >
>   >   2d Platoon, Company C, Third Engineer Battalion
>   >
>   >   Helicopter Support Team, 2d Platoon, Company A,
>   >   3d Shore Party Battalion

>   >   >   Signed:    Paul H. Nitze
>   >   >             Secretary of the Navy

THE MEDAL OF HONOR IS PRESENTED TO

CAPTAIN HARVEY C. BARNUM, JR., USMC
WHILE ON TEMPORARY ASSIGNMENT, ON THE 18TH OF DECEMBER
1965,
TO COMPANY H, SECOND BATTALION, NINTH MARINE REGIMENT
WHICH WAS ON THAT DATE
ATTACHED TO SECOND BATTALION, SEVENTH MARINES

for service as set forth in the following

CITATION:

For conspicuous gallantry and intrepidity at the risk of his life above and beyond the call of duty. When the company was suddenly pinned down by a hail of extremely accurate enemy fire and was quickly separated from the remainder of the battalion by over 500 meters of open and fire swept ground, and casualties mounted. Captain Barnum quickly made a hazardous reconnaissance of the area, seeking targets for his artillery. Finding the rifle company commander mortally wounded and the radio operator killed, he, with complete disregard for his safety, gave aid to the dying commander, then removed the radio from the dead operator and strapped it on himself. He immediately assumed command of the rifle company, and moving at once into the midst of the heavy fire, rallying and giving encouragement to all units, reorganized them to replace loss of key personnel and led their attack on enemy positions from which deadly fire continued to come. His sound and swift decisions and his obvious calm served to stabilize the badly decimated units and his gallant example as he stood exposed repeatedly to point out targets served as an inspiration to all. Provided with two armed helicopters, he moved fearlessly through enemy fire to control the air attack against the firmly entrenched enemy positions while skillfully directing one platoon in a successful counterattack on the key enemy positions. Having thus cleared a small area, he requested and directed the landing of two transport helicopters for the evacuation of the dead and wounded. He then assisted in the mopping up and seizure of the battalion's objective. His gallant initiative and heroic conduct reflected great credit upon himself and were in keeping with the highest traditions of the Marine Corps and the United States Naval Service.

THE NAVY CROSS IS PRESENTED TO

**FIRST LIEUTENANT NICHOLAS H. GROZ, JR., USMC
COMMANDING OFFICER, HEADQUARTERS AND SERVICE COMPANY
SECOND BATTALION, SEVENTH MARINE REGIMENT**

for service as set forth in the following

CITATION:

For extraordinary heroism as Commanding Officer of Headquarters and Service Company, Second Battalion, Seventh Marines, in the Republic of Vietnam on 18 December 1965, during OPERATION HARVEST MOON in Quang Tin Province near the hamlet of Ky Phu. When savage small arms, automatic weapons and mortar fire pinned his company down in a muddy and exposed rice paddy area, Lieutenant Groz immediately informed his battalion commander of the seriousness of the situation and summoned help. Completely ignoring his own personal safety, he repeatedly ran the gauntlet of intense enemy fire to personally evacuate four wounded Marines. He returned to his men and gave them encouragement as he rallied them and directed their fire toward the Viet Cong positions. In order to permit a few of the lesser wounded to make their way to safety while rifle company was coming to the rescue, he personally engaged automatic weapons with a grenade launcher while enemy rounds were striking his pack and equipment. After returning to retrieve weapons and sundry abandoned gear, and to make certain that none of his men were left behind, he finally made his way to the main battle position and organized his company to support the battalion in its subsequent attack and mopping up operations. By his daring actions, indomitable fighting spirit, and loyal devotion to duty in the face of great personal danger, Lieutenant Groz reflected distinct credit upon himself and the Marine Corps and upheld the highest traditions of the United States Naval Service.

# REFERENCES

**Books:**
    Fall, Bernard, *Street Without Joy*
    Hymoff, Edward, *First Marine Division in Vietnam*
    McMasters, H. R., *Dereliction of Duty*

**Magazines:**
    *Leatherneck,* April 1966, "Operation Harvest Moon." Author: Sergeant Frank Beardsley
    *Marine Corps Gazette,* April 1966, "Solid Contact for 2/7." Author: Lieutenant Colonel Leon N. Utter
    *Time,* August 17, 1965

**Newspapers:**
    *Los Angeles Times,* December 15, 1965
    *Miami Herald,* December 15, 1965
    *Stars and Stripes,* Far East Edition, August 9, 1965

**Archival Materials from Headquarters, United States Marine Corps:**
Commanding Officer, Second Battalion, Seventh Marines, Letters
    3/AJD/3000 of 25 December 1965, After Action Report, "Operation Harvest Moon"
    3/JNJ/gwr/3120 of 7 January 1966, Command Chronology—18 May 1965 to 31 December 1965

3/al/der/3000 of 5 March 1966, After Action Report, "Operation Double Eagle, Phase II"

3/AJD/der/3000 of 12 March 1966, After Action Report, "Operation Utah"

3/AJD/der/3000 of 2 April 1966, After Action Report, Company Search and Destroy Operation

3/AJD/www/3000 of 3 April 1966, After Action Report, "Operation Indiana"

3/AJD/der/3000 of 25 April 1966, After Action Report, "Operation Nevada"

3/AJD/der/3000 of 28 April 1966, After Action Report, "Operation Hot Springs"

3/AJD/der/3000 of 1 May 1966, After Action Report, Company Search and Destroy Operation

3/AJD/www/3000 of 17 May 1966, After Action Report, "Operation Montgomery"

3/JJR/gac/3120 of 2 July 1966, Command Chronology, June 1966


Second Battalion, Seventh Marines Command Diaries (Pages with 29, 30, and 31 May are not in archives)
Period 0001 01 January 1966 to 2400 31 January 1966
Period 0001 01 February 1966 to 2400 28 February 1966
Period 0001 01 March 1966 to 2400 31 March 1966
Period 0001 01 April 1966 to 2400 30 April 1966
Period 0001 01 May 1966 to 2345 28 May 1966

# INDEX

A-4 aircraft, 322, 324
Adams, Maj. Sammy T., 247
ADCON (administrative
    control), 57
AK-47 rifle, 220, 224–226,
    253, 268, 316
Allen, S.Sgt., 61–62
Ammunition
    blank, 49
    live-fire training, 49
    loading on ship, 68–73
Amphibious tractors, LVTP-5,
    99, 172
An Hoa, Republic of Vietnam,
    314, 315
An Ke, Republic of Vietnam,
    127, 132, 150, 151,
    156, 165
AN/MRC 38 jeep, 36
AN/PRC-10 radio, 129, 130
AN/PRC-25 radio, 129
Antipersonnel mines, 154–155,
    297
Antiwar movement, 279, 280
Archer, 1st Lt. Jack, 191
Arc Light, 195–196

*Arizona* Memorial, Pearl
    Harbor, 84
Armed Forces Radio and
    Television Station
    (AFRTS), 171
Army of the Republic of
    Vietnam (ARVN), 111,
    119, 120, 159, 185,
    194, 197–199, 228,
    229, 241, 242, 275,
    276, 298, 320, 328
    Rangers, 252, 253, 265
Arnett, Peter, 143

B-52 bomber, 196, 199, 202
"Baldomero Lopez Battalion,"
    37–41
Barber, Capt. William, 4
Barnum, Capt. Harvey C., Jr.,
    212, 338, 341
Basketball (C-47 flareship),
    271, 272, 294
Bataan, Philippine Islands, 3
Batangan Peninsula, Republic
    of Vietnam, 121, 295,
    296

Battalion Landing Team 1/7 (BLT 1/7), 70, 121, 336

Battalion Landing Team 2/7 (BLT 2/7), 58, 66–67, 69–115 (see also Second Battalion, Seventh Marines)

Battalion Landing Team 3/7 (BLT 3/7), 70, 93, 94, 121

Battery M, Fourth Battalion, Eleventh Marines, 188, 248

Best, S. Sgt., 211

Binh Son, Republic of Vietnam, 248

Blakeman, Maj., 167, 168

Body counts, 216, 280–281

Booth, Paul, 8

Boxes, mount-out, 15

Boxing Smoker, 83–84

Bronze Star, 162

C-47 flareship "Basketball," 271, 272, 294

C-130 aircraft, 95

Ca Mau Peninsula, Republic of Vietnam, 321

Cam Lai, Republic of Vietnam, 192

Camp Las Pulgas, 13, 25, 26, 67, 70

Camp Pendleton, California, 7–10, 13, 22, 24, 26, 46, 47, 53–54, 68

Camp Schwab, Okinawa, 89

Castro, Fidel, 23, 24

Causery, Gunnery Sgt., 205

Central Highlands, Republic of Vietnam, 127

Chapelle, Dickie, 44

Chau Ngai, Republic of Vietnam, 247–248, 259–260, 274

CH-34 helicopter, 93, 98, 168, 180, 200, 249, 251, 268, 271, 272, 302, 322

CH-46 helicopter, 296, 299, 322

CH-47 helicopter, 132, 133

Ch'in Peng, 75

Choisin Reservoir, Korea, 4–5, 33

"Chop to" (report to work), 57

Chu Lai, Republic of Vietnam, 96, 166–167, 172, 176, 177, 184, 190, 199, 202–203, 205, 213, 214, 229, 242, 247, 273, 275, 283, 293, 294, 296, 299, 301, 302, 307, 309, 313, 322–330

Chu Luc forces (Interprovincial Force Viet Cong), 169, 218, 321

Clancy, 1st Lt. John, 159

Clark, PFC James, 211

Combat Infantryman Badge, 130

Communications Platoon, 63

Company C, First Reconnaissance Battalion, 237, 301, 302

Company D, First Battalion, Seventh Marines, 191

Company E (2/7), 43, 53, 124–126, 159, 160, 162, 171, 240, 294

    Chu Lai airfield security, 327–330

    Operation Double Eagle, 219–225, 228

Operation Harvest Moon, 184, 190–193, 195, 199
Operation Hot Springs, 313
Operation Mixmaster, 234
Operation Montgomery, 314–316
Operation Nevada, 295–296, 301
Operation Utah, 248, 253
Company F (2/7), 43, 52, 53, 144, 284–286, 288, 292, 293
Chu Lai airfield security, 323–330
Operation Double Eagle, 220
Operation Harvest Moon, 184, 190–193, 195–197, 200–211, 213–215
Operation Montgomery, 314–317
Operation Nevada, 296–298
Operation Utah, 237, 238, 244–245, 248–250, 252–275, 277
Tho An, 302–309
Company G (2/7), 43, 52, 53, 294
Operation Double Eagle, 220, 221, 226, 228
Operation Harvest Moon, 190, 192–195, 199, 200, 203–207, 213, 214
Operation Hot Springs, 310–313
Operation Montgomery, 314–316
Operation Nevada, 296, 298, 300, 301
Operation Utah, 245,

249–255, 262, 263, 267, 268, 274, 275
Company H (2/7), 43, 53
Operation Double Eagle, 219–224, 226–228
Operation Harvest Moon, 192, 194, 196–199, 202–204, 213
Operation Hot Springs, 310–313
Operation Montgomery, 314–317
Operation Nevada, 296, 299
Operation Utah, 248, 253, 255, 263, 267, 268, 274
Company H, Second Battalion, Ninth Marines (H/2/9), 199–204, 206, 211–213
Company L, Third Battalion, First Marines, 224
Condon, Sgt. John, 277
Cornelius, 1st Lt. Jerry, 276–277
Corregidor, Philippine Islands, 3
Crosswait, Sgt., 159–162
Cuba, 14, 22–24

Dai Trang, Republic of Vietnam, 203
Da Lat, Republic of Vietnam, 127
Da Nang, Republic of Vietnam, 94–97, 134, 322, 327
D day, World War II, 128
Demilitarized Zone (DMZ), 149, 189
*Dia Phoung* forces (Regional Force Viet Cong), 110, 123, 140, 321

Diem, Ngo Dinh, 322
Direct air support center
    (DASC), 305–307
Doublet, Capt. A.J., 29, 48, 59,
    60, 64, 94, 98, 100,
    101, 103, 160, 164,
    167, 176, 181, 182,
    184, 192, 218, 239,
    246, 262
Duan, Le, 123, 322
*Du Kich* forces (Local Force
    Viet Cong), 110, 140,
    321
"Dustoff" (evacuation)
    helicopter, 132
Duval, S.Sgt., 211

81mm mortar, 191, 200, 203,
    222, 268, 294, 311
85th Evacuation Hospital, Qui
    Nhon, 137
Eleventh Marine Regiment,
    237
Emerson, Lt. Col. Hank, 129
Enfilade fire, 192–193

Fagan, 1st Lt. Fred, 327–329
Fall, Bernard, 101
Fallbrook Naval Ammunition
    Depot, 77
Feille, 1st Lt. William, 211
Fifth Marine Regiment, 3, 36,
    37, 282–283
First Air Cavalry Division, 121,
    127, 132, 150, 152,
    156, 166
First Air-Ground Task Force,
    22*n*
First Battalion, Fifth Marines,
    40
First Brigade, 101st Airborne,

127–132, 150, 166,
    168
I Corps Tactical Zone (ICTZ),
    103, 166
I Field Force, 116, 130, 140,
    144, 145, 165, 174
First Marine Air Wing, 180
First Marine Brigade, 22*n*, 27
First Marine Division, 11,
    13–15, 21–24, 35, 53,
    56, 59, 60, 283, 331
First Motor Transport
    Battalion, 48, 70
First Reconnaissance Battalion,
    237, 301, 302
Flamethrowers, 40, 210–211
Fleet Marine Forces, Pacific
    (FMFPAC), 8, 85, 317
.45 caliber pistol, 210, 259
4.2 inch mortar, 200–201, 203
Fourth Marine Regiment, 3, 4,
    22*n*, 27, 240
French Foreign Legion, 3, 83,
    128

Gallaher, Bob, 144
Gas, 140–141
    CN, 142, 148
    CS, 142–148, 299
Gatchell, Capt. Ted G., 296,
    314, 327*n*
Gentry, Maj. George H., Jr.,
    207–208, 210, 246,
    254, 329
Giang River, Republic of
    Vietnam, 315
Graeboske, Fred, 18
Grenades (*see* Hand grenades)
Groz, 1st Lt. Nicholas, 114,
    115, 208–209, 335,
    338, 342

Guadalcanal, Solomon Islands, 6, 84
*Guidebook for Marines,* 47

Hackworth, Col. David, 128
Hand grenades, 119–120, 135, 204–205, 224, 229
Hanoi Hannah, 114
Headquarters and Service Company (H&S), 34, 154, 174, 191, 203, 204, 216, 219, 233, 251, 253, 268, 294
Henderson, Brig. Gen. Melvin D., 177, 178
Hien Loc, Republic of Vietnam, 197
Hiep Duc, Republic of Vietnam, 185
Hill 49, 174, 282, 283, 284–287, 323
Hill 85, 251–253, 255, 267
Hill 97, 251, 252, 317
Hill 100, 297, 298
Hill 110, 222
Hill 407, 192, 195–199
Hill 488, 221
Hill 671, 307
Hiskett, Lt. Walter (Chaplain Corps), 65, 141, 142
Ho Chi Minh, 131
Howze, Lt. Gen. Hamilton, 131–132
Howze Board Report, 132
Hua, Father, 321
Huk-Bala-Hap, 75

Immersion foot, 163, 175, 197–199, 205, 215
Iwo Jima, Volcano Islands, 6, 81, 82

Johnson, Lyndon B., 68, 145
Johnson, Maj., 85
Jolley, 1st Lt. Nate, 35, 64
Jungle rot, 163, 175

Kehn, 1st Lt. Al, 63, 94, 98, 153
Kelly, Lt. Col. Paul X., 244, 247
Kelly, S.Sgt. John, 304
Kerr, Gunnery Sgt., 103
Kesselring, 1st Lt. Steve, 201, 207, 210
Ketchem, 1st Lt. Hank, 102–103
Korean Tiger Division, 165, 166
Korean War, 2, 4–6, 45, 48, 64, 65, 76, 141, 247, 290
Kue army hospital, Japan, 137
Ky Phu, Republic of Vietnam, 206, 208, 210, 212, 213, 223–226, 228

Lao Dong (Communist) Workers Party, 123
Laos, 44, 143, 239, 281
Larsen, Lt. Gen. Stanley R. "Swede," 146–147, 174, 239
Lau, 1st Lt. James, 52, 53, 117–118, 251–253, 267, 310–312
L-Form munitions, 68–69
Lindauer, Capt. Jerry, 237, 244, 245, 248, 253–254, 260, 263
Lloyd, 1st Lt. Joe, 102–103, 207
Lock-on cycle, 44–55

Logistics support area (LSA), 108, 110, 188, 190
Long, Sgt. Joseph, 304–305
Los Alimitos Naval Ammunition Depot, 77
Losse, Capt. Jim, 201
Luan, Sgt. Nguyen Van, 104, 210, 336

M-1 rifle, 88
M-2 carbine, 259
M-3 submachine gun, 112, 304
M-14 rifle, 125, 210, 256–259, 261, 265, 266
M-35 truck, 2½ ton, 174, 184
M-60 machine gun, 62, 124, 159, 258
M-1937 field ranges, 14, 15, 48
Madeo, 1st Lt. Bob, 190, 195, 203, 210, 211, 213
Malaria, 135–137, 158–159, 239
Malaya, 75
Marine Corps Air Station, El Toro, California, 24
Marine Corps Air Station, Kaneohe, Hawaii, 22n
Marine Medium Helicopter Squadron 161, 44
McCreight, Lt. Col. J.K., 43, 52, 59
McElwain, Lt. Al, 90, 104, 115
McNamara, Robert, 68, 96, 105
Medal of Honor, 4, 81, 111, 112, 212, 338, 341
Mekong River Delta, Republic of Vietnam, 44
*Miami Herald,* 216
Mighty Mite (¼ ton, M-422) jeep, 61, 158

Mike boat (LCM-6 landing craft), 103
Mike docks, Pearl Harbor, Hawaii, 84
Military Assistance Command–Vietnam (MAC-V), 96, 127, 132, 144
Miller, Sgt. August O., 265–266
Miller, 1st Lt. Jim, 225
Mills, 1st Sgt. Gene, 263–264, 269, 272, 306, 318
Mines, antipersonnel, 154–155, 297
Mobile Groupment 100, 128
Mogas, 12
Monsoons, northeast, 149–151, 157–163, 183
Morale and attitude, 51–52, 138, 158, 279
Moss, Maj. Roy E., 329
Mountain Warfare Training Camp, Pickle Meadows, 50–51
Muir, Lt. Col. Joe, 38

Napalm, 311
National Command Authority, 22
*National Geographic,* 44–45
National Highway 1, 228
National Route 1, 101, 115, 117, 119, 121, 123, 140, 155, 156, 172, 174, 214, 228, 248, 296, 298, 313
National Route 19, 127, 136, 150, 156, 165
Naval Station, Guantanamo Bay, Cuba, 23, 67

Navy Cross, 209, 335, 338, 342
Nha Trang, Republic of Vietnam, 96, 116, 149, 239
Nolan, Capt. James M., 34–35, 98, 103–104, 126–127, 159, 163, 169, 190, 191, 195–196, 201, 202, 205–207, 209–215, 237, 238, 245
North Vietnamese Army (NVA), 189, 216–218, 241, 260, 295, 313

O'Connor, Capt. Martin E., 43, 53, 118, 191, 196, 198, 199, 203, 251, 268–270, 335
Okinawa, battle of (1945), 6, 81, 82
Okinawa, Ryukyu Islands, 22, 23, 25, 49, 89, 232
Old Chu Lai, 167
106mm recoilless rifle, 191, 298
155mm guns, 308, 309
173d Airborne Brigade, 239
Ontos vehicles, 298–299
OPCON (operational control), 57
Operation Blue Marlin, 169–170, 172–173, 190
Operation Double Eagle, 217
Operation Double Eagle, Phase II, 217–230, 244, 245
Operation Harvest Moon, 177–216, 218, 229, 237, 251, 277, 282, 290, 339–340
Operation Hot Springs, 310–313, 317, 318
Operation Indiana, 293–295

Operation Mixmaster, 231–240, 244, 245
Operation Montgomery, 313–319
Operation Nevada, 295–301
Operation Ramrod, 127
Operation Silver Lance, 53–54
Operation Starlight, 121, 216, 295
Operation Stomp, 139–148
Operation Utah, 237, 241–277, 282, 290, 313, 317–319, 334–335

Paige, 1st Lt. Roswell, IV, 43
Panama Canal, 24
Pearl Harbor, Hawaii, 84–85
Peatross, Col. Oscar F., 67, 68, 148, 167, 173–174, 218–219, 234
Philippine Islands, 3, 75
Phu Thanh Valley, Republic of Vietnam, 101, 114, 152–155
Pineapple Patch, 228
Platt, Brig. Gen. Jonas, 178
Pleiku, Republic of Vietnam, 127, 239
"Port Huron Statement, The," 8
Preda, Lt., 205
Purple Heart, 233

Quang Ngai City, Republic of Vietnam, 241, 242, 248, 293, 294
Quang Ngai Province, Republic of Vietnam, 121, 241, 313
Que Son Mountains, Republic of Vietnam, 178, 185, 187, 217

Qui Nhon, Republic of
Vietnam, 95–101, 103,
104, 107, 115, 121,
122, 127, 131–134,
149, 152, 165, 166,
170, 239, 283

Radio Battalion, 241–243
Radios, 63–64, 114, 129, 130
Red Hat One, 251–253, 257,
265
Regimental Landing Team 7
(RLT 7), 56, 57, 67–68,
77, 78, 84–92, 96, 231,
232, 278
Regimental Landing Team 9
(RLT 9), 91
Rider, Col. Jon, 236
Rivers, 1st Lt. John, 113
RMK-BRJ construction
consortium, 282, 325,
326, 328
Rocket-propelled grenade
(RPG), 135
Rood, Pvt. Gary, 268
Roothoff, Lt. Col. John J., 330
Rotation policy, 231–240

Seabees, 282, 325, 326
2/7 (*see* Second Battalion,
Seventh Marines)
Second Battalion, Fifth
Marines (2/5), 38–41
Second Battalion, First
Marines (2/1), 26,
192–197
Second Battalion, Fourth
Marines (2/4), 244,
273, 274
Second Battalion, Ninth
Marines (2/9), 199

Second Battalion, Seventh
Marines (2/7), 2, 4, 5,
11–19, 238
"Baldomero Lopez
Battalion," 37–41
call signs, 131
at Camp Las Pulgas, 25–43
Chu Lai airfield security,
323–330
command change, 59
command post in Phu Thanh
Valley, 101, 114,
152–155
deployment and embarkation
to Republic of Vietnam,
56–73
equipment of, 60–66
landing at Qui Nhon,
98–101, 103–104, 111
local operations, 116–138
lock-on cycle, 44–55
mountain warfare training,
50–53
Operation Blue Marlin,
169–170, 172–173
Operation Double Eagle,
Phase II, 217–230, 244,
245
Operation Harvest Moon,
177–216, 229, 237,
251, 277, 282, 290,
339–340
Operation Hot Springs,
310–313, 317, 318
Operation Indiana, 293–295
Operation Montgomery,
313–319
Operation Nevada, 295–301
Operation Stomp, 139–148
Operation Utah, 237,
241–277, 282, 290,

313, 317–319,
357–358
trip across Pacific, 74–94
Second Field Force
Headquarters, 239
II Corps Tactical Zone
(IICTZ), 95–96, 116
Second Marine Division, 53
Second Platoon of Company C,
First Reconnaissance
Battalion, 237, 301, 302
7.62mm RPD machine gun,
252, 253, 260
Seventh Marine Regiment, 14,
15, 25, 56, 59, 65, 67,
121, 165–167,
173–174, 177, 229,
232, 240, 243, 283,
293, 299, 322, 327
Seymour, Capt. William D., 43,
119, 190, 194, 206,
207, 210, 214, 220,
221, 226, 251, 252,
258, 262–263, 268,
296, 299, 300
Sixth Marine Regiment, 3
60mm mortar, 227, 271
Society of Jesus (Jesuits), 12
Song Chang Valley, Republic
of Vietnam, 178,
185–187, 194, 202,
217, 219, 222, 223
Soon, S.Sgt. Ah, 30
South China Sea, 149, 172
Special Landing Force (SLF),
177
*Stars and Stripes* newspaper,
121, 175
Stockton, Lt. Comdr. Bill, 214
Students for a Democratic
Society (SDS), 8

Tackett, S.Sgt. Reginald D.,
30–33, 66, 90, 92, 103,
108
Tactical areas of responsibility
(TAORs), 202
Tam Ky, Republic of Vietnam,
181, 184, 185, 187,
188, 190, 213, 218,
219, 229, 244
Tan Vinh, Republic of Vietnam,
226
Tarawa, Gilbert Islands, 6, 84
Task Force Delta, 177, 178,
181, 182, 187, 192,
194, 195, 197, 199,
200, 202, 204,
219–222, 228, 244,
245, 249, 251, 273
Thang Binh, Republic of
Vietnam, 188
Theer, Capt. Richard E.,
191–193, 199, 236,
237, 248
Third Battalion, Eleventh
Marines (3/11), 293,
294
Third Battalion, First Marines
(3/1), 10–11, 16, 273
Third Battalion, Ninth Marines
(3/9), 25, 26, 35, 42
Third Battalion, Seventh
Marines (3/7), 42
Third Battalion, Third Marines
(3/3), 192, 195, 197
Third Marine Aircraft Wing,
56
III Marine Amphibious Force,
233, 234, 331
Third Marine Division, 20–21,
25, 56–57, 91, 94–96,
146, 181

Tho An, Republic of Vietnam, 302–309

Thon Hai, Republic of Vietnam, 205

*Time* magazine, 143

Tok Tong Pass, Korea, 4, 65

Tolleson, Capt. Fredrick L., Jr., 27–29, 36, 43, 191*n*

Tra Bong River, Republic of Vietnam, 308

Transplacement system, 21, 22, 28, 42

Tu Cam, Republic of Vietnam, 224

12.7mm antiaircraft machine gun, 200, 210, 217, 252, 256, 257, 263, 268, 269, 310–312

UH-1E helicopter (Hueys), 132, 133, 295, 303, 304

Uniforms, 105–106, 289–290

U.S. Naval Station, Long Beach, California, 77, 78

U.S. Naval Station, San Diego, California, 72, 74

U.S. Navy Hospital, Guam, Marianas Islands, 137

USS *Kemper County*, 214–215

USS *Okanogan*, 90, 93, 94, 103

USS *Pickaway*, 66, 72, 74–90

USS *St. Paul*, 297

Utter, Lt. Col. Leon N., 19, 59, 86, 90, 108–109, 167, 170, 173, 174, 188, 240, 246, 287, 288, 290, 291, 305, 310, 329
  leadership abilities of, 59,

76, 80, 138, 175–176, 212–213, 239, 331–332
  mixmaster concept and, 236, 237
  Operation Double Eagle and, 220, 224–230
  Operation Harvest Moon and, 177, 181, 182, 184, 189, 194, 197, 199, 202, 204, 206–208, 211–215
  Operation Hot Springs and, 310, 313
  Operation Indiana and, 293, 294
  Operation Montgomery and, 314, 316, 319
  Operation Nevada and, 295, 298–300
  Operation Stomp and, 139, 141, 145–148
  Operation Utah and, 243–245, 248, 250, 252, 253, 255, 267–268, 270–273, 275–276, 334–335
  relieved, 330
  as speech writer, 335
  trip across Pacific, 75–77, 79–80

Vergalitto, S.Sgt. John, 235–236

Viet An, Republic of Vietnam, 199, 201

Viet Cong, 74, 95, 99, 101, 102, 110–112, 115, 116–124, 127–129, 131–134, 153–156, 159–162, 169, 170,

174, 281, 321–323,
326, 334
Operation Double Eagle,
217, 218, 220–226,
228, 229
Operation Harvest Moon,
178–180, 184–188,
190, 191, 193, 194,
196–198, 200, 201,
203–214, 216, 218
Operation Hot Springs,
310–313
Operation Montgomery,
313–317, 319
Operation Nevada, 295,
297–301
Operation Stomp, 140, 141,
143, 147
Operation Utah, 241, 250,
255–268, 271–275
Tho An, 301–309
Viet Cong sympathizers
(VCS), 194, 197, 216,
223, 224, 274, 294,
296, 315
Viet Minh, 128
Vietnamese National Police,
120, 194
Vietnamese Regional Force
(RF), 202

Walt, Maj. Gen. Lewis W., 56,
57, 94, 146, 147
Ware, Cpl. George A., 171–172
Weather, 149–151, 157–163,
178, 180, 183
Welty, Capt. Michael F., 43
White Beach, Camp Pendleton,
California, 37–38
White Beach, Okinawa, Japan,
89, 91, 92
Williams, 1st Lt. Dal, 221, 301,
302
Wilson, Col. Louis H., 67
Wilson, Maj. Raymond W., 43,
58–59, 62, 63, 73, 80,
175–176, 208$n$, 329
WOIS (worn out in service),
12
Woodall, Sgt., 54
World War I, 3
World War II, 3, 4, 6, 23, 45,
48, 76, 81, 82, 84, 128,
141, 242, 247, 259

Xuan Hoa, Republic of
Vietnam, 317

Yoshida, 1st Lt. Herbert,
117–118
Young, S.Sgt., 211

# FORCE RECON COMMAND
## 3rd Force Recon Company in Vietnam, 1969–70

## by Lt. Col. Alex Lee, USMC (Ret.)

In order to prevent surprise attacks on U.S. forces as they were pulling out of Vietnam in 1969, someone had to be able to pinpoint the NVA's movements. That dangerous job was the assignment of then-major Alex Lee and the Marines of the 3rd Force Reconnaissance Company. Whether tracking NVA movements, recovering downed air crews, or making bomb-damage assessments after B-52 strikes, each time one of Lee's small, well-led, and wildly outnumbered teams was airlifted into the field, the men never knew if the day would end violently.

Forthright and unabashed, Lieutenant Colonel Lee leaves no controversy untouched and no awe-inspiring tale untold in this gripping account.

**Published by The Ballantine Publishing Group.**
**Available in bookstores everywhere.**

# THE ONLY WAR WE HAD
## A Platoon Leader's Journal of Vietnam

## by Michael Lee Lanning

During his tour in Vietnam with the 199th Light Infantry Brigade, Lt. Michael Lee Lanning and his men slogged through booby-trapped rice paddies and hacked their way through triple-canopy forest in pursuit of elusive Viet Cong and North Vietnamese Army regulars. Lanning's entire year in Vietnam was spent in the field, and he saw a lot of combat, as an infantry platoon leader, as a reconnaissance platoon leader, and as a first-lieutenant company commander.

In this book, based on the journal he kept in Nam, Lanning writes of his experiences—and of the terror, boredom, rage, and excitement he shared with countless other American soldiers.

Published by The Ballantine Publishing Group.
Available in bookstores everywhere.

# A SNIPER IN THE ARIZONA

2nd Battalion, 5th Marines,
in the Arizona Territory, 1967

## By John J. Culbertson

In 1967, death was the constant companion of the
Marines of Hotel Company, 2/5, as they patrolled the
paddy dikes, mud, and mountains of the Arizona Territory
southwest of Da Nang. Chosen from the 1st Division's
twenty thousand Marines, John Culbertson was part of an
elite class of just eighteen top marksmen who attended
Sniper School in Da Nang. In graphic terms, he describes
the daily, dangerous life of a soldier fighting in a country
where the enemy was frequently indistinguishable from
the allies.

This riveting, bloody first-person account offers a stark
testimony to the stuff U.S. Marines are made of.

Published by The Ballantine Publishing Group.
Available at bookstores everywhere.